A LEVEL
GERMAN

John H Davies
Former Headteacher of Beauchamps
Grant-maintained School, Essex

Keith Watson
Chief Examiner, A level, Oxford Delegacy
Former Head of German
St Austell College

EDUCATIONAL

Every effort has been made to trace copyright holders and to obtain their permission for the use of copyright material. The authors and publishers will gladly receive information enabling them to rectify any reference or credit in subsequent editions.

First published 1996

Letts Educational
Aldine House
Aldine Place
London W12 8AW
0181 740 2266

British Library Cataloguing in Publication Data
A CIP record for this book is available from the British Library

ISBN 1 85758 391 4

Printed and bound in Great Britain by Bemrose, Derby DE21 6XG

Letts Educational is the trading name of BPP (Letts Educational) Ltd

PREFACE

This book is designed as a study guide for all students who are studying for the recently revised A/AS-Level examinations in England, Wales and Northern Ireland and the Higher Grade/CSYS examinations in Scotland. The authors have a wealth of experience between them, both as teachers and examiners at this level. This is not an A-level course book, but affords students the opportunity to work on their own alongside their studies at school or college, as it shows them how to succeed in their own preparation for their examinations and what to do in the actual examinations themselves.

It would be sensible to supplement this book with a reference grammar such as Hammer's *German Grammar and Usage*, revised by Martin Durrell and published by Edward Arnold and to make use of one or more of the Advanced German Vocabulary books which are currently available, such as the Mary Glasgow publication by H. Lanzer & R. Parikh or *Wort für Wort* by P. Stocker published by Hodder & Stoughton.

The authors would like to acknowledge the contributions made to the book by a student at St Austell College whose coursework essay is included as an example of an excellent piece of research and writing and the scheme of work provided by N.J. Davies (teaching A level in Coalville) which formed the basis for the two-year plan of action in section 1.

ACKNOWLEDGEMENTS

The authors and publishers would like to thank the following for the use of extracts from their publications.

pp37–39 *The Collins German Dictionary* for the extracts from a German-English dictionary.

pp40–42 *Langenscheidts Großwörterbuch, Deutsch als Fremdsprache* for the extracts from a monolingual dictionary.

p174 'Der blonde Engel der deutschen Straßenkinder', reproduced from *Ditmarscher Landeszeitung*, 24.12.94.

p176 'Weight Watchers', reproduced from *Badische Zeitung*, 30.10.93.

p177 'Blindes Vertrauen', reproduced from *Hamburger Abendblatt*.

p183 'Kinder Stark Machen', reproduced from an advert by the Bundesministeriums für Gesundheit.

p186 'Eine Ära der neuen Chancen und Pflichten', reproduced from *Hamburger Abendblatt*, 4.4.91.

p189 'Das unglaubliche Glück', reproduced from *Hamburger Abendblatt*, 4.4.91.

The authors and publishers would also like to thank the following Examination Boards for permission to reproduce questions:

AEB
NEAB
Oxford
Oxford & Cambridge
UCLES
ULEAC

CONTENTS

SECTION 3: APPENDICES

STARTING POINTS

In this section:

How to use this book
        The structure of this book

Syllabus checklists and paper analysis
        Examining Boards and addresses

Studying and revising German
        The transition from GCSE to A/AS-level
        The four skills: Listening, Reading, Speaking and
        Writing

How to revise for each element of the examination

A two-year plan of action

HOW TO USE THIS BOOK

This book has been written to help those of you who are preparing for either A-level or AS-level German examinations. The examples used in the text are taken mostly from sample papers made available to the authors by the Examining Boards listed at the end of this section. They have been carefully chosen to show the kinds of language task which you will be expected to undertake and are used to illustrate how you can complete them successfully, even if you are working on your own.

The first thing you will need to do is decide which Board's syllabus you are going to work towards, unless this decision is made for you by your school or college. To do this thoroughly, you will need to read in this section a statement of the aims and objectives of the examination as a whole and an analysis of each Board's papers. Once you know which examination you will be taking, then you must acquire a copy of the detailed syllabus for your particular Board and read it through very carefully.

The various sections of this book are designed to bridge the gap between the standard of GCSE and the much more demanding A-(or AS-) level German examination. There are lots of language learning strategies for you to use and thereby consolidate and improve your competence in the four recognised language skills. The book tells you what you need to know in order to succeed and gives you a chance to practise your newly acquired skills using relevant material from examination-type questions. The advice on how to answer a particular question is given by an actual practising examiner who tells you what marks would have been awarded for a particular answer. Clearly this is advice well worth following as you are told how to achieve good marks.

Each section of this book deals with strategies for success in your examination. There are sections on how to plan your work, how to learn vocabulary and use a dictionary, the essentials of German grammar and a section on each of the language skills in which you will need to show competence in order to tackle the examination with a real chance of knowing you will be successful.

You should work systematically through the book in accordance with your own plan of action, ensuring that you have thoroughly understood what is expected of you and leaving yourself time to revise properly what you have learnt.

THE STRUCTURE OF THIS BOOK

The various sections of this book follow a logical sequence, enabling you to work on any particular aspect of your course, concentrating on the area(s) where you feel you might need some extra help or practice. **Section One** gives you general information about what will be expected of you, when you embark on a course of study leading to German A- or AS-level. There is also some introductory advice about how to approach the tasks you will be expected to undertake along with a two-year plan of action.

Chapters 1 and 2 are concerned with the essentials of **Vocabulary** and **Grammar** in German which will obviously form the basis of your course of study.

There are then four further chapters, each devoted to one of the core language skills, which explain in detail what you are expected to do and how to prepare yourself for the kinds of examination task you will have to perform. In each of these chapters there are several examples for you to work through with comments on what would be an appropriate answer and the marks that would have been awarded to such answers.

Chapter 7 is about **Coursework** or **Topic** work and shows you how to tackle this major area of your work which can include the reading of literature texts and is a new type of test in languages which you have not had to do in a similar way before. Chapter 8 gives advice on studying literature.

The book is designed to allow you to have a 'hands on' approach to your learning. It can be used independently or in conjunction with any A-level course book in a school or college. It has a CD incorporated as an integral part of the approach to revision and guidance. This CD contains recorded material which gives examples of the oral and aural elements of the examination.

The appendices include a list of topics, a brief description of the texts listed by the Boards for study and a transcription of the material on the accompanying CD. Finally, the material as a whole represents most of the themes to be found in the A- and/or AS- level examinations, the syllabuses of which have been revised for 1997. You should therefore find it an invaluable exercise to use this book to prepare yourself for your examination. You should be rewarded with the success you deserve.

THE SYLLABUS CHECKLIST

The general aims and objectives of the examination

All Boards are required to state the aims of a course of study in German at Advanced Level or Advanced Supplementary Level. They are summarised here:

- to build on positive attitudes to language learning acquired through earlier study and experience;
- to enable a student to use German for the purpose of communication in both spoken and written forms and to understand the use of German in a variety of registers;
- to form a sound base of skills, language and attitude required for further study, the world of work, training and leisure;
- to foster the ability of the student to collect, analyse and exchange information, ideas, attitudes and opinions through the medium of German;
- to encourage in the student an interest in and an awareness of the contemporary society, institutions, way of life and culture of Germany or any other German-speaking country;
- to provide for the student enjoyment and intellectual stimulation;
- to further the student's intellectual and personal development by promoting learning and social skills.

The assessment objectives of all the Boards in summary indicate that the examination will assess the candidate's ability to:

- understand texts written in German, drawn from a variety of sources, including magazines, books, reports, publicity and information leaflets and other forms of extended writing;
- understand contemporary spoken German from a variety of authentic sources such as recorded news items, telephone messages, announcements, talks and discussions;
- manipulate German accurately in spoken and written forms and in ways which demonstrate a capacity to choose appropriate examples of lexis and structures and to transfer meaning from and into German;
- select information and present it in German, organising arguments and ideas logically;
- provide opinions and information in a sustained spoken interchange in German;
- demonstrate knowledge of contemporary German culture and society from a study of selected topic areas including literature.

SYLLABUS CHECKLISTS AND PAPER ANALYSIS

THE ASSOCIATED EXAMINING BOARD
A-level (0655)

Paper	Skills tested	Time	% of Total marks
1	Listening 20%, Reading 5%, Writing 5%,	$1\frac{1}{2}$ hrs.	30%
2	Reading 10%, Writing 15%,	$2\frac{1}{2}$ hrs.	30%
3	Cultural Background – Essays on Topics	$2\frac{1}{2}$ hrs.	20%
4	Cultural Background – Coursework	-	20%
5	Speaking – Oral (External Examiner)	20 mins.	20%
6	Speaking – Oral (Teacher Examiner)	20 mins.	20%

Notes: You are required to do Papers 1 and 2 with either Paper 3 or 4 plus either Paper 5 or 6. The total number of papers is therefore four.

Paper analysis

Paper 1 is in four parts. Parts 1 and 2 are Listening.

Part 1: Three to four short items lasting about a minute each, recorded in German on tape. There will be a range of tasks set in German designed to test comprehension.

Part 2: A longer passage recorded in German on tape thematically linked to Parts 3 and 4. Questions and Answers will be in English

N.B. In both Parts 1 and 2 notes can be made at any time and answers will be assessed for content and effective communication.

Part 3 is Reading consisting of a passage of about 200 words in German. Questions and Answers will be in German testing comprehension with similar tasks to those in Part 1.

N.B. As in Parts 1 and 2 answers will be assessed for content and effective communication.

Part 4 is Writing. You will write about 100 words in German based on the instructions given. There will be a thematic link with Parts 2 and 3 and you are encouraged to include aspects of what you have heard and read in your response and will be expected to include a personal reaction to all three parts. Your response will be assessed for content, effective communication and the ability to manipulate German accurately.

Paper 2 is in three parts.

Part 1 consists of four or five short reading passages (60–300 words each). A range of tasks will be set in German to be answered in German.

Part 2a: One longer passage will be set (about 400 words). A range of tasks will be set in German to be answered in German.

Part 2b: A translation into English of a section of the text in Part 2a will be required.

N.B. In Parts 1 and 2a answers will be assessed for content and effective communication. In Part 2b the answer will be assessed on your ability to render accurately and appropriately the German text into English.

Part 3: Two sets of stimulus materials in German will be provided for study. You will be asked to write about 250 words in German in response to **one** of the sets of material. Answers should include personal reaction and opinion.

N.B. Answers will be assessed on content, quality of language and accuracy of the German.

Paper 3 Prescribed Topics

Two essays of not less than 350 words each in German on different topics. There will be a choice of two questions on each topic in this Paper. Essays will be assessed for content relevant to the question chosen, organisation of the material and the ability to analyse and comment on the material chosen.

Paper 4 Coursework

Four pieces of work in German, two on each of two topics. The list of Topics is the same as for Paper 3. On each topic, one piece of writing should be an in-depth study of 700 to 1000 words, showing evidence of personal research, analysis and comment as well as expressing opinion or personal reaction; the other piece of writing should be creative and about 300 words long. A video or audio cassette lasting 5–10 minutes may also be submitted, provided that there is supporting written commentary.

70% of the marks for this Paper will be awarded to the In-depth Studies. The other 30% will go to the pieces of creative writing.

The coursework will be assessed as for Paper 3. All coursework will be assessed at the examination centre (school or college) and then sent to the Board for moderation. Centre-assessed coursework must be submitted to the Board by 30 April each year.

Papers 5 and 6 Oral

There are three sections to both versions of the Oral which are recorded on tape for subsequent moderation. The oral examination is conducted either by a visiting examiner (Paper 5) or by a teacher at the centre (Paper 6). The assessment of Paper 6 will be carried out by an examiner appointed by the Board to whom the recorded tape will be sent.

Each section will last about 6 or 7 minutes. There will be 20 minutes preparation time for each candidate.

Section (i) will consist of a discussion between you and the examiner on a theme or themes suggested by the Board in the stimulus material provided. You will choose one of two sets of material offered and can study it during the preparation period.

Section (ii) will consist of a dialogue between you and the examiner on a pre-prepared topic chosen by you from a prescribed list. You will provide the examiner with notes in German on the main points of personal interest within the topic before the examination starts. Your treatment of the topic should include opinions on broader issues and implications and avoid obviously rehearsed material.

Section (iii) will consist of general conversation across a range of topics.

In all three sections you will be assessed on your linguistic performance, your ability to handle ideas, to give descriptions, to seek and offer explanations and information and to give opinions with supporting reasons.

The Topics prescribed for the whole of this examination are listed in Appendix 1 page 242.

AS-level (0968)

The AS examination is a complete sub-set of the A-level. AS candidates will take Paper 1 and either version of the Oral (Paper 5 or 6).

UNIVERSITY OF CAMBRIDGE LOCAL EXAMINATIONS SYNDICATE
A-level (9915)

Paper	Skills tested	Time	% of Total marks
1	Speaking	20 mins.	25%
2	Listening	1 hr.	20%
3	Reading and Writing	$2\frac{1}{2}$ hrs.	25%
4	Essay on Prepared Topic – Writing	$1\frac{1}{2}$ hrs.	10%
5	Coursework on Topics	–	20%
6	Texts and Thematic Studies	$2\frac{1}{2}$ hrs.	20%
55	Coursework	–	10%
66	Texts and Thematic Studies	$1\frac{1}{4}$ hrs.	10%
0	Special (Optional)	3 hrs.	–

Notes: All papers are called Components in this syllabus. You are required to do Components 1, 2, 3 and 4 with either Component 5 or 6 or with both Components 55 and 66. Component 0 is optional and not part of the A-level examination as such. The total number of Components required is therefore five or six.

Paper analysis

Component 1 Speaking – Oral
There are three parts to this test which is conducted by a visiting examiner and recorded on tape.

> Part 1: Presentation – 3 minutes on a specific topic. The subject matter must not be closely related to any topic chosen for the coursework Component (5 or 55) or the themes of Components 6 or 66. The examiner needs at least one week's notice of your choice of topic. This is worth 5% of the oral marks.

> Part 2: Topic Conversation on the topic chosen in Part 1 lasting 7–8 minutes, worth 10% of the marks.

> Part 3: General Conversation lasting 8–9 minutes, worth 10% of the marks.

Sample tests are available, together with notes on the marks awarded.

Component 2 Listening
There are two sections in this test, both recorded on cassette. You have your own cassette in the examination.

> Section (i) 10% – Part A 5% – Short factual items will be heard and tasks of different kinds will be set to test comprehension. All rubrics and task descriptions will be in German. Part B 5% – Extended piece of listening; questions and answers will be in German and will test comprehension of the text as a whole and of specific details.

> Section (ii) 10% – Extended piece of listening and you will be required to act as an interpreter. Questions and answers will therefore be in English.

Component 3 Reading and Writing
There are three sections. In Sections (i) and (ii) two passages in German will be set on related themes.

> Section (i) $7\frac{1}{2}$% – Non-verbal response, recognition, manipulation expected. Comprehension questions will be in English

> Section (ii) $7\frac{1}{2}$% – Comprehension and interpretation will be tested through questions in German. Summary and comparison of issues raised in both texts will be tested through a writing task of up to 140 words in German.

You are expected to spend one and a half hours on Sections (i) and (ii).

> Section (iii) 10%, 1 hr – A single text in English will be used as source material. You will be expected to act as an interpreter answering questions in German and writing a guided composition based on the text and inviting your opinions.

Component 4 Essay on Prepared Topic

Six topic areas will be notified to the centre on 1 February before the examination in June to allow time for preparation. The Essay Paper will contain one essay title on each of the six notified topic areas. You will write 250 to 400 words in German on one of the six titles.

Component 5 Coursework

Normally coursework will come from within the prescribed topic areas. A total of 2000 words in German is required, made up of either two short pieces 500 words long plus one long piece 1000 words long or two long pieces of a 1000 words each. All planning and bibliography should be in German. All coursework will be marked by the teacher and moderated by the Board. Coursework must be completed and marked ready for moderation by 30th April.

Component 6 Texts and Thematic Studies

There are two sections to this paper. You will be expected to answer two questions in total. Any two questions can be answered from either or both sections. Answers will be in German and any monolingual/bilingual dictionary will be allowed in the examination room.

Section (i) Texts – five texts will be set and there will be two questions on each text to choose from. One of these questions will consist of an extended passage from the text, inviting you to comment on a particular aspect or to indicate how the passage reflects the book as a whole. Both questions will focus on issues central to the text under discussion. Detailed knowledge of the text is therefore essential.

Section (ii) Thematic Studies – a choice of four themes will be set with three questions on each theme. The questions will focus on the themes rather than on any one particular text. There is a list of named texts which are related to the themes in this section. (See pp 245–247 for list of prescribed texts) You are allowed to take into the examination room texts which are not too heavily annotated in either section of this paper. In answering the question in section (ii) you will be required to refer in detail to one named text (the one which you have taken into the examination room with you). You are not allowed to use the same text in both sections as the main stimulus or source material for your answers.

Component 55 Coursework

This component is half of Component 5. (See above) i.e. 1000 not 2000 words in German either as a long 1000 word essay or two short 500 word pieces of work. All the details are as for Component 5.

Component 66 Texts and Thematic Studies

This paper is in two sections and is half of Component 6. You will answer one question in German from any part of the paper. For all the other details see Component 6 above.

Component 0 Optional Special Paper

Three sections:

Section A – A text drawn from the list of Advanced Level topics will be set. You may be expected to answer questions requiring summary, analysis, general/specific comprehension or to show an understanding of linguistic points. The tasks and your responses will be in German.

Section B – An essay of about 250–300 words in German on a subject related to the topic area of the passage in Section A.

Section C – A short translation into German.

AS-level (8617)

For the AS-level examination you are required to do only the following:

Component 1: Speaking 40% of the marks. Component 2: Listening (Section (i) Parts A and B only) 20% of the marks with **either** Component 3: Reading and Writing (Sections (i) and (ii) only) 40% of the marks **or** Component 33: Reading 20% Section (i) **and** Component 5: Coursework 20%.

Details of each Component:

Component 1 is the same as the A-level Oral. The three parts are given an increased percentage of the total marks, viz. Part 1 8%, Parts 2 and 3 16%.

Component 2 is similar, where Parts A and B of section (i) are given 10% each.

Component 3 is sections (i) and (ii) only and each section is given 20% of the marks.

Component 33 is section (i) of Component 3 only, worth 20%.

Component 5 is half of the A-level component 5 only, requiring 1000 words to be written in German as coursework, i.e. one long or two short pieces of work. This version of Component 5 can only be done with Component 33.

UNIVERSITY OF LONDON EXAMINATION & ASSESSMENT COUNCIL
A-level (9234)

Module	Skills tested	Time	% of Total marks
1	Listening	$\frac{3}{4}$ hr.	15%
2	Reading and Writing	$1\frac{1}{2}$ hrs.	15%
3	Speaking – Oral	15 mins.	20%
4	Paper 1 – Speaking, Oral Extension	10 mins.	15%
	or Paper 2 – Speaking, Interpreting	15 mins.	15%
5	Paper 1 – Topics and Texts	$2\frac{1}{2}$ hrs.	20%
	or Paper 2 – Coursework – Cultural Background	-	20%
6	Writing in Registers	$1\frac{1}{4}$ hrs.	15%

Notes: There are four Pathways through the Syllabus. Modules 1, 2, 3 and 6 are compulsory for A-level. You can choose either Paper in Modules 4 and 5. The Pathways are:

1 The compulsory modules plus Paper 1 in both Modules 4 and 5.
2 The compulsory modules plus Module 4 Paper 1 with Module 5 Paper 2.
3 The compulsory modules plus Module 4 Paper 2 with Module 5 Paper 1.
4 The compulsory modules plus Paper 2 in both Modules 4 and 5.

The examination can be taken at the end of the normal two-year course, i.e. all six modules or if you choose the modular approach, you can take any module in any order over a period of four years as long as the last exam you take is worth a total of 30% of the marks. Examination sessions are available in January and June each year. The first time these modules will be available is June 1997.

Paper analysis

Module 1 will consist of recorded authentic material in German. You will have control of your own cassette in the examination. Questions mostly in German will elicit answers of different types – some non-verbal, some in English and some in German.

Module 2 is similar to Module 1 except that the stimulus material will be in written German.

Module 3 is the Oral which is conducted either by a teacher at the centre or a visiting examiner and is recorded on tape for moderation purposes. You will be expected to discuss a prepared topic dealing with an aspect of contemporary society in a German-speaking country. The chosen topic cannot be the same as for Module 5. A list of topics is on page 242.

Module 4 Paper 1 is optional and consists of a free-ranging conversation in German with the examiner on an issue of general interest which has been pre-prepared in advance and which is introduced by you the examination.

Module 4 Paper 2 can be done instead of Paper 1. It is an interpreting task involving two teachers, one a non-German speaker; you have to act as the interpreter between them. The task will be recorded on tape for assessment by an external examiner.

Module 5 Paper 1 is a written paper requiring two essays to be written in German. You may choose to write on two Topics, two Texts or one of each. Two questions will be set on each Topic or Text. You cannot choose to write on the same Topic as you prepared for Module 3.

Module 5 Paper 2 is an alternative to Paper 1 and consists of Coursework involving two pieces of extended writing in German (about 1000 words each) on a different free choice subject. Coursework must be available for moderation after assessment by the teacher by 31 May. Coursework cannot be submitted for the January examination session.

Module 6 is called Writing in Registers. It is in three sections: (a) Creative Writing – you will be expected to write an essay of 300–350 words in German based on an imaginative German text, a visual source or a combination of both. There will be a choice of questions. (b) Discursive Essay – similar choice and length of essay required involving the organisation of arguments and ideas in a structured consideration of a general issue. Task-based Assignment – you are required to carry out a typical office 'in-tray' exercise involving: analysis of a German letter, fax, memorandum or report; English summary of the document in note-form or headings; a draft reply in German. There will be a choice of questions.

You choose one question from one of these sections.

AS-level (8234)

To obtain an AS certificate you need to complete Modules 1, 2 and 3 only. The % marks are doubled for AS-level.

N.B. Monolingual or bilingual dictionaries are allowed in the examination for Modules 1, 2, 5 and 6.

THE NORTHERN EXAMINATIONS AND ASSESSMENT BOARD
A-level (4216A coursework/4216W written)

Paper	Skills tested	Time	% of Total marks
1	Coursework – Cultural Background	-	20%
or	Writing – Culture and Society	3 hrs.	20%
2	Reading and Writing	3 hrs.	40%
3	Listening	1 hr.	20%
4	Speaking	15 mins.	20%

Notes: Syllabus 4216A is the Coursework option in Paper 1 and is not available to private candidates. Syllabus 4216W is the Writing option in Paper 1. A Special Paper (Syllabus No. 5216) is also available (see details below).

Paper analysis

Paper 1 either (a) Coursework which is internally assessed and externally moderated.
or (b) Culture and Society, a 3-hour written paper.

(a) Coursework – Two essays in German totalling about 2000 words. Essay 1–800 words, Essay 2–1200 words. Essays must be based on the study of one work of German fiction or non-fiction with **either** a second work of fiction or non-fiction **or** German spoken and/or written material equivalent in scope to a second work of fiction/non-fiction.

One essay can be based on information gained from staying abroad in a German-speaking environment. Closing date for the receipt of marked Coursework at the Board is 30 April. A list of suggested areas of interest/topics with possible essay titles and source materials is available from the Board.

(b) Culture and Society – This paper is in three sections. You must answer three questions with a maximum of two from any one section.

Section A: Prescribed Texts – Two alternative questions will be set in German on each of eight texts. Answers will be in German.

Section B: Prescribed Literary Texts – Two alternative questions will be set in English on each of eight texts. Answers may be in German or English and will be marked for content only.

Section C: Prescribed Topics – Two alternative questions will be set on each of three topics. Questions and answers will be in German.

N.B. for all three sections a list of Prescribed Topics and texts is available from the Board including suggested source materials (see page 243).

Paper 2 will consist of two texts in German totalling 600–700 words. A series of questions arising from the texts will be set in German, requiring answers in German for the most part. Three types of question will always be included: (a) translation into English of part of a text, (b) translation into German of 80 words of English based on the text(s), (c) 250 words free composition in German covering a range of different types of writing (e.g. letter, narrative, dialogue, discursive, descriptive, imaginative) on a choice of themes either directly, loosely or in no way connected with texts.

Paper 3 Listening material will be recorded in German on cassette tapes, consisting of one extended item and a number of shorter items. You will be expected to answer several types of question – to answer questions in English, to summarise particular sections, to answer multiple-choice questions or transcribe German phrases you have heard after being given their English equivalents. This is the only time you will be expected to produce written German.

Paper 4 Speaking will be conducted by the Board's examiner and recorded on tape. 20 minutes preparation time will be allowed. Notes on parts (a) and (b) can be taken into the examination room. The examination is in three parts.

Part (a): Role-playing (2–3 mins.) 4% of marks, transactional type task – outline in English given to you before your examination on the day to prepare.

Part (b): Reporting (about 3 mins.) 4% of marks, expected to convey in German information suggested by written or visual material given to you on the day before your examination to prepare, e.g. the gist of a newspaper article in English.

Part (c): General Conversation (8–9 mins.) 12% of marks, conversation will range over a variety of topics and you must be prepared and able to defend or counter opinions expressed by the examiner. Topics can include those prepared for Paper 1.

Special Paper is designed to test your intellectual grasp and capacity to think about the subject. It consists of a 3-hour written paper in two sections.

Section A 60% of the marks – You are required to study a passage of modern German prose (about 500 words) and answer a variety of questions on it.

(i) translate part of the text into English; (ii) show precise understanding of the passage by answering comprehension questions in German; (iii) write 200–250 words in German expressing your own ideas and reactions to the contents of the passage in answer to a question based on it. Questions in (i) and (ii) will be in German.

Section B 40% of the marks – You are expected to attempt one question from this section. Questions will consist of the following:

(a) Critical appreciation of a passage of German. A choice of poetry will be offered.

(b) Literary criticism – a choice of four essay questions will be set based on the candidate's reading of literature. Answers should refer to more than one text.

(c) Essay on social, political, economic and historical developments in the German-speaking world. Four essay titles to choose from, answers may be in German or English and will be assessed on content only.

AS-level (3216)

There are three components to this examination.

(a) Speaking Test (40% of the marks) – exactly the same requirements as for A-level.

(b) Paper 1: Listening Comprehension (30% of the marks) – as Paper 3 A-level, but you will not be required to write any German in your responses.

(c) Paper 2: Reading Comprehension (30% of the marks) – a 2-hour paper with a number of functional passages of varying length in German to study and answer questions on. Questions will be in either English or German and you will not be required to write any German in your responses.

Dictionaries are not allowed in this examination.

NORTHERN IRELAND COUNCIL FOR THE CURRICULUM, EXAMINATIONS AND ASSESSMENT

A-level

Paper	Skills tested	Time	% of Total marks
1	Speaking	20 mins.	20%
2	Listening	45 mins.	20%
3	Reading	2 hrs.	20%
4	Writing	$2\frac{1}{2}$ hrs.	20%
5	Literature and Culture	$2\frac{1}{2}$ hrs.	20%

Paper analysis

Details of each paper:

Paper 1 The Oral is in two parts. 20 minutes preparation time is allowed. You will have an external examiner and the Speaking Test will be recorded on tape for subsequent moderation. Part 1 – a discussion of stimulus material provided on the day, based on a topic from list A, see page 243. Part 2 – a general conversation. You may use a bilingual dictionary in the preparation time.

Paper 2 You will have a cassette tape to listen to with various items in German. Questions and answers will be in English.

Paper 3 There will be two sections. A) 500 words of German for reading, questions and answers in English set on the passage. B) Translation into English – two passages of German will be set.

Paper 4 Three sections: A) a passage of English based on the topics in List A – questions and answers based on it in German. B) Translation from English into German. C) Essay in German (250 words) on one of three titles. Each title will be accompanied by stimulus material drawn from the 10 topic areas in List A.

A) is worth 4%; B) 8%; C) 8% of total marks.

Paper 5 Two sections: A) will contain two questions on each of six literary texts. B) will offer two questions on each of four topics. Questions and answers will be in English. Details of texts and topics are given in List B, see page 243. You will be required to answer three questions, at least one from each section.

UNIVERSITY OF OXFORD DELEGACY OF LOCAL EXAMINATIONS
A-level (9922)

Unit	Skills tested	Time	% of Total marks
1	Work and Leisure – Reading; Listening; Writing	2 hrs.	25%
2	Contemporary Society (skills as unit 1)	$2\frac{1}{2}$ hrs.	30%
3	Terminal Oral – Speaking	15 mins.	15%
4	Terminal Oral (Extension) – Speaking	10 mins.	15%
5	Oral Coursework – Speaking	15/20 mins.	15%
6	Written Coursework – Writing	-	15%
7	Topic Essay – Writing	$1\frac{1}{2}$ hrs.	15%

Notes: This is a modular syllabus which allows you to accumulate Units over a maximum of four years. Alternatively all units can be taken at one sitting at the end of your course. Assessment is three times a year in March, May/June, December. You must take units totalling 30% of the marks in the final examination session of your award. Monolingual and bilingual dictionaries are allowed in all units. There are three routes through the syllabus:

Option A – Units 1, 2, 3, 4 and 6 – includes written coursework
Option B – Units 1, 2, 3, 4 and 7 – no coursework
Option C – Units 1, 2, 3, 5 and 7 – includes oral coursework

Paper analysis

Unit 1 Reading 15%, Listening 5%, Writing 5%. Part 1 Work – three tasks will be set to test comprehension, (a) Reading text, (b) Listening material on tape, (c) Writing in German (a short piece of directed writing). (a) and (b) questions and answers will be in English. Part 2 Leisure – short Reading texts with comprehension tests set on them which will usually not involve productive writing in German. One task will be set requiring 180 words of German to be written arising out of one of the Reading texts.

Unit 2 Listening 15%, Reading $7\frac{1}{2}$%, Writing $7\frac{1}{2}$%. Part 1 – Comprehension Tests on a passage of German to be answered in German. Part 2 – Listening material on tape, answers in German to a series of different comprehension exercises, one of which will require a short piece of extended writing in German. The material used in this unit will reflect contemporary society.

Unit 3 must be offered at the same time as either Unit 4 or Unit 5. You will be expected to discuss a topic or text from the prescribed list (see p244). You cannot choose the same topic for discussion as the topics you have chosen in Units 6 and 7 if you are doing them. This oral can be internally or externally assessed and will be recorded on tape for future moderation.

Unit 4 is taken before Unit 3 and will be a Role-play exercise. 30 minutes preparation time is allowed to study and make notes on a sheet of background information in English. This part of the oral will be conducted by an external examiner or your own teacher and will be recorded for moderation purposes.

Unit 5 involves assessment over the final year of the course of your contribution in role-playing situations, pair work and small group discussion. Over the period of time a recording will be compiled lasting about 15–20 minutes on an individual tape. The tape must be finished and assessed by 30 April for despatch to the Board for moderation.

Unit 6 Either one piece of extended writing in German (1000–1200 words) or two pieces of writing (500–700 words each) must be submitted and assessed at the centre by 30 April on a topic from the prescribed list or an approved own choice topic. If you choose the two shorter pieces of writing they must be on different aspects of the same topic. N.B. topics chosen for this unit must be different from those for Unit 3 or 6, especially if literary texts are chosen. They must be different texts by different authors.

Unit 7 One essay (450–500 words) is required in German on one of the 24 titles which will be available on this paper. Eight of these titles will relate to the literature-based topics and the others will be two questions on each of the eight non-literary topics prescribed for this syllabus (see page 244).

AS-level (8722)

This examination comprises Units 1, 3 and 4.

Unit 1 Work and Leisure, 2 hours. Reading; Listening; Writing; 50% of total marks.

Unit 2 Terminal Oral, 15 minutes. Topic Discussion, 25% of total marks.

Unit 4 Terminal Oral (Extension), 10 minutes. Extended Role-play, 25% of total marks.

You can 'cash in' an AS-level award once you have successfully completed these units or continue for a full A-level certificate.

OXFORD & CAMBRIDGE SCHOOLS EXAMINING BOARD
A-level (9611)

Module	Skills tested	Time	% of Total marks
1	Listening and Speaking I	1 hr.	16.6%
2	Listening and Speaking II	1 hr.	16.6%
3	Reading and Writing I	$1\frac{1}{2}$ hrs.	16.6%
4	Reading II	$1\frac{1}{2}$ hrs.	16.6%
5	Writing	2 hrs.	16.6%
6	Literature and Civilisation	$2\frac{1}{2}$ hrs.	16.6%

Notes: All six Modules must be completed for an A-level award. You have up to four years to complete all six modules, but the final examination session must include modules worth 30% and either Module 1 or 2 as part of that 30%. Examination sessions are only available in the Summer. You can of course take the complete assessment of all six modules for A-level at a single sitting.

Paper analysis

Module 1 Two parts – Part 1: Listening Comprehension, individual cassettes containing items recorded in German. Questions and Answers on this material will be in German. Bilingual dictionaries are allowed. 45 minutes; about 8% of total marks.

Part 2: Oral – 15 minutes plus 15 minutes preparation time; about 8% of total marks.

(a) Role-play 4–5 minutes, dictionaries may be used.

(b) Discussion 10 minutes; 7 days to prepare topic for discussion, no notes allowed in the examination. Oral conducted by teacher and recorded on cassette. Assessed tapes will be sent to the Board for moderation. A bilingual dictionary may be used during the preparation time only.

Module 2 Part 1: Listening similar to Module 1 but with longer and more complex answers required in German. A bilingual dictionary is allowed in this examination.

Part 2: Oral 15 minutes; 10–15 minutes discussion on a prepared topic. Subject matter is not prescribed.

It must be a genuine discussion. No notes are allowed but you can take into the exam room realia, pictures, books or artefacts. Orals will be conducted at the centre by a teacher, recorded on cassette and assessed before being sent to the Board for moderation. A bilingual dictionary is allowed in the preparation phase of Part 2.

Module 3 is Responsive Reading I which is in two parts. Part 1 is Comprehension and Translation. Question 1 is a passage of German on which questions in German to be answered in German will be set. Question 2 will be a Translation into English of a short extract from the passage. Part 2: Letter or short report (140–150 words) in German based on instructions or a brief which may be in German. There will be a link with the subject matter of the passage in Part 1.

Module 4 is Responsive Reading II, also in two parts. Part 1: Comprehension questions will be set in German to be answered in German on one or more passages in German.

Part 2: Translation of about 150 words of German into English. A bilingual dictionary can be used in both parts of this Module.

Module 5 is in four parts. You must answer any two parts. Dictionaries are not allowed in any part of this Module. Part 1: Guided Writing – 250 words in German in response to a brief, e.g. a passage of German and/or visual or statistical material. Part 2: Translation into German of a passage of English (200 words approx.) Part 3: Free Composition I – 250 words in German based on one of five titles on the paper requiring a discursive or argumentative response. Part 4: Free Composition II – as for Part 3 but requiring a descriptive or imaginative essay to be written.

Module 6 is in two parts. You are required to answer three questions chosen freely from part 1 and/or part 2. Part 1: Literary Texts – 10–12 texts will be prescribed, three questions will be set on each text, a commentary question and two essay titles. You must answer in German either the commentary question or one of the essay titles on up to three of the prescribed texts. Part 2: Civilisation and Society – four prescribed themes with two questions set on each of them. You will be expected to answer in German up to a maximum of three questions.

AS-level (8465)

This examination consists of Modules 1, 2 and 3 of the A-level Syllabus above. You can take up to four years to complete these Modules.

A-level for Professional Use (9616)

This is a Modular Syllabus with Assessment by accumulation of credits which can be banked and remain valid for three years. There are three Areas of Study each comprising two Modules. You are required to complete all six Modules to obtain an A-level Certificate.

AREA OF STUDY – LISTENING AND SPEAKING

Module 1 Part 1: Listening Comprehension 1 hour. Questions and Answers in German based on recorded material. You have your own cassette in the examination and can listen to the stimulus material as often as you like within the time allocated.

Part 2: Oral Test 20 minutes (a) Two Role-plays (b) Discussion. A bilingual dictionary is allowed in Part 1 and is available in the examination room in Part 2.

Module 4 Part 1: Listening Comprehension Viewing Test 1 hour 20 minutes. A video will be shown, you will have the soundtrack available on cassette. You have to write a report in German on what you have seen and heard. Bilingual dictionaries are allowed in this part. Part 2: Oral 30 mins. (a) A presentation leading to a discussion about a commercial or industrial theme. (b) A presentation and description of a guided tour for a business or tourist visit to a UK town or area.

AREA OF STUDY – READING AND WRITING

Module 2 Part 1: Translation – Letter in German to be translated into English plus a reply in German. ($1\frac{1}{4}$ hours)

Part 2: Summary Writing – Passage in German about 500–600 words to be summarised in English in about 175–200 words. ($1\frac{1}{4}$ hours)

Module 5 Part 1: Report Writing – Write report in German based on German articles or reports providing information on a theme or event. ($1\frac{1}{2}$ hours)

Part 2: Translation into English (1 hour) – (a) German text(s) provided with a translation by a non- English speaking person. You have to revise the English version. (b) Translate a German text into accurate English.

Bilingual dictionaries are permitted in both these Modules.

AREA OF STUDY – SOCIETY AND CULTURE

Module 3 Part 1: Contemporary References – comprehension of contemporary journalistic texts/extracts where background and cultural knowledge are also being assessed (1 hour). Part 2: Project (1500–2000 words in German), final version to be written under supervised conditions over 4 hours. You are expected to have prepared this Project beforehand.

Module 6 Project(s) either one project (2500–3000 words in German) or two shorter projects (1250–1500 words in German) dealing with a business, scientific, political, environmental or geographical theme, which must be approved beforehand by the Board. Final version written under supervised conditions over 6 hours.

NB: Bilingual dictionaries are permitted in Part 1 of Module 3.

SCOTTISH EXAMINING BOARD
Higher Grade (1300)

Paper	Skills tested	Time	% of Total marks
1	Reading	2 hrs.	30%
2	Listening and Writing	1 hr.	20%
3	Writing	$1\frac{1}{4}$ hrs.	13.33%
4	Cloze Test	30 mins.	6.66%
5	Oral	15 mins.	30%

Paper analysis

Paper 1 Two passages totalling up to 1200 words of German will be set. A range of questions will test comprehension. Answers will mostly be in English and you will be required to translate parts of both passages into English.

Paper 2 Section A: Listening 10% – recorded material on tape in German with questions and answers in German to test communication and understanding.
Section B: Writing 10% – You will be required to write 100–120 words in German expressing your views on the topic of the taped material in section A.

Paper 3 You are required to write a narrative essay in German of 200–250 words in response to a reading stimulus.

NB. In papers 1-3 a dictionary may be used.

Paper 4 Two passages in German will be set, each containing 10 gaps to be filled in by the candidate. In the first passage a choice of three words for each gap will be available, in the second passage no help will be given.

Paper 5 The oral test will be in two parts. The first part will be a short talk by the candidate on a topic selected on the day. This will be followed by a discussion on the chosen topic with the teacher-examiner. The second part will be a discussion of a book read during the course of the year by the student. Both parts of the oral will be recorded on tape and sent to the Board for moderation after assessment has been completed by the centre. Books and topics will be chosen by the teaching staff of the school or college.

NB. Dictionaries are not allowed in papers 4 and 5.

Certificate of sixth year studies CSYS.

Paper	Skills tested	Time	Marks Total 350
1	Reading	$1\frac{1}{4}$ hrs.	50 marks
2	Critical Reading	$1\frac{1}{2}$ hrs.	50 marks
3	Listening	45 mins.	30 marks
4	Writing	1 hr.	50 marks
5	Folio – Coursework	–	100 marks
6	Oral – Speaking	15 mins.	70 marks

Paper analysis

This examination is more advanced than the Higher Grade examination.

Paper 1 A passage of 600–800 words in German will be set. Questions will be set on the passage to test comprehension, translation into English and language study.

Paper 2 Two passages of literary German will be set, one in prose and one in verse. You will be required to answer the questions on one passage only. Questions and answers will be in English. You will be expected to understand and react to language in its imaginative, literary mode and show awareness of the functions of structure, imagery, rhyme, rhythm and metre.

Paper 3 You will hear a discussion in German on tape which you will be expected to summarise in 150–200 words of German, comparing and contrasting the positions taken by the speakers. You are allowed to make notes during the playing of the tape. You will hear the material twice.

Paper 4 You will be required to write an essay in German of 250–300 words on one of five topics on the paper.

NB. You may use a dictionary in any of the papers 1–4 above.

Paper 5 Your folio should include the following: 3 essays in German, each about 200–250 words long, one essay on current affairs plus **either** two essays on culture/civilisation topics **or** two essays on literary texts **or** one essay on a cultural topic with one essay on a literary text. In addition 2 essays in English of about 400–500 words are required, one on a culture/civilisation topic and one on a literary text. Folios must be completed and sent to the Board by 1 April in the year of the examination.

Paper 6 The oral test will be conducted by a visiting examiner and will be based on work carried out for the folio.

WELSH JOINT EDUCATION COMMITTEE
A-level

Paper	Skills tested	Time	% of Total marks
A1	Reading	$2\frac{1}{2}$ hrs.	20%
A2	Writing	3 hrs.	20%
A3	Listening	1 hr.	20%
A4	Speaking – Oral Test (plus one of the following)	15–20 mins.	20%
A5	Literature and Coursework	$2\frac{1}{2}$ hrs.	20%
A6	Extended Language – Writing, Speaking, and Coursework	$1\frac{1}{2}$ hrs.	20%
A7	Project Work	-	20%
There is also a Special Paper available.			

Paper analysis

Paper A1 Questions and Answers will be in English/Welsh. Texts in German will be set to test your understanding. One question will require you to translate into English/Welsh selected parts from the texts in the other questions.

Paper A2 Bilingual dictionaries are allowed in this paper. You will be required to write a letter in German (150 words), an essay in German (250 words) and **either** a resumé in German (150 words) of an English/Welsh text **or** a translation into German of a short English/Welsh text (120 words) **or** a short report in German (150 words) using information in English/Welsh or German in the form of tables, diagrams, surveys etc.

Paper A3 Questions and Answers will be in English/Welsh. You will have 10 minutes to read through the paper. There will be a 10-minute break after Section 2. Sections 1 and 2 will be short items, heard twice, Section 3 will be a longer stimulus which will be heard three times.

Paper A4 5 minutes preparation time for this test. Dictionaries may be used during this preparation period and you may use your notes during the Role-play only. There are three elements – Role-play, Conversation about studies, interests and future plans, and Discussion of an issue related to one of the prescribed topics.

Paper A5 Optional paper – (a) There will be questions on extracts from three prescribed texts; you will choose one to answer questions on. (b) Two essays required on any two texts from the prescribed list. (c) Paper A5 also includes an element of teacher-assessed coursework, i.e. the two best pieces of your work completed during your normal work in year 2 of your course. The work must be related to Literature prescribed for Paper A5.

Paper A6 Optional paper – bilingual dictionaries may be used in the written part of this paper. (a) Two essays in German (120–150 words), one on each of two prescribed texts will be required. Questions will be in German. (b) An oral exposition in German followed by discussion with the external examiner lasting 10 minutes. (c) An element of teacher-assessed coursework as for Paper A5, but based on the prescribed texts for Paper A6. Coursework must be completed in German.

Paper A7 You will be required to produce about 1500 words in German on an approved subject. It can be one extended piece or two/three shorter pieces on related topics.

Special Paper has four elements; you choose two to answer. They are:
(a) prose composition, i.e. translation into German, (b) an unprepared commentary, (c) a general essay in English/Welsh on a literary topic, (d) an essay in German.

AS-level

Paper	Skills tested	Time	% of Total marks
	Option 1		
(a)	Listening	1 hr.	40%
(b)	Reading	$2\frac{1}{2}$ hrs.	40%
(c)	Speaking – Oral Test	10 mins.	20%
	Option 2		
(a)	Listening	1 hr.	40%
(b)	Reading	$1\frac{1}{2}$ hrs.	20%
(c)	Speaking – Oral Test	15–20 mins.	40%

Paper analysis

(a) The Listening Comprehension in both options is as for Paper A3 above.

(b) The Reading Comprehension in Option 1 is as for Paper A1 above, in Option 2 there are only two questions based on texts and visual stimuli to be answered in English/Welsh.

(c) The Oral Test in Option 2 is as for Paper A4 above, in Option 1 there is no Role-play.

QUALITY OF LANGUAGE

It is now a requirement for all Boards that quality of English language is assessed at GCE A and AS-level. This will be applied particularly where continuous prose is used in an examination answer. If your Board requires you to write continuous prose – for example in a literature question – make sure that:

1 You write in complete sentences that convey meaning clearly.

2 Punctuation – capital letters, full stops, commas, semi colons and colons – are used properly (for example when referring to the title of a book, play or poem this should be either underlined or put in inverted commas).

3 Spelling is correct.

Most of these details also apply when you are doing a German to English translation or answering a comprehension question in English.

EXAMINING BOARDS AND ADDRESSES

AEB	The Associated Examining Board Stag Hill House, Guildford, Surrey GU2 5XJ
Cambridge	University of Cambridge Local Examinations Syndicate Syndicate Buildings, 1 Hills Road, Cambridge CB1 2EU
London	University of London Examinations and Assessment Council Stewart House, 32 Russell Square, London WC1 5DN
NEAB	Northern Examinations and Assessment Board 12 Harter Street, Manchester M1 6HL
Northern Ireland	Northern Ireland Council for the Curriculum Examinations and Assessment, Beechill House, 42 Beechill Road, Belfast BT8 4RS
Oxford	Oxford Delegacy of Local Examinations Ewert House, Ewert Place, Summertown, Oxford OX2 7BZ
Oxford & Cambridge	Oxford and Cambridge Schools Examination Board Purbeck House, Purbeck Road, Cambridge CB2 2PU or Elsfield Way, Oxford OX2 8EP
Scottish	Scottish Examinations Board Ironmills Road, Dalkeith, Midlothian EH22 1LE
WJEC	Welsh Joint Education Committee 245 Western Avenue, Cardiff CF5 2YX

STUDYING AND REVISING GERMAN

THE TRANSITION FROM GCSE TO A/AS-LEVEL

It is assumed that the user of this book has already successfully completed a GCSE course in German and has achieved one of the higher grades A*, A, B or C. It is possible of course that you are a mature student who has taken GCSE recently at an adult evening class or even that you took an O-level course a number of years ago, passing with a good grade. In both cases you should have a good grasp of the basics of the German language and you now wish to embark on a course of study leading to either the achievement of a good grade at Advanced level in German or at the Advanced Supplementary level.

You may be surprised to know that there are now modular A-level courses available in German and you should therefore look carefully at the section of this book which details the choice of syllabus which you could be studying. You could be equally surprised to discover that these modular courses enable you to do so many modules per year and to spread the accumulation of credits over as much as four years, 'cashing in' an AS-level on the way. One word of warning though, most Examining Boards do not allow external or private candidates to enter for the coursework section of the examination.

Clearly the first thing you need to do is to consider carefully the aims and objectives of the examination at A or AS-level. Every Board is obliged to state them in their syllabus information booklets. These are detailed and very well worth reading closely, because they not only give you details about the aims and objectives but they also give precise information about mark schemes, topic areas and texts for study or reference; they tell you what to expect and what the examiners' assessment criteria are.

Another interesting point is the fact that many Examining Boards allow you to take texts and/or dictionaries into the examination room. There is even advice from a number of Boards as to which dictionary or text they recommend. This book shows you how to use a dictionary properly and how to get the best out of what you are allowed to do. See the section which deals with **Using a Dictionary** on page 37.

There is no doubt that the change from a GCSE-type course to A-level (or AS-level) is quite dramatic, in spite of the Examining Boards' claims that the new A-level syllabuses being introduced, (subsuming AS-level in most cases) are based on the concept of GCSE and form a continuity with the requirements of the National Curriculum. The level of knowledge and the skills you need to acquire for A-level in particular are nevertheless much more rigorous than at GCSE. You must therefore plan your work with the greatest care over the period of your A-level course. In most cases this will still be, for the majority of students, the traditional two-year course. There is a plan of action on how to check your progress over the two years included in this book and you should try to follow it; you will find it a worthwhile exercise.

The four skill areas of learning a foreign language are the same as for Key stages 3 and 4. They are Listening, Speaking, Reading and Writing. To these is added the skill of demonstrating your knowledge of contemporary German culture and society through a study of topics related to a German-speaking country – usually Germany itself. In the syllabuses of at least two Boards there is an opportunity to give your study of culture and society a vocational bias. The National Curriculum and the GCSE/Key stage 4 syllabuses contain quite specific references to the context of language learning and the use of the target language. At A and AS-level the context of the whole course is contemporary. You will be expected to have opinions and be able to express them fluently in German on a number of contemporary, often contentious issues. Frequently these issues are caught up with the political, financial, cultural or social changes in Germany of recent date. This provides you with a specific challenge, but it also makes your work significantly more interesting. The authors you will be expected to read will often be ones who are still alive and writing today. If we look more closely at the four skill areas, you will be required to use German in most of your answers to the different tasks set.

THE FOUR SKILLS

Listening

Listening skills will require you to have a high degree of understanding and be able to respond to authentic, spoken German in a contemporary context. Most of your responses will be in German. The sources of spoken German which you will listen and respond to will be taken from recorded news items, telephone messages, announcements, talks and discussions. On the face of it, this does not seem all that different from what you did in GCSE listening tasks, but here your understanding will include the ability to identify important points of themes, including attitudes, ideas, opinions and emotions in what you hear.

Reading

In Reading you will be expected to understand authentic written German in a variety of registers and from a variety of sources. Your comprehension will be assessed in a number of different ways. These will include some translation from German into English (i.e. interpreting), translation from English into German (re-translation), showing how you can manipulate the language used in the comprehension passage set and questions expecting you to find other words or phrases in German which are equivalent to the ones in the German text. How to tackle questions of this sort is discussed more fully later in this book, but it is obvious that they make demands on your grasp and understanding of German which are far more searching than anything you had to attempt at GCSE (or O-level in the past).

Speaking

Speaking is another skill where for both A-level and AS-level what is demanded is much more exacting. You will be expected to be able to communicate your own views and opinions on a wide range of topics in discussion with the oral examiner. Much more emphasis is laid on your ability to communicate fact and opinion and to do this in fluent, accurate, well-pronounced German, showing a good range of vocabulary and structure.

Writing

Writing in German becomes a major part of the assessment procedures at A-level – much more so than in GCSE. Consequently this is probably the area where you will need to make the most specific efforts to improve your skills and technique. All syllabuses expect extended pieces of writing in German. If you choose the coursework options, you will have up to 2,000 words of German to write on at least one topic. Once again you are expected to express your own opinions and analyse the arguments for and against in a discursive type of essay. Creative writing is also on the agenda in some tasks and literary appreciation, criticism and analysis are required in a number of Boards' examinations.

Coursework

Finally coursework is an option which is new to students of German who have done GCSE. There is a full explanation of how to approach coursework in a later section of this book.

The important thing to remember is not to be daunted or put off by the considerable increase in the level of skills required to succeed at A or AS-level when comparing them with what you had to do for GCSE. Admittedly it would be unwise to try and study A-level German, if you have not achieved at least a grade 'C' at GCSE or its equivalent, but if you are genuinely interested in learning German at a higher level and if you organise your learning progress properly, you should have little difficulty in having the great personal satisfaction of achieving success at A or AS-level. Using this book will help you achieve your aim.

HOW TO REVISE FOR EACH ELEMENT OF THE EXAMINATION

When revising for the various parts of the examination it is important that you give yourself as much time as possible. Learning a language cannot be hurried. An essential element for understanding both spoken and written German and for building your own sentences, both in speech and writing, is as large a vocabulary as you can manage to acquire in the time available. This is so important that there is a whole section of this book devoted to showing you how to learn the vocabulary you will need to ensure success in your examination.

Most A/AS-level syllabuses lay equal stress on the four skills and give roughly equal marks to all four. You will need to practise them often and regularly to improve. To do this you will need access to extra materials. This study guide contains some and working through them will give you practice. You should also become familiar with the format of the particular A/AS-level examination that you will be taking. How many papers are there? What skills are being tested in each one? How long does each one last? What will you be asked to do in each of the various papers? The details about each Board's papers are given on pp 4–17, but it is a good idea to get hold of some past papers and work through them. This study guide contains examples of most types of examination question with help and advice on how to approach each one.

LISTENING

This is a skill that is often neglected, yet it is essential if you are to understand what is being said to you. If you do not understand what Germans and the oral examiner are saying to you, then you will be unable to respond in an appropriate way. So you will need to listen to as much German as you can.

If you can make a recording of some German being spoken, it is often useful to transcribe (write out) what you have heard. If there are bits that you find particularly difficult, you can listen to the tape two or three times.

In the Listening examination you will be tested in a number of ways to see how well you can do a variety of things:

- pick out details from what you have heard;
- understand the gist of a passage and summarise its main details;
- draw inferences from what you have heard.

You will probably need to make notes to help your memory and before formulating an answer to a question. A good strategy is to make your notes in German and put them into shape when you read what you have noted down. Don't just write down what you hear! Think what it means!

Opportunities for getting access to spoken German are much better now than even a few years ago. Below are some suggestions:

1 Five times a year a newspaper is published containing a wide range of extracts from the German press, together with a tape of items from the German media. The transcription of the whole tape is included in the newspaper, so that you have the opportunity of listening to the tape and comparing it with the text, if you have not understood something. The newspaper is called *Authentik*, and is published by **Authentik Language Learning Resources Ltd, 27 Westland Square, Dublin 2, Tel. (01) 6771478 or 677152.**

2 The BBC brings out a number of radio and television programmes for schools and individual learners. One that is intended for A-level learners of German is *Deutschlandspiegel*. You can get details of programmes by writing to **BBC Education Information, White City, London, W12 7TS.**

3 Most modern course books come with a tape that will provide you with valuable listening opportunities. Usually the teacher's book also contains transcripts, so that you can check anything that you have found difficult to understand.

4 If you have access to Astra satellite channels you can view a number of German television programmes and films regularly. There are also some radio broadcasts. Two of the more well known radio stations outside Germany are *Deutsche Welle* and *Deutschlandradio*. You can get their broadcasting schedules from: **Deutsche Welle, 50588 Köln, Germany** and **Deutschlandradio Marketing GmbH, Raderberggürtel 40, 50968 Köln, Germany**. German films are also often shown on terrestrial channels with subtitles. Keep an eye open for them!

5 Many Further Education Colleges and schools now have Flexible Learning Centres which contain self access listening material, for use by students working on their own. Often for a small registration fee (where charged) you can use their materials on a regular basis.

6 If you have a pen-friend or some other contact in Germany, or another German speaking country, you could ask him/her to record some material from the radio or television and send it to you. Rather than writing letters you might also record onto a cassette in English. Your German friend could reciprocate in German.

7 The *Goethe Institut* has a large amount of recorded and printed material which can be borrowed by post, once you have become a member of their library. Their address is: **Goethe Institut, 50 Prince's Gate, Exhibition Road, London, SW7 2PH.**

To get the practice that you will need you must listen to German regularly. As the examination approaches, it is a good idea to do some past listening papers of the Board whose examination you intend doing. Past papers can be obtained from the Board. You will find the addresses of all the Boards on p18. Examples of the types of listening questions are included elsewhere in this guide and on the tape which accompanies it.

READING

Like the other skills this requires a lot of regular practice and a good vocabulary. In the examination you will have to read a range of different texts fulfilling different functions. The examination syllabus may talk about texts in different 'registers'. That means texts written in different types of language according to the audience they are addressing. There are literary texts in a formal register and texts in a more colloquial register. The type of exercise set by the various Boards will vary, but for all of them you will need to understand what you have read. Sometimes it will be a question of understanding the gist or main argument of the text. Sometimes you will be asked questions about the details. Some questions may require only a one-word answer. To answer others you will need to write some continuous German.

Most of the reading material in A-level papers consists of authentic texts. By this is meant that the texts were originally intended for native German speakers. They have not been concocted specially for teaching or examining purposes. They are taken mainly from the German language press, magazines, pamphlets and literature.

This guide gives you help in how to answer the various types of question. You must familiarise yourself with the format of the reading questions set by your particular Board. Practising how to answer past questions is useful, but if you have the ability to understand what you read you should not find unexpected question types too difficult.

Read as much different material as you can get your hands on as well as practising on the material in this guide and on past papers. Remember you do not need to understand every word that you read to get the gist of what the text is all about. It is a good idea to get into the habit of looking up words that are unknown to you and writing them down in your vocabulary notebook. You should of course spend some time learning them afterwards.

Getting hold of printed authentic material in German is fortunately not difficult. The following suggestions give some ideas of where to look:

1 You can buy German newspapers and magazines at most good newsagents. Avoid some of the quality press, such as *Frankfurter Allgemeine* and *Die Süddeutsche Zeitung*, which contain excellent German, but which will probably be too difficult initially. *Die Welt*, a local newspaper from one of the regions, or even a tabloid such as *Bildzeitung* will be much easier to understand. One of the national German magazines such as *Stern, Bunte Illustrierte, Das Blatt, Brigitte* or *Focus* is also much more accessible. Your school or college could very well have some of these in the Language Department or the Library.

❷ The new A-level course books contain a wealth of reading material with exercises.

❸ German novels are often available in libraries or large book shops. They should also be available in a school or college library. German paperbacks can be ordered from most book shops or from European Schoolbooks, who also have a catalogue available. Their address is: **European Schoolbooks Ltd., The Runnings, Cheltenham, Gloucestershire, GL51 9PQ. (Tel. 01242 245252)**

❹ If your town has a twinning arrangement with a German speaking area, it should be possible to get in touch with somebody over there who would be prepared to correspond in German with you and to send you occasional copies of the local paper, in return perhaps for a similar service from you.

❺ As mentioned in the previous paragraph on Listening your local FE College or your school could have a Flexible Learning Centre. You should find that there will be lots of suitable A-level reading materials there which you should have no difficulty in being able to use.

SPEAKING

It is not impossible to practise this skill on your own, but it is difficult. Again it needs regular practice if you are to feel confident in using the language. In most localities there are German speaking nationals with whom you might arrange conversation lessons for a reasonable fee. Most secondary schools and local Further Education or Sixth Form colleges will have a German assistant, usually a young student who is in Great Britain to learn English. A letter to the Head of the Language Department in a school or college could put you in touch with somebody who is prepared to give you some conversation lessons, particularly just before your oral examination, if you do not have easy access to an assistant in your own institution.

You need to familiarise yourself with the format of the oral examination you will be taking and concentrate on those elements with which you need most help. Most oral examinations carry a large proportion of the marks available for the whole paper. Many of the things you are asked to do require careful preparation beforehand, either of material or strategies. You will find more about the oral later in this guide.

Probably the best way of getting intensive speaking (and listening) practice is by taking part in an exchange with a German speaker. Living with a German-speaking family for two or three weeks and having to survive without speaking any English will be of enormous benefit to you. Many schools and colleges organise such exchanges, but if this is not the case you could find that the area where you live is twinned with a similar German-speaking area, so the possibilities for finding a family that would be prepared to take you as a paying guest or as an exchange partner are available. It requires discipline on your part to use German the whole time you are there, particularly since foreigners often like to use their English on visitors. You just have to make it clear that you have come to improve your speaking and listening skills and that you do not wish to speak any English. When that is made clear people will normally go along with your wishes. Contact your local town hall or county hall to find out if there is a twinning arrangement or even if there is an exchange trip organised by them.

If you cannot get to a German-speaking country, then some of the following strategies will help to improve your speaking skills for the examination:

❶ Join an evening class. Most areas run conversation classes for a range of ability levels. Make some enquiries at your local Further Education establishment. If you join a class, make sure you speak! It is much easier to sit and listen, but you will only get speaking practice by speaking!

2 Hold conversations in German with yourself. If you imagine some of the questions that you might be asked in an oral examination, try speaking your reply out loud. This is best done when you are alone as people may think you have gone mad if they hear you talking to yourself!

3 Record some questions on to a tape with gaps for your replies. Vary your responses.

4 Keep asking yourself how you would express specific ideas in German and try vocalising them.

5 Learn some specific phrases and expressions that are useful in conversation. Here are some of the more common ones, but learn some of your own as well. There is another longer list of useful expressions in Chapter 5 (Speaking):

wie bitte?	*pardon?*
könnten Sie das bitte wiederholen?	*could you repeat that please?*
das ist sehr umstritten	*that is very controversial*
im Vergleich zu uns hat Deutschland…	*in comparison to us Germany has…*
im Gegensatz zu	*in contrast to*
das ist furchtbar/schrecklich/	*that is dreadful/terrible/*
unglaublich	*unbelievable*
der große Unterschied zwischen	*the big difference between England*
England und Deutschland liegt	*and Germany lies in the fact that…*
darin, daß…	
trotzdem	*nevertheless*
davon bin ich nicht ganz überzeugt	*I'm not completely convinced about that*
das glaube ich nicht	*I don't believe that*
da bin ich nicht so sicher	*I'm not so sure*
das könnte man wohl sagen	*I suppose you could say that*
das läßt sich nicht machen	*that can't be done*
das wäre mir lieber, weil…	*I would prefer that because…*
ich ziehe den Autos Fahrräder vor	*I prefer bikes to cars*
die heutige Situation sieht schlecht aus	*the present situation looks bad*
nehmen wir zum Beispiel	*let's take as an example*
so etwas kann man nie rechtfertigen	*you can never justify something like that*
ich erinnere mich sehr genau daran,	*I remember very well that…*
daß…	
was halten Sie von…?	*what do you think of…?*
glauben Sie persönlich, daß…?	*do you personally think that…?*
ich mag…	*I like…*

WRITING

This is probably the most difficult of all skills. The more you write the better you will get. Fortunately when you write you have time to shape what you want to say, to check what you have written and to improve bits that you are not satisfied with. When you are speaking you do not get this opportunity to the same extent.

Most errors are caused by making mistakes with the basics of the language, although you obviously also need to have at your disposal a good stock of words and phrases. To write accurately you must know the German case system and how it works. Knowing how to use verbs is also important, as is knowing about prepositions and the cases which follow them. Finally German word order is very different from that in English and creates the opportunity for lots of mistakes. To write well therefore, you must revise these four basics:

- the case system;
- verbs – what the various endings are and how the different tenses are formed;
- prepositions and the cases that follow them;
- word order.

Because you have more time when you write German you can be more systematic in checking what you have written, although it is much better to get it right first time. Once it is written down it tends to look correct. If at all possible do a rough version first and leave it for a few days before coming back to it. You should then see it with a fresh eye. Check it carefully through as you produce your final version. Check your final version again.

Be systematic in your checking. You can check the following aspects of your work fairly easily.

Check all verbs. Ask yourself these questions:

- Does it agree with the subject? Have I written a plural subject with a singular verb? (*Die Kinder geht*: it should be *Die Kinder gehen*).
  This usually happens when the verb is at the end of the sentence and you have forgotten what the subject is.
- Is the verb in the correct tense? It is often easier to use the simple past, rather than the perfect tense, which requires an auxiliary verb and a past participle.
- Is the verb regular or irregular?
- Is the verb in the correct position – usually second idea or at the end of the clause?

Check all nouns:

- Is the gender correct? (*der, die, das*). Check in a dictionary.
- Is the plural form correct?
- Is the noun in the correct case? (nominative, accusative, genitive, dative)
- Is it spelled with a capital letter? Is the spelling correct?
- Is it a weak noun? (see Chapter 2 Grammar pp 69–76).

Check all prepositions:

- Have I used the correct case after this preposition? Take particular care with those prepositions which can take either the accusative or the dative case.

Check all adjectives:

- If an adjective comes in front of a noun it will require an ending. Has it got the correct ending?

You will find all these points dealt with in the grammar chapter of this book.

Checking your work will not come naturally. It is something that you will have to practise. The majority of the mistakes made are to do with the mechanical aspects of the language. With care nearly all of them can be eliminated by checking.

Most of what you write will be marked for the language that you use (usually vocabulary, idiom, structures and accuracy) and for content (structure, relevance, analysis and illustrative material). The mark for language is usually greater than the mark for content. Nevertheless you need to have a clear idea of what you want to say and how you are going to say it. So an outline showing how you will introduce the topic, what ideas you will put in each paragraph (usually one idea per paragraph) and how you will finish off your piece of work is essential if you are to express your ideas clearly and give your reader an idea of where your argument is heading.

Most writers have their own phrases and expressions which occur frequently in their work. It is a good idea for you to learn a number of phrases and expressions that will make your work read more like that of a native German speaker. Choose also some constructions that will enable you to give your work a skeleton of language on which you will hang the flesh of your ideas. It can start with a number of language elements that you know are good German; then you are a good way along the road for producing a good piece of work. Some examples are shown below.

Some good constructions to include might be:

- a passive   es wird oft gesagt, daß…
- some modal verbs   man könnte behaupten, daß…
- some subordinate clauses
  introduced by conjunctions   weil, wenn, obgleich, vorausgesetzt daß…
- verbs with prepositions   ich erinnere mich sehr gut daran, daß…

- verbs taking the dative case   das entspricht unseren Vorstellungen
- an expanded adjectival phrase   ein schön aussehendes Kind
- an infinitive with *zu*   um eine Lösung zu finden, ohne ... zu, anstatt ... zu
- some reported speech   man sagte, das sei...
- a conditional sentence with *wenn*   wenn ich reich wäre, würde ich ein Auto kaufen
- a preposition with the genitive   wegen des Wetters
- the construction *je ... desto*   je mehr Geld man hat, desto mehr will man haben

A selection of useful idiomatic phrases will also help to make your written work read more like natural German. Collect your own from your reading, but you may find some of the following worthwhile learning along with the list of 'useful expressions' in the writing chapter later in the book.

wie dem auch sein mag	*however that may be*
in erster Linie	*mainly*
wir sind alle über die Lösung dieses Problems einig	*we are all agreed about the solution to this problem*
dieses Problem geht alle sozialen Schichten an	*this problem affects all social classes*
viele stehen auf dem Standpunkt, daß...	*many have the view that...*
beim Betrachten dieses Problems dürfen wir nicht außer Acht lassen, daß...	*when looking at this problem we must not forget that...*
es besteht kein Zweifel, daß...	*there is no doubt that...*
es besteht die Gefahr, daß...	*the danger exists that...*
im allgemeinen	*in general*
im großen und ganzen	*on the whole*
nach fachmännischen Schätzungen	*according to expert estimations*
nach den letzten Meinungsumfragen	*according to the latest opinion polls*
Vorteile und Nachteile müssen gegen einander abgewogen werden	*the pros and cons have to be carefully weighed*
einige sagen, daß ... andere dagegen...	*some say that ... on the other hand others...*
sich etwas vor Augen halten	*to bear something in mind*
es versteht sich von selbst, daß...	*it goes without saying that...*
im Gegenteil	*on the contrary*
es lohnt sich nicht...	*it is not worth...*
man könnte fast sagen, daß...	*one might almost say that...*
ich halte es für vernünftig	*I consider it sensible*

A TWO-YEAR PLAN OF ACTION

An A-level course of study is expected to be between 240 and 270 hours of teaching time usually spread over a period of two years. This should then be supplemented by at least five hours a week private study during term time. If we assume 34 weeks' teaching time in the first year and 30 weeks in the second year, allowing for end of year and 'Mock' examinations plus study leave, 320 hours of private study time are available and should be devoted to your study of German to ensure success at A-level. This means that you should be averaging one and a half to two hours of study per working day for the 64 weeks spread over the two years. Remember most academic years have a total of 38 weeks or 190 working days in attendance at school, but this will be less for a college student or someone at school in the private sector where terms are shorter.

On the face of it this does not seem a very long time, so you need to plan your workload with care, given that you will be studying for other A-level subjects as well. You also need to use the private study time you have on your timetable wisely and sort out your priorities at home on a weekly basis, leaving yourself time for recreational pursuits and the part-time job many of you will almost certainly have by then.

What follows is a suggested plan of action divided into five and a half terms which allows you to schedule your work and concentrate on your priorities. Depending on which syllabus you are studying there will be deadlines to meet and examinations to take – even internal ones.

Year one

AUTUMN TERM   12 WEEKS   60 HOURS PRIVATE STUDY

Priorities:

❶ Build up the level of your linguistic competence, improve your language skills, listening, reading, speaking and some easier writing.

❷ From the work you are doing in lessons, learn all new vocabulary and idioms and list by topic area.

❸ Learn the items of grammar which occur in your work and check that you understand them by using the summary in Chapter 2 of this book.

Concentrate this term on (a) nouns – gender and plurals, (b) the case structure, (c) adjectives and adjective endings – all three declensions, (d) verbs – formation of the main tenses of weak and strong verbs.

SPRING TERM   10 WEEKS   50 HOURS PRIVATE STUDY

Priorities:

❶ Continue to improve your language skills through practising different language tasks. Include more writing and begin to give it more emphasis.

❷ Continue to learn and list all new vocabulary and idioms, paying particular attention to the vocabulary and idioms which will enhance your written work, essay writing especially.

❸ Continue to learn items of grammar. Concentrate on (a) verbs – the formation of the other tenses of weak and strong verbs plus the passive voice, (b) the use of pronouns, (c) word order, (d) adverbs and the comparison of adjectives and adverbs.

SUMMER TERM   12 WEEKS   60 HOURS PRIVATE STUDY

Priorities:

❶ There will be some sort of end of year examination during this term. You will need to leave time to revise your vocabulary and grammar notes to date.

❷ Continue to practise and improve the four main skill areas, using all the hints given in the sections of this book.

❸ Continue to consolidate learning and listing vocabulary and idioms by topic area.

❹ Give serious consideration to the subject you might choose as your topic for your coursework or the literature texts you intend to read. Preliminary planning and reading should begin this term.

❺ Grammar – (a) use of prepositions, (b) use of co-ordinating and subordinating conjunctions, (c) use of tenses, including the subjunctive, (d) modal auxiliaries, (e) separable and inseparable verbs.

During the Summer Holidays further work should be done on your coursework and your prescribed texts – research on background material and/or reading in German.

Year two

AUTUMN TERM   12 WEEKS   60 HOURS PRIVATE STUDY

Priorities:

❶ You should aim to have completed your learning of grammar by the end of this term.

2 You should continue to extend your knowledge of vocabulary and idioms based on the topic areas listed in Chapter 1.

3 You must decide on and have a written plan in German for your coursework. With some Boards you will need to notify them of the title of your coursework before Half Term.

4 **Either** complete your first piece of coursework before Christmas, if you are doing more than one, **or** finish reading in detail at least half of your prescribed texts, if you are taking that option.

5 Use every opportunity to practise all four skills, increasingly using material based on the sort of tasks you will be expected to tackle in your examinations in the coming Summer Term.

6 Depending on the policy of your school or college you may have a 'Mock' examination before Christmas. You should allow for this in your work schedule. With feedback afterwards it is likely to take up at least three weeks of your precious time. Use the feedback to inform your revision programme.

SPRING TERM 10 WEEKS 50 HOURS PRIVATE STUDY

Priorities:

1 Complete the rest of your coursework and submit it to your teacher by the middle of March. Your teacher has to have assessed it and sent it to the Board to arrive no later than 30th April. Complete any reading of prescribed texts by the same time.

2 Your 'Mock' examinations could be this term – allow time for revision and use the results to identify weaknesses in skill areas.

3 Plan a revision programme to start at the beginning of next term, giving emphasis to those skills or elements of your examination syllabus which need extra attention.

4 Continue to practise examination-type questions in all the skill areas. Speaking should be given some additional priority as your Oral Test is imminent, either at the end of this term or at the start of next term.

5 Continue to expand your knowledge of vocabulary, idioms and grammatical points – make notes and write down words and idioms in your vocabulary note book under the appropriate topic heading.

SUMMER TERM 8 WEEKS 40 HOURS PRIVATE STUDY

Priorities:

1 Continue practising all types of examination question.

2 Revise all skill areas and how to approach a task.

3 Revise all topic area material.

4 Revise all vocabulary and idioms, but continue to add new material as it occurs.

5 Revise all grammar rules.

Here are some tips on how to revise successfully:

- You must have a realistic and achievable revision timetable.
- Choose the time you do your revision with care, i.e. when you are at your most receptive – include the times in your timetable.
- Ensure you have a suitable place to do your revision properly, away from distractions like TV or loud music. You need a table, a chair, adequate light (a table lamp will often help you concentrate) and a comfortable temperature – not too hot nor too cold.
- It is better to revise indoors rather than outdoors lying in the sun.
- When revising vocabulary try to learn the words in context. Learn lists of words in fairly short spells and always give yourself a written test.

- When revising grammar it is a good idea to make notes on a postcard. Distil the grammar into key facts. You will find that you can use these cards for quick revision on the night before your examinations.

- Plan your revision in relatively short bursts, depending on your span of concentration. Remember you learn most by studying for 30–45 minutes and then testing yourself to see how much you remember.

- Take regular breaks and give yourself a reward at the end of a revision period, e.g. watch TV or a video, read a book, play a computer game, listen to a CD, a record or the radio, go out.

- Have a definite start and finish time. Learning efficiency tends to fall at the beginning of a revision session but rises towards the end.

- Build into your timetable an increasing amount of revision time per day during the last few weeks before your examinations start. Remember that German should get its fair proportion of the time you have planned for revision.

- Don't waste revision time – recognise when your mind begins to wander; if you have things on your mind deal with them first or make a list of the things you need to do, then go back to revising; get up and move about – do something different like making a cup of tea; think with your day dream – it will probably go away; change your revision subject, work on another subject for a while, then come back to the German.

- Some things can often be better revised working with someone else, e.g. learning vocabulary – you can test one another; talking German together; listening to German radio broadcasts together.

- Make sure you understand what you are revising, refer to the relevant section in this book. Remember – **work, test, rest, reward.**

- Do not give up; stick to your programme. Recognise that you may feel irritable and depressed, don't worry, it is a common problem.

DURING THE EXAMINATION PERIOD

The night before:
- Don't do any in-depth revision – key points only. Read the hints in the section on the related skill area. Set yourself a time limit.
- Make sure everything is ready for the examination – pens, materials, dictionary, etc.
- Relax for most of the evening.
- Go to bed at a reasonable time.

The morning of the examination:
- Get up early, don't rush, don't be late and don't arrive flustered.
- Don't get there too early, you might be put off by those who seem more confident.
- Eat breakfast.

During the examination itself:
- Read all instructions carefully.
- Read the paper through before deciding which question to answer, if you have a choice.
- Make sure you have understood the question – what is it asking you to do?
- Budget the amount of time you are going to spend on each question where this is appropriate.
- For an essay in German always produce a plan in German.
- Try to leave time to check your work, go back and re-read your answers.
- Try to write legibly as the examiner has to be able to read what you have written in order to assess it.

A-LEVEL GERMAN

VOCABULARY

Units in this chapter

1.1 *An introduction*
1.2 *Different kinds of vocabulary*
1.3 *The structure of German - how complex words are formed - deductive vocabulary*
1.4 *Using a dictionary*
1.5 *Lists of words by topic area*

1.1 INTRODUCTION

We cannot overemphasise the importance of acquiring as wide a range of vocabulary as possible in the time you have for studying A/AS-level. Unfortunately you will find that at this level no lists of vocabulary are provided by the Boards. Instead there are only themes or topics listed which you will be able to absorb in detail by looking in the syllabus details for the Examining Board of your choice. These themes or topics form the basis on which the materials for the various sections of the examination are chosen.

What we have tried to do here is give you some tips on how to learn vocabulary, tell you something about the structure of the German language and provide lists of German words and phrases which are grouped according to the topic areas mentioned by the Boards.

From research into the frequency of word-usage we know that more than 80% of the vocabulary of all normal texts is included in the basic 1,000 words of a language; a further 8 to 10% in the second 1,000, approximately 4% in the third 1,000, a further 2% in the fourth and likewise another 2% in the fifth. The first 4,000 words therefore comprise on average 95% of the vocabulary of all normal texts and dialogues. It is not too daunting a task to expect that you will be able to learn this basic and essential vocabulary during your A/AS-level course, but you must start straight away and not leave the serious work on learning vocabulary until the last few weeks before the examination.

1.2 DIFFERENT KINDS OF VOCABULARY

One of the aims of any A/AS-level course is to enable the candidate to use German for the purpose of communication. To do this with confidence you need to acquire this basic and essential vocabulary as described in the previous paragraph. There are in fact three kinds of vocabulary, which all students at this level should be aware of – they are **receptive**, **productive** and **deductive**. Receptive vocabulary is made up of words or phrases in German which you have seen or heard at some stage in your experience, but which you would not normally use in your own work, even though you know the meaning. Productive vocabulary contains words and phrases which you can use accurately and with confidence in any part of the examination or in any context. Deductive vocabulary is, as its name implies, words or phrases which you do not know the meaning of exactly, but you can make a good guess at the meaning from the context or from the formation of the words themselves. The knowledge of all three kinds of vocabulary can be improved in a number of different ways.

RECEPTIVE VOCABULARY

Receptive vocabulary can be extended by keeping a vocabulary note-book and writing in it any new words you come across in your work, whatever the task may be. Look up the words in a large dictionary and record the meanings in your note-book. It would also be worth including any idiomatic phrase in which the word occurs listed in the dictionary, as this will give you a context for the use of the word in future. The form in which you compile your vocabulary note-book is a matter of personal taste, but as the material used in the examination is topic-based, we suggest you make your vocabulary entries in your note-book under topic areas.

PRODUCTIVE VOCABULARY

Productive vocabulary can be improved in much the same way. There is no short cut to learning vocabulary properly, you just have to keep working at it and devise your own system for ensuring that you learn as much as you can in the time available. Here are some tips on increasing your productive vocabulary:

- Set yourself a target of so many words to be learned each week. Remember to learn the gender and plural of each noun and the principal parts of each strong verb. Remember the secret is to establish a routine and keep to it.

- Be systematic, work through the lists in this book and make use of one or more of the excellent published *Advanced German Vocabulary* books on the market.

- Do not try to learn too many words at one go and always ensure that you test yourself in writing.

- It is a good idea to work with a friend and test one another when you think you have both learned the list properly.

- Do be careful about the way you set out the words you enter into your note-book. Remember the conventions for showing the plural of nouns and the importance of indicating the details of verbs – strong, weak, separable, inseparable, regular or irregular, takes *sein* or *haben* etc.

- Listen to German radio programmes, especially daily news bulletins which often have similar items to ours. Note down any words you are not fully conversant with and look them up in your dictionary, then learn them. German radio programmes can be heard in most parts of this country; you can get details about frequencies by writing to Deutsche Welle, 50588 Köln, Deutschland.

- Read German newspapers and magazines and do the same thing.

- Make arrangements to go to a German-speaking country and stay in a family home for a short period. Most schools and colleges organise exchanges to Germany, so do take advantage of the opportunity to visit and immerse yourself in the German-speaking atmosphere. There is nothing better than this for helping to improve your productive or receptive vocabulary.

- Set up a correspondence with a German-speaking friend and ask him/her to write letters to you, half in German and half in English; you do the same thing by return and that way you both get to extend your productive vocabulary.

● When working on any task in preparation for your examination, devise a method for writing down new vocabulary as you come across it and recording words and phrases by topic in your notebook. The fact that you are writing them down and deciding which topic area to assign them to, will actually help you to commit them to memory.

● Remember that there is only one way of extending your knowledge of vocabulary and that is to have a system for learning words and phrases on a very regular basis. Little and often is the watchword and you must keep it up; once learned, try to use it!

DEDUCTIVE VOCABULARY

How to deduce the meaning of a word or phrase in German which is new to you, requires some knowledge of the formation of German words. Armed with this knowledge you will be able to improve your deductive vocabulary.

You will already have realised that German is a much more formalised language than, for example English. German vocabulary consists of comparatively few basic words or roots and lots of compounds which are derived from them. It is worth knowing how these complex words in German are formed, as it will clearly help you to extend your deductive vocabulary. Here is a list of words which are related in this way and illustrate a number of the principles involved:

suchen	*to look for, to seek*
die Suche (-n)	*the search*
besuchen	*to visit*
der Besuch (-e)	*the visit*
versuchen	*to try, to attempt*
der Versuch (-e)	*the attempt*
die Versuchung (-en)	*the temptation*
untersuchen	*to investigate*
die Untersuchung (-en)	*the investigation*
die Untersuchungshaft	*custody, imprisonment awaiting trial*
aufsuchen	*to look up, to find (in a book)*
aussuchen	*to seek out, to pick*
durchsuchen	*to search, to frisk*
nachsuchen	*to look and see if*
die Nachsuchung (-en)	*the application, request*

This group of words is based on the root of the verb **suchen**. It shows how words can be derived from one another in German. By looking at the parts of a long word you can frequently guess at the meaning of the whole word. What you need to know is how complex words are formed from simpler words and how different parts of speech can be connected in German. There are several ways in which this can be done:

● by adding a prefix or a suffix;

● by changing the vowel sound;

● by joining two existing words together, sometimes with a linking element.

Here are some examples:

● adding a prefix e.g. **ver-**: suchen – *to look for*, **ver**suchen – *to try*

● adding a suffix e.g. **-ung**: untersuchen – *to investigate*, die Untersuch**ung** – *the investigation*

● changing a vowel sound: sprechen – *to speak*, das Gespräch – *the conversation*

● joining words together: der Rat + das Haus = das **Rathaus** – *the town hall*

● joining with a linking letter: die Untersuchung + die Haft = die Untersuchung**s**haft – *custody, imprisonment while awaiting trial*

Knowing how to form words from other parts of speech is another way of improving your deductive vocabulary. Have a look at these examples:

● masculine nouns can usually be formed from the stem of a verb: besuchen – *to visit*, der **Besuch** – *the visit*; fallen – *to fall*, der **Fall** – *the fall*, in diesem **Fall** - *in this case*.

- neuter nouns which have the suffixes **-chen** or **-lein** are the diminutives of the words to which they are attached: die Frau – *woman, wife*, das Frau**lein** – *young lady, unmarried woman;* die Stadt – *town*, das Städt**chen** – *small town.*

- adding the suffix **-e** to the stem of a verb forms a feminine noun which usually denotes the action or an instrument: suchen – *to seek*, die Such**e** – *the search*; bremsen – *to brake* die Brems**e** – *the brake.*

- adding the suffixes **-heit, -(ig)keit** to form feminine abstract nouns from adjectives denoting a quality: krank – *ill*, die Krank**heit** – *illness*; dankbar – *grateful*, die Dankbar**keit** – *gratitude*; geschwind - *fast*, die Geschwind**igkeit** – *speed.*

- adding the suffixes **-nis, -schaft, -ung** to form neuter and feminine nouns from nouns, adjectives or parts of verbs as follows:

  - **-nis** is added to part of a verb or to an adjective to form an abstract noun. The gender is usually neuter, but there are a few feminine nouns formed this way: erkennen – *to recognise*, die Erkennt**nis** – *recognition*; finster – *dark*, die Finster**nis** – *darkness*; but (more usually) erleben – *to experience*, das Erleb**nis** – experience; geheim – *secret*, das Geheim**nis** – *secret.*

  - **-schaft** is used to form feminine nouns from other nouns and implies a collective group or state: der Freund – *friend*, die Freund**schaft** – *friendship*; der Mann – *man*, die Mann**schaft** – *team, crew.*

  - **-ung** is added to the stem of verbs to form feminine nouns which refer to   the action of the verb: bedeuten – *to mean*, die Bedeut**ung** – *meaning*; heizen – *to heat*, die Heiz**ung** – *heating*; landen – *to land*, die Land**ung** – *landing;* aufteilen – *to divide, share out*, die Aufteil**ung** – *division, sharing out.*

- adding the suffixes **-ei, -erei** to form feminine nouns from other nouns or verbs as follows:

  - **-ei** is added to another noun usually indicating the place where something is done: der Bäcker – *baker*, die Bäcker**ei** – *bakery*; der Konditor – *pastry cook*, die Konditor**ei** – *cake shop, patisserie;* der Maler – *painter*, die Maler**ei** – *art, painting;* der Schläger – *thug, ruffian*, die Schläger**ei** – *fight, brawl.*

  - **-erei** is added to the stem of a verb and shows an action which is repetitive: fischen – *to fish*, die Fisch**erei** – *catching fish, fishing industry*; fragen – *to ask*, die Frag**erei** – *lots of questions*; schwatzen – *to chatter*, die Schwätz**erei** – *prattling, gossip.*

- adding the suffix **-in** forms a feminine noun usually denoting someone who does something. Here are some examples: die Lehrer**in** – *female teacher*; die Freund**in** – *female friend*; die Schüler**in** – *schoolgirl*; die Verkäufer**in** – *saleswoman, shop assistant*; die Kellner**in** – *waitress*; die Beamt**in** – *female official*; die Enkel**in** – *granddaughter*; die Pfleger**in** – *nurse*; die Rassist**in** – *female racist*; die Schaffner**in** – *female conductor*; (e.g. on bus); die Schmeichler**in** – *female flatterer.*

- using the suffixes **-er, -ler** to form masculine nouns from other nouns or verbs:
  - **-er** when added to the stem of a verb indicates the person doing the action: anhängen – *to attach, to subscribe to*, der Anhäng**er** – *trailer, supporter*; backen – *to bake*, der Bäck**er** – *baker*; verbrechen – *to commit a crime*, der Verbrech**er** – *criminal.* **-er** when added to a place name forms a noun showing the person who lives there: Frankfurt – der Frankfurt**er**, Berlin – der Berlin**er**, Österreich – der Österreich**er** – *Austrian.*
  - **-ler** is commonly used to form a noun from another noun denoting a person who does something: der Tisch – *table*, der Tisch**ler** – *carpenter*; die Kunst – *art*, der Künst**ler** – *artist*; der Sport – *sport*, der Sport**ler** – *sportsman*; die Wissenschaft – *science*, der Wissenschaft**ler** – *scientist*; der Handel – *trade;* der Händ**ler** – *trader.*
  Please note all nouns formed using these two suffixes are masculine and an Umlaut is often used where possible.

The suffix **-ling** is used to form masculine nouns as well from verbs or adjectives. When formed from verbs the noun refers to a person who is the recipient of the action of the verb: lehren – *to teach*, der Lehr**ling** – *the apprentice*; prüfen – *to examine*, der Prüf**ling** – *examinee, examination candidate.* When the noun is formed from an adjective it denotes a person who has the quality the adjective describes: feig – *cowardly*, der Feig**ling** – *the coward*; fremd – *strange*, der Fremd**ling** – *stranger*; früh – *early*, der Früh**ling** – *spring* (not a person, but the idea is the same).

There are other prefixes and suffixes which are used particularly with verbs (see section on inseparable and separable verbs, pp105–108). Some are used to form adjectives. Here are some of the more common examples of suffixes used to form adjectives:

- **-bar** is added to the stem of a verb and is used like *-able* or *-ible* in English: brauchen – *to use*, brauch**bar** – *usable*; danken – *to thank*, dank**bar** – *grateful*; essen – *to eat*, eß**bar** – *edible*; trinken – *to drink*, trink**bar** – *drinkable*.

- **-ig** is commonly added to a noun to form an adjective, either showing that a person or thing possesses what the noun refers to, or it indicates a quality similar to the person or thing denoted by the noun: der Blut – *blood*, blut**ig** – *bloody*; der Staub – *dust*, staub**ig** – *dusty*; das Holz – *wood*, holz**ig** – *woody*; die Milch – *milk*, milch**ig** – *milky*; der Riese – *giant*, ries**ig** – *gigantic*.

- **-los** is added to a noun in the same way as the English – *less*: die Hoffnung – *hope*, hoffnungs**los** – *hopeless*; die Sorge – *worry, care*, sorg**los** – *careless* (i.e. *carefree*); die Furcht – *fear*, furcht**los** – *fearless*.

- **-mäßig** is often used in modern German to form adjectives from nouns, having the sense of *in accordance with*: die Gewohnheit – *habit*, gewohnheits**mäßig** – *habitual*; der Plan – *plan*, plan**mäßig** – *according to plan;* die Regel – *rule*, regel**mäßig** – *regular*.

Here are a few of the most common prefixes used to form adjectives and nouns:

- **grund-** has the effect of intensifying the meaning, making the sense of the adjective stronger and more fundamental: **grund**anständig – *thoroughly decent*, **grund**falsch – *utterly wrong*. With nouns it means 'basic/essential': der **Grund**gedanke – *basic idea*; der **Grund**zug – *essential feature*.

- **hoch-** also intensifies the meaning literally meaning *highly*: begabt – *talented*, **hoch**begabt – *highly talented*; entwickelt – *developed*, **hoch**entwickelt – *highly developed*; fliegend – *flying*, **hoch**fliegend – *ambitious, high flying*; fein – *fine*, **hoch**fein – *high quality*. With nouns it usually means high: der **Hoch**betrieb – *peak period, rush hour*; der **Hoch**druck – *high pressure*; die **Hoch**ebene – *plateau*; die **Hoch**achtung – *deep respect*.

- **ur-** is another prefix which intensifies the meaning of the word to which it is attached: alt – *old*, **ur**alt – *ancient, very old*; weltlich – *worldly*, **ur**weltlich – *primeval, primordial*. It can also be used with other parts of speech when it has a similar effect: die **Ur**sache (-n) – *cause*, **ur**sächlich – *causal*; der **Ur**sprung (**Ur**sprünge) – *origin*, **ur**sprünglich – *original*, die **Ur**sprünglichkeit – *naturalness, simplicity*; das **Ur**teil (-e) – *judgement, verdict*, **ur**teilsfähig – *competent to judge*.

- **un-** is used in the same way as in English to indicate the opposite meaning: abhängig – *dependent*, **un**abhängig – *independent*, die **Un**abhängigkeit – *independence*; ähnlich – *similar*, **un**ähnlich – *dissimilar*, die **Un**ähnlichkeit – *dissimilarity*; angenehm – *pleasant*, **un**angenehm – *unpleasant*; anständig – *decent, respectable*, **un**anständig – *ill-/bad-mannered, rude*, die **Un**anständigkeit – *bad manners, rudeness, indecency*; freundlich – *friendly*, **un**freundlich – *unfriendly*, die **Un**freundlichkeit – *unfriendliness*.

The following are further examples of word groups which indicate how words are linked to one another. Being aware of this in learning German will help to improve your deductive vocabulary.

- hoffen – *to hope*, hoffentlich – *hopefully, it is to be hoped that*, die Hoffnung – *hope*, hoffnungslos – *hopeless*, die Hoffnungslosigkeit – *hopelessness, despair*, hoffnungsvoll – *hopeful*.

- antworten – *to answer*, die Antwort (-en) – *the answer*, der Antwortschein (-e) – *the (international) reply coupon*, beantworten – *to answer, reply to*, die Beantwortung – *answer, response*, verantworten – *to accept responsibility for*, verantwortlich – *responsible*, der/die Verantwortliche (-n) – *person responsible*, die Verantwortlichkeit (no pl.) – *responsibility*, die Verantwortung – *responsibility*, verantwortungslos – *irresponsible*, die Verantwortungslosigkeit (no pl.) – *irresponsibility*, verantwortungsvoll – *responsible*.

- stehen – *to stand*, stehenbleiben – *to stop, come to a halt*, stehenlassen – *to leave behind*, gestehen – *to confess*, das Geständnis (-sse) – *confession*, verstehen – *to understand*, der Verstand (no pl.) – *reason*, verstandesmäßig – *rational*, verständig – *sensible*, sich verständigen mit jedem – *to communicate with someone*, die Verständigung (no pl.) – *understanding, agreement*, verständlich – *understandable, comprehensible*, die Verständlichkeit (no pl.) – *comprehensibility*, das Verständnis (no pl.) – *understanding, comprehension*, verständnislos – *uncomprehending*, die Verständnislosigkeit – *lack of understanding or sympathy*.

1.3 USING A DICTIONARY

- Choosing a dictionary
- How to use your dictionary
- Choosing the right word
- Using a monolingual dictionary

CHOOSING A DICTIONARY

To complete an A/AS-level course in German successfully you must own your own dictionary. The majority of the Examining Boards now allow you to take a dictionary into most parts of the examination. Sometimes they stipulate the edition you should use and if this is the case for your Examining Board you should acquire the specified dictionary at the start of your course and make sure you understand and are fully conversant with the way in which that particular dictionary presents information to you.

The choice of a dictionary, if not specified, is important. Here are some things you should take into account when choosing the right dictionary for you:

- Remember that the dictionary should be large enough to contain the range of vocabulary and idiom which you are expected to know and use productively in your work.

- Ascertain before buying whether you are allowed to use only a monolingual dictionary (i.e. German–German) in your examination or one which is German–English, English–German. (For details see the Board's syllabus.)

- Make sure that the dictionary you acquire has the **gender, plural, genitive ending** and **idiomatic uses** of the nouns listed, full details about verbs, i.e. whether they are **regular** or **irregular**, **weak** or **strong**, **transitive** or **intransitive** and whether the **principal parts** are included and the categories of all other words, i.e. **parts of speech**.

- Ask your teacher or tutor to recommend a dictionary to you which will satisfy all the requirements of your Examining Board and the way s/he wants you to work.

You can expect to pay up to £20 for a suitably sized German–English dictionary and slightly more for a similar sized German–German one. Finally make sure that your dictionary is as up to date as possible – in other words the most recently revised edition.

HOW TO USE YOUR DICTIONARY

When you first look at a large German–English dictionary, you will obviously see words in German listed alphabetically with their English meanings, but that is not all. There is a lot of other information given and you need to understand it in order to use your dictionary to its full potential and to enhance your knowledge of German.

All dictionaries use abbreviations. You will need to familiarise yourself with them. Here are some typical examples taken from one of the large German–English dictionaries currently available.

acc	accusative case	n	noun
adj	adjective	neg	negative
adv	adverb	nom	nominative case

art	article	npl	plural noun
aux	auxiliary	nt	neuter
coll	colloquial	pass	passive
comp	comparative	pl	plural
conj	conjunction	poss	possessive
cpd	compound	pref	prefix
dat	dative case	prep	preposition
decl	declined	pres	present
def	definite	pret	preterite/imperfect
dem	demonstrative	pron	pronoun
dial	dialect	prp	present participle
dim	diminutive	ptp	past participle
dir obj	direct object	reg	regular
esp	especially	sep	separable
f	feminine	sing	singular
fig	figurative	sl	slang
gen	genitive case	subjunc	subjunctive
imp	imperative	usu	usually
impers	impersonal	vb	verb
indef	indefinite	vi	intransitive verb
indir obj	indirect object	vr	reflexive verb
infin	infinitive	vt	transitive verb
insep	inseparable	vti	transitive and intransitive verb
inv	invariable		
irreg	irregular	vtir	transitive/intransitive and reflexive verb
m	masculine		
		vtr	transitive and reflexive verb

Have a look at these entries from a large German–English dictionary:

- a feminine noun

Tr<u>ä</u>ne *f* -, **-n** tear, (*einzelne Träne*) tear(drop), **den Tränen nahe sein** to be near to *or* on the verge of tears.

The underlined letter <u>ä</u> shows that this is a long vowel sound when you say the word in German.

The *f* shows the gender – *feminine*.
The - shows there is no genitive ending.
The **-n** shows the plural ending, so *tears* are **dieTräne<u>n</u>** in German.

The rest of the entry reproduced here shows another specific meaning *teardrop* plus an idiomatic phrase. The full entry includes several other phrases in which the word **Träne** occurs.

- a masculine noun

Tr<u>o</u>st *m* **-(e)s**, *no pl* consolation, comfort
jemandem Trost zusprechen/bringen to console *or* comfort somebody.

The <u>o</u> shows that this is a long vowel sound.
no pl means that this noun is only used in the singular.

The *m* shows the gender – *masculine*.
-(e)s is the genitive singular ending, the **e** is optional, hence the brackets.

The phrase **jemandem Trost ... bringen** is idiomatic and forms part of the rest of the entry for this word.

- a verb

zurücktreten *sep irreg vi aux sein*, *pres* **tritt zurück**, *pret* **trat zurück**, *ptp* **zurückgetreten** to step back.

a separable verb, an irregular verb, an intransitive verb, auxiliary *sein* for the perfect tenses, e.g. **er ist zurückgetreten.**

The principal parts are 3rd pers sing *pres* – present tense, *pret* – imperfect tense (preterite) and *ptp* – the past participle.

- another verb

  trennen *vt* to separate (*von* from)

  vt = a transitive verb, *von* (+ dat) is the preposition used with this verb meaning *from*.

- **treu 1** *adj* loyal, faithful, true, devoted **2** *adv* loyally, faithfully, devotedly

  1 adj = adjective **2** adv = adverb. The entries for this word give other German words which show when the word **treu** has the meanings listed, e.g. **ein treuer Freund** – a loyal friend, **ein treuer Diener** – a devoted servant.

- **wenn** *conj* **a)** (*konditional*) if **b)** (*zeitlich*) when

  conj = conjunction **a)** introducing a *conditional* clause **b)** introducing a *time* clause – in both uses this conjunction introduces a subordinate clause.

- **wider** *prep* (+ *acc*) against, contrary to

  prep = preposition always followed by the *accusative* case.

In the English–German section of the dictionary the lay-out is very similar. The main addition is the inclusion of the phonetic spelling of the word in English in square brackets immediately after the alphabetical entry. This has been omitted in the examples which follow.

- **environment** *n* Umwelt *f*, (*of town etc, physical surroundings*) Umgebung *f*,

  (*social, cultural surroundings also*) Milieu *nt*.

  working-class environment Arbeitermilieu *nt*.

  n means noun,   *f* is the gender – feminine,   *nt* is also the gender – *neuter*.

This gives three possible translations for the word **environment** and one compound. The explanation in italics gives you the meaning/context for each of the three German nouns. You have to choose the right one accordingly.

- **enchanting** *adj*, **-ly** *adv* bezaubernd, entzückend
  both words in German can be used as adjectives or adverbs.

- **and** *conj* **(a)** und **(b)** (*in repetition, continuation*) und, (*between comparatives*) immer, **better and better** immer besser **(c)** (*with numbers*) **three hundred and ten** dreihundertzehn, **one and a half** anderthalb

From these few examples you can see that using a dictionary needs care.

CHOOSING THE RIGHT WORD

On any page of a large dictionary in the German–English section you will obviously find a lot of alternatives listed as possible English versions for the German word you are looking up. It is usual for the most common translation to be listed first. You have to decide, however, which of the versions listed is the right one, given the context in which the word occurs.

It is possible of course that the word you are looking for will not be listed where you expect to find it. The most likely reason for this will be that it is part of a verb which is usually listed in its infinitive form. The past participle of most verbs begins with **ge-** for example; you will not find the meaning of past participles listed under **ge-,** only the verbs themselves, e.g. **geflogen** *ptp of* **fliegen**. You need to look up **fliegen** to find the meaning *to fly*.

When you look up an English word you find frequently that there are a number of possible German equivalents. If you follow these simple rules there is every chance that you will choose the right German word.

- What sort of word are you looking for – a noun, an adjective, a verb or what? Clearly you must choose the same part of speech.

- When you think that you have found the right German word for the context, look it up in the German–English section of your dictionary and you should find the English word you were looking up in the first place. This a good check for the right word.

- Do be careful not to choose the word in German which looks the same as the English automatically. It is probably not used in an exact equivalent sense.

● Prepositions in English are used in all kinds of ways especially with verbs, so if you are looking for a word which is followed by a preposition in English then great care is needed to ensure that you choose the same word with the right preposition in German. Please remember it is vitally important that you check the case which is used with any preposition in German. More mistakes are made with prepositions than any other construction. The golden rule is to crosscheck the meanings both ways.

USING A MONOLINGUAL DICTIONARY

● A *Deutsch–Deutsch* dictionary is quite difficult to use, especially at the beginning of your course. However, it is worth persevering with trying to use one, as it is so good for improving your knowledge of German. These dictionaries are compiled for native speakers and therefore make specific demands on anyone learning German. The examples given after the initial definition in German will be wide-ranging and no concessions will be made to the non-native speaker. You can now obtain a monolingual dictionary specially compiled for people learning the language. It is: Langenscheidts Großwörterbuch Deutsch als Fremdsprache.

● The conventions about lay out and the abbreviations used will be much the same as in the German–English dictionaries discussed already, except that they will be in German.

● Perhaps the best way to become adept at using a monolingual dictionary is to use it in conjunction with a German–English dictionary at first, so that you can cross check words and meanings as you go along. When you become more proficient and more confident of your knowledge of vocabulary and grammar as your course progresses, you will find that your monolingual dictionary becomes an invaluable source of idiomatic German which you can use in your work. Your reliance on your other dictionary will become less necessary.

Here are some entries taken from a German–German dictionary:

● **Umwelt** *die, nur Sg, Kollekt,* **1** die Erde, die Luft, das Wasser und die Pflanzen als Lebensraum für die Menschen und Tiere: *gegen die Verschmutzung der U. kämpfen*

die is the gender – feminine, *nur Sg* means *only singular, Kollekt* indicates that this is a collective noun.

A literal translation of definition **1** is – *the earth, the air, the water and the plants as living space for humans and animals,* i.e. the environment.

2 die gesellschaftlichen Verhältnisse, in denen ein Mensch lebt und die seine Entwicklung beeinflussen.

Definition **2** – *the social conditions in which a human being lives and which influence his development,* i.e. the environment in that sense.

3 die Menschen, zu denen man Kontakt hat: *sich von seiner U. mißverstanden fühlen*

Definition **3** – *the human beings with whom one has contact,* – i.e. one's human environment, circle of human contacts.

Besides these entries quoted here there are a number of compounds listed involving the word **Umwelt** and phrases which show the context in which the word can be used.

● **Lampe** *die, -, -n,* **1** ein (*mst* elektrisches) Gerät (*z. B.* an der Decke od. an der Wand), das Licht erzeugt: *e-e L. an die Decke hängen.*
-K: **Schreibtisch-, Tisch-, Zimmer- 2** das Teil e-s technischen Geräts, das künstliches Licht erzeugt: *Glühbirnen, Neonröhren u. Scheinwerfer sind Lampen.* Abb. unter **Fahrrad**. K-: **Lampen-, -licht -schein**. -K: **Glüh-, Öl-, Paraffin-**

die is the gender – feminine, -, means no change in genitive singular, -n, is the plural ending.

Definition **1** – a (*mostly* electric) piece of equipment (e.g. on the ceiling or on the wall) which produces light. **2** – the part of a technical piece of equipment which produces artificial light.

The abbreviations used here are:

mst – meist – *mostly*; *z. B.* – zum Beispiel – *e.g.* ; *od.* – oder – *or*; *e-e* – eine - *a*; *e-s* – eines – of a (genitive of ein); *-K* – Kompositum - compound ending with **-lampe**, so **Schreibtischlampe** – *desklamp*; *K-* – Kompositum – compound starting with **Lampen-** – **Lampenlicht** – *artificial light*; *u.* – und – *and*; *Abb.* – Abbildung – *illustration* or *diagram*.

Words in *italics* after the definitions in German are examples of how the word is used in context.

> ● **betonen**; *betonte, hat betont*; *Vt* **1 etw. b.** e-e Silbe od. ein Wort hervorheben, indem man es kräftig spricht (ein Wort richtig, falsch, auf der Stammsilbe b.; e-e betonte Silbe): *Das Wort „Katze" wird auf der ersten Silbe betont* **2 etw. b.** auf etw. besonders hinweisen – hervorheben: *Der Redner betonte, daß er mit dieser Regelung nicht zufrieden sei* **3 etw. betont etw.** etw. macht etw. deutlich, hebt es hervor: *Die enge Kleidung betont ihre Körperformen*

This is a weak verb with an inseparable prefix **be-** and therefore no **ge-** in the past participle. The principal parts of the verb, i.e. imperfect and perfect tenses, are in *italics* immediately after the infinitive. The abbreviations used here are:

e-e is eine; *od.* is oder; *etw.* is etwas; *Vt* is a transitive verb

Definition **1** means *by saying it forcefully (to emphasise or stress a word rightly, wrongly, on the root syllable; a stressed syllable)*. Definition **2** means *to point something out especially, to emphasise something*. Definition **3** means *something makes something clear, emphasises it*. The sentences in *italics* are examples showing the shades of meaning.

> ● **singen**; *sang, hat gesungen*; *Vt/i* **1 (etw.) s.** e-e Melodie od. ein Lied mit der Stimme produzieren (ein Lied s.; falsch, richtig, laut, leise, schön, gut s.; nach Noten/vom Blatt s.; solo, Sopran s.): *Weihnachtslieder s.* K-: **Sing-, -stimme, -weise**; *Vt* **2 j-n in den Schlaf s.** leise s. (1), bis *bes* ein Kind einschläft; *Vi* **3** beruflich od. als Hobby regelmäßig s. (1): *im Kirchenchor, am Theater s.* **4** *gespr*; *mst* vor der Polizei ein Verbrechen gestehen (j-n zum Singen bringen) **5 ein Vogel singt** ein Vogel produziert melodische Töne

This is a strong verb, the imperfect and perfect tenses are in *italics* as before. The abbreviations are:

> *Vt/i* means a verb which is either transitive or intransitive;
> *K-* Kompositum i.e. a compound which starts with **Sing-**;
> *Vt* and *Vi* are a transitive and intransitive verb respectively;
> *bes* is *besonders* and means 'especially';
> j-n is jemanden meaning 'someone';
> *gespr* is *gesprochene Sprache, umgangssprachlich* meaning 'colloquial' use.

Definition **1** means *to produce a melody or a song with the voice (to sing a song; to sing wrongly, correctly, loudly, softly, beautifully, well; to sing from music/to sightread; to sing solo, soprano)*

Definition **2** means *to sing someone to sleep, to sing softly until one, especially a child falls asleep*

Definition **3** means *to sing regularly on a professional basis or as a hobby*

Definition **4** means *to sing* (slang for *to confess a crime*) *mostly to the police*

Definition **5** means *a bird sings, i.e. a bird produces melodic sounds or notes*

> ● **melodisch** *Adj*; **1** so, daß der Klang angenehm für den Zuhörer ist (e-e Stimme; etw. klingt m.) **2** in bezug auf die Melodie

This is an adjective. Definition **1** means *so that the sound is pleasant to the listener*, i.e. melodic or melodious. **2** means *regarding the melody*.

> ● **genügsam** *Adj.* mit wenig zufrieden, anspruchslos (ein Mensch, ein Tier; g. leben)

This is an adjective which can also be used as an adverb. The definition means *satisfied with little, undemanding/modest (a human, an animal, to live modestly)*

- **während** *Präp; mit Gen*; im Laufe der genannten Zeit, im Verlauf der genannten Tätigkeit *o. ä.; w. des Sommers, w. der Ferien, w. der letzten Jahre, w. des Essens*

This is a preposition with the Genitive case. The abbreviations used here are:

Präp – Präposition – *preposition*; *Gen* – Genitiv – *genitive case*; *o. ä.* – oder ähnliche(s) – *or similar.*

The definition means *in the course of the named time, during the course of the activity* hence 'during'. The examples of the use of this preposition are printed in *italics* after the definition.

- **während** *Konjunktion*; **1** drückt e-e Gleichzeitigkeit aus; *W. ich koche, kannst du den Tisch decken; W. wir beim Essen saßen, läutete das Telefon* **2** drückt e-e Gegensätzlichkeit aus; *W. sie sehr sparsam ist, kauft er sich teure Bücher*

This is a subordinating conjunction. Definition **1** means *expresses a simultaneity*, i.e. two actions going on together at the same time hence 'while/whilst'. Definition **2** means *expresses a contrast* hence it can be translated as 'whereas'. The examples in *italics* illustrate the differences between the two uses.

The most commonly used abbreviations in a monolingual dictionary are:

Abk.	Abkürzung	*abbreviation*
Adj.	Adjektiv	*adjective*
Adv.	Adverb	*adverb*
Akk.	Akkusativ	*accusative case*
bes	besonders	*especially*
Dat.	Dativ	*dative case*
etw.	etwas	*something*
Gen.	Genitiv	*genitive case*
geschr	geschriebene Sprache, förmlich	*written language formal*
gespr	gesprochene Sprache, umgangssprachlich	*spoken language, colloquial*
ID	idiomatische Wendung	*idiomatic expression*
mst	meist	*mostly*
Nom.	Nominativ	*nominative case*
o. ä.	oder ähnliches	*or similar*
Pl.	Plural	*plural*
Präp.	Präposition	*preposition*
Sg.	Singular	*singular*
Subst.	Substantiv	*noun*
u.	und	*and*
usw	und so weiter	*and so on, etc.*
Vi	intransitives Verb	*intransitive verb*
Vimp	unpersönlich gebrauchtes Verb	*impersonal verb*
Vr	reflexives Verb	*reflexive verb*
Vt	transitives Verb	*transitive verb*
Vt/i	transitives Verb, das auch ohne Akkusativobjekt verwendet werden kann	*transitive verb that can also be used without an accusative object*
z. B.	zum Beispiel	*for example, e.g.*

Using a dictionary needs practice throughout your course, but it is an effort in time and application that is well worthwhile and will reward you handsomely.

1.4 VOCABULARY LISTED BY TOPIC AREA

In this section you will find lists of vocabulary on 12 topic areas which are linked to the topics mentioned in the A/AS-level syllabuses. This is not intended to be an exhaustive list but every effort has been made to include the essential vocabulary to assist you in compiling your own lists. The topic areas covered here are:

The Family, Education, Leisure Activities, Society Today, Life in Germany Today, Environmental Issues, The Third World, Geography, Transport and Communication, Current Affairs, Technology and Research, The Arts.

THE FAMILY

- **die Familie (-n)** *the family*

das Adoptivkind (-er)	*adopted child*	die Kindesmißhandlung	*child abuse*
die Ehefrau (-en)	*wife*	die Kindheit	*childhood*
der Ehemann (¨er)	*husband*	die Kleinfamilie (-n)	*small (nuclear) family*
das Einzelkind (-er)	*only child*	das Kleinkind (-er)	*toddler*
die Eltern (pl)	*parents*	die Pflegeeltern (pl)	*foster parents*
die Elternpflicht (-en)	*parental duty*	das Pflegekind (-er)	*foster child*
der/die Erwachsene (-n)	*adult, grown up*	der Säugling (-e)	*baby, infant*
die Familienplanung (-en)	*family planning*	der Schwager (¨)	*brother-in-law*
die Großfamilie (-n)	*extended family*	die Schwägerin (-nen)	*sister-in-law*
die Hausfrau (-en)	*housewife*	die Schwangerschaft (-en)	*pregnancy*
der Hausmann (¨er)	*house husband*	die Schwiegereltern (pl)	*in-laws*
die Kindererziehung (no pl)	*upbringing of children*	die Tagesmutter (¨)	*childminder*
der Kinderhort (-e)	*creche*	die Verwandtschaft	*relations, relatives*
die Kinderkrankheit (-en)	*childhood illness*	die Zwillinge (pl)	*twins*

abstammen	*to descend from*	erben	*to inherit*
ein Kind erziehen	*to bring up a child*	ernähren	*to nourish, feed*
empfangen	*to conceive*	im Kindesalter	*at an early age*

das gehört zu den Kindheitserinnerungen	*that's part of one's childhood memories*
Familie und Beruf unter einen Hut bringen	*to manage family and career*
mehr Männer als früher helfen im Haushalt sich die Hausarbeit teilen	*more men than before help in the house to share the housework*

- **die Ehe (-n)** *marriage*
- **die Scheidung (-en)** *divorce*

die Affäre (-n)	*affair*	der Junggeselle (-n)	*bachelor*
der Alleinerzieher (-)	*single parent*	die Junggesellenbude (-n)	*bachelor pad*
das Baby (-s)	*baby*	der Mädchenname (-n)	*maiden name*
die Beziehung (-en)	*relationship*	der Polterabend (-e)	*pre-wedding party*
die Braut (¨e)	*bride*	der Scheidungsprozeß (-sse)	*divorce proceedings*
der Bräutigam (-e)	*bridegroom*	die Scheidungsrate (-n)	*divorce rate*
das Brautpaar (-e)	*bride & bridegroom*	der Seitensprung (no pl)	*infidelity*
die Eheberatung (no pl)	*marriage guidance*	die kirchliche Trauung (-en)	*church wedding*
der Ehebruch (no pl)	*adultery*	die standesamtliche	
das Ehepaar (-e)	*married couple*	Trauung (-en)	*civil wedding*
die Eifersucht (no pl)	*jealousy*	der Trauzeuge (-n)	*best man*
die Einelternfamilie (-n)	*single parent family*	die Trennung (-en)	*separation*
der Familienname (-n)	*surname*	der/die Verlobte (-n)	*fiancé(e)*
die Flitterwochen (pl)	*honeymoon*	der Verlobungsring (-e)	*engagement ring*
die Hausarbeit (-en)	*housework*	das Vertrauen (no pl)	*trust*
die Hochzeit (-en)	*wedding*	die Verlobung (-en)	*engagement*

ledig	*single*	verheiratet	*married*
heiraten	*to marry*	zusammenleben	*to live together*

die Ehe geht in die Brüche	*the marriage is breaking up*
die Ehescheidung wird zu einfach gemacht	*divorce is being made too easy*
auf jemanden eifersüchtig sein	*to feel jealous of someone*

fremdgehen	*to have an affair*
häufig den Partner wechseln	*to live promiscuously, change partner frequently*
einen gemeinsamen Haushalt führen	*to live together*
sie leben getrennt	*they live apart, separated*
sich scheiden lassen	*to get divorced*
mit jemandem schlafen	*to sleep with someone*
sich mit jemandem verheiraten	*to marry someone*
sich bis über beide Ohren in jemanden verlieben	*to fall head over heels in love with someone*
sich Hals über Kopf verlieben	*to fall in love in a rush/hurry*
in jemanden verliebt sein	*to be in love with someone*
sich mit jemandem verloben	*to become engaged to someone*
die Verlobung lösen	*to break off the engagement*

- **die Jugend** (no pl) *youth*
- **der Konflikt** (-e) *conflict*

die Autorität (no pl)	*authority*	altmodisch	*old-fashioned*
die Clique (-n)	*group, set, gang*	angesehen	*respected*
die Emotion (-en)	*emotion*	anständig	*respectable, decent*
die Empfindung (-en)	*feeling*	aufgeschlossen	*open-minded*
der/die Halbstarke (-n)	*young hooligan*	böse auf (+acc)	*angry with someone*
das Jugendalter (no pl)	*adolescence*	böse mit (+dat)	*angry at something*
das Jugendgericht (-e)	*juvenile court*	deprimiert	*depressed*
der/die Jugendliche (-n)	*youngster*	engstirnig	*narrow-minded*
das Jugendschutzgesetz (-e)	*law for the protection of young people*	gebildet	*well-bred, educated*
die Kluft ("e)	*rift, gulf*	gleichgültig	*indifferent*
das Recht (-e)	*right*	höflich	*polite*
die Pflicht (-en)	*duty, responsibility*	kompromißbereit	*ready to compromise*
die Spannung (no pl)	*tension*	minderjährig	*under-age*
das Stiefkind (-er)	*stepchild*	naiv	*naive*
die Stiefmutter (")	*stepmother*	selbständig	*independent*
der Stiefvater (")	*stepfather*	selbstbewußt	*self confident*
das Streitgespräch (-e)	*argument*	unsicher	*insecure*
der Streitpunkt (-e)	*contentious issue*	verständnisvoll	*understanding*
der Teenager (-)	*teenager*	volljährig	*of age, over 18*
das Verhältnis (-se)	*relationship*	vorwurfsvoll	*reproachful*
		wohlmeinend	*well-meaning*

ärgern	*to annoy*	kritisieren	*to criticise*
beleidigen	*to insult*	lügen	*to tell lies*
sich benehmen	*to behave*	meckern	*to moan, groan*
bestehen auf (+dat)	*to insist on*	nörgeln an (+dat)	*to carp about*
diskutieren über (+acc)	*to discuss something*	strafen	*to punish*
fluchen	*to swear*	sich streiten	*to squabble*
haften für (+acc)	*to be responsible for*	übereinstimmen	*to agree*

mit jemandem schlecht auskommen	*to get on badly with someone/not to get on with*
seinen Willen durchsetzen	*to get one's own way*
Probleme durchsprechen	*to talk problems through*
jemandem auf die Nerven gehen	*to get on someone's nerves*
über etwas (acc) reden	*to talk about something*
mit jemandem schimpfen	*to tell someone off*
die Beherrschung verlieren	*to lose control*
sich in die Lage versetzen	*to put oneself in the position of*
sich gut verstehen	*to get on well together*
gegen etwas/jemanden voreingenommen sein	*to be prejudiced against something/someone*
Respekt vor (+dat) zeigen	*to show respect for*
bei etwas (dat) ein Auge zudrücken	*to turn a blind eye to something*

- **das Alter** (no pl) *old age*

die Alten (pl)	*old people*	der Lebensabend (no pl)	*twilight of one's life*
das Altersheim	*old people's home*	die Lebenserwartung	*life expectancy*
die Altersrente (-n)	*old age pension*	die Pflege (no pl)	*care*
der/die Angehörige (-n)	*relative, relation*	die Senioren (pl)	*senior citizens/OAPs*
das Essen auf Rädern	*meals on wheels*	der Seniorenpaß ("e)	*OAP's travel pass*
das Hospiz (-e)	*hospice*	das Seniorenwohnheim (-e)	*old people's home*

zur Gesellschaft etwas beitragen	*to contribute something to society*
mit 60 Jahren in Rente gehen	*to retire at 60*
sich an den Ruhestand gewöhnen	*to get used to retirement*

an der Alzheimerschen Krankheit leiden	to suffer from Alzheimer's disease
in den Ruhestand treten	to retire
in den Vorruhestand treten	to retire early
im Vollbesitz seiner geistigen Kräfte	in full possession of one's faculties

EDUCATION

● **die Ausbildung** (pl rare) *education*

die Schultypen	*types of school*	das Internat (-e)	*boarding school*
die Abendschule (-n)	*night school*	der Kindergarten (")	*kindergarten*
die Berufsschule (-n)	*vocational school*	die Privatschule (-n)	*private school*
die Gesamtschule (-n)	*comprehensive school*	die Realschule (-n)	*secondary school*
die Grundschule (-n)	*primary school*	die Sonderschule (-n)	*special school*
das Gymnasium (-ien)	*grammar school*	die staatliche Schule (-n)	*state school*
die Hauptschule (-n)	*secondary school*		

die Noten	*marks*		
(1) sehr gut	*very good*	(4) ausreichend	*fair*
(2) gut	*good*	(5) mangelhaft	*poor*
(3) befriedigend	*satisfactory*	(6) ungenügend	*unsatisfactory*

das Abitur (no pl)	*A-level equivalent*	das Nachsitzen (-)	*detention*
die Anstrengung (-en)	*effort*	das Nebenfach ("er)	*subsidiary subject*
die Aufnahmeprüfung (-en)		die Oberstufe (-n)	*sixth form*
	entrance exam	die Partnerschule (-n)	*partner school*
der Ausflug ("e)	*trip, excursion*	die Partnerstadt ("e)	*twinned town*
der Austauschpartner (-)	*exchange partner* (m)	das Pflichtfach ("er)	*compulsory subject*
die Austauschpartnerin (-nen)		die mittlere Reife (-n)	*1st public secondary*
	exchange partner (f)		*school exam (GCSE)*
die Bildungslücke (-n)	*gap in one's education*	die mündliche Prüfung (-en)	
die Disziplin (no pl)	*discipline*		*oral examination*
das Fach ("er)	*subject*	die schriftliche Prüfung (-en)	
die Fächerauswahl (no pl)	*subject choice*		*written examination*
der Förderkurs (-e)	*special course*	der Rowdy (-s)	*bully*
der Förderunterricht	*special instruction*	die Schikane (no pl)	*bullying*
das Hauptfach ("er)	*main subject*	der Schüleraustausch (-e)	*school exchange*
der Hausmeister (-)	*caretaker*	der Schulminibus (-se)	*school minibus*
der Klassensprecher (-)	*class representative*	die Schulpflicht (no pl)	*compulsory schooling*
die Konzentrationsschwäche (-n)		das Schulsystem (-e)	*school system*
	weak concentration	der Stundenplan ("e)	*timetable*
der Kurs (-e)	*course*	der Unterricht (no pl)	*lessons, classes*
der Kurs für Anfänger	*beginner's course*	das Wahlfach ("er)	*optional subject*
der Lehrplan ("e)	*syllabus*	das Zeugnis (-se)	*report*
das Lieblingsfach ("er)	*favourite subject*		

akademisch	*academic*	pünktlich	*punctual*
begabt	*gifted*	schulfrei	*no school*
faul	*lazy*	streng	*strict*
gerecht	*fair, just*	überfordert	*overstretched*
hitzefrei	*no school because*	unberechenbar	*unpredictable*
	of the heat	unnahbar	*unapproachable*
ordentlich	*tidy, orderly*	unterhaltsam	*entertaining*

abschreiben	*to copy, cheat*	die Prüfung machen	*to take an exam*
bestehen	*to pass (exam)*	motivieren	*to motivate*
begreifen	*to understand, grasp*	schwänzen	*to play truant*
sich bemühen	*to try hard*	sitzenbleiben	*to repeat a year*
durchfallen	*to fail*	studieren	*to study*
erklären	*to explain*	unterrichten	*to teach*
Unterricht geben	*to teach*	versetzt werden	*to move up a year*
lernen	*to learn*	wiederholen	*to repeat*

das Wesentliche beherrschen	*to know the basics*
einen Schüler nachsitzen lassen	*to put a schoolboy in detention*
etwas auswendig lernen	*to learn something by heart*
Fortschritte machen	*to make progress*
am Unterricht teilnehmen	*to attend lessons*
sich auf (+acc) vorbereiten	*to prepare oneself for*
den Kopf zerbrechen	*to rack one's brains*

- **die Fortbildung** (no pl) *further education*
- **das Hochschulwesen** (no pl) *higher education*

der Absolvent (-en)	*graduate (m)*	der Hochschulabschluß ("sse)	
die Absolventin (-nen)	*graduate (f)*		*university degree*
der Ausbildungsplatz ("e)	*trainee place*	die Lehre (-n)	*apprenticeship*
der/die Auszubildende (-n)	*trainee*	der Lehrling (-e)	*apprentice*
die Berufsausbildung	*vocational training*	der Numerus Clausus	*restricted entry*
der Bewerber (-)	*applicant*		*to university*
das Darleh(e)n (-)	*loan*	der Studienplatz ("e)	*place at university*
der Dozent (-en)	*lecturer (m)*	die Universität (-en)	*university*
die Dozentin (-nen)	*lecturer (f)*	das Universitätsgelände (no pl)	
die Fachhochschule (-n)	*tertiary technical college*		*university campus*
die Fakultät (-en)	*faculty*	die Vorlesung (-en)	*lecture*
die Forschung (-en)	*research*	die Wohnungsnot ("e)	*lack of*
die Hochschule (-n)	*college, university*		*accommodation*

berufsorientiert	*vocational*	überfüllt	*overcrowded*
leistungsorientiert	*results orientated*	zinnlos	*interest free*

absolvieren	*to graduate*	promovieren	*to do/get a PhD*
abgewiesen werden	*to be turned down*	sich weiterbilden	*to continue one's*
dozieren	*to lecture*		*education*
forschen	*to research*	weiterstudieren	*to continue studying*
nachholen	*to make up (something missed)*		

das Studium abbrechen	*to drop out of the course*
nach Abschluß des Studiums	*after qualifying*
sich um einen Studienplatz bewerben	*to apply for a place at university*
einen akademischen Grad erhalten	*to be awarded a degree*
auf die Universität gehen	*to go to university*
Forschung treiben	*to do research*
die Schule verlassen	*to leave school*
bei jemandem zur Untermiete wohnen	*to lodge with someone*

LEISURE ACTIVITIES

- **die Freizeit** (no pl) *spare/leisure time*
- **der Sport** (Sportarten) *sport*

der Athlet (-en)	*athlete (m)*	die Olympiade (no pl)	*Olympic Games*
die Athletin (-nen)	*athlete (f)*	das Preisgeld (-er)	*prize money*
der Amateur (-e)	*amateur*	der Professional (-s)	*professional*
die Anstrengung (-en)	*exertion, effort*	der Profi (-s) (coll.)	*pro. (coll.)*
die Ausdauer (no pl)	*stamina*	der Professionalismus	*professionalism*
der Behindertensport	*sport for the disabled*	die Professionalität	*professionalism*
der Berufssportler (-)	*professional sportsman*	der Sieger (-)	*winner*
die Berufssportlerin (-nen)	*professional sportswoman*	der Sportler (-)	*sportsman*
das Doping (-s)	*drug taking*	die Sportlerin (-nen)	*sportswoman*
die Dopingkontrolle (-n)	*drug test*	die Sportmedizin (no pl)	*sports medicine*
der Gegner (-)	*opponent*	der Sportplatz ("e)	*sportsground*
der Gewinn (-e)	*win*	der Sportverein (-e)	*sports-club*
die Leistung (-en)	*achievement*	das Trimm-dich-Gerät (-e)	*keep fit apparatus*
die Mannschaft (-en)	*team*	die Weltmeisterschaft (-en)	*world championship*
das Mannschaftsspiel (-e)	*team game*	der Wettkampf ("e)	*competition*
die Medaille (-n)	*medal*	der Zuschauer (-)	*spectator (m)*
die Niederlage (-n)	*defeat*	die Zuschauerin (-nen)	*spectator (f)*

beliebt	*popular*	siegreich	*victorious*
biegsam	*supple*	sportlich	*sporting, sporty*
ehrenamtlich	*honorary*	sportbegeistert	*keen on sport*

skifahren	*to ski*	sich trimmen	*to keep fit*
trainieren	*to train*	üben	*to practise*
Sport treiben	*to go in for sport*	wetten	*to bet*

die Zeit ausnützen	*to make good use of the time*
ins Schwitzen kommen	*to break out in a sweat*
trimm dich durch Sport!	*keep fit through/with sport!*

mit Abstand das beste sein		*to be far and away the best*	
ein Mitglied in einem Verein sein		*to be a member of a club*	

● **das Hobby** (-s) *hobby*

der Abendkurs (-e)	*evening class*	das Interesse (-n)	*interest*
die Belastung (-en)	*stress*	die Langeweile (no pl)	*boredom*
die Beschäftigung (-en)	*activity*	die Leidenschaft (-en)	*passion*
die Betätigung (-en)	*exercise, activity*	die Popmusik (no pl)	*pop music*
das Diskotanzen (no pl)	*disco dancing*	die Sammlung (-en)	*collection*
die Entspannung (no pl)	*relaxation*	der Spaß (no pl)	*fun*
die Erholung (no pl)	*recuperation, rest*	das Tasteninstrument (-e)	*keyboard instrument*
der Fanatiker (-)	*fanatic (m)*	die Töpferei (no pl)	*pottery*
die Fanatikerin (-nen)	*fanatic (f)*	die Vielfalt (no pl)	*variety*
der Feierabend (-e)	*end of daily work*	das Vergnügen (-)	*pleasure*
die Geselligkeit (no pl)	*social gathering*	die Volkshochschule (-n)	*adult education centre*
aktiv	*active*	musikalisch	*musical*
faszinierend	*fascinating*	nützlich	*useful*
gelegentlich	*occasionally*	praktisch	*practical*
genießbar	*enjoyable*	regelmäßig	*regular*
gesellig	*sociable*	selbsterlernt	*self-taught*
lebenslang	*lifelong*	sinnvoll	*sensible*
lohnend	*rewarding*	vorzugsweise	*preferably*
abschalten	*to switch off*	sich erholen	*to recuperate*
sich ausruhen	*to rest*	malen	*to paint*
sich betätigen	*to get some exercise*	modellieren	*to make models*
beieinandersitzen	*to sit together*	töpfern	*to make in clay*
sich entschließen	*to decide*	unterschätzen	*to underestimate*
sich entspannen	*to relax*	verbringen	*to spend (of time)*

ohne Arbeit ist Freizeit nichts wert		*without work free time has no value*
die Belastungen des heutigen Lebens		*the stresses and strains of modern life*
etwas als Hobby betreiben		*to do something as a hobby*
nach Dienstschluß		*after work*
Radio hören		*to listen to the radio*
ein Instrument spielen		*to play an instrument*
auf etwas/jemanden stehen (slang)		*to be mad about something/someone (slang)*
in einer Popgruppe spielen		*to play in a pop group*

● **das Reisen** (no pl) *travel*

der Abenteuerurlaub (-e)	*adventure holiday*	der Passagier (-e)	*passenger*
die Abreise (-n)	*departure*	die Pauschalreise (-n)	*package holiday*
der Aufenthalt (-e)	*stay*	der Reiseboom (-s)	*travel boom*
die Besichtigung (-en)	*sight seeing tour*	das Reisebüro (-s)	*travel agency*
der Charterflug ("e)	*charter flight*	der Reiseführer (-)	*guide book*
die Entfernung (no pl)	*distance*	der Reiseleiter (-)	*tour leader (m)*
die Fähre (-n)	*ferry*	die Reiseleiterin (-nen)	*tour leader (f)*
das Faulenzen (no pl)	*lazing around*	der/die Reisende (-n)	*traveller, passenger*
die Ferien (pl)	*holidays*	der Reisepaß (-pässe)	*passport*
der Ferienort (-e)	*holiday resort*	die Reiseroute (-n)	*itinerary*
die Ferienwohnung (-en)	*holiday flat*	der Rucksackurlaub (-e)	*back packing trip*
der Fernflug ("e)	*long haul flight*	die Sehenswürdigkeit (-en)	*sight*
die Flugkarte (-n)	*plane ticket*	der Strandurlaub (-e)	*beach holiday*
der Fremdenverkehr (no pl)	*tourism*	die Tour (-en)	*tour*
die Gastfreundlichkeit	*hospitality*	der Tagesausflug ("e)	*day trip*
die Hauptsaison (-s)	*high season*	der Tourismus (no pl)	*tourism*
die Impfung (-en)	*vaccination*	die Tourismusbranche (-n)	*tourist industry*
die Jugendherberge (-n)	*youth hostel*	die Übernachtung (-en)	*overnight stay*
die Kreuzfahrt (-en)	*cruise*	die Unterkunft ("e)	*accommodation*
die Küste (-n)	*coast*	das Verkehrsamt ("er)	*tourist office*
die Landschaft (-en)	*landscape, scenery*	die Wanderung (-en)	*walk, hike*
der Linienflug ("e)	*scheduled flight*	der Wanderurlaub (-e)	*walking holiday*
der Mietwagen (-)	*hire car*	die Weltreise (-n)	*world tour*
abenteuerlich	*adventurous*	reizvoll	*charming, delightful*
anspruchslos	*unpretentious*	romantisch	*romantic*
bezaubernd	*enchanting, charming*	sehenswert	*worth seeing*
malerisch	*picturesque*	sehenswürdig	*worth seeing*

mittelalterlich	*medieval*	urlaubsreif	*ready for a holiday*
preisgünstig	*good value*	weltberühmt	*world famous*
buchen	*to book*	reservieren	*to reserve*
entdecken	*to discover*	streichen	*to cancel*
kennenlernen	*to get to know*	trampen	*to hitch-hike*
organisieren	*to organise*	verreisen	*to go away on holiday*
reisen	*to travel*	übernachten	*to stay overnight*

viele Arbeitsplätze hängen von der Tourismusnachfrage ab	*many jobs rely on the demand from tourists*
ein Zelt aufschlagen	*to pitch a tent*
per Anhalter fahren	*to hitch-hike*
ins Ausland fahren	*to go abroad*
ein Gebiet außerordentlicher Schönheit	*a region of exceptional beauty*
eine Tour machen	*to go on a tour/touring*
Tourismus als Wirtschaftszweig	*tourism as a branch of the economy*
unterwegs sein	*to be travelling/on one's way*
die Zeitumstellung überwinden	*to overcome the time difference/jet-lag*

● **das Wetter (-)** *weather*

der Bodenfrost (no pl)	*ground frost*	der Tageswert (-e)	*daytime temperature*
die Dürre (-n)	*drought*	der Tau (no pl)	*dew*
die Eintrübung (no pl)	*clouding over*	das Tauwetter (no pl)	*thaw*
die Feuchtigkeit (no pl)	*humidity*	das Tief (-s)	*low*
die Hitzewelle (-n)	*heat wave*	der Tiefdruck (no pl)	*low pressure*
das Hoch (-s)	*high*	der Tiefswert (-e)	*minimum temperature*
der Hochdruck (no pl)	*high pressure*	die Trockenheit (-en)	*drought*
das Hochdruckgebiet (-e)	*high pressure area*	das Unwetter (-)	*bad weather*
der Höchstwert (-e)	*maximum temperature*	die Wetteransichten (pl)	*weather prospects*
die Kaltfront (-en)	*cold front*	der Wetterbericht (-e)	*weather report*
das Klima (-s)	*climate*	die Wetterlage (-n)	*weather situation*
der Luftdruck (no pl)	*atmospheric pressure*	der Wettersatellit (-en)	*weather satellite*
der Niederschlag ("e)	*precipitation*	die Wetterverhältnisse (pl)	*weather conditions*
der Rauhreif (no pl)	*hoar frost*	die Wettervoraussage (-n)	*weather forecast*
der Regenbogen (-)	*rainbow*	die Wettervorhersage (-n)	*weather forecast*

auffrischend	*freshening*	nebelig	*foggy*
bedeckt	*overcast*	schwül	*sultry, close*
dunstig	*hazy*	stellenweise	*in places*
drohend	*threatening*	unbeständig	*changeable*
feucht	*damp*	verhangen	*overcast*
frostig	*frosty*	wetterempfindlich	*sensitive to weather*

durchnässen	*to soak through*	tröpfeln	*to drip, trickle*
frösteln	*to shiver*	überschwemmen	*to flood, inundate*
rieseln	*to drizzle*	sich verbessern	*to improve*

SOCIETY TODAY

● **die heutige Gesellschaft** *society of today*
● **Frauenfragen – Männerfragen** *questions of women's and men's rights*

die Berufsrückkehr (no pl)	*return to a career*	die Frauenemanzipation	*emancipation of women*
das Bewußtsein (no pl)	*consciousness*	die Frauenrechte (pl)	*women's rights*
die Chancengleichheit	*equal opportunity*	die Karrierefrau (-en)	*career woman*
die Eigenständigkeit	*independence*	der Konkurrenzkampf ("e)	*rivalry*
die Feministin (-nen)	*feminist*	das Retortenbaby (-s)	*test tube baby*
der Feminismus (no pl)	*feminism*	die Schwangerschaft (-en)	*pregnancy*
die Frauenbewegung (-en)	*feminist movement*	die Vergewaltigung	*rape*
die Gleichberechtigung	*equality, equal rights*	die Weiblichkeit	*femininity*

alleinstehend	*living alone*	erwerbstätig	*working*
emanzipiert	*emancipated*	gleichberechtigt	*with equal rights*
erfolgreich	*successful*	partnerschaftlich	*as partners*
benachteiligen	*to discriminate against*	verdrängen	*to suppress*
sich durchsetzen	*to assert oneself*	sich verwirklichen	*to fulfil oneself*
mißhandeln	*to abuse*	vorankommen	*to make headway*
die Pille nehmen	*to take the pill*	sich zutrauen	*to have confidence*

der Aufstieg der Frauen	the promotion of women
die sexuelle Belästigung	sexual harassment
mehr Frauen mit Familie wollen zurück in den Beruf	more women with families want to go back to their careers
Frauen sind noch relativ selten in beruflichen Führungspositionen	women are still relatively rare in leading positions in professions
gleicher Lohn für gleiche Arbeit	equal pay for equal work
der traditionelle Männerberuf (-e)	job traditionally done by men
sich selbst im Wege stehen	to be one's own worst enemy

● die Mode (-n) *fashion*

das Atelier (-s)	studio, workshop	der Modeausdruck ("e)	in-phrase
die Boutique (-n)	boutique	das Modehaus ("er)	fashion house
der Futterstoff (-e)	lining material	die Modeschau (-en)	fashion show
die Konfektion (no pl)	manufacture of ready-to-wear clothing	der Modeschöpfer (-)	fashion designer
das Konfektionskleid (-er)	off-the-peg dress	die Modeschöpferin (-nen)	fashion designer (f)
die Kreativität (no pl)	creativity	die Nähmaschine (-n)	sewing machine
der Laufsteg (-e)	catwalk	die Phantasie (no pl)	imagination
das Mannequin (-s)	fashion model	der Schneider (-)	tailor
der Modeartikel (-)	fashion accessory	die Schneiderin (-nen)	tailor (f)
		der Stil (-e)	style

abgetragen	worn out	schäbig	shabby
bügelfrei	non-iron	schick	smart
modebewußt	fashion conscious	verkäuflich	saleable
provozierend	provoking	wasserdicht	waterproof

ablegen	to take off	herstellen	to manufacture
aussuchen	to choose	nähen	to sew
bügeln	to iron, press	passen	to fit
entwerfen	to design	schaffen	to create

aus dem Katalog bestellen	to order from a catalogue
Furore machen	to cause a stir
Kleider machen Leute	clothes make the man
mit/nach der Mode gehen	to keep up with the latest fashion
sich nach der Mode kleiden	to dress in the height of fashion
in Mode kommen	to come into fashion
aus der Mode kommen	to go out of fashion
die Mode mitmachen	to keep up with fashion
sich nach der Mode richten	to keep up with the latest fashion
Mode sein	to be fashionable
im Stil der achtziger Jahre	in the style of the 80s

● das Rauchen (-) *smoking*

die Auswirkung (-en)	effect	die Pfeife (-n)	pipe
die Kippe (-n)	stub	das passive Rauchen	passive smoking
die Krebsgefahr (-en)	danger of cancer	der Raucher (-)	smoker
der Lungenkrebs	lung cancer	die Raucherin (-nen)	smoker (f)
das Mitrauchen	passive smoking	der Raucherhusten	smoker's cough
der Nichtraucher (-)	non smoker	die Sorge (-n)	worry
die Nichtraucherin (-nen)	non smoker (f)	die Zigarettenwerbung	cigarette advertising

asozial	antisocial	aufgeben	to give up
nikotinarm	low-nicotine	aufhören	to stop
nikotingelb	nicotine stained	inhalieren	to inhale
schlicht und einfach	plain and simple	kettenrauchen	to chain-smoke
unbestritten	indisputably	paffen	to puff away
ungesund	not healthy	rauchen	to smoke
verboten	banned, forbidden	überreden	to persuade

sich (dat) das Rauchen abgewöhnen	to give up smoking
Jugendlichen vom Rauchen abraten	to advise young people against smoking
sich (dat) eine Zigarette drehen	to roll oneself a cigarette
die Werbung einschränken	to restrict advertising
außer Atem kommen	to get out of breath
einen lässigen Eindruck machen	to make a 'cool' impression
das Rauchen gefährdet die Gesundheit	smoking endangers health
seine Gesundheit schädigen	to damage one's health

nach Rauch stinken — *to smell of smoke*
seine Unsicherheit überspielen — *to cover up one's insecurity*
das Rauchverbot am Arbeitsplatz — *ban on smoking in the work place*
das Zimmer ist verraucht — *the room is full of smoke*

- **die Droge (-n)** *drug*
- **Aids (no pl)** *aids*
- **der Alkohol (-e)** *alcohol*

die Abhängigkeit (no pl)	dependency, addiction	das 'Gras'	pot
der Cannabis (no pl)	cannabis	das Heroin	heroin
der Dealer (-)	dealer	das Kokain	cocaine
die weiche Droge (-n)	soft drug	aus Neugierde	out of curiosity
der Drogenkonsum (-s)	drug taking	der Pusher (-) (slang)	pusher
der Drogenmißbrauch	drug abuse	der Rausch ("e)	high, intoxication
der/die Drogensüchtige (-n)	drug addict	das Rauschgift (-e)	drug (addictive)
		der Rauschgifthandel (-)	drug trafficking
die Entzugserscheinungen (pl)	withdrawal symptoms	das Rehabilitationszentrum (-zentren)	rehabilitation centre
die Entziehungskur (-en)	withdrawal therapy	die Sucht ("e)	addiction
der Fixer (-)	junkie	die Überdosierung (-en)	overdose
die Flucht (-en)	means of escape	die Wiedereingliederung	rehabilitation
der AIDS-Test (-s)	AIDS test	der Alkoholiker (-)	alcoholic
die Blutprobe (-n)	blood test	die Alkoholikerin (-nen)	alcoholic (f)
die HIV-Antikörper (pl)	HIV antibodies	die Alkoholvergiftung	alcohol poisoning
der/die HIV-Betroffene (-n)	HIV sufferer	der Blutalkoholspiegel (-)	blood-alcohol level
die Immunschwäche (-n)	immune deficiency	der Kater (-)	hangover
das Kondom (-e)	condom	die Kneipentour (-en)	pub crawl
die Prävention	prevention	die Promillegrenze (-n)	legal (alcohol) limit
der Virus (Viren)	virus	der/die Säufer/in (-/-nen)	drunkard (m/f)
drogensüchtig	addicted to drugs	HIV-infiziert	HIV infected
stumpfsinnig	mindless	HIV-kontaminiert	HIV contaminated
süchtig	addicted	HIV-positiv	HIV positive
alkoholfrei	alcohol free	besoffen (coll.)	stoned, smashed (coll)
alkoholsüchtig	addicted to alcohol	betrunken	drunk
aussteigen	to drop out	schlucken	to swallow
beschlagen	to impound, confiscate	schnüffeln	to sniff
sich einspritzen	to inject oneself	schnupfen	to snort
legalisieren	to legalise	zittern	to shake, shiver
anstecken	to infect	sich betrinken	to get drunk
sich verbreiten	to spread	sich übergeben	to be sick, vomit

nur der Dealer macht Kasse — *only the dealer makes gains (money)*
Euphoriegefühle erzeugen — *to produce feelings of euphoria*
zur Abhängigkeit führen — *to lead to addiction/dependency*
eine tödliche Dosis nehmen — *to take a fatal dose*
Alleskleber schnüffeln — *to glue sniff*
auf harte Drogen umsteigen — *to change to hard drugs*
unter dem Einfluß von Drogen stehen — *to be under the influence of drugs*
rückfällig werden — *to go back (onto drugs)*
heroinsüchtig werden — *to become addicted to heroin*
die Persönlichkeit verändern — *to change one's personality*
Beim Geschlechtsverkehr sollte man vorsichtig sein — *one ought to be careful during sexual intercourse*
die Hemmungen verlieren — *to lose one's inhibitions*
jemanden zum Alkohol treiben — *to drive someone to drink*
die Trunkenheit am Steuer vermeiden — *to avoid drinking and driving*
die Reflexe nachlassen — *to slow one's reflexes down*
einen Unfall verursachen — *to cause an accident*
in die Tüte blasen — *to take a breath test*
sich mit HIV infizieren — *to contract the HIV virus*
den Virus auf den Intimpartner/die Intimpartnerin übertragen — *to pass the virus on to a sexual partner*
an AIDS sterben — *to die of AIDS*
am Virus erkranken — *to contract the virus*

- **die Abtreibung** (-en) *abortion*

die Beratung (-en)	*counselling*	die Frauenklinik (-en)	*women's clinic*
der Embryo (-s)	*embryo*	das Urteil (-e)	*verdict, judgement*

der Schwangerschaftsabbruch ("e)	*termination of pregnancy*
eine ungewollte Schwangerschaft	*an unwanted pregnancy*
der Schutz des ungeborenen Lebens	*protection of unborn life*
der/die Gegner/in der Abtreibung	*anti-abortion campaigner (m/f)*

- **Essen und Trinken** *food and drink*

der Apppetit (-e)	*appetite*	der Geschmack ("e)	*taste*
die Ballaststoffe (pl)	*roughage*	das Getränk (-e)	*drink*
der Bluthochdruck (no pl)	*high blood pressure*	die Gewichtkontrolle (-n)	*weight control*
das Cholesterin (no pl)	*cholesterol*	das Grundnahrungsmittel (-)	
der Cholesterinspiegel	*cholesterol level*		*basic food stuff*
der Diabetes (no pl)	*diabetes*	das Hauptgericht (-e)	*main course*
der Diabetiker (-)	*diabetic (m)*	der Kaloriengehalt (-e)	*calorific value*
die Diabetikerin (-nen)	*diabetic (f)*	die Lebensmittel (pl)	*groceries*
die Diät (no pl)	*diet*	die Magersucht	*anorexia*
der Durstlöscher (-)	*thirst-quencher*	das Rezept (-e)	*recipe*
die Energiezufuhr (no pl)	*energy intake*	das Übergewicht (-e)	*overweight*
die Ernährung (no pl)	*nutrition*	der/die Vegetarier/in (-/nen)	
der Farbstoff (-e)	*artificial colouring*		*vegetarian (m/f)*
das Fertiggericht (-e)	*ready-to-serve meal*	die Zutaten (n. sing)	*ingredients*
das Fett (-e)	*fat*	das Zusatzmittell (-)	*additive*
das Gericht (-e)	*dish*		

abgepackt	*pre-packed*	lecker	*tasty*
aromatisch	*aromatic*	lieblich	*sweet (of wine)*
dickmachend	*fattening*	nahrhaft	*nourishing*
eßbar	*edible*	pflanzlich	*vegetable (adj)*
gesüßt	*sweetened*	saftig	*juicy*
herb	*dry (of wine)*	tierisch	*animal (adj)*
künstlich	*artificial*	vollmundig	*full-bodied (of wine)*
abnehmen	*to lose weight*	verschlingen	*to devour*
dünsten	*to steam, stew*	verzehren	*to consume*
schmoren	*to braise*	würzen	*to season*
verkochen	*to boil away*	zunehmen	*to put on weight*

guten Appetit!	*enjoy your meal!*
auf vernünftige Ernährung achten	*to eat sensibly*
gesunde Ernährungsgewohnheiten haben	*to have healthy eating habits*
nach einer ausgewogenen Ernährung leben	*to be on a balanced diet*
einen geringen Nährwert haben	*to have a low nutritional value*

LIFE IN GERMANY TODAY

- **das heutige Deutschland** *Germany of today*
- **die Geschichte ab 1914** *history from 1914*

1914 Erzherzog Ferdinand ermordet	*Archduke Ferdinand assassinated*
Deutschland erklärt den Franzosen und Russen den Krieg	*Germany declares war on the French and the Russians*
1914–1918 Erster Weltkrieg	*First World War*
Millionen kommen ums Leben	*Millions lose their lives*
1919 die Weimarer Republik beginnt	*The Weimar Republic begins*
1923 Hitler versucht einen Putsch	*Hitler attempts a putsch*
1932 die Nationalsozialisten bekommen 38% der Stimmen	*The National Socialists (Nazis) get 38% of the votes*
1933 die Machtergreifung – Hitler ergreift die Macht nach dem Reichtagsbrand in Berlin; die Nazizeit beginnt	*The seizure of power – Hitler seizes power after the Reichstags fire in Berlin; the Nazi era begins*
1938 der Anschluß von Österreich	*The annexation of Austria*
1939 Hitler marschiert in Polen ein	*Hitler invades Poland*
Großbritannien erklärt den Deutschen den Krieg	*Great Britain declares war on the Germans*

1939–1945 Zweiter Weltkrieg	*Second World War*
1945 die Potsdamer Konferenz teilt Deutschland und Österreich in vier Zonen ein	*the Potsdam Conference divides Germany and Austria into four zones*
1949 Im Mai wird die Bundesrepublik Deutschland von den Westlichen Alliierten gegründet	*In May the Federal Republic of Germany is founded by the Western Allies*
Im Oktober wird die Sowjetische Zone die Deutsche Demokratische Republik	*In October the Soviet Zone becomes the German Democratic Republic*
1953 der Aufstand in Ostberlin wird von den russischen Truppen niedergeschlagen	*Uprising in East Berlin is put down by Russian troops*
1957 BRD wird Gründer-Mitglied vom Gemeinsamen Markt. Zu dieser Zeit genießt die BRD das Wirtschaftswunder	*West Germany becomes a founder member of the Common Market. At this time West Germany is enjoying the economic miracle*
Während der 50er Jahre flüchten Millionen aus der DDR, um ein neues Leben in der BDR zu suchen	*During the fifties millions flee East Germany to seek a new life in West Germany*
1961 Die Berliner Mauer wird gebaut	*The Berlin Wall is built*
1989 die Berliner Mauer wird abgerissen	*The Berlin Wall is demolished/pulled down*
1990 die deutsche Wiedervereinigung	*German Reunification*
Tag der deutschen Einheit (3. Oktober)	*German unification day (3rd October)*

● **die Nazizeit** *the Nazi period*

die Besatzungsmacht ("e)	*occupying force*	der Holocaust (-s)	*Holocaust*
die Besatzungszone (-n)	*occupation zone*	der Kriegsverbrecher (-)	*war criminal*
die Braunhemden (pl)	*'the Brownshirts'*	der Jude (-n)	*Jew (m)*
die Bücherverbrennung(-en)	*book burning*	die Jüdin (-nen)	*Jewess*
der Faschismus (no pl)	*fascism*	der Judenhaß (no pl)	*anti-Semitism*
der Führer (-)	*leader, (Hitler)*	die Judenverfolgung (-en)	*persecution of Jews*
die Gaskammer (-n)	*gas chamber*	das Konzentrationslager (-)	
das Getto (-s)	*ghetto*		*concentration camp*
das Hakenkreuz (-e)	*swastika*	die Vernichtung (-en)	*extermination*
die Hitlerjugend (no pl)	*Hitler youth*	das Vernichtungslager (-)	*extermination camp*

● **die ehemalige DDR** *the former GDR*

die Abgrenzung (-en)	*separation, isolation*	die Meinungsfreiheit (no pl)	*freedom of speech*
die Arbeiterbewegung	*labour movement*	die Nationalisierung (no pl)	*nationalisation*
die Arbeiterklasse (-n)	*working class*	der Ostblock	*Eastern bloc*
das Ausreisevisum (-sen)	*exit visa*	die Pressefreiheit (no pl)	*freedom of the press*
der Diktator (-en)	*dictator*	der Sozialismus	*socialism*
die Diktatur (no pl)	*dictatorship*	die Staatssicherheit (Stasi)	*state security service*
die Genossenschaft (-en)	*co-operative*	die Stasi-Akten (pl)	*state security files*
der Grenzübergang ("e)	*border crossing point*	der Stacheldraht ("e)	*barbed wire*
der Kommunismus (no pl)	*Communism*	die Überwachung (-en)	*surveillamce*

Wunden hinterlassen	*to leave scars*	inhaftieren	*to imprison*
kommunistisch	*communist*	sozialistisch	*socialist*
radikal	*radical*	volkseigen	*nationally-owned*

Staatsgewalt ausüben	*to assume the authority of the state*
die Folgen des Zweiten Weltkrieges	*the consequences of the Second World War*
der Kalte Krieg	*the Cold War*
der Eiserne Vorhang	*the Iron Curtain*
der Warschauer Pakt	*the Warsaw Pact*

● **die deutsche Wiedervereinigung** *German Reunification*

der Aufschwung (no pl)	*upturn*	die Verbitterung	*bitterness*
die Freiheit (no pl)	*freedom*	die Verhandlung (-en)	*negotiation*
die Freizügigkeit	*freedom of movement*	die Volksvertretung (-en)	*body representing people*
der Ossi (-s)	*east German (person)*	die Währungsunion (no pl)	*monetary union*
die Pleitewirtschaft (-en)	*bankrupt economy*	der Wessi (-s)	*west German (person)*
die Preisfreigabe (-n)	*lifting of price controls*	der Wiederaufbau	*reconstruction*
die Reisefreiheit (-en)	*freedom to travel*	der Wohlstand	*affluence*
die Staatsfürsorge (no pl)	*state welfare*	die Wohnungsknappheit	*shortage of*
die Übergangsfrist (-en)	*transitional peiod*		*accommodation*
der Umbruch ("e)	*radical change*	die Zuversicht (no pl)	*confidence*
der Umsiedler (-)	*resettler*		

wirtschaftlich	*financial, economic*	sozial	*social*
Truppen abziehen	*to withdraw troops*	zurücktreten	*to resign*
demonstrieren	*to demonstrate*	zusammenwachsen	*to grow together*

Arbeitsplätze in der DDR sind ausgefallen	*jobs in the GDR have been cut*
einen Vertrag billigen	*to ratify a treaty*
der Demokratisierungsprozeß	*process of democratisation*
die Grenzkontrollen beseitigen	*to abolish border controls*
die Privatisierungstreuhand	*privatisation trust/agency*
Steuererhöhungen zur Finanzierung der Einheit	*tax increases to finance unification*
der Übergang zu einer Marktwirtschaft	*transition to a market economy*
die Verlegung des Regierungssitzes von Bonn nach Berlin	*transfer of the seat of government from Bonn to Berlin*
die Verteilung des Wohlstandes	*distribution of wealth*
die Wettbewerbswirtschaft (-en)	*competitive economy*

- ## Soziale Probleme *social problems*
- ## die Arbeit und die Arbeitslosigkeit *work and unemployment*

die Absage (-n)	*refusal*	die Dauerarbeitslosen (pl)	*long term unemployed*
der Abteilungsleiter (-)	*head of department*	der Dienstleistungsbetrieb (-e)	
der/die Angestellte (-n)	*(salaried) employee*		*service industry*
die Annonce (-n)	*advertisement*	das Einkommen (no pl)	*income*
der/die Arbeiter/in (-/nen)	*worker (m/f)*	die Entlassung (-en)	*dismissal*
der Arbeitgeber (-)	*employer*	die Ganztagsarbeit	*full time work*
der Arbeitnehmer (-)	*employee*	das Gehalt ("er)	*salary*
das Arbeitsamt ("er)	*job centre*	die Gelegenheitsarbeit	*casual work*
die Arbeitsbeschaffung	*creation of jobs*	die Gewerkschaft (-en)	*trade union*
die Arbeitskraft (no pl)	*capacity for work*	die Gleitzeit	*flexitime*
der/die Arbeitslose (-n)	*unemployed person*	die Halbtagsarbeit	*part time work*
das Arbeitslosengeld (-er)	*unemployment benefit*	das Krankengeld (-er)	*sick pay*
die Arbeitslosenrate (-n)	*rate of unemployment*	die Kündigung (-en)	*dismissal notice*
der Arbeitsmangel	*lack of work*	der Personalabbau (no pl)	*staff cutbacks*
der/die Arbeitssuchende (-n)		die Qualifikation (-en)	*qualification*
	job hunter/seeker	die Schichtarbeit	*shift work*
der Arbeitsvertrag ("e)	*work contract*	die Sozialversicherung	*social security*
die Arbeitszeit (-en)	*working hours*	die Stelle (-n)	*post, job*
der Aufsichtsrat ("e)	*board of directors*	das Stellenangebot (-e)	*job offer*
die Beförderung (-en)	*promotion*	der Tarif (-e)	*rate of pay*
der Beruf (-e)	*career, vocation*	die Tarifverhandlung (-en)	*pay negotiation*
der Berufsberater (-)	*careers advisor*	die Überstunde (-n)	*overtime*
die Berufswahl (-en)	*choice of career*	die Umschulung	*retraining*
der/die Bewerber/in (-/nen)	*applicant (m/f)*	der Verkaufsleiter (-)	*sales manager*
die Bewerbung (-en)	*application*	der Zahltag (-e)	*payday*

arbeitslos	*unemployed*	überflüssig	*superfluous*
ehrgeizig	*ambitious*	unentbehrlich	*indispensible*
fleißig	*hard working*	überqualifiziert	*overqualified*
gesichert	*secure*	unterqualifiziert	*underqualified*

sich anpassen	*to adapt*	entlassen	*to dismiss*
beschäftigen	*to employ*	entlassen werden	*to be made redundant*
betragen	*to amount to*	sich arbeitslos melden	*to sign on*
sich um etwas bewerben	*to apply for something*	verhandeln	*to negotiate*

der/die leitende Angestellte (-n) (adjectival noun)	*middle manager (m/f)*
jemanden als Referenz angeben	*to give someone's name as a referee*
sich arbeitslos anmelden	*to sign on unemployed*
Gegenmaßnahmen ergreifen	*to take counter measures*
jemandem eine Absage erteilen	*to refuse/reject someone*
frühzeitig in den Ruhestand gehen	*to take early retirement*
Anspruch auf Arbeitslosengeld haben	*to be entitled to unemployment benefit*
freie Stellen haben	*to have vacancies*
um eine Stelle konkurrieren	*to compete for a job*
der Lohn liegt unter dem Existenzminimum	*the wage is below the subsistence level*
einen Auftrag auf Arbeitslosengeld machen	*to make an application for unemployment benefit*
Arbeitsplätze schaffen	*to create new jobs*
in den Anzeigenteil der Zeitung sehen	*to look in the advertising section of the paper*
bei der Arbeit sein	*to be at work*

eine Stelle suchen	*to look for a job*
eine Stelle verlieren	*to lose a job*
mit dem technischen Wandel zurechtkommen	*to cope with technical change*
die Arbeitsbedingungen sind schrecklich	*working conditions are awful*
die Arbeitsbeschaffungsmaßnahmen sind nötig	*job creation measures are necessary*
die Arbeitslosenunterstützung ist unzureichend	*unemployment benefit is inadequate*
die Aufstiegsmöglichkeiten existieren nicht	*promotion possibilities/prospects do not exist*
die Arbeitszeitverkürzung ist eine Möglichkeit	*reduction in working hours is a possibility*
der Schlichtungsversuch fiel durch	*the attempt at arbitration failed*
er hat viele Vorstellungsgespräche gehabt	*he has had many job interviews*

● **die Obdachlosigkeit** *homelessness*

die Armut (no pl)	*poverty*	die Scham (no pl)	*shame*
das Elend (no pl)	*misery*	der Straßenmusikant (-en)	*busker (m)*
der Hausbesetzer (-)	*squatter (m)*	die Straßenmusikantin (-nen)	*busker (f)*
die Hausbesetzerin (-nen)	*squatter (f)*	die Wohlstandsgesellschaft (-en)	
die Innenstadt ("e)	*inner city*		*affluent society*
der Lebensstandard	*standard of living*	das Wohngeld	*housing benefit*
der/die Obdachlose (-n)	*homeless person*	die Wohnungsnot ("e)	*housing shortage*
das Obdachlosenheim (-e)	*hostel for the homeless*	die Wohnverhältnisse (pl)	*living conditions*
der Pappkarton (-s)	*cardboard box*		

betteln	*to beg*	überleben	*to survive*
schnorren (coll)	*to cadge, scrounge*	unterbringen	*to house*
beengt	*cramped*	unhygienisch	*insanitary*

die Gesellschaft ablehnen	*to reject society*
der soziale Abstieg ist offensichtlich	*social decline is evident*
er lebt unter der Armutsgrenze	*he is living below the poverty line*
ein verwahrlostes Aussehen haben	*to have an unkempt appearance*
ohne festen Wohnsitz sein	*to be of no fixed abode*
das Haus wieder in Besitz nehmen	*to repossess the house*
im Freien schlafen	*to sleep rough*
von zuhause weglaufen	*to run away from home*
zuhause rausgeschmissen werden	*to be thrown out of one's home*

● **das Verbrechen (-)** *crime*

der/die Angeklagte (-n)	*defendant (m/f)*	der Ladendiebstahl ("e)	*shop lifting*
der/die Angreifer/in (-/nen)	*attacker (m/f)*	der/die Mittäter/in (-/nen)	*accomplice (m/f)*
der/die Autodieb/in (-/nen)	*car thief (m/f)*	der Mord (-e)	*murder*
der Betrug (no pl)	*fraud*	der Mörder (-)	*murderer*
der Beweis (-e)	*proof*	der Prozeß (-sse)	*trial*
der Dieb (-e)	*thief*	der Richter (-)	*judge*
der Diebstahl ("e)	*theft*	die Schlägerei (-en)	*fist fight*
der Einbrecher (-)	*burglar*	der Sträfling (-e)	*prisoner*
der Einbruch ("e)	*burglary, break in*	der Taschendieb (-e)	*pickpocket*
die Erpressung (no pl)	*black mail, extortion*	die Überführung (-en)	*conviction*
das Gefängnis (-se)	*prison*	die Untersuchung (-en)	*investigation*
die Gerechtigkeit (no pl)	*justice*	der Vandalismus (no pl)	*vandalism*
das Gericht (-e)	*court of law*	die Verbrechungsrate (-n)	*crime rate*
das Gesetz (-e)	*law*	die Verbrechensverhütung	*crime prevention*
das Geständnis (-se)	*confession*	die Verbrechenswelle (-n)	*crime wave*
die Gewalttätigkeit (no pl)	*violence*	der Verbrecher (-)	*criminal*
die Haft (no pl)	*custody*	der/die Vorbestrafte (-n)	*person with record*

bewaffnet	*armed*	gewaltsam	*violent, by force*
gesetzwidrig	*unlawful, illegal*	kaltblütig	*cold bloodied*

bedrohen	*to threaten*	rauben	*to rob*
bestechen	*to bribe*	töten	*to kill*
entführen	*to kidnap*	überfallen	*to attack, assault*
ermorden	*to murder*	verhaften	*to arrest*

er ist des Diebstahls angeklagt	*he is accused of theft*
er bleibt in Untersuchungshaft	*he has been remanded in custody*
ein Verbrechen begehen	*to commit a crime*
die Unschuld beteuern	*to protest one's innocence*
jemanden auf frischer Tat ertappen	*to catch someone red handed/in the act*
die Bekämpfung der Kriminalität	*the fight against crime*
das Recht selbst in die Hand nehmen	*to take the law into one's own hands*

gegen das Gesetz verstoßen		*to break the law*	
einen Bankraub verüben		*to commit a bank robbery*	

- **die Einwanderung** *immigration*
- **der Rassismus** *racialism*

das Asyl (no pl)	*asylum*	die Integration (no pl)	*integration*
der Asylant (-en)	*asylum seeker*	die Integrierung (no pl)	*integration*
der Asylbewerber (-)	*asylum seeker (m)*	das Mißtrauen (no pl)	*mistrust*
die Asylbewerberin (-nen)	*asylum seeker (f)*	der Neo-Nazismus (no pl)	*neo-nazism*
der Ausländer (-)	*foreigner*	das Notaufnahmelager (-)	*transit camp*
der Aussiedler (-)	*emigrant*	die Rassendiskriminierung	*racial discrimination*
der Einwanderer (-)	*immigrant*	die Rassenunruhen (pl)	*racial disturbances*
die Einwanderung (pl rare)	*immigration*	die Staatsbürgerschaft	*nationality*
der Flüchtling (-e)	*refugee*	der Übersiedler (-)	*migrant*
der Fremde (-n)	*foreigner*	die Ungleichheit (no pl)	*inequality*
der Gastarbeiter (-)	*foreign worker*	die Unterbringung (-en)	*accommodation*
das Herkunftsland ("er)	*country of origin*	das Vorurteil (-e)	*prejudice*
ausländerfeindlich	*xenophobic*	politisch	*political*
doppelt	*dual*	schlechtbezahlt	*badly paid*
anwerben	*to recruit*	repatriieren	*to repatriate*
enteignen	*to dispossess*	terrorisieren	*to terrorise, intimidate*
integrieren	*to integrate*	verfolgen	*to persecute*
gegen .... protestieren	*to protest against...*	zusammenschlagen	*to beat up*

die Ausländerfeindlichkeit erleben	*to experience hatred of foreigners*
den Groll anfachen	*to inflame resentment*
gegen jemanden diskriminieren	*to discriminate against someone*
finanzielle Anreize zur Rückkehr in die Heimat	*financial incentives to return home*
der kulturelle Konflikt ist unvermeidlich	*the cultural clash is unavoidable*
er hat das Recht auf Einbürgung in Deutschland	*he has the right to German citizenship*
aus politischen Gründen	*for political reasons*
Rassenvorurteile haben	*to be racially prejudiced*
in die Bundesrepublik übersiedeln	*to emigrate to the Federal Republic*
auf beiden Seiten bekunden sie ihren Abscheu für	*on both sides they demonstrate their disgust for*
den Zuzug sperren	*to stop the influx of immigrants*

- **der Wehrdienst** (no pl) *military service*
- **der Zivildienst** (no pl) *community service*

der/die Wehrdienstpflichtige (-n)	*person liable for military service*
der Wehrdienstverweigerer (-)	*conscientious objector*
der/die Zivildienstleistende (-n)	*person doing community service*
seinen Wehrdienst ableisten	*to do one's military service*
jemanden zum Wehrdienst einberufen	*to call someone up for military service*
er war aus Gewissensgründen dagegen	*he had conscientious objections*

wehrdienstpflichtig	*liable for military service*	zivildienstpflichtig	*liable for community service*
die Wehrpflicht	*conscription*	der Militärdienst	*military service*

ENVIRONMENTAL ISSUES

- **die Umwelt** (no pl) *environment*

der Abfall ("e)	*rubbish/litter*	der Schadstoff (-e)	*harmful substance*
die Abgase (pl)	*exhaust gases*	die Sprühdose (-n)	*aerosol can*
das Abwasser ("er)	*sewage*	der Stausee (-n)	*reservoir*
die Altpapiersammlung	*waste paper collection*	der Treibhauseffekt	*greenhouse effect*
der Atommüll (no pl)	*radioactive waste*	das Umweltbewußtsein	*environmental awareness*
der Auspuff (-e)	*car exhaust*		
die Belastung (+gen)	*pollution (of)*	die Umwelterziehung	*environmental education*
die Energiequelle (-n)	*source of energy*		
die geothermische Energie	*geothermal energy*	der Umweltschaden	*damage to environment*
die Gezeitenenergie	*tidal power*	der Umweltschutz (no pl)	*protection of environment*
das Gift (-e)	*poison*		
die Isolierung (-en)	*insulation*	der Umweltschützer (-)	*environmentalist*
der Katalysator (-en)	*catalytic convertor*	die Verschmutzung	*pollution*
die Katastrophe (-n)	*catastrophe*	die Verseuchung	*contamination*

die Kernenergie (-n)	*nuclear power*	das Waldsterben (no pl)	*dying of the forests*
die Klimaveränderung (-en)	*climatic change*	die Wasserkraft	*hydroelectric power*
die Lärmbelästigung (no pl)	*noise pollution*	das Wasserverschmutzung	*water pollution*
die Luftverschmutzung	*air pollution*	die Wasserversorgung (-en)	
der Müll (no pl)	*waste*		*water supply*
der Ölteppich (-e)	*oil slick*	die Wasservorräte (pl)	*water reserves*
das Ozonloch ("er)	*hole in ozone layer*	die Wegwerfgesellschaft	*throw away society*
die Ozonschicht	*ozone layer*	die Windenergie	*wind power*
alternativ	*alternative*	global	*global*
atomar	*nuclear, atomic*	künstlich	*artificial*
biologisch abbaubar	*bio-degradeable*	schädlich	*harmful*
krebserregend	*carcinogenic*	umweltbewußt	*environmentally aware*
krebserzeugend	*cancer producing*	umweltfeindlich	*ecologically harmful*
energiesparend	*energy-saving*	umweltfreundlich	*ecologically friendly*
erneubar	*renewable*	verseucht	*contaminated*
durchführen	*to carry out*	bleifrei tanken	*to use lead free petrol*
entwickeln	*to develop*	wegwerfen	*to throw away*
isolieren	*to insulate*	verbrauchen	*to use, to consume*
konsumieren	*to consume, use*	vergiften	*to poison*
säubern	*to clean*	vernichten	*to destroy*
schaden (+ dat)	*to damage*	verschmutzen	*to pollute*
sparen	*to save*	verseuchen	*to contaminate*
schonen	*to protect, conserve*	zerstören	*to destroy*

Abfälle auf die Straßen werfen	*to throw litter in the streets*
industrielle Abwässer (pl)	*industrial effluent*
das Abschmelzen der Polkappen	*the melting of the polar ice-caps*
der Anstieg des Meeresspiegels	*the rise in sea-level*
das Aussterben von gefährdeten Tieren	*the extinction of endangered animals*
Autos müssen reduzierten Abgaswerten genügen	*cars must satisfy reduced exhaust fumes values*
einen Ölteppich beseitigen	*to clean up an oil slick*
die fossilen Brennstoffe	*fossil fuels*
die Entsorgung von radioaktiven Abfallprodukten	*disposal of radioactive waste products*
den Verbrauch auf das Nötigste einschränken	*to limit consumption to the minimum*
die Erwärmung der Erdatmosphäre	*global warming*
die FCKWs (Fluorchlorkohlenwasserstoffe)	*CFCs (chlorofluorocarbons)*
die Folgen sind kaum absehbar	*the consequences are scarcely forseeable*
in Grenzen halten	*to keep in bounds*
im Laufe unseres Lebens	*in our life time*
Rücksicht auf etwas/jemanden nehmen	*to show consideration for something/someone*
ein empfindliches Öko-system	*a delicate eco-system*
mit etwas sparsam umgehen	*to use something economically*
in die Praxis umsetzen	*to put into practice*
sich zu etwas verpflichten	*to commit oneself to something*
die Verteilung des Ölteppichs	*the spreading of the oil slick*
künstliche Düngemittel verwenden	*to use artificial fertilisers*
auf etwas/jemanden verzichten	*to do without something/someone*
die Folgen voraussagen	*to predict the consequences*
jemanden vor etwas warnen	*to warn someone of something*
eine Wende in der öffentlichen Einstellung zum Umweltschutz	*a change in public attitude to environmental protection*
es gibt kein Zurück	*there is no going back*

THE THIRD WORLD

● **die dritte Welt** *The Third World*

der Analphabetismus	*illiteracy*	das Industrieland ("er)	*industrialised country*
die Armut	*poverty*	die Industrialisierung (-en)	*industrialisation*
die Ausbeutung	*exploitation*	die Kindersterblichkeit	*child mortality*
die Bevölkerungsexplosion (-en)		die Landwirtschaft (-en)	*agriculture*
	population explosion	die Lebenserwartung (-en)	*life expectancy*
das Bevölkerungswachstum		die Regenzeit (-en)	*rainy season*
	population growth	die Schulden (pl)	*debts*
das Dritte-Welt-Land ("er)	*Third World Country*	die Spende (-n)	*donation*

die Entwicklungshilfe (-n)	*development aid*	die Überbevölkerung (-en)	*over-population*
die Familienplanung	*family planning*	die Unterdrückung	*oppression*
die Geburtenkontrolle (-n)	*birth control*	die Unterernährung	*malnutrition*
die Geburtenrate (-n)	*birth rate*	das Wirtschaftswachstum	*economic growth*
der Geburtenzuwachs.	*increase in birth rate*	die Weltgesundheits-	*World Health*
die Hungersnot ("e)	*famine*	organisation	*Organisation*

abgemagert	*emaciated*	niedrig	*low*
gezielt	*targeted*	unterentwickelt	*underdeveloped*

mangeln	*to lack*	verdursten	*to die of thirst*
schicken	*to send*	verhungern	*to starve*

die Armut bekämpfen	*to fight poverty*
Hilfe zur Selbsthilfe	*helping people to help themselves*
der Unterschied zwischen Arm und Reich	*the difference between the rich and the poor*

GEOGRAPHY

- **das Stadtleben** *town life*
- **das Landleben** *country life*

die Anonymität	*anonymity*	das Ackerland ("er)	*arable land*
der Bürger (-)	*citizen*	der Bauer (-n)	*farmer*
die Einbahnstraße (-n)	*one way street*	der Bauernhof ("e)	*farm*
das Einkaufszentrum (-ren)	*shopping centre*	die Bergkette (-n)	*mountain range*
die Einsamkeit	*loneliness*	die Dorfkneipe (-n)	*village pub*
die Fabrik (-en)	*factory*	die Ernte (-n)	*harvest*
das Fachwerkhaus ("er)	*half-timbered house*	die Forstwirtschaft	*forestry*
die Fußgängerzone (-n)	*pedestrian zone*	der Getreidebau	*arable farming*
das Gedränge	*hustle*	das Häuschen (-)	*cottage*
das Graffiti	*graffiti*	die Heide (-n)	*heath, moor*
die Großstadt ("e)	*big city*	der Kleinbauer (-n)	*smallholder*
der Grüngürtel (-)	*green belt*	die Landluft	*country air*
die Hauptstadt ("e)	*capital city*	die Milchviehhaltung	*dairy farming*
die Litfaßsäule (-n)	*advertising column*	das Moor (-e)	*fen*
der Pendler (-)	*commuter*	die Pflanzung	*planting*
die Schlafstadt ("e)	*dormitory town*	die Ruhe	*peace, quiet*
der Stadtbewohner (-)	*town dweller*	der Steinbruch ("e)	*quarry*
die Stoßzeit (-en)	*rush hour*	die Scheune (-n)	*barn*
der Straßenraub	*mugging (crime)*	das Strohdach ("er)	*thatched roof*
die Umgehungsstraße (-n)	*by-pass*	der Teich (-e)	*pond*
die Vorstadt ("e)	*suburb*	die Viehzucht (no pl)	*cattle breeding*
der Wohnblock ("e)	*block of flats*	das Weideland ("er)	*pasture land*
das Wohngebiet (-e)	*housing area*	der Weinbauer (-n)	*wine grower*
die Wohnsiedlung (-en)	*housing estate*	der Weinberg (-e)	*vineyard*
der Wolkenkratzer (-)	*sky scraper*	die Weinlese (-n)	*grape harvest*

bebaut	*built up*	abgeschieden	*isolated*
benachteiligt	*deprived*	abgeschnitten	*cut off*
städtisch	*municipal, urban*	bewaldet	*wooded*
übervölkert	*overpopulated*	geruhsam	*leisurely*
voll	*crowded*	hügelig	*hilly*
verstopft	*congested*	ländlich	*rural*

besetzen	*to occupy*	ernten	*to harvest*
besitzen	*to own*	pflügen	*to plough*
leerstehen	*to stand empty*	säen	*to sow*

einen Einkaufsbummel machen	*to go shopping*
öffentlicheVerkehrsmittel (pl)	*public transport*
auf das Auto angewiesen sein	*to be dependent on the car*
einen Stadtbummel machen	*to go for a stroll in town*
einen Ausflug aufs Land machen	*to go on a trip to the country*
unberührte Natur erleben	*to enjoy unspoiled countryside*

TRANSPORT AND COMMUNICATION

- **der Transport** (-e) *transport*
- **der Straßenverkehr** (no pl) *road traffic*

der Ärmelkanal-Tunnel	*Channel Tunnel*	der Lieferwagen (-)	*delivery van*
die Autobahn (-en)	*motorway*	der Nahverkehr (no pl)	*local traffic*
die Auffahrt (-en)	*slip road onto m/way*	das Parkhaus ("er)	*multi-storey car-park*
die Ausfahrt(-en)	*motorway exit*	der Parkplatz ("e)	*car-park*
das Autobahnkreuz (-e)	*motorway junction*	das Parkverbot (-e)	*no parking area*
die Baukosten (pl)	*building costs*	der Personenkraftwagen (-)	*private car*
die Beförderung (-en)	*movement of goods/people*	die Radkralle (-n)	*wheel clamp*
der Busbahnhof ("e)	*bus station*	die Raststätte (-n)	*service area (m/way)*
die Busspur (-en)	*bus lane*	die Ringstraße (-n)	*ring road*
der Engpaß ("sse)	*bottleneck*	der Schwerlastverkehr (no pl)	
das Fahrzeug (-e)	*vehicle*		*heavy goods traffic*
der Fernverkehr (no pl)	*long distance traffic*	die Straßenbauarbeiten (pl)	*road works*
der Führerschein (-e)	*driving licence*	das Straßenbauprogramm (-e)	
der Gebrauchtwagen (-)	*second-hand car*		*road building programme*
die Gebühr (-en)	*toll*	das Straßennetz	*road network*
die Geldstrafe (-n)	*fine*	die Strecke (-n)	*stretch of road*
die Gescwindigkeit (-en)	*speed*	die Tiefgarage (-n)	*underground car-park*
die Geschwindigkeitsbegrenzung (-en)		das Überholverbot (-e)	*no overtaking area*
	speed limit	die Umleitung (-en)	*diversion*
das Halteverbot (-e)	*no waiting area*	das Verkehrsministerium	*transport ministry*
der Kombi (-s)	*estate car*	das Verkehrsopfer (-)	*road casualty*
das Kraftfahrzeug (-e)	*motor vehicle*	die Verkehrsplanung	*traffic planning*
die Kreuzung (-en)	*crossroads*	die Verkehrsstauung (-en)	*traffic jam*
die Kurve (-n)	*bend*	der Zeitgewinn (-e)	*time saving*
der Lastkraftwagen(-)	*lorry*	der Zusammenstoß ("sse)	*collision*

frontal	*head on*	unentbehrlich	*essential/indispensible*
kurvenreich	*full of bends*	verkehrssicher	*safe, roadworthy*

abschleppen	*to tow away*	Vorfahrt haben	*to have the right of way*
Abstand halten	*to keep one's distance*	einen Helm tragen	*to wear a helmet*
anschnallen	*to fasten seatbelt*	jemanden überfahren	*to knock someone down*
vorsichtig fahren	*to drive carefully*	überholen	*to overtake*
Gas geben	*to put one's foot down*	verunglücken	*to have an accident*
eine Panne haben	*to break down*	einen Unfall verursachen	*to cause an accident*

verkehrsberuhigende Maßnahmen	*traffic calming measures*
sich an etwas (dat) beteiligen	*to share in something*
ins Schleudern geraten	*to go into a skid*
für alle Fahrzeuge gesperrt	*closed to all vehicles*
sich nach etwas (dat) richten	*to gear something towards*
die Geschwindigkeitsbegrenzung überschreiten	*to exceed the speed limit*
den Idividualverkehr auf öffentliche	*to transfer/switch private transport users*
Verkehrsmittel umstellen	*on to public transport*

- **der Schienenverkehr** (no pl) *rail traffic*

der Anschluß ("sse)	*connection*	die Notbremse (-n)	*communication cord*
der Bahnwärter (-)	*signalman*	die Oberleitung (-en)	*overhead cable*
die Eisenbahn (-en)	*railway*	das Schienennetz	*rail network*
die Entgleisung (-en)	*derailment*	der Schlafwagen (-)	*sleeping-car*
der Fahrkartenschalter (-)	*ticket office*	der Speisewagen (-)	*restaurant car*
der Fahrplan ("e)	*time table*	die Stadtbahn (-en)	*urban railway*
der Gepäckwagen (-)	*luggage van*	die Straßenbahn (-en)	*tramway*
der Güterzug ("e)	*goods train*	die Streckensstillegung (-en)	
die Hauptstrecke (-n)	*main line*		*line closure*
die Lokomotive (-n)	*locomotive*		
der Lokomotivführer (-)	*engine driver*	die Subvention (-en)	*subsidy*
die Nebenstrecke (-n)	*branch line*	die Zeitkarte (-n)	*season ticket*
		der Zugführer (-)	*guard*

belastet	*heavily used*	überfüllt	*overcrowded*
besetzt	*occupied, engaged*	wenig frequentiert	*little used*
regelmäßig	*regular*	zuschlag(s)pflichtig	*incurs supplement*

anhalten	*to stop*	einsteigen	*to get on/in*
aussteigen	*to get off/out*	umsteigen	*to change*
das Defizit abbauen	*to reduce the deficit*		

finanzielle Hilfen (pl)	*financial aid*
dem Schienen gegenüber dem Straßenverkehr Priorität einräumen	*to give priority to rail as opposed to road traffic*
verstärkte Investitionen (pl)	*increased investment*
das Schienennetz modernisieren	*to modernise the rail network*
mit der Untergrundbahn fahren	*to go by underground*

● **der Flugverkehr** (no pl) *air traffic*

der Abflug ("e)	*take off*	der Fluglotse (-n)	*air traffic controller*
der Absturz ("e)	*crash*	der Flugschreiber (-)	*flight recorder*
der Aufenthaltsraum ("e)	*airport lounge*	der Hubschrauber (-)	*helicopter*
die Bruchlandung (-en)	*crash landing*	der Informationsschalter	*information desk*
der Charterflug ("e)	*charter flight*	der Luftraum	*air space*
das Düsenflugzeug (-e)	*jet plane*	die Notlandung (-en)	*emergency landing*
die Einflugschneise (-n)	*approach path*	der Pendelverkehr (no pl)	*shuttle service*
der Fallschirm (-e)	*parachute*	das Segelflugzeug (-e)	*glider*
der Flug ("e)	*flight*	die Sichtweite (-n)	*visibility*
der Fluggast ("e)	*passenger*	die Startbahn (-en)	*runway*
die Fluggesellschaft (-en)	*air line*	das Transportflugzeug (-e)	*cargo aircraft*
der Flughafen (")	*airport*	das Überschallflugzeug	*supersonic aircraft*
die Flugleitung	*air traffic control*	die Vergütung (-en)	*re-imbursement*

abstürzen	*to crash*	schweben	*to hover*
auftanken	*to refuel*	starten	*to take off*
landen	*to land*	vergüten	*to refund*

mit einer Höhe von 3000 Meter	*at an altitude of 3000 meters*
lange Wartezeiten bei der Abfertiging sind ärgerlich	*long waiting times when checking in are annoying*
den Flugverkehr lahmlegen	*to paralyse air traffic*
der Flug wurde umgeleitet	*the flight was diverted*
die Überschallgeschwindigkeit	*supersonic speed*

● **die Schiffahrt** *shipping*

der Anker (-)	*anchor*	der Lastkahn ("e)	*barge*
die Binnenschiffahrt	*inland shipping*	der Leuchtturm ("e)	*lighthouse*
die Binnenwasserstraßen	*inland waterways*	der Lotse (-n)	*pilot*
das Bullauge (-n)	*porthole*	die Mannschaft (-en)	*crew*
der Dampfer (-)	*steamer*	der Matrose (-n)	*sailor*
das Deck (-s)	*deck*	das Rettungsboot (-e)	*lifeboat*
die Fähre (-n)	*ferry*	die Rettungsleine (-n)	*lifeline*
der Fischdampfer (-)	*trawler*	der Rettungsring (-e)	*lifebelt*
die Flagge (-n)	*flag*	der Schiffbruch (no pl)	*shipwreck*
der Frachter (-)	*freighter*	der Schlepper (-)	*tug*
der Hafen (")	*harbour*	die Schleuse (-n)	*lock*
die Hafenstadt ("e)	*port*	die Seereise (-n)	*voyage*
das Handelsschiff (-e)	*merchant ship*	das Segelboot (-e)	*sailing boat*
die Jacht (-en)	*yacht*	der Tanker (-)	*tanker*
der Kai (-s)	*quay*	der Taucher (-)	*diver*
der Kran ("e or -e)	*crane*	die Überfahrt (-en)	*crossing*
der Laderaum ("e)	*hold*	die Untiefe (-n)	*shallows*
die Landungsbrücke (-n)	*landing stage*	die Werft (-en)	*shipyard*
der Landungssteg (-e)	*gangway*	das Wrack (-s)	*wreck*

ankern	*to anchor*	kentern	*to capsize*
auslaufen	*to set sail*	vom Stapel lassen	*to launch*
sich nach... einschiffen	*to embark for...*	auf Grund laufen	*to run aground*
Schiffbruch erleiden	*to be shipwrecked*	vor Anker liegen	*to ride at anchor*
ertrinken	*to be drowned*	an Bord sein	*to be on board*

schiffbar	*navigable*	seetüchtig	*sea-going*
schwer	*heavy*	stürmisch	*stormy*

● **die Raumfahrt** *space travel*

die Abschußrampe (-n)	*launching pad*	der Raumtransporter (-)	*space shuttle*
der Astronaut (-en)	*astronaut*	der Satellit (-en)	*satellite*

die Bodenstation (-en)	*ground station*	die Schwerelosigkeit (no pl)	*weightlessness*
der Fernsehsatellit (-en)	*TV satellite*	die Sternwarte (-n)	*observatory*
die Forschungsgeräte (pl)	*research equipment*	das Teleskop (-e)	*telescope*
der Lotse (-n)	*pilot*	der Treibstoff (-e)	*fuel*
die Mond(lande)fähre (-n)	*lunar module*	die Umlaufbahn (-en)	*orbit*
die Rakete (-n)	*rocket*	das Vacuum (no pl)	*vacuum*
der luftleere Raum	*vacuum*	der Weltraum (no pl)	*(outer) space*
der Raumanzug ("e)	*space suit*	der Weltraumfahrer (-)	*space traveller*
das Raumfahrzeug (-e)	*space-vehicle*	das Weltraumrennen	*space-race*
die Raumkapsel (-n)	*space capsule*	die Weltraumstation (-en)	*space station*
das Raumschiff (-e)	*space ship*	das Weltraumzeitalter(no pl)	*space age*
die Raumsonde (-n)	*space probe*	der Wettersatellit (-en)	*weather satellite*

CURRENT AFFAIRS

● **Politik und Aktualitäten** *Politics and current affairs*

der/die Abgeordnete (-n)	*member of parliament*	die Regierung (-en)	*government*
der Antrag ("e)	*motion*	der Sieg (-e)	*victory*
die Beliebtheit (no pl)	*popularity*	die Sitzung (-en)	*sitting*
die Briefwahl (-en)	*postal vote*	die Sozialdemokraten (pl)	*social democrats*
die Debatte (-n)	*debate*	die Stimme (-n)	*vote*
die Demokratie	*democracy*	die Umbildung (-en)	*reshuffle*
die Fraktion (-en)	*group, faction*	der Vertrag ("e)	*treaty*
das Gesetz (-e)	*law, bill*	die Wahl (-en)	*election, vote*
die Gesetzgebung (no pl)	*legislation*	der Wähler (-)	*voter*
das Kabinett (-e)	*cabinet*	der Wahlkampf ("e)	*election campaign*
der Kandidat (-en)	*candidate*	der Wahlkreis (-e)	*constituency*
die Koalition (-en)	*coalition*	die Wahlniederlage (-n)	*election defeat*
die Krise (-n)	*crisis*	das Wahlrecht	*right to vote*
das Machtkartell (-e)	*monopoly of power*	die Wahlrede (-n)	*election speech*
die Mehrheit (-en)	*majority*	die Wahlversprechungen	*election promises*
die Meinungsumfrage (-n)	*opinion poll*	der Wahlzettel (-)	*voting paper*
die Nachwahl (-en)	*by-election*	der Außenminister (-)	*Foreign Minister*
die Opposition (-en)	*opposition*	der Bundeskanzler (-)	*Chancellor (= PM)*
das Parlament (-e)	*parliament*	der Bundespräsident (-en)	*President*
die Partei (-en)	*party*	der Finanzminister (-)	*Finance Minister*
der Politiker (-)	*politician*	der Innenminister (-)	*Home Secretary*
die Redefreiheit (no pl)	*freedom of speech*	der Kultusminister (-)	*Education Minister*
die Reform (-en)	*reform*	der Verteidigungsminister	*Defence Minister*

CDU die Christliche Demokratische Union	*Christian Democratic Union (Conservative)*
FDP die Freie Demokratische Partei	*Free Democratic Party (Liberal)*
die Grünen, die Alternative Liste (AL)	*The Green Party, the Alternative List*
KPD die Kommunistische Partei Deutschlands	*The German Communist Party*
PDS Partei des Demokratischen Sozialismus	*the former SED in East Germany*
die Republikaner	*Republicans (extreme right wing)*
SPD die Sozialdemokratische Partei Deutschlands	*The German Social Democratic Party*
SED die Sozialistische Einheitspartei Deutschlands	*The German Socialist Party (in GDR)*

absolut	*absolute*	liberal	*liberal*
aufrührerisch	*inflammatory*	parlamentarisch	*parliamentary*
geheim	*secret*	reaktionär	*reactionary*
gering	*small, slim*	rechtskräftig	*with the force of law*
künftig	*future*	revolutionär	*revolutionary*
konservativ	*conservative*	sozialdemokratisch	*social democratic*
kurzfristig	*short term*	totalitär	*totalitarian*
langfristig	*long term*	wahlberechtigt	*entitled to vote*

anspornen	*to spur on, encourage*	stimmen für (acc)	*to vote for*
aufheben	*to repeal*	verwerfen	*to reject*
auflösen	*to dissolve*	unterzeichnen	*to sign*
bilden	*to form*	wählen	*to vote, elect*
einbringen	*to introduce*	zunehmen	*to gain*
entwerfen	*to draw up*	zurücktreten	*to resign*

eine Wahl ankündigen	*to call an election*
aus politischen Gründen	*for political reasons*

an die Macht kommen	*to come to power*
die Sache schleifen lassen	*to drag one's feet*
den Kopf in den Sand stecken	*to bury one's head in the sand*
auf der Tagesordnung stehen	*to be on the agenda*
einen Antrag auf etwas (acc) stellen	*to put a motion on something*
die Vertrauensfrage stellen	*to ask for a vote of confidence*
sich zur Wahl stellen	*to stand for election*
die Unterschriftensammlung (-en)	*petition*
eine Resolution verabschieden	*to pass a resolution*
das Verhältniswahlrecht (no pl)	*proportional representation*
das Blaue vom Himmel versprechen	*to promise the earth*
rechtskräftig werden	*to become law*

● die Religion *Religion*

das Abendmahl (no pl)	*communion*	die Kommunion	*communion*
der Aberglaube (-n)	*superstition*	der Koran	*Koran*
der Agnostiker (-)	*agnostic*	der Kult (-e)	*cult*
die Andacht (-en)	*worship, prayer*	der Lama (-s)	*Lama*
der/die Atheist/in (-/nen)	*atheist (m/f)*	die Lebensphilosophie	*philosphy of life*
die Beerdigung (-en)	*funeral, burial*	die Meditation (-en)	*meditation*
die Beichte (-n)	*confession*	der/die Missionär/in (-/nen)	*missionary (m/f)*
die Bibel (-n)	*bible*	die Moschee (-n)	*mosque*
der Buddha	*Buddha*	der Moslem (-s)	*moslem*
der Buddhismus	*Buddhism*	der Prophet (-en)	*prophet*
der/die Buddhist/in (-/nen)	*Bhuddist (m/f)*	der Protestantismus	*Protestantism*
das Christentum	*Christianity*	der Rabbiner (-)	*Rabbi*
der/die Christ/in (-/nen)	*Christian (m/f)*	der Sabbat (-e)	*Sabbath*
das Dogma (-men)	*dogma*	das Schicksal (-e)	*fate, destiny*
das Evangelium	*gospel*	die Seele (-n)	*soul*
der Friedhof ("e)	*cemetry*	die Sekte (-n)	*sect*
das Gebet (-e)	*prayer*	der/die Sünder/in (-/nen)	*sinner*
der Glaube (-n)	*belief, faith*	die Synagoge (-n)	*synagogue*
der Gott ("er)	*God*	die Taufe (-n)	*baptism*
der Gottesdienst (-e)	*church service*	der Tempel (-)	*temple*
der Himmel (-)	*Heaven*	der Teufel (-)	*devil*
der Hinduismus	*Hinduism*	die Theologie (-n)	*theology*
der Hindu (-s)	*Hindu*	die Toleranz (no pl)	*tolerance*
die Hoffnung (-en)	*hope*	die Überzeugung (-en)	*conviction*
die Hölle (-n)	*Hell*	die Versuchung (-en)	*temptation*
der Islam	*Islam*	die Wahrheit	*truth*
das Judentum	*Judaism*	die Wiedergeburt	*reincarnation*
die Kirche	*church*	die Zeremonie (-n)	*ceremony*
Ostern	*Easter*	anbeten	*to worship*
Pfingsten	*Whitsuntide*	bekehren zu	*to convert to*
Weihnachten	*Christmas*	an Gott glauben	*to believe in God*
anglikanish	*Anglican*	heidnisch	*pagan*
evangelisch	*Protestant*	katholisch	*Catholic*
fromm	*pious*	orthodox	*orthodox*
geistig	*spiritual*	religiös	*religious*
gläubig	*religious*	reumütig	*remorseful/repentant*
göttlich	*divine*	römisch-katholisch	*Roman Catholic*
heilig	*holy*	unsterblich	*immortal*

● der Krieg (-e) *war*

die Abschreckung (-en)	*deterrent*	der Luftangriff (-e)	*air attack*
die Armee (-n)	*army*	der Luftschutzkeller (-)	*air raid shelter*
die Aufrüstung (-en)	*armament*	die Luftwaffe (-n)	*air force*
die Ausrüstung (-en)	*equipment*	das Manöver (-)	*manoeuvre*
die Besatzungstruppen (pl)	*occupying forces*	der Marschflugkörper (-)	*cruise missile*
die Bombe (-n)	*bomb*	das Maschinengewehr (-e)	*machine gun*
die Bundeswehr (no pl)	*German army*	die Munition (no pl)	*ammunition*
der Bürgerkrieg (-e)	*civil war*	die Neutralität (no pl)	*neutrality*
die Entwarnung (-en)	*all clear*	der Panzer (-)	*tank*
die Fahne (-n)	*flag, colours*	der Rekrut (-en)	*recruit*
das Feldlazarett (-e)	*field hospital*	die Schlacht (-en)	*battle*

der Flugalarm (no pl)	*air raid warning*	die Sirene (-n)	*siren*
der Flugzeugträger (-)	*aircraft carrier*	der Soldat (-en)	*soldier*
der Freiwillige (-n)	*volunteer*	der Straßenkampf ("e)	*street fighting*
die Gasmaske (-n)	*gas mask*	die Streitkräfte (pl)	*armed forces*
das Gewehr (-e)	*rifle*	der Tornister (-)	*kit bag*
der Heckenschütze (-n)	*sniper*	die Verluste (pl)	*casualties*
die Kapitulation (-en)	*capitulation*	die Waffe (-n)	*weapon*
die Kaserne (-n)	*barracks*	der Waffenhandel (no pl)	*arms trade*
der Kriegsgefangene (-n)	*prisoner of war*	der Waffenstillstand (no pl)	*cease fire*
die Kugel (-n)	*bullet*	der Zerstörer (-)	*destroyer*

bedingungslos	*unconditional*	luftdicht	*airtight*
biologisch	*biological*	kriegerisch	*warlike*
blutig	*bloody*	schutzlos	*defenceless*
bombensicher	*bomb-proof*	wehrlos	*defenceless*
chemisch	*chemical*	vermißt	*missing*
entscheidend	*decisive*	verzweifelt	*desperate*

abfeuern	*to fire off*	schießen	*to shoot*
angreifen	*to attack*	in die Luft sprengen	*to blow up*
ausrüsten	*to equip*	überrennen	*to overrun*
beschießen	*to shell*	sich verbünden	*to form an alliance*
im Heer dienen	*to serve in the army*	verletzen	*to wound*
erobern	*to conquer*	verteidigen	*to defend*
explodieren	*to explode*	verwüsten	*to devastate*

diplomatische Beziehungen abbrechen	*to break off diplomatic relations*
der Ausbruch von Feindseligkeiten	*the outbreak of hostilities*
jemandem den Krieg erklären	*to declare war on someone*
ein Flugzeug entführen	*to hijack a plane*
für den Krieg rüsten	*to arm for war*
außer/in Schußweite	*out of/in range*
Truppen stationieren	*to station troops*
mit jemandem im Krieg stehen	*to be at war with someone*
die alliierten Truppen	*the allied troops*
die allgemeine Wehrpflicht (no pl)	*general conscription*

● **der Friede** (-n) *peace*

die Abrüstung (no pl)	*disarmament*	die Friedenstruppen (pl)	*peace-keeping force*
die Beschwichtigung (-en)	*appeasement*	das Gipfelgespräch (-e)	*summit talks*
der Blauhelm (-e)	*UN soldier/blue helmet*	der Truppenabbau (no pl)	*troop reduction*
die Entspannung (no pl)	*easing of tension*	die Vereinten Nationen (pl)	*United Nations*
die Friedensbewegung (-en)	*peace movement*	das Zugeständnis (-se)	*concession*

vereinbaren	*to agree*	vermitteln	*to mediate*

Truppen abziehen	*to withdraw troops*
die Verhandlungen aufnehmen	*to enter into negotiations*
internationale Beziehungen	*international relations*
über etwas (acc) Einigung erzielen	*to reach agreement on something*
Friedensverhandlungen führen	*to hold peace negotiations*
diplomatische Beziehungen herstellen	*to establish diplomatic relations*
ein Abkommen schließen	*to conclude an agreement*
am Scheideweg stehen	*to be at a crossroads*
den Krieg vermeiden	*to avoid war*

● **der Handel** (no pl) *trade*

● **die Wirtschaft** (pl rare) *economy*

der Absatz ("e)	*sale*	der Exportmarkt ("e)	*export market*
die Aktiengesellschaft AG	*joint stock company (Plc)*	die Flaute (-n)	*depression*
die Aktie (-n)	*share*	das Geschäft (-e)	*business*
der/die Aktionär/in (-/nen)	*shareholder (m/f)*	der Großhandel (no pl)	*wholesale trade*
die Analyse (-n)	*analysis*	die Haftung (-en)	*liability*
die Anlage (-n)	*investment*	die Handelsbilanz (-en)	*balance of trade*
die Anleihe (-n)	*bond*	die Herstellung (no pl)	*manufacture*
der Aufschwung ("e)	*upturn*	die Hochkonjunktur (-en)	*boom*
der Auftrieb (-e)	*upward trend*	die Industrie (-n)	*industry*
der Außenhandel (no pl)	*foreign trade*	die Konjunktur (-en)	*economic situation*

die Aussicht (-en)	prospect	der Konkurrent (-en)	competitor
das Bankwesen (no pl)	banking	die Konkurrenz (-en)	competition
der Bedarf (-e)	need	der Kurseinbruch ("e)	stock market crash
die Bestellung (-en)	order	die Partnerschaft (-en)	partnership
die Bestimmung (-en)	regulation	die Planwirtschaft	planned economy
die Bitte (-n)	request	die Privatisierung (-en)	privatisation
die Börse (-n)	stock market	die Rezession (-en)	recession
die Branche (-n)	trade sector	die Tochtergesellschaft (-en)	subsidiary
das Defizit (-e)	deficit	die Übernahme (-n)	take over
die Dividende (-n)	dividend	das Unternehmen (-)	company
der Einzelhandel (no pl)	retail trade	die Verwaltung (-en)	administration
die Erneuerung (no pl)	regeneration	der/die Volkswirt/in (-/nen)	economist
das Erzeugnis (-se)	product	das Werk (-e)	works, factory
der Export (-e)	export	die Zahlungsbilanz (-en)	balance of payments

aktuell	current	ökonomisch	economical
effektiv	effective	rückläufig	declining
flau	slack	unabhängig	independent
konkurrenzfähig	competitive	unternehmerisch	entrepreneurial

abbestellen	to cancel (an order)	erzeugen	to produce
anlegen	to invest	reduzieren	to reduce
bestellen	to order	spekulieren	to speculate

- **die Bank** (-en) *bank*
- **Finanzen** (pl) *finances*

die Abwertung (no pl)	devaluation	die Kosten (pl)	costs
die Ausgaben (-n)	expenditure	der Kredit (-e)	credit, loan
das Bankkonto (-ten)	bank account	die Kreditgrenze (-n)	credit limit
das Bargeld (no pl)	cash	die Kreditkarte (-n)	credit card
die Bausparkasse (-n)	building society	die Mehrwertsteuer	value added tax/ VAT
die Buchhaltung (-en)	book keeping, accounts	der Preisanstieg (-e)	price increase
das Budget (-s)	budget	der Preiskampf ("e)	price war
der Einkaufspreis (-e)	cost price	der Preisnachlaß ("sse)	price reduction
die Einkommenssteuer	income tax	die Quittung (-en)	receipt
der Euroscheck (-s)	Eurocheque	die Rechnung (-en)	invoice, bill
die Filiale (-n)	branch	der Scheck (-s)	cheque
die Geheimzahl (-en)	PIN number	die Scheckkarte (-n)	cheque card
der Geldautomat (-en)	cash dispenser	die Schulden (pl)	debts
das Girokonto (-ten)	current account	das Sparkonto (-ten)	savings account
der Haushaltsplan ("e)	budget	die Steuer (-n)	tax
die Hypothek (-en)	mortgage	die Steuerbelastung	tax burden
die Inflationsrate (-n)	inflation rate	das Steuerparadies (-e)	tax haven
der Kaufpreis (-e)	purchase price	die Währung (-en)	currency
die Kaution (-en)	deposit	die Versicherung (-en)	insurance
der Kontoauszug ("e)	bank statement	die Zahlung (-en)	payment
die Körperschaftssteuer	corporation tax	das Zinsenkonto (-ten)	interest account

ausgabefähig	disposable	netto	net
bankrott	bankrupt	preisgünstig	low cost
bargeldlos	cashless	stabil	stable
brutto	gross	zahlungsfähig	solvent
multinational	multi-national	zahlungsunfähig	insolvent

ankurbeln	to boost	gutschreiben	to credit
berechnen	to calculate	überweisen	to transfer
einlösen	to cash (a cheque)	überziehen	to overdraw
einzahlen	to pay in	verleihen	to lend

bar bezahlen	to pay cash
mit Scheck bezahlen	to pay by cheque
der Einzelhandelspreisindex (-e)	retail price index
in Konkurs gehen	to go bankrupt
Geld auf der Bank haben	to have money in the bank
GmbH – Gesellschaft mit beschränkter Haftung	private limited company (Ltd)
in Aktien investieren	to invest in shares
wie Gott in Frankreich leben	to live a life of luxury
über seine Verhältnisse leben	to live beyond one's means
seinen Verhältnissen entsprechend leben	to live within one's means

der Lebenshaltungskostenindex (-e)	cost-of-living index
Abstriche machen	to make cutbacks
in den roten Zahlen stecken	to be in the red
die Preise steigen/sinken	prices are rising/falling
einen Betrieb stillegen (or still-legen)	to close down a business
sich nach der Decke strecken	to cut one's coat according to one's cloth
mit jemandem Handel treiben	to do business with someone
Soll und Haben	debit and credit
ein Unternehmen mit einem Jahresumsatz von mehr als...	a firm with an annual turnover of more than...
das Geld auf die Straße werfen	to spend money like water
etwas mit Verlust verkaufen	to sell something at a loss

- **die Medien** (pl) *media*
- **die Presse** *the press*

das Abonnement (-s/-e)	subscription	der Leitartikel (-)	leading article
das Anzeigeblatt ("er)	local advertising paper	die Leserschaft (no pl)	readership
die Auflage (-n)	circulation	die Meldung (-en)	announcement
das Boulevardblatt ("er)	tabloid newspaper	die Nachricht (-en)	news item
die Boulevardpresse	popular/gutter press	die Ortszeitung (-en)	local paper
der Bericht (-e)	report	die Pressefreiheit	freedom of the press
die Berichterstattung	reporting	die Pressezensur	censorship
das Farbmagazin (-e)	colour supplement	der/die Redakteur/in (-/nen)	editor (m/f)
das Feuilleton (-s)	feature/review section	die Redaktion	editorial staff
die Informationsfreiheit	freedom of information	der Reporter (-)	reporter
der Journalismus	journalism	die Reklame (-n)	advertising
der Journalist (-en)	journalist	die Schlagzeile (-n)	headline
der Knüller (-) (coll)	scoop	die Verleumdung	libel
der Kommentar (-e)	comment, analysis	der Zeitungshändler (-)	newsagent
angesehen	quality, respected	reißerisch	sensational
auflagenstark	with big circulation	richtunggebend	influential
einseitig	onesided, biased	sachlich	objective
illustriert	illustrated	unsachlich	subjective
monatlich	monthly	voreingenommen	biased
objektiv	objective	wöchentlich	weekly
abonnieren	to subscribe to	durchblättern	to leaf/flick through
beeinflussen	to influence	erscheinen	to be published
berichten über (acc)	to report on	kommentieren	to comment on
drucken	to print	melden	to announce

in die Privatsphäre eingreifen	to invade one's privacy
ein Zerrbild entwerfen	to give a distorted picture
aktuelle Ereignisse	current events
eine Zeitung herausgeben	to publish a newspaper
seine Macht mißbrauchen	to misuse one's power
die überregionale Zeitung	national newspaper

- **das Fernsehen** (no pl) *television*
- **das Radio** (-s) *radio*

die Ankündigung (-en)	announcement	die Kurzmeldung (-en)	newsflash
die Antenne (-n)	aerial	die Live-Sendung (-en)	live broadcast
der/die Ansager/in (-/nen)	announcer	die Magazinsendung (-en)	current affairs programme
die Aufnahme (-n)	recording		
der Bildschirm (-e)	screen	das Mikrofon (-e)	microphone
der Diskjockey (-s)	discjockey	der Musiksender (-)	music station
der Dokumentarfilm (-e)	documentary	die Parabolantenne (-n)	satellite dish
die Einschaltquote (-n)	viewing figures	der Radiosender (-)	radio station
der Empfang	reception	der Rundfunksprecher (-)	broadcaster (m)
der Fernsehapparat (-e)	television set	die Rundfunksprecherin	broadcaster (f)
der Fernsehkanal ("e)	television channel	das Satellitenfernsehen	satellite television
der Fernseher (-)	television set	die Scheinwelt	sham world
die Fernsehserie (-n)	soap opera	die Seifenoper (-n) (coll)	soap opera
die Funkstation (-en)	radio station	die Sendung (-en)	broadcast
der Glotzkasten (") (coll)	goggle box	die Serie (-n)	series, serial
die Haupteinschaltzeit (-en)		der Spielfilm (-e)	feature film
	peak viewing time	die Tagesschau	news programme

der/die Hörer/in (-/nen)	listener (m/f)	die Tonqualität (-en)	tone quality
der Horrorfilm (-e)	horror film	der Überblick (-e)	overview, summary
das Hörspiel (-e)	radio play	das Wellenband ("er)	waveband
die Hörspielserie (-n)	soap opera on radio	die Wellenlänge (-n)	wavelength
das Kabelfernsehen (no pl)	cable television	die Werbung	advertising
das Kamerateam (-s)	camera crew	die Wiederholung (-en)	repeat
der Kanal ("e)	channel	der Zuhörer (-)	listener (audience pl)
das Kanalhüpfen (-)	channel hopping	der Zuschauer (-)	viewer (audience pl)
farbig	colour	stereo	stereo
gewaltsam	violent	synchronisiert	dubbed
lokal	local	uralt	ancient
aufzeichnen	to record	empfangen	to receive
aufnehmen	to record, video	fernsehen	to watch television
ausschalten	to switch off	unterhalten	to entertain
ausstrahlen	to broadcast	verharmlosen	to play down
einschalten	to switch on	vorführen	to show

zu viel Zeit für das Fernsehen aufwenden	to spend too much time watching television
die Auswirkung auf das Verhalten	the effect on one's behaviour
die Gewaltdarstellung ist wichtig	the depiction of violence is important
im Radio hören	to hear on the radio
Live-Sendungen lassen den Zuschauern	live broadcasts allow viewers to
am aktuellen Geschehen teilhaben	participate in what is currently happening
im Fernsehen sehen	to see on television
einen Sender stören	to jam a radio station
auf ein anderes Programm umschalten	to switch to another channel
mit Untertiteln für Hörgeschädigte	with subtitles for the hard of hearing
die Gewalt verherrlichen	to glorify violence
seine Phantasie verlieren	to lose one's imagination

TECHNOLOGY AND RESEARCH

● **die Technik** (no pl) *technology*

die Akte (-n)	file	der Farbdrucker (-)	colour printer
der Aktenschrank ("e)	filing cabinet	die Faseroptik	fibre optics
das Autotelefon(-e)	car phone	der Fernschreiber (-)	teleprinter
das Bildschirmgerät	VDU visual display unit	die Hardware (-s)	hardware
die Bearbeitung	editing	die Informatik (no pl)	information technology
der Bildschirmtext (no pl)	viewdata	das Laufwerk (-e)	disk-drive
die Compact Disc (-s)	compact disc	die Software (no pl)	software
die Compact Platte (-n)	compact disc	die Tastatur (-en)	keyboard
der Computer (-)	computer	das Telefon (-e)	telephone
die Datenbank (-en)	database	das Telefonnetz (-e)	telephone network
die Datenfernübertragung	data transmission	das Telefax (no pl)	fax
das Datenschutzgesetz	data protection act	das Telefaxgerät (-e)	fax machine
die Diskette (-n)	floppy disc	die Textverarbeitung	word processing
das Dokument (-e)	document	der Videotext	teletext
der Drucker (-)	printer	die Wissensexplosion	information explosion
die Eingabe (-n)	input	die Zugriffszeit	access time
drahtlos	cordless, wireless	computerunterstützt	computer-supported
computergesteuert	computer controlled	kompatibel	compatible
anzeigen	to display	ersetzen	to replace
archivieren	to archive	löschen	to delete
bearbeiten	to edit	rationalisieren	to rationalise
beschleunigen	to speed up	speichern	to save
entlasten	to free from	vereinfachen	to simplify

Computer dringen in fast alle Lebensbereiche ein	computers are penetrating almost every aspect of our lives
menschliche Arbeitskraft durch Technik ersetzen	to replace human labour by technology
die elektronische Post	electronic mail
die Papieremenge reduzieren	to reduce the volume of paper
per Telefax senden	to fax

Zeit sparen	*to save time*		
neue Arbeitsplätze schaffen	*to create new jobs*		
Routinevorgänge übernehmen	*to take over routine processes*		

● **die Forschung** (no pl) *research*

der Entdecker (-)	*discoverer*	das Resultat (-e)	*result*
die Erkenntnisse (pl)	*knowledge*	das Retortenbaby (-s)	*test-tube baby*
der Fachmann ("er)	*expert*	das Risiko (-en)	*risk*
der Forscher (-)	*researcher*	die Überlebensrate (-n)	*survival rate*
der Fortschritt (-e)	*progress*	das Verfahren (-)	*procedure*
der Herzschrittmacher (-)	*heart pacemaker*	der Versuch (-e)	*experiment*
das Laboratorium (-ien)	*laboratory*	der Wissenschaftler (-)	*scientist*

abstoßen	*to reject (an organ)*	manipulieren	*to manipulate*
ausmerzen	*to eradicate*	rechtfertigen	*to justify*
erproben	*to put to the test*	steigern	*to raise*
über etwas (acc) forschen	*to research into…*	zurückliegen	*to lag behind*

sie haben das durch Ausprobieren entdeckt	*they have discovered that by trial and error*
in dieser Forschung gibt es immer ethische Bedenken	*in this research there are always ethical considerations*
wir haben ein Problem zu bewältigen	*we have a problem to overcome*
sie sollten Versuche an Tieren und Experimente mit menschlichen Embryonen einstellen	*they ought to discontinue experiments on animals and human embryos*
die Heilung von Erbkrankheiten ist kein Grund zur Sorge	*the treatment/ curing of hereditary diseases is no cause for concern*
er leistete die Pionierarbeit für die Heilung von Krebs	*he pioneered the treatment of cancer*
sie konnten dieses Problem nicht lösen	*they could not solve this problem*
sie haben eine narrensichere Methode perfektioniert	*they have perfected a foolproof technique*
sie mußten Abhilfe schaffen	*they had to take remedial action*
sie stoßen an die Grenzen des Wissens	*they are reaching the limits of knowledge*
sie unterzog sich einer Organverpflanzung	*she underwent an organ transplant*
die Forschung kann die Lebensqualität verbessern	*research can improve the quality of life*
diese Hypothese ist Wirklichkeit geworden	*this hypothesis has become reality*

THE ARTS

● **das Kulturleben** (no pl) *cultural life*
● **die Literatur** (-en) *literature*

die Anschauung (-en)	*view*	der/die Kritiker/in (-/nen)	*critic (m/f)*
der Antiheld (-en)	*anti-hero*	das Leitmotiv	*leitmotiv*
die Antiheldin (-nen)	*anti-heroine*	das Märchen (-)	*fairy tale*
die Ausgabe (-n)	*edition*	die Novelle (-n)	*short story, novella*
der/die Autor/in (-/nen)	*author (m/f)*	die Poesie (no pl)	*poetry*
der Charakter (-)	*character*	die Prosa (no pl)	*prose*
der Dichter (-)	*poet*	die Prosaliteratur	*fiction*
das Drama (-men)	*drama*	der Roman (-e)	*novel*
die Epik (no pl)	*epic*	das Sachbuch ("er)	*non-fiction book*
der Erzähler (-)	*narrator*	die Sage (-n)	*legend*
die Erzählung (-en)	*narrative*	der Schriftsteller (-)	*author*
die Figur (-en)	*character*	der Stil (-e)	*style*
das Gedicht (-e)	*poem*	das Taschenbuch ("er)	*paperback*
die Ironie (no pl)	*irony*	der Verfasser (-)	*author, writer*
das Kapitel (-)	*chapter*	der Verlag (-e)	*publisher*
die Kreativität (no pl)	*creativity*	das Vorwort (-e)	*preface*
der Kriminalroman (-e)	*detective novel*	das Zitat (-e)	*quotation*

ausführlich	*detailed*	romantisch	*romantic*
lebendig	*lively*	satirisch	*satirical*
moralisch	*moral*	symbolisch	*symbolic*
poetisch	*poetic*	ungekürzt	*unabridged*

betonen	*to stress*	sich reimen	*to rhyme*
sich in (acc) hineinsetzen	*to empathise with…*	vergleichen	*to compare*
erzählen	*to narrate*	veröffentlichen	*to publish*
nachahmen	*to imitate*	zitieren	*to quote*

- **der Film** (-e) *film*
- **das Theater** (no pl) *theatre*

die Aufnahme (-n)	*shot*	der Akt (-e)	*act*
der Auftritt (-e)	*appearance*	die Aufführung (-en)	*performance*
das Drehbuch ("er)	*script*	die Auflösung (-en)	*denouement*
der Drehort (-e)	*location*	der Beifall ("e)	*applause*
der Filmemacher (-)	*film maker (m)*	die Besetzung (-en)	*cast*
die Filmemacherin (-nen)	*film maker (f)*	die Bühne (-n)	*stage*
die Filmmusik (pl rare)	*film music*	das Bühnenbild (-er)	*stage set*
der Filmstar (-s)	*filmstar*	die Darstellung (-en)	*acting*
die Folge (-n)	*sequel*	der Dramatiker (-)	*dramatist (m)*
die Hauptrolle (-n)	*leading role*	die Dramatikerin (-nen)	*dramatist (f)*
der Held (-en)	*hero*	der Erfolg (-e)	*success*
die Heldin (-nen)	*heroine*	die Gestalt (-en)	*figure*
das Kino (-s)	*cinema*	die Handlung (-en)	*plot*
das Kinocenter	*multi-screen cinema*	die Hauptfigur (-en)	*main character*
der Kinogänger (-)	*cinema-goer (m)*	das Hauptthema (-men)	*main theme*
die Kinogängerin (-nen)	*cinema-goer (f)*	das Kabarett (-e)	*cabaret*
die Leinwand ("e)	*screen*	die Komödie (-n)	*comedy*
die Nahaufnahme (-n)	*close up*	die Kulissen (pl)	*scenery*
der Produzent (-en)	*producer (m)*	das Lampenfieber	*stage fright*
die Produzentin(-nen)	*producer (f)*	die Pause (-n)	*interval*
die Regie (no pl)	*direction*	die Premiere (-n)	*premiere*
die Rolle (-n)	*role*	das Publikum (no pl)	*audience*
der Schwarzweißfilm (-e)	*black and white film*	der Schauspieler (-)	*actor*
der Stummfilm (-e)	*silent film*	die Schauspielerin (-nen)	*actress*
die Toneffekte (pl)	*sound effects*	das Schicksal (-e)	*fate*
die Tricks (pl)	*special effects*	die Stimmung (-en)	*atmosphere*
die Verfilmung (-en)	*filming*	die Tragödie (-n)	*tragedy*
die Vorschau (-en)	*trailer, preview*	die Vorstellung (-en)	*performance*
ausverkauft	*sold out*	dramaturgisch	*dramatic*
abbilden	*to portray*	Regie führen	*to direct*
aufführen	*to put on*	inszenieren	*to produce*
auftreten	*to appear*	laufen	*to run*
ausdrücken	*to express*	leiten	*to direct*
drehen	*to shoot*	präsentieren	*to present*
herausbringen	*to release*	eine Rolle spielen	*to play a part*

- **die Bildhauerkunst** *sculpture*
- **die Musik** *music*
- **die Malerei** *painting*
- **der Tanz** *dance*

das Album (-ben)	*album*	die Landschaft (-en)	*landscape*
das Aquarell (-e)	*water colour*	der Lautsprecher (-)	*loudspeaker*
der Aspekt (-e)	*aspect*	das Lied (-er)	*song*
das Atelier (-s)	*studio*	die Melodie (-n)	*melody*
die Ausstellung (-en)	*exhibition*	das Mischpult (-e)	*sound mixer*
die Ballerina (-nen)	*ballerina*	der/die Musiker/in (-/nen)	*musician*
das Ballett (-e)	*ballet*	die Noten (pl)	*sheet music*
die Blechbläser (pl)	*brass instruments*	das Ölgemälde (-)	*oil painting*
der Bildhauer (-)	*sculptor*	die Oper (-n)	*opera*
die Bildhauerin (-nen)	*sculptress*	das Orchester (-)	*orchestra*
die Bildhauerei (no pl)	*sculpture*	das Originalölgemälde (-)	*original painting*
der Chor ("e)	*choir*	die Ovation (-en)	*ovation*
der Choreograph (-en)	*choreographer (m)*	der Pinsel (-)	*paint brush*
die Choreographin (-nen)	*choreographer (f)*	die Plastik (-en)	*piece of sculpture*
der Dirigent (-en)	*conductor (m)*	die Popgruppe (-n)	*pop group*
die Dirigentin (-nen)	*conductor (f)*	der Popsänger (-)	*pop singer*
die Fotografie (no pl)	*photography*	der Popstar (-s)	*popstar*
die Galerie (-n)	*gallery*	die Popszene (-n)	*pop scene*
der Gegenstand ("e)	*object*	das Porträt (-s)	*portrait*
der Gesang ("e)	*singing*	die Probe (-n)	*rehearsal*
die Harmonie (-n)	*harmony*	der Rhythmus (-men)	*rhythm*
der Hintergrund ("e)	*background*	die Sammlung (-en)	*collection*
die Hitliste (-n)	*charts (pop)*	der/die Sänger/in (-/nen)	*singer (m/f)*
die Hitparade	*hit parade*	der Schlager (-)	*pop-song*
die Holzbläser (pl)	*woodwind*	das Schlagzeug (no pl)	*percussion*
das Instrument (-e)	*instrument*	die Schnitzerei (-en)	*wood carving*

der Klang ("e)	*sound*	der/die Tänzer/in (-/nen)	*dancer (m/f)*
der Komponist (-en)	*composer*	die Truppe (-n)	*troupe, company*
die Komposition (-en)	*composition*	die Volksmusik (no pl)	*folk music*
der Künstler (-)	*artist (m)*	der Vordergrund ("e)	*foreground*
die Künstlerin (-nen)	*artist (f)*	der Vortrag ("e)	*recital*
das Kunstwerk (-e)	*work of art*	die Zeichnung (-en)	*drawing*
abstrakt	*abstract*	langweilig	*boring*
ausdrucksfähig	*expressive*	melodisch	*melodic*
instrumental	*instrumental*	vielversprechend	*very promising*
klassisch	*classical*	zeitgenössisch	*contemporary*
bekommen	*to get*	malen	*to paint*
darbieten	*to perform*	schnitzen	*to carve*
einstudieren	*to rehearse*	steppen	*to tap dance*
hauen	*to sculpture*	üben	*to practise*
komponieren	*to compose*	verewigen	*to immortalise*
aktionsreich	*action-packed*	hervorragend	*magnificent*
amüsant	*amusing*	historisch	*historic*
atemberaubend	*breathtaking*	innovativ	*innovative*
ausdruckslos	*inexpressive*	katastrophal	*disastrous*
beachtlich	*remarkable*	kompliziert	*complicated*
beklemmend	*oppressive*	kurzweilig	*entertaining*
belanglos	*trivial*	lobenswert	*praiseworthy*
charmant	*charming*	mittelmäßig	*mediocre*
durchschnittlich	*average*	neuartig	*new*
ehrgeizig	*ambitious*	packend	*exciting*
eindrucksvoll	*impressive*	rührselig	*tear-jerking*
einmalig	*unique*	sachlich	*objective*
enttäuschend	*disappointing*	schonungslos	*savage*
experimentell	*experimental*	sentimental	*sentimental*
erfolgreich	*successful*	stimmungsvoll	*atmospheric*
ergreifend	*moving*	subjektiv	*subjective*
ernsthaft	*serious*	überzeugend	*convincing*
fesselnd	*engrossing*	ungewöhnlich	*unusual*
genießbar	*enjoyable*	unterhaltsam	*entertaining*
gewagt	*risqué*	virtuos	*virtuoso*
glanzvoll	*brilliant*	wirkungsvoll	*effective*
großartig	*splendid*	zeitlos	*timeless*
handlungsarm	*thin on plot*	zutreffend	*accurate*

ein Film läuft im Kino	*a film is showing at the cinema*
sie sehen sich einen Film an	*they are watching a film*
das Stück handelt von Liebe und Haß	*the play is about love and hatred*
sie warten hinter den Kulissen	*they wait backstage*
die zweite Szene spielt in einem Wald	*the second scene takes place in a wood*
er hat den Werther dargestellt	*he has played the part of Werther*
sie waren bei Außenaufnahmen	*they were on location*
er malte mit Ölfarben	*he painted in oils*
sie können die Musik vom Blatt spielen	*they can sight read the music*
leider kann er die Noten nicht lesen	*unfortunately he cannot read music*
die meisten haben kein absolutes Gehör	*most people do not have perfect pitch*
nur wenige können nach Gehör spielen	*only a few can play by ear*
er hat einen Roman in der Ich-Form geschrieben	*he has written a novel in the first person*

GRAMMAR

The aim of this chapter is to set out in straightforward terms the essentials of German Grammar. You may think that Grammar is unimportant, a boring irrelevance but it is not. If words are the bricks of a sentence then grammar is the mortar enabling you to build sentences which convey ideas and meaning.

In this chapter you will find information about the following:
nouns, cases, articles, adjectives and adjective declensions, adverbs, pronouns, numerals and expressions of time, verbs (including strong and irregular verbs), the passive, the subjunctive, modal auxiliaries, conjunctions, prepositions, word order, punctuation.

2.1 NOUNS

GENDER

Nouns in German are written with a capital letter. There are three genders – masculine, feminine and neuter. All nouns are assigned to one of them unlike English where gender is determined by sex or 'natural gender'. This means that in German inanimate objects can be masculine or feminine as well as neuter. When listing vocabulary you should always list and learn nouns with their gender and where appropriate their plural form. To indicate the gender you use the definite article as follows:

Masculine	Feminine	Neuter
der Mann ("er) *man,*	die Frau (-en) *woman,*	das Kind (-er) *child,*
but note		
der Stuhl ("e) *chair,*	die Schule (-n) *school,*	das Buch ("er) *book*

A few rules exist which can help you learn the gender of nouns, but in general these are not hard and fast and you have to learn the gender when you learn the noun. Remember that if you cannot recall the gender of a noun under the stress of an examination, it is usually the first thought that comes into your mind which is right, assuming that you learned the gender correctly the first time you met the word.

Masculine

The following groups of nouns are masculine.

- all nouns referring to male gender including animals:
  der Kater (-) *tomcat,* **der Arzt ("e)** *doctor,* **der Onkel (-)** *uncle.*

- seasons, months, days of the week, points of the compass:
  der Herbst *autumn,* **der Februar** *February,* **der Dienstag** *Tuesday,* **der Norden** *north.*

- alcoholic drinks with the exception of beer:
  der Wein (-e) *wine,* **der Cocktail (-s)** *cocktail,* **der Schnaps ("e)** *schnapps,*
  but **das Bier (-e)** *beer.*

- the designation of professions or occupations, although a feminine form will also exist, often ending in **-in**:
  der Lehrer (-) *teacher,* **der Bäcker (-)** *baker,* **der Rechtsanwalt ("e)** *solicitor.*

- nouns ending in the following are masculine by form:

-ant	der Passant (-en)	*passer-by*	**-ast**	der Ast ("e)	*branch*
-ich	der Teppich (-e)	*carpet*	**-ig**	der Honig (no pl)	*honey*
-ismus	der Realismus (no pl)	*realism*	**-ling**	der Feigling (-e)	*coward*
-or	der Rotor (-en)	*rotor*	**-us**	der Passus (-)	*passage*

- nouns formed from the stem of a verb are usually masculine:
  besuchen - **der Besuch (-e)** *visit*,   raten - **der Rat** (no pl) *advice*.

Feminine

The following groups of nouns are feminine.

- all nouns referring to female gender including animals:
  die Katze (-n) *cat*, **die Ärztin (-nen)** *doctor*, **die Tante (-n)** *aunt*.

- the names of most German rivers:
  die Donau, die Elbe, die Spree, die Mosel, but there are some notable exceptions such as **der Main, der Neckar, der Rhein.**

- the majority of nouns ending in **-e**:
  die Liebe (no pl) *love*, **die Mitte (-n)** *middle*, **die Hilfe** (no pl) *help*.

  The exceptions are names of male persons and animals as in
  der Junge (-n) *boy*, **der Löwe (-n)** *lion*.

- almost all nouns ending in the following:

-ei	die Konditorei (-en)	*cakeshop*	**-heit**	die Kindheit (-en)	*childhood*
-in	die Studentin (-nen)	*female student*	**-keit**	die Einsamkeit (no pl)	*loneliness*
-schaft	die Freundschaft (-en)	*friendship*	**-tät**	die Universität (-en)	*university*
-ung	die Wohnung (-en)	*flat*			

  plus words of foreign origin ending in

-nz	die Existenz (no pl)	*existence*	**-ie**	die Chemie (no pl)	*chemistry*
-ik	die Musik (-en)	*music*	**-ion**	die Pension (-en)	*guest-house, pension, retirement, board (half or full board)*

- aeroplanes, motor-bikes and ships:
  die Boeing, die Honda, die „Belgrano".

- names of numerals:
  die Drei (-en), die Tausend (-en), die Million (-en).

Neuter

The following groups of nouns are neuter.

- infinitives used as nouns – gerunds and other parts of speech e.g. colours:
  das Singen (no pl) *singing*, **das Leiden (-)** *suffering*, **das Grün (-)** *green*.

- the young of persons and animals:
  das Kind (-er) *child*, **das Baby(-s)** *baby*, **das Kalb ("er)** *calf*, **das Lamm ("er)** *lamb*.

- the letters of the alphabet:
  das A (-), das Ypsilon (-) '*y*'.

- the names of towns and almost all countries, continents and provinces:
  das London der Nachkriegszeit *postwar London*, **das schöne Frankreich** *beautiful France*, **das Kleinasien** *Asia Minor*, **das alte Bayern** *old Bavaria*.

  die Schweiz *Switzerland* and **die Türkei** *Turkey* are the commonest exceptions and are always used with the article.

- nouns ending as follows are neuter:
  -chen das Mädchen *girl*   **-lein** das Fräulein *young lady (unmarried)*

  These two endings are used to form diminutives and are neuter by form.

  Other mainly neuter nouns include those ending as follows:

-ment	das Element (-e)	*element*	**-nis**	das Ereignis (-se)	*event, occurrence*
-sal	das Schicksal (-e)	*fate*	**-um**	das Studium (Studien)	*study*

- the majority of nouns with the prefix **Ge-**:
  das Gebäck (-e) *biscuits, cookies*   **das Gebet (-e)** *prayer*
  das Gelände (-) *open country, ground*

  Those that are **not** neuter refer (i) to living beings:
  der Gehilfe (-n)/die Gehilfin (-nen) *male/female assistant*

  or (ii) include a few masculine and feminine nouns:
  der Gewinn (-e) *profit*, **die Geschichte (-n)** *story, history* (no pl).

- metals and chemical elements:
  das Aluminium (no pl) *aluminium*, **das Messing** (no pl) *brass*.

  Exceptions include **der Stahl** (no pl) *steel*, **der Sauerstoff** (no pl) *oxygen*.

- physical units:
  das Ampere (-) *amp*, **das Atom (-e)** *atom*, **das Pfund (-e)** *pound*.

Compounds

The gender of **compounds** is determined by the last part of the word:
der Fahrplan ("e) *timetable*, or **die** Bushaltestelle (-n) *bus stop*.

Two genders

Some nouns have two genders with different meanings. The following is a list of the most common in this category:

der Band ("e)	*volume*	**das Band ("er)**	*ribbon*
		das Band (-e)	*bond, fetter*
der Bund ("e)	*alliance*	**das Bund (-e)**	*bundle, bunch*
der Erbe -n (-n)	*heir*	**das Erbe (Erbschaften)**	*inheritance*
der Gefallen (-)	*favour*	**das Gefallen** (no pl)	*pleasure*
der Gehalt (-e)	*content*	**das Gehalt ("er)**	*salary*
der Golf (-e)	*gulf*	**das Golf** (no pl)	*golf*
der Heide (-n)	*heathen*	**die Heide (-n)**	*heath*
der Hut ("e)	*hat*	**die Hut** (no pl)	*guard*
der Kunde -n (-n)	*customer*	**die Kunde** (no pl)	*knowledge*
der Leiter (-)	*leader*	**die Leiter (-n)**	*ladder*
der Messer (-)	*surveyor*	**das Messer (-)**	*knife*
der Pony (no pl)	*fringe (hair)*	**das Pony (-s)**	*pony*
der See (-n)	*lake*	**die See** (no pl)	*sea*
die Steuer (-n)	*tax*	**das Steuer (-)**	*steering-wheel*
der Tau (no pl)	*dew*	**das Tau (-e)**	*rope, hawser*
der Tor -en (-en)	*fool*	**das Tor (-e)**	*gate*
der Verdienst (no pl)	*earnings*	**das Verdienst (-e)**	*merit*
die Wehr (no pl)	*defence*	**das Wehr (-e)**	*weir*

Recent words

The gender of the most recent words taken into the language from English is mainly masculine as in **der Boom (-s)**, **der Hit (-s)**, **der Computer (-)**, **der Job (-s)**, **der Sex** (no pl), **der Streß** (no pl), **der Trend (-s)** etc.

THE FORMATION OF NOUN PLURALS

There are seven ways of forming the plural of German nouns.

Group 1

Nouns which do not change in the plural. Most masculine and neuter nouns which end in **-el, -en, -er** belong to this group.

The majority are in fact masculine, many ending in **-er** which is added to the stem of a verb forming nouns like **der Bäcker (-)** *baker*, **der Diener (-)** *servant* etc.

Example: **der Onkel** *uncle*

	Singular	Plural
N	der Onkel	die Onkel
A	den Onkel	die Onkel
G	des Onkels	der Onkel
D	dem Onkel	den Onkeln

- Here are some examples of **masculine nouns** in this group:

Ärmel	*sleeve*	**Arbeiter**	*worker*	**Felsen**	*rock*
Enkel	*grandson*	**Bettler**	*beggar*	**Kuchen**	*cake*
Gipfel	*summit*	**Bürger**	*citizen*	**Rasen**	*lawn*
Himmel	*sky*	**Fehler**	*mistake*	**Reifen**	*tyre*
Nebel	*fog*	**Gegner**	*opponent*	**Rücken**	*back*
Titel	*title*	**Schalter**	*booking office*	**Streifen**	*stripe*
Zweifel	*doubt*	**Teller**	*plate*	**Wagen**	*car*

N.B. Nouns which end in **-en** do not add an extra **-n** in the dative plural.

- **Neuter nouns** which belong to this group include:

Dunkel	*darkness*	**Abenteuer**	*adventure*	**Becken**	basin
Möbel	*item of furniture*	**Fenster**	*window*	**Examen**	*exam*
Segel	*sail*	**Theater**	*theatre*	**Zeichen**	*sign*

- The fractions: **das Drittel** *third*, **das Viertel** *quarter* etc.

- All nouns ending in **-chen** or **-lein**: **Mädchen** *girl*, **Fräulein** *young lady* etc which are diminutives.

- **Neuter nouns** which begin with **Ge-** and end in **-e** belong to this group also:
  e.g. **das Gebirge** *range of mountains*

Group 2

No ending in the plural but an Umlaut is added to the vowels **a, o, u**, which are stressed. These are mainly **masculine nouns** which end in **-el, -en, -er.**

Example: **der Nagel** *nail*

	Singular	Plural
N	der Nagel	die Nägel
A	den Nagel	die Nägel
G	des Nagels	der Nägel
D	dem Nagel	den Nägeln

- To this group belong the following **masculine nouns**:

Apfel	*apple*	**Bruder**	*brother*	**Boden**	*ground*
Mantel	*coat*	**Hammer**	*hammer*	**Garten**	*garden*
Sattel	*saddle*	**Schwager**	*brother-in-law*	**Hafen**	*harbour*
Vogel	*bird*	**Vater**	*father*	**Laden**	*shop*

This is not a complete list.

- Two **feminine nouns** are in this group: **die Mutter (")** *mother* and **die Tochter (")** *daughter*

- One **neuter noun** is in this group: **das Kloster (")** *monastery*

Group 3

Nouns forming their plural by adding **-e**. To this group belong most **neuter nouns** of one syllable with the exception of those belonging to groups 1 and 4 and other **neuter nouns** ending in **-tum** and **-um.**

Example: **das Jahr** *year*

	Singular	Plural
N	das Jahr	die Jahre
A	das Jahr	die Jahre
G	des Jahres	der Jahre
D	dem Jahr	den Jahren

- Here are some examples of single-syllable **neuter nouns** in this group:

Bein	*leg*	**Kinn**	*chin*	**Rohr**	*tube*	**Tier**	*animal*
Bier	*beer*	**Mal**	*time*	**Schiff**	*ship*	**Tor**	*gate/goal*
Boot	*boat*	**Meer**	*sea*	**Seil**	*rope*	**Zelt**	*tent*
Haar	*hair*	**Recht**	*right*	**Stück**	*piece*	**Ziel**	*aim*

This is not a complete list.

- Most **neuter nouns** of more than one syllable also belong to this group. Here are some examples:

Alphabet	*alphabet*	**Paket**	*parcel*	**Talent**	*talent*
Dutzend	*dozen*	**Problem**	*problem*	**Telegramm**	*telegram*
Gegenteil	*opposite*	**Prozent**	*percentage*	**Telephon**	*telephone*
Konzert	*concert*	**System**	*system*	**Verbot**	*prohibition*

- To this group belong most **masculine nouns** of more than one syllable (not listed so far) plus many one-syllable **masculine nouns** which do not take an Umlaut in the plural as in group 4. Here are some examples:

Dialekt	*dialect*	**Erfolg**	*success*	**Monat**	*month*	**Versuch**	*attempt*
Arm	*arm*	**Dom**	*cathedral*	**Hund**	*dog*	**Schuh**	*shoe*

Group 4

Nouns forming their plural by adding an **-e** with an Umlaut on the vowel that is stressed. To this group belong the great majority of **masculine nouns**, especially monosyllables, not listed elsewhere.

Example: **der Sohn** *son*

	Singular	Plural
N	der Sohn	die Söhne
A	den Sohn	die Söhne
G	des Sohnes	der Söhne
D	dem Sohn	den Söhnen

- Most **masculine nouns** of one syllable belong to this group. There are therefore a very large number of them. Some obvious examples are: **der Arzt ("e)** *doctor*, **der Stuhl ("e)** *chair* and there are many more.

- To this group also belong a small number of **masculine nouns** of more than one syllable. These include:

  Altar *altar* **Bischof** *bishop* **Kanal** *canal* **Kardinal** *cardinal* **Palast** *palace*

- There is one **neuter noun** belonging to this group: **das Floß ("e)** *raft*

- An important group of **feminine nouns** belongs to this group, e.g. **die Angst ("e)** *fear*. Others include:

Axt	*axe*	**Bank**	*bench*	**Braut**	*bride*	**Brust**	*breast*	**Faust**	*fist*
Frucht	*fruit*	**Gans**	*goose*	**Hand**	*hand*	**Haut**	*skin*	**Kraft**	*strength*
Kuh	*cow*	**Kunst**	*art*	**Luft**	*air*	**Lust**	*desire*	**Macht**	*power*
Magd	*maid*	**Maus**	*mouse*	**Nacht**	*night*	**Not**	*need*	**Nuß**	*nut*
Schnur	*string*	**Stadt**	*town*	**Wand**	*wall*	**Wurst**	*sausage*		

N.B. This group of **feminine nouns** does not follow the normal pattern (see group 6) in the formation of the plural of **feminine nouns**, so learn them carefully.

Group 5

Nouns forming their plural by adding **-er** with an Umlaut on the stressed vowel where possible.

Example: **das Dorf** *village*

	Singular	Plural
N	das Dorf	die Dörfer
A	das Dorf	die Dörfer
G	des Dorfes	der Dörfer
D	dem Dorf	den Dörfern

- About a quarter of all **neuter nouns** belong to this group. Most of them are monosyllabic. Remember that an Umlaut can only be used on the vowels **a, o, u, au**.
  e.g. **das Blatt ("er)** *leaf* **das Kind (-er)** *child*

- A number of **neuter nouns** of more than one syllable are included in this group:
  Gehalt *salary* **Gemüt** *mind* **Geschlecht** *sex* **Gesicht** *face*
  Gespenst *ghost* **Gewand** *garment* **Regiment** *regiment* **Spital** *hospice*

- To this group belong a small number of masculine nouns:
  Geist *spirit* **Gott** *God* **Mann** *man* **Mund** *mouth* **Rand** *edge*
  Ski *ski* **Strauch** *shrub* **Wald** *forest* **Wurm** *worm*

- Nouns ending in **-tum** belong to this group:
  e.g. **der Irrtum ("er)** *error* **das Altertum ("er)** *antiquity (antiquities)*

Group 6

Nouns forming their plural by adding **-n** or **-en**. This is the ending of the plural of virtually all **feminine nouns**.

Example: **die Blume** *flower*

	Singular	Plural
N	die Blume	die Blumen
A	die Blume	die Blumen
G	der Blume	der Blumen
D	der Blume	den Blumen

- Please note that **feminine nouns** ending in **-in** double the 'n' before adding **-en**, so the plural of **die Lehrerin** (*teacher female*) is **die Lehrerinnen**.

- Please note that **-n** is added to **feminine nouns** ending in **-e, -l, -r** in this group.
  e.g. **die Ecke (-n)** *corner* **die Gabel (-n)** *fork* **die Mauer (-n)** *wall*.

- The **masculine nouns** in this group are known as the 'weak' declension as they have the ending **-n** or **-en** in every case except the nominative singular.

Examples: **der Junge** *boy*   **der Mensch** *human being*

	Singular	Plural	Singular	Plural
N	der Junge	die Jungen	der Mensch	die Menschen
A	den Jungen	die Jungen	den Menschen	die Menschen
G	des Jungen	der Jungen	des Menschen	der Menschen
D	dem Jungen	den Jungen	dem Menschen	den Menschen

- Other common **masculine nouns** in this group ending in **-e** are:
  Affe *monkey* **Bote** *messenger* **Franzose** *Frenchman* **Hase** *hare* **Hirte** *shepherd*
  Löwe *lion* **Matrose** *sailor* **Neffe** *nephew* **Russe** *Russian* **Schotte** *Scotsman*
  N.B. Exceptions are: **der Käse** *cheese* which has no plural like this, **Käsesorten** is used for *cheeses* and **der Charme** (no pl) *charm* plus those ending in **-e** listed under group 6a.

- Other **masculine nouns** with the same pattern as **der Mensch** include:
Bär	*bear*	**Bauer***	*farmer*	**Elefant**	*elephant*	**Fink**	*finch*
Graf	*count*	**Held**	*hero*	**Herr***	*gentleman*	**Kamarad**	*comrade*
Komponist	*composer*	**Nachbar***	*neighbour*	**Narr**	*fool*	**Ochs**	*ox*
Papagei	*parrot*	**Pfau**	*peacock*	**Präsident**	*president*	**Soldat**	*soldier*
Spatz	*sparrow*	**Student**	*student*	**Tor**	*fool*	**Untertan**	*subject*

  * Please note **Bauer** and **Nachbar** add **-n** not **-en**, Herr adds **-n** in the singular and **-en** in the plural:
  e.g. ich habe den Bauern, meinen Nachbarn und Herrn Kittel neulich gesehen.
  Meine Damen und Herren.

Group 6a

Similar to Group 6 but having **-ens** in the genitive singular.

Example: **der Name** *name*

	Singular	Plural
N	der Name	die Namen
A	den Namen	die Namen
G	des Namens	der Namen
D	dem Namen	den Namen

Seven other **masculine nouns** belong to this group:

Buchstabe	*letter* (of alphabet)	**Funke**	*spark*	**Glaube**	*belief*
Friede	*peace*	**Same**	*seed*	**Wille**	*will*
Gedanke	*thought*				

Group 6b

Plural ending in **-en**.

Example: **der Staat** *state*

	Singular	Plural
N	der Staat	die Staaten
A	den Staat	die Staaten
G	des Staates	der Staaten
D	dem Staat	den Staaten

- Not many nouns belong to this group. The following **masculine nouns** are worth noting:

Direktor	*headteacher*	**Professor**	*professor*	**Stachel***	*sting*
Doktor	*doctor* (title)	**Schmerz**	*pain*	**Strahl**	*ray*
Dorn	*thorn*	**See***	*Lake*	**Vetter***	*cousin*
Pantoffel*	*slipper*				

  * have **-n** in the plural.

- There are twelve **neuter nouns** in this group:

Auge	*eye*	**Fakt**	*fact*	**Insekt**	*insect*	**Ohr**	*ear*
Bett	*bed*	**Hemd**	*shirt*	**Interesse**	*interest*	**Statut**	*statute*
Ende	*end*	**Herz***	*heart*	**Juwel**	*jewel*	**Verb**	*verb*

  * **Herz** is irregular in the singular: **das Herz, das Herz, des Herzens, dem Herzen.** Note also **das Museum** *museum* and **das Studium** *study* have the plurals **Museen** and **Studien** respectively.

Group 7

Plural ending in **-s**.
These are words in the main with foreign origins:

Example: **das Auto** *car*

	Singular	Plural
N	das Auto	die Autos
A	das Auto	die Autos
G	des Autos	der Autos
D	dem Auto	den Autos

- Here is a short list of some of these words which are in different genders:

der Bankier	*banker*	**die Kamera**	*camera*	**das Restaurant**	*restaurant*
das Hobby	*hobby*	**der Klub**	*club*	**der Streik**	*strike*
das Hotel	*hotel*	**der Park**	*park*	**der Tunnel**	*tunnel*

- This ending is also used for family names in the plural:
  e.g. die Dinkelborgs, die Winklers

THE DECLENSION OF NOUNS

This is really very straightforward. There are only changes to the masculine and neuter singular in the genitive where **-es** is added usually to a one syllable noun and **-s** is added if there is more than one syllable. In the dative plural of all nouns **-en** or **-n** is added except where the plural ends in **-s** or already ends in **-n**.

This is illustrated by the following pattern with the definite article:

	Singular			*Plural*		
	M	F	N	M	F	N
N	der Mann	die Frau	das Kind	die Männer	die Frauen	die Kinder
A	den Mann	die Frau	das Kind	die Männer	die Frauen	die Kinder
G	des Mannes	der Frau	des Kindes	der Männer	der Frauen	der Kinder
D	dem Mann(e)	der Frau	dem Kind(e)	den Männern	den Frauen	den Kindern

Please note that an **-e** can be added to the dative singular of masculine and neuter nouns of one syllable in a formal written register.

The other noun declension is the so-called 'weak' declension which refers to a group of masculine nouns where all cases end in **-en** except the nominative singular. See Group 6 above and Group 6b for those with **-ens** in the genitive singular.

2.2 CASES

If you are going to succeed in German you must know what the four cases are and how to use them. They are crucial to your understanding of what you read, hear, speak and write.

THE NOMINATIVE

- This is the case used for the subject of a finite verb as in:
  Wir singen ein Weihnachtslied. *We are singing a christmas carol.*

- You use it after the verbs **sein, werden, bleiben, heißen, scheinen** and the passive of **nennen**:

  Du wirst immer **mein bester Freund** bleiben. *You will always remain my best friend.*
  Diana wurde **die Prinzessin** von Wales genannt. *Diana was called the Princess of Wales.*

THE ACCUSATIVE

- This is the case used for the direct object of transitive verbs:
  Ich habe **meinen Aufsatz** geschrieben.   *I have written my essay.*

- You use this case in expressions of definite time:
  Es hat **den ganzen Tag** geregnet.   *It rained all day.*
  Nächste Woche werde ich nicht zu Hause sein. *I shall not be at home next week.*
  It is also used for the date at the head of a letter:
  Dienstag, **den fünften Dezember** or **den 5. Dezember**.

- It is used for greetings and wishes:
  Guten Morgen.   *Good morning.*

- For the use of the accusative with prepositions please see pp130–138.

THE GENITIVE

- This is the case which denotes possession. It means in English 'of the', 'of a', 'of my' etc, although it is often rendered by apostrophe s or s apostrophe.
  Here are some examples:

der Garten **meines Bruders**   *my brother's garden (the garden of my brother)*
das Haus **meiner Eltern**   *my parents' house (the house of my parents)*
die Fenster **der Kirche**   *the windows of the church*

- With proper names of people, countries or towns the genitive in German is like the English without the apostrophe:
  Peters Weinkeller   *Peter's wine-cellar*

- To express indefinite time you use this case:
  eines Tages letztes Jahr   *one day last year*
  Montags gehen wir normalerweise in die Stadt.   *We normally go to town on Mondays.*

- Note that the genitive occurs in some very useful set phrases like:
  Ich bin **der Meinung/Ansicht**, daß...   *I am of the opinion that...*
  Er ist **schlechter Laune**.   *He is in a bad mood.*
  Wir sind **der festen Überzeugung**, daß...   *We are firmly convinced that...*

- Some prepositions are followed by the genitive (see pp138–139).

- The genitive also follows some adjectives (see p81).

- Frequently in German the genitive is replaced by the preposition **von** + the dative:
  das Bild **vom Hause** meines Vaters   *the picture of my father's house*
  In this example it is clearly to avoid having two genitives together.

- A few verbs are followed by a noun in the genitive case (see p112).

THE DATIVE

- The indirect object of a verb is in the dative. Be careful because English does not always make it clear which the indirect object is. In English the indirect object is indicated by the use of the words 'to' or 'for' or the word order. Look at these examples in English of basically the same sentence each containing an indirect object:
  (a) *The parents gave **the children** some toys.*
  (b) *The parents gave some toys **to the children**. Or a slightly different sentence:*
  (c) *The parents brought some toys **for the children**.*
  In German, sentences (a) and (b) would read:
  Die Eltern gaben **den Kindern** einige Spielzeuge.
  (c) would be: Die Eltern brachten **den Kindern** einige Spielzeuge.

- Certain verbs are followed by the dative (see list on p112).

- The dative is also used to show an advantage or disadvantage for someone as in the following examples:
  Er kaufte **seiner Schwester** einen neuen Kugelschreiber.
  He bought his sister a new ballpoint pen./ He bought a new ballpoint pen for his sister.
  Sie haben **uns** den Wagen gestohlen. *They stole our car./ They stole the car from us.*

- The dative is the most commonly used case with adjectives as in:
  Er ist **seinem Onkel** sehr ähnlich. *He is very like his uncle.*
  In most instances the adjective follows the noun in the dative which it governs.
  The following are the adjectives most frequently used in this construction:

ähnlich	*similar to*	gemeinsam	*common*
begreiflich	*comprehensible*	gerecht	*just*
behilflich	*helpful*	günstig	*favourable*
bekannt	*known, familiar*	klar	*obvious*
bequem	*comfortable*	möglich	*possible*
böse	*angry*	nötig	*necessary*
dankbar	*grateful*	peinlich	*embarrassing*
ergeben	*devoted, attached*	schuldig	*owing*
erwünscht	*desirable*	schwer	*difficult*
fern	*distant*	teuer	*expensive*
fremd	*strange*	treu	*faithful*
gefährlich	*dangerous*	überlegen	*superior*
gefällig	*obliging*	verständlich	*comprehensible*

nicht geheuer	*scary*	wichtig	*important*
gehorsam	*obedient*	willkommen	*welcome*
geläufig	*familiar*	zuträglich	*beneficial*

- The dative of a personal pronoun is used to indicate possession in sentences where you do not use the possessive adjective:
  Ihr Vater wusch **ihr** die Hände.   *Her father washed her hands.*

  Where the subject of the verb and the possessor are the same, then the dative of the reflexive pronoun is used as in:
  Ich putzte **mir** die Zähne.   *I cleaned my teeth.*

- In impersonal constructions with **sein** and **werden** when the person experiencing a sensation or feeling is in the dative:
  Es ist **ihm** kalt.   *He is cold.*
  Mir wurde unwohl.   *I felt unwell/ I became indisposed.*

  These adjectives can be used in this sort of construction:

bang(e)	*scared*	schwindlig	*dizzy, giddy*
gut	*good*	übel	*bad*
heiß	*hot*	warm	*warm*
kalt	*cold*	(un)wohl	*(un)well*
schlecht	*bad*		

APPOSITION

When nouns are used in apposition with one another, usually they are in the same case:

Heute sah ich **Herrn Major, den Premierminister**, in London.
I saw Mr. Major, the Prime Minister, in London today.

2.3   ARTICLES

THE DEFINITE ARTICLE

	Masculine	*Feminine*	*Neuter*	*Plural*
N	der	die	das	die
A	den	die	das	die
G	des	der	des	der
D	dem	der	dem	den

These are the words used in German to translate 'the' in English. They are used with nouns. The pattern of the endings in the four cases, the three genders and the plural is repeated in all kinds of other instances, so make sure you know it well.

dieser *this*, **jener** *that*, **jeder** *each*, **solcher** *such*, **welcher** *which* and **alle** *all* (plural) have the same endings as **der** above.

Some forms of the definite article can be contracted when used with certain prepositions. **das**, **der** and **dem** contract as follows:

an das	becomes	ans	in das	becomes	ins
an dem	becomes	am	in dem	becomes	im
auf das	becomes	aufs	um das	becomes	ums
bei dem	becomes	beim	von dem	becomes	vom
durch das	becomes	durchs	zu der	becomes	zur
für das	becomes	fürs	zu dem	becomes	zum

USES OF THE DEFINITE ARTICLE

Generally the definite article in German is used in the same way as its English counterpart. There are, however, some special uses which should be noted.

- with abstract nouns, in most instances:

  Die Zeit ist für uns.   *Time is on our side.*

- usually with the days of the week, months and seasons:

  am Montag   *on Monday*

  im August   *in August*

  im Frühling   *in spring*

- usually with the masculine, feminine and plural names of countries and with street names and rivers:

  Wir fahren in **die** Schweiz.   *We are going to Switzerland.*

  Er wohnt in **der** Friedrichstraße.   *He lives in Friedrich street.*

  London liegt an **der** Themse.   *London is on the Thames.*

- with proper names when qualified by an adjective:

  der kleine Peter   *little Peter*

  das heutige Deutschland   *present-day Germany*

- to replace a possessive adjective in expressions with parts of the body and clothes:

  Er hob **den** Arm.   *He raised his arm.*

  Sie zog **den** Mantel aus.   *She took off her coat.*

  Er hielt **den** Hut in **der** Hand.   *He held his hat in his hand.*

- in talking about meals and in common phrases about transport:

  beim Frühstück   *at breakfast*   mit **dem** Zug   *by train*

  nach **dem** Mittagassen *after lunch*   mit **dem** Flugzeug   *by air*

- usually in a distributive sense when in English we use the indefinite article:

  zwei Mark **das** Kilo   *two marks a kilo*

  Er kommt zweimal in **der** Woche.   *He comes twice a week.*

  Wir fuhren 80 Kilometer **die** Stunde: *We were doing 80 kilometres an hour.*

- the definite article is omitted in German in pairs of nouns which are linked:

  Tag und Nacht   *day and night*

  The names of the major festivals have no article:

  Weihnachten   *Christmas*

  Pfingsten   *Whitsuntide*

  Ostern   *Easter*

  The neuter names of countries and towns have no article when used on their own:

  Wir wohnen in Deutschland.   *We live in Germany.*

  Der Rhein fließt durch Köln.   *The Rhine flows through Cologne.*

THE INDEFINITE ARTICLE

The indefinite article **ein** (*a* or *an*) has no plural as in English. The negative form of the indefinite article **kein** (*not a*) does have plural forms. Here it is used to illustrate the declension of the indefinite article.

	Masculine	*Feminine*	*Neuter*	*Plural*
N	kein	keine	kein	keine
A	keinen	keine	kein	keine
G	keines	keiner	keines	keiner
D	keinem	keiner	keinem	keinen

The indefinite article **ein** has the same endings as **kein** above. Remember that the plural of 'a book' is 'books'. German is exactly the same: *ein Buch*, plural *Bücher*.

The possessive adjectives **mein** *my*, **dein** *your*, **sein** *his*, **ihr** *her*, **unser** *our*, **euer** *your*, **Ihr** *your* (polite form), **ihr** *their* have the same endings as **kein** above.

The indefinite article is omitted in the following examples:

● with nationalities or professions:
Er ist Lehrer. *He is a teacher.*
Sie ist Französin. *She is French.*

● in phrases beginning with **als**:
Er sprach als Freund. *He spoke as a friend.*

2.4 ADJECTIVES AND ADJECTIVE DECLENSIONS

Adjectives are words which describe nouns or pronouns. They can be used without endings as in English, but when used attributively, i.e. preceding a noun, they have endings according to the following three patterns or declensions.

DECLENSIONS

The strong declension

Here the adjective is used with a noun and without any preceding determining word. The endings are the same as **dieser** (*this*) except in the masculine and neuter genitive singular. Compare this pattern with the endings of **dieser** in the 'weak' declension below.

The adjective endings show the case and the gender of the noun they qualify.

	Masculine	*Feminine*	*Neuter*	*Plural*
N	guter Wein	frische Milch	kaltes Bier	frische Eier
A	guten Wein	frische Milch	kaltes Bier	frische Eier
G	guten Weines	frischer Milch	kalten Bier(e)s	frischer Eier
D	gutem Wein	frischer Milch	kaltem Bier	frischen Eiern
	(good wine)	*(fresh milk)*	*(cold beer)*	*(fresh eggs)*

These adjective endings are also used after the determining words **ein**, **kein** and the possessive adjectives **mein**, **dein**, **sein**, **ihr**, **unser**, **euer**, **Ihr**, **ihr** (their) when there is no indication of the case or the gender, i.e. in the nominative masculine and neuter singular and in the accusative neuter singular only. In all other cases after these words the adjective ending is **-en** as in the 'weak' declension below.

This is sometimes called the 'mixed' declension. Here is the mixed declension in full, with **kein**, showing that the strong declension endings are used when the determining word does not show the gender or the case.

The mixed declension

	Masculine	*Feminine*	*Neuter*	*Plural*
N	kein guter Wein	keine gute Milch	kein kaltes Bier	keine frischen Eier
A	keinen guten Wein	keine gute Milch	kein kaltes Bier	keine frischen Eier
G	keines guten Weines	keiner guten Milch	keines kalten Bier(e)s	keiner frischen Eier
D	keinem guten Wein	keiner guten Milch	keinem kalten Bier	keinen frischen Eiern
	(no good wine)	*(no good milk)*	*(no cold beer)*	*(no fresh eggs)*

e.g. Mein junger Bruder hat ein großes Haus. *My young brother has a big house.*

Sein schönes Haus liegt an einem kleinen See. *His beautiful house is situated by a small lake.*

Meine alte Mutter liest ihr neues Buch. *My old mother is reading her new book.*

Seine hübsche Schwester hat eine unartige Tochter. *His pretty sister has a naughty daughter.*

Ich habe keinen grünen Bleistift. *I do not have a green pencil.*

The weak declension

This is used after **der** and words declined like **der**, i.e. **dieser** (*this*), **jener** (*that*), **jeder** (*each, every*), **solcher** (*such*), **welcher** (*which*) and **alle** (*all*).

There are only two endings **-e** and **-en** in this declension as the determining word shows the gender and case of the words being qualified. There is very little therefore to remember. The rule is, if the word preceding the adjective has a case ending the adjective ending will be weak, i.e. either **-e** or **-en** as in the pattern of endings below:

	Masculine	*Feminine*	*Neuter*	*Plural*
N	dieser gute Mann	diese gute Frau	dieses gute Kind	diese guten Eltern
A	diesen guten Mann	diese gute Frau	dieses gute Kind	diese guten Eltern
G	dieses guten Mannes	dieser guten Frau	dieses guten Kindes	dieser guten Eltern
D	diesem guten Mann(e)	dieser guten Frau	diesem guten Kind(e)	diesen guten Eltern

When there are two or more adjectives used attributively in this way, the endings are the same:

diese schöne, rote Rose	*this beautiful red rose*
die Lösung wichtiger sozialer Probleme	*the solution of important social problems*

OTHER USES OF ADJECTIVES

Town names

Adjectives from town names do not have any endings:

die Leipziger Messe	*the Leipzig trade fair*
Wir haben eine Rundfahrt um den Hamburger Hafen gemacht.	*We have been on a trip round the port of Hamburg.*

Adjectives as nouns

Almost all adjectives can be used as nouns. To do this, simply write the adjective with a capital letter and add the ending from one of the three patterns above in the appropriate case and gender:

Der Alte ist fast blind.　　　　*The old man is almost blind.*
(masc. sing. nominative, weak declension ending)
Ein Angestellter arbeitet 39 Stunden pro Woche. *A (male) employee works 39 hours a week.*
(masc. sing. nominative, mixed declension ending)

Adjectives with cases

- Adjectives which govern the dative are listed above on pp77–78.
- Some adjectives take the genitive. Usually they correspond to the English 'of' and follow the noun they govern.
  Er ist des Betrugs fähig.　　　　*He is capable of deceit.*
  The most common adjectives in this group are:

bewußt	*conscious of*	voll	*full of*
fähig	*capable of*	wert	*worthy of*
schuldig	*guilty of*	würdig	*worthy of*

Adjectives with prepositions

There are a considerable number of adjectives which are linked to nouns by prepositions. The list which follows gives you the most frequent combinations but there are many others and you should make a note of them as you come across them in your work. Please note **auf** and **über** in these instances always take the accusative.

abhängig von (+dat)	*dependent on*	gierig nach (+dat)	*greedy for*
angewiesen auf (+acc)	*to have to rely on*	hungrig nach (+dat)	*hungry for*
aufmerksam auf (+acc)	*attentive to*	interessiert an (+dat)	*interested in*
begeistert von (+dat)	*enthusiastic about*	neugierig auf (+acc)	*curious about*
berechtigt zu (+dat)	*justified in*	reich an (+dat)	*rich in*

bereit zu (+dat)	*ready for*	schuld an (+dat)	*to be blamed for*
besorgt um (+acc)	*anxious about*	stolz auf (+acc)	*proud of*
bezeichnend für (+acc)	*characteristic of*	typisch für (+acc)	*typical of*
böse auf (+acc)	*angry with*	überzeugt von (+dat)	*convinced of*
charakteristisch für (+acc)	*characteristic of*	unabhängig von (+dat)	*independent of*
dankbar für (+acc)	*grateful for*	verheiratet mit (+dat)	*married to*
einverstanden mit (+dat)	*in agreement with*	verliebt in (+acc)	*in love with*
empfindlich gegen (+acc)	*sensitive to*	verschieden von (+dat)	*different from*
fertig mit (+dat)	*to have finished with*	verwandt mit (+dat)	*related to*
gewöhnt an (+acc)	*accustomed to*	vorbereitet auf (acc+)	*prepared for*

Spelling changes in some adjectives

Adjectives ending in **-el** and **-er** frequently drop the **-e-** when they have endings:

das **dunkle** Haus	*the dark house*
Wir sitzen in **unsrem** kleinen Garten.	*We are sitting in our small garden.*

hoch *high* drops the **-c-** when it precedes a noun:

Der Berg ist hoch.	*The mountain is high.*
ein **hoher** Berg	*a high mountain*

After 'etwas' and 'nichts'

Adjectives used after **etwas** or **nichts** have a capital letter and the ending **-es**:

etwas **Gutes**	*something good*	nichts **Neues**	*nothing new*

Please note the phrase **alles Gute** *all the best*, which works in a similar way.

Comparisons

For the comparative and superlative forms of adjectives please see 2.5 on pp84–85.

2.5 ADVERBS

Adverbs are words which describe or amplify the action of a verb. They can also qualify an adjective or another adverb. They fall into several groups. There are adverbs of **place**, **direction**, **manner**, **degree** and **interrogative adverbs**. Fortunately they are easy to use in German and usually cause no difficulties for English students. Most adjectives and participles can be used in German as adverbs without any modification to the original word. They are easily recognised in English because they usually end in **-ly**. Here are some examples:

ein **schnell** geschriebener Brief	*a quickly written letter*
eine **überraschend** langsame Reise	*a surprisingly slow journey*
Er sprach **aufgeregt**.	*He spoke excitedly.*

Adverbs of place

- **dort, da, hier, mitten, oben** and **unten** are the most common:

Hier und **dort/da** standen ein paar einzelne Häuser.	*Here and there stood a few solitary houses.*
Mitten in der Nacht hörte ich eine Eule rufen.	*In the middle of the night I heard an owl hooting.*
Er lief nach **oben**.	*He ran upstairs.*
von **oben** bis **unten**	*from top to bottom*

Please note that **mitten, oben** and **unten** are usually used with prepositions.

- **außen, draußen, innen** and **drinnen**:
außen and **innen** mean on the outside and inside referring specifically to the outer or

inner surface of an object, whereas **draußen** and **drinnen** mean outside and inside away from the object or contained within it.

Er steht **draußen** vor der Tür.	*He stood outside in front of the door.*
Der Mantel hat **innen** Pelz und **außen** Leder.	*The coat has fur on the inside and leather on the outside.*

- **irgendwo, überall, nirgendwo/nirgends** and **anderswo/woanders:**
  These are indefinite adverbs of place, meaning respectively *somewhere* or *anywhere*, *everywhere*, *nowhere* or *not … anywhere*, *somewhere else*, *elsewhere* or *anywhere else*.

Hast du mein Buch **irgendwo** gesehen?	*Have you seen my book **anywhere**?*
Ich suchte meinen Onkel **überall**.	*I looked **everywhere** for my uncle.*
Er war **nirgends/nirgendwo** zu finden.	*He was **nowhere** to be found.*
Er wohnte **anderswo/woanders**.	*He used to live **somewhere else**.*

Adverbs of direction

hin and **her** are used to indicate 'motion away from' and 'motion towards' the speaker. They can be added to a large number of adverbs and prepositions to emphasise these ideas of 'motion to' and 'motion from'. They are also combined with verbs as separable prefixes to indicate the direction of the movement:

Er ist aus Bonn hier**her** gekommen.	*He came **here** from Bonn.*
Er ging die Treppe **hinunter**.	*He went **downstairs**.*
Sie kam die Treppe **herauf**.	*She came **upstairs**.*

Adverbs of manner

These adverbs are mostly adjectives used as adverbs and they describe **how** something is done. Er lief **schnell**. *He ran **quickly**.*

Some adverbs of manner are not used as adjectives. These include the following:

allerdings	*though, mind you*	leider	*unfortunately*
anscheinend	*apparently*	möglicherweise	*possibly*
beinahe	*almost*	sicherlich	*surely*
ebenfalls	*likewise*	sonst	*otherwise*
einigermaßen	*to some extent*	umsonst	*in vain*
freilich	*admittedly*	unversehens	*inadvertently*
gleichfalls	*likewise*	vergebens	*in vain*
größtenteils	*largely*	vielleicht	*perhaps*
hoffentlich	*hopefully*	vielmehr	*rather*
immerhin	*all the same*	zweifellos	*without doubt*

Adverbs of manner can also be formed by adding the suffix **-weise** to nouns, verbs or adjectives; it usually has the meaning of 'by way of'. Here are some examples:

ausnahmsweise	*by way of exception*	probeweise	*on approval*
beispielsweise	*by way of example*	schrittweise	*step by step*
beziehungsweise	*as the case may be*	stundenweise	*by the hour*
gruppenweise	*in groups*	teilweise	*partly*

You can create adverbs of manner by adding the suffix **-erweise** to adjectives and participles with the added implication that the speaker is expressing a judgement on, or an attitude towards the action involved. The following could be useful in expressing your views on a subject:

begreiflicherweise	*understandably*	möglicherweise	*possibly*
erstaunlicherweise	*amazingly*	normalerweise	*normally*
glücklicherweise	*fortunately*	unglücklicherweise	*unfortunately*
komischerweise	*funnily*	unerwarteterweise	*unexpectedly*

Adverbs of degree

You all know a selection of these but there are many more that you could easily learn to use to make your written and spoken German more lively and interesting. Here is a list of the most common adverbs used to modify the meaning of adjectives or other adverbs:

außerordentlich	*extraordinarily*	höchst	*extremely, highly*

äußerst	*extremely*	kaum	*hardly, scarcely*
beinahe	*almost, nearly*	mäßig	*moderately*
besonders	*especially*	sehr	*very*
durchaus	*absolutely, thoroughly*	verhältnismäßig	*relatively*
etwas	*a little*	völlig	*completely*
fast	*almost, nearly*	vollkommen	*completely*
ganz	*quite*	ziemlich	*fairly, rather*
genug	*enough*	zu	*too*

Heute abend ist mein Großvater **etwas** müde. *My grandfather is a little tired this evening.*
Mein Bruder fährt **ziemlich** schnell. *My brother drives rather fast.*

Adverbs which ask questions – interrogatives

As well as asking direct questions, all of the following can introduce indirect questions in reported speech which requires the subjunctive in German (see pp118–123).

They are grouped under **time**, **place**, **manner** and **cause**.

- **Time**
  wann? *when?*
  Wann wird der Bus in Münster ankommen? *When will the bus arrive in Münster?*
  bis wann? *until when? by when?*
  Bis wann wirst du hier sitzen? *Until when will you sit here?*
  seit wann? *how long for?*
  Seit wann wohnst du hier in Köln? *For how long have you lived in Cologne?*
  wie lange? *how long?*
  Wie lange willst du im Bett bleiben? *How long do you want to stay in bed?*
  wie oft? *how often?*
  Wie oft kommt er nach Hause? *How often does he come home?*

- **Place**
  wo? *where?*
  Wo wohnt deine Mutter? *Where does your mother live?*
  wohin? *where (to)?*
  Wohin fährt dieser Zug? *Where is this train going (to)?*
  woher? *where from?*
  Woher stammst du? *Where do you come from?*

- **Manner**
  wie? *how?*
  Wie alt sind unsre Eltern? *How old are our parents?*

- **Cause**
  warum? *why?*
  Warum weint das Mädchen? *Why is the girl crying?*
  weshalb? *why?*
  Weshalb hast du nicht geschlafen? *Why did you not sleep?*
  wozu? *what ... for?*
  Wozu benutzt man das? *What is that used for?*

COMPARISON OF ADJECTIVES AND ADVERBS
Adjectives

In English the comparative and superlative of adjectives can be formed in two ways:

Positive	*Comparative*	*Superlative*
small	smaller	smallest
beautiful	more beautiful	most beautiful

The '-er/-est' endings are used on short adjectives but long adjectives require 'more' and 'most' to be used. In German **-er** and **-st** are used whatever the length of the adjective concerned, the other form with **mehr** and **meist** is only used in very special circumstances.

In general the comparative form is used to compare two items, the superlative more than two. Here are some examples:

Positive	Comparative	Superlative	
klein	kleiner	der/die/das kleinste	(*small*)
intelligent	intelligenter	der/die/das intelligenteste	(*intelligent*)

Die **kleinere** der beiden Schwestern heißt Maria.
The smaller of the two sisters is called Maria.
Heute habe ich den **intelligentesten** Schüler in meiner Klasse nicht gesehen.
I have not seen the most intelligent schoolboy in my class today.

Points to note about these examples are:

● Comparative and superlative forms of adjectives when used attributively must be declined, i.e. have the endings of the appropriate declension, so 'die klein**ere**', and 'den intelligent**esten**' are weak declension endings in the nom. fem. sing. and the acc. masc. sing. respectively.

● Adjectives ending in **-t, -d, -sch, -s, -ß, -z**, will nearly always form the superlative with **-est** making it easier to pronounce.

There are a number of adjectives which form their comparative and superlative in the normal way but with an Umlaut. An Umlaut is only possible on the vowels **a, au, o, u**. Here is an example:

arm *poor*,   ärmer *poorer*,   der/die/das ärmste *the poorest*

The following list contains the ones you are most likely to come across in your work:

alt	*old*	jung	*young*	scharf	*sharp*
arg	*bad*	kalt	*cold*	schwach	*weak*
dumm	*stupid*	klug	*clever*	schwarz	*black*
gesund	*healthy**	krank	*ill*	stark	*strong*
grob	*coarse*	kurz	*short*	warm	*warm*
hart	*hard*	lang	*long*		

*gesund – the Umlaut is usual in modern German – **gesünder, der/die/das gesündeste**

There is a handful of irregular comparatives which should be noted carefully:

groß	größer	der/die/das größte	(*big*)
gut	besser	der/die/das beste	(*good*)
hoch	höher	der/die/das höchste	(*high*)
nah	näher	der/die/das nächste	(*near*)
viel	mehr	der/die/das meiste	(*much*)

Note the Umlaut on the comparatives of **groß, hoch** and **nah**.

Adverbs

The comparatives of adverbs are similar to adjectives except that the superlative has a different form. It is written as a phrase **am ...-sten.**

schnell *quickly*   schneller *more quickly*   am schnellsten *most quickly*

The rules about some comparatives being formed with an Umlaut and being slightly irregular apply here too.

bald	eher	am ehesten	(*soon*)
gern	lieber	am liebsten	(*gladly, willingly*)
oft	öfter	am öftesten	(*often, frequently*)*
oft	häufiger	am häufigsten	(*often, frequently*)

*öfter and **am öftesten** are much less common than **häufiger** and am **häufigsten.**

Other comparative phrases

● The repeated comparison is translated by **immer**:
Die Ferien werden **immer kürzer**.   *The holidays are getting shorter and shorter.*

● 'than' in a comparison of unequals is usually **als** in German:
Mein Onkel ist älter **als** mein Vater.   *My uncle is older **than** my father.*

● **so ... wie** is used for the comparison of equals:
Hans ist **so** groß **wie** Fritz.   *Hans is **as** tall **as** Fritz.*

- **ebenso ... wie** or **genauso ... wie** are both used in the same sort of phrase as **so ... wie** but mean 'just as':
  Mein Vater ist **ebenso** alt **wie** sein Bruder.   *My father is **just as** old **as** his brother.*

- **je ... desto** or **je ... um so** are both used to express the 'more ... the more':
  Je früher die Sonne aufgeht, **desto** später   *The earlier the sun rises the later it sets.*
    geht sie unter.
  In spoken German **um so** would probably replace **desto**. Please note **je** is a subordinating conjunction introducing a subordinate clause with the verb at the end, and **desto** or **um so** introduce the main clause with the verb as the second idea (see 2.15 on pp139–144).

- **weniger ... als** is used for comparisons of inferiority:
  Karl ist **weniger** angenehm **als** sein Bruder.   *Karl is **less** pleasant **than** his brother.*

- **nicht so ... wie** can also be used:
  Karl ist **nicht so** angenehm **wie** sein Bruder.   *Karl is **not so** pleasant **as** his brother.*
  Please note **weniger** is indeclinable.

SUPERLATIVES

We need to be careful in the use of superlatives.

- 'Most' in English is sometimes an adverb of degree and not part of a true superlative:
  Das ist ein sehr interessantes Buch.   *That is a **most** interesting book.*
  Jenes Buch ist gut, aber dieses Buch   *That book is good but this book is*
    ist **das beste**.   **the best**.

- The adverbial superlative **am ...-sten** is always used to describe the action of a verb:
  Nachts arbeitet er **am besten**.   *He works **best** at night.*

  It can also be used with **sein** especially where there is no noun to be understood:
  Ein Minicar wäre **am billigsten**.   *A minicab would be **the cheapest**.*

- There are a few special superlative formations which have no comparative meanings. Here are some of those worth learning:
  Ending in **-st**
  äußerst *extremely*, herzlichst *most cordially*, höchst *highly, extremely*,
  längst *for a long time, a long time ago*, meist *mostly*, möglichst *as ... as possible*.
  Ending in **-stens**
  bestens *very well*, höchstens *at the most*, meistens *mostly*, mindestens *at least*,
  nächstens *shortly, soon*, spätestens *at the latest*, wenigstens *at least*.

- Some examples in context:
  Wir sehen uns **spätestens** morgen, in   *We shall see each other tomorrow week*
    einer Woche.   **at the latest**.
  Ich danke Ihnen **bestens** dafür.   *I thank you **very much** for it.*
  Ich warte **höchstens** eine Viertelstunde. *I'll wait a quarter of an hour **at the most**.*
  Das hättest du mir **längst** sagen können. *You could have told me that **a long time ago**.*

NEGATIVES

Most of the following negatives are used adverbially:

nicht	*not*	nein	*no*
gar nicht	*not at all*	nichts	*nothing*
nicht mehr	*no more, no longer*	niemand	*nobody*
nie	*never*	nichts als	*nothing but*
noch nicht	*not yet*	nirgendwo	*nowhere*
nicht einmal	*not even*	gar nichts	*nothing at all*
noch nie	*never yet*	weder ... noch	*neither ... nor*
nicht ... sondern	*not ... but ...*		
nicht wahr	*isn't it*, etc. (used like *n'est-ce pas* in French)		

Some examples:

Ich habe ihn **nicht** gesehen.	*I have **not** seen him.*
Sie ist **noch nicht** angekommen.	*She has **not** arrived yet.*
Sie haben Ihren Aufsatz geschrieben, **nicht wahr?**	*You have written your essay, haven't you?*
Er spricht **nichts als** die Wahrheit.	*He speaks **nothing but** the truth.*

THE POSITION OF ADVERBS

In German the adverb is usually placed next to the word it qualifies, but remember this can be overruled by the other rules of word order which are explained in detail on pp139–144.

Er lief **schnell** die Straße entlang.	*He ran quickly along the street.*
Er mußte den Brief von seiner Tante **schnell** lesen.	*He had to read the letter from his aunt quickly.*

2.6 PRONOUNS

PERSONAL PRONOUNS

The personal pronouns in German are declined in the four cases, although the genitive case is very rarely used and has therefore been omitted from the following table.

	Nominative		Accusative		Dative	
1st person sing.	ich	*I*	mich	*me*	mir	*to me*
2nd person sing. (familiar)	du	*you*	dich	*you*	dir	*to you*
3rd person masc. sing.	er	*he, it*	ihn	*him, it*	ihm	*to him, it*
3rd person fem. sing.	sie	*she, it*	sie	*her, it*	ihr	*to her, it*
3rd person neut. sing.	es	*it*	es	*it*	ihm	*to it*
1st person plur.	wir	*we*	uns	*us*	uns	*to us*
2nd person plur. (familiar)	ihr	*you*	euch	*you*	euch	*to you*
2nd person sing. and plur. (polite)	Sie	*you*	Sie	*you*	Ihnen	*to you*
3rd person plur.	sie	*they*	sie	*them*	ihnen	*to them*

● Pronouns stand for nouns and in the 3rd person they must agree in gender and number with the noun they are replacing. The case is determined by the role the pronoun has in the sentence.

> Hast du meinen Kamm gesehen? **Er** (subject – nominative) war gestern auf der Frisierkommode, ich muß **ihn** (direct object – accusative) verlegt haben.
> *Have you seen my comb?* **It** *was on the dressing-table yesterday, I must have mislaid* **it**.

● Sometimes there is a problem over whether to use a pronoun in the grammatical gender or in the natural gender, such as when replacing **das Fräulein** or **das Mädchen** for example. Both of these are grammatically neuter but refer to females. In most instances the pronoun would follow the natural gender in German and would therefore be a form of **sie**.

> Dieses kleine Mädchen ist gestern in London angekommen; **sie** kommt aus Bayern.
> *This little girl arrived in London yesterday;* **she** *comes from Bavaria.* But you also see **es** kommt aus Bayern.

● In the 2nd person German distinguishes between the familiar and the formal or polite forms of address.

Sie is the formal or polite form of address and is used for both singular and plural references to 'you' in English when speaking to adult strangers.

du (singular) and **ihr** (plural) are the familiar forms of address when speaking to children, animals, inanimate objects, God, relatives and close friends.

When writing letters it is a convention in German to use capital letters for **du, ihr** and their associated forms **dich, dir, dein, euch, euer.**

Ich danke **Dir** für **Deinen** letzten Brief. *I thank you for your last letter.*

Es

- With sein and werden **es** is used as a general subject as 'it' in English. It can also be used in this way with a plural verb, but there is no English equivalent:
  Es ist wunderbar in Berlin.   ***It** is wonderful in Berlin.*
  Es sind Apfelbäume, die in diesem Garten wachsen.
  They are apple trees growing in this garden. or
  It's apple trees that are growing in this garden.

- It can refer back to a complete phrase, sentence or situation:
  Kannst du meine Bücher finden?   *Can you find my books?*
  Hans macht **es** schon.   *Hans is already doing **it**.*

- It translates the English 'so' when used as an object of the verbs 'to say' and 'to do':
  Mein Vater hat **es** gesagt.   *My father said **so**.*
  Warum hast du **es** getan?   *Why did you do **so**?*

- It is used as the subject in a large number of impersonal verb constructions:
  Es schneit.   *It is snowing.*
  (For more examples of impersonal verbs see pp108–109)

- It can be the object in a range of idiomatic verbal constructions:
  Wir hatten **es** eilig, in die Stadt zu fahren. *We were in a hurry to go to town.*

- Please note that **es** is never used after a preposition (except **ohne**). It is replaced by **da(r)** + preposition:
  Ich freue mich sehr **darauf**.   *I am looking forward **to it**.*
  Ohne **es** kann ich nicht weitermachen. *Without **it** I cannot continue.*

REFLEXIVE AND RECIPROCAL PRONOUNS

The best way to illustrate reflexive pronouns is to give an example of a reflexive verb **sich waschen** *to wash oneself*. A verb is described as reflexive when the action of the verb reflects on the subject.

ich wasche **mich**	*I wash **myself***	wir waschen **uns**	*we wash **ourselves***
du wäschst **dich**	*you wash **yourself***	ihr wascht **euch**	*you wash **yourselves***
Sie waschen **sich**	*you wash **yourself***	Sie waschen **sich**	*you wash **yourselves***
er wäscht **sich**	*he washes **himself***		
sie wäscht **sich**	*she washes **herself***	sie waschen **sich**	*they wash **themselves***

This is a transitive verb and all the reflexive pronouns are in the accusative case.

The second example shows the reflexive pronouns in the dative case.

ich wasche **mir** die Hände	*I wash my hands*
du wäschst **dir** die Hände	*you wash your hands*
Sie waschen **sich** die Hände	*you wash your hands* (sing. formal)
er wäscht **sich** die Hände	*he washes his hands*
sie wäscht **sich** die Hände	*she washes her hands*
wir waschen **uns** die Hände	*we wash our hands*
ihr wascht **euch** die Hände	*you wash your hands*
Sie waschen **sich** die Hände	*you wash your hands* (plur. formal)
sie waschen **sich** die Hände	*they wash their hands*

Please note that **mir** and **dir** are the only two reflexive pronouns that change in the dative.

There is an emphatic form of 'myself', 'yourself' etc. which is translated by **selbst** or **selber** in German.

Er hat **selbst** mit dem Pfarrer gesprochen.   *He spoke with the priest himself.*

The reciprocal pronoun 'each other' is indicated in German with the plural of the appropriate reflexive pronoun or **einander**.

Wir sehen **uns** morgen.   *We shall see **each other** tomorrow.*

To render 'each other' with a preposition **einander** must be used and it is written as one word.

Sie sprachen **miteinander**.   *They were talking with each other.*

RELATIVE PRONOUNS

The relative pronouns in English are 'who', 'whom', 'whose' referring to people, or 'which' and 'that' referring to things. The relative pronoun is often omitted in English but **must** be present in German. You must also be careful to ensure that 'that' is actually a relative pronoun. The way to check this is to replace 'that' with 'who' or 'which' and if the sense is not changed it is a relative and must be translated accordingly.

Examples:
Where is the book I bought yesterday?
The relative pronoun has been omitted and 'which' or 'that' should be supplied.
Where is the book that I bought yesterday?
Wo ist das Buch, **das** ich gestern gekauft habe?
We believe that you bought this book yesterday.
Substitute 'which' for 'that' and the sentence does not make sense any more.
We believe which you bought this book yesterday.
The word for 'that' in this sentence is **daß**.
Wir glauben, **daß** du dieses Buch gestern gekauft hast.

The form of the relative pronoun

	Masculine	Feminine	Neuter	Plural	
N	der	die	das	die	*who, which, that*
A	den	die	das	die	*whom, which, that*
G	dessen	deren	dessen	deren	*of whom, of which, whose*
D	dem	der	dem	denen	*to whom, to which*

The most obvious thing about this declension is that it looks like the declension of the definite article **der**. Only the genitives and the dative plural are different.
The rules about which of these to choose in a given context in German are as follows:

- The relative pronoun takes its number and gender from the noun (or pronoun) for which it stands, i.e. its **antecedent**.

- The case of the relative pronoun is determined by its function in the relative clause.

- The finite verb in a relative clause in German must be placed at the end of the clause (see pp139–144 Word order).

- The relative clause must be separated from the rest of the sentence by a comma.

Look at these examples:

Nominative feminine   Wo ist die Frau, **die** letztes Jahr in diesem Haus **wohnte?**
Where is the woman who lived in this house last year?

Accusative masculine   Der Mann, **den** ich gestern **sah**, verließ heute das Hotel.
The man (whom) I saw yesterday left the hotel today.

Genitive masculine   Mein Freund, **dessen** jüngster Sohn sehr klug **ist**, wohnt in Münster.
My friend, whose youngest son is very clever, lives in Münster.

Dative plural   Ich wohne bei den Eltern meiner Brieffreundin, mit **denen** ich viel Deutsch **spreche**.
I am living with the parents of my pen friend with whom I speak a lot of German.

Be careful when using prepositions at the start of a relative clause because the preposition may not govern the case of the relative pronoun as in this example.

Genitive plural   Die Freunde, mit **deren** Bruder ich **arbeite**, wohnen in Bonn.
The friends whose brother I work with, live in Bonn.

i.e. 'with the brother **of whom** I work', the **friends** are the antecedent.

Other points

- The relative pronoun **der** etc. can be replaced by **welcher** etc. to avoid too much repetition:
  Die, **welche** die Geschichte hörten... *Those who heard the story...*
  The declension of **welcher** is like **dieser** but when used as a relative pronoun in this way, the genitive case is not used; it is **dessen, deren, dessen, deren** as below:

	Masculine	*Feminine*	*Neuter*	*Plural*
N	welcher	welche	welches	welche
A	welchen	welche	welches	welche
G	(dessen)	(deren)	(dessen)	(deren)
D	welchem	welcher	welchem	welchen

- After **alles** and **nichts** the relative is **was** as in:
  Alles, **was** er **sagte**, war nicht treu.   *Everything he said was not true.*
  Nichts, **was** sie tun **konnte**, befriedigte mich.   *Nothing she could do satisfied me.*

- **Wo-** and **wor-** sometimes replace the relative pronoun with prepositions when the antecedent is a thing or things, not people:
  Der Tisch, **worauf** viele Bücher **liegen**,...   *The table on which there are lots of books...*

  Der Zug, **womit** er **fuhr**, hatte 5 Minuten Verspätung.   *The train by which he was travelling was 5 minutes late.*
  Wo can also replace the relative pronoun in idioms of place.
  Die Stadt, **wo** ich wohne, ist klein.   *The town where (in which) I live is small.*

- In English 'when' can be used as a relative pronoun; in this instance German will use a preposition + a relative pronoun:
  Der Tag, an dem ich sie zum ersten Mal sah...
  The day when (on which) I saw her for the first time...

INTERROGATIVE PRONOUNS

These are pronouns which introduce questions. In German they fall into two categories, those referring to people and those referring to things. They correspond to 'who' and 'what' in English.

	Referring to people (m. and f.)		*Referring to things*	
N	wer	*who*	was	*what*
A	wen	*whom*	was	*what*
G	wessen	*whose*	wessen	*of what* (rarely used)
D	wem	*to whom*	(wem)	(*to what*) (rarely used)

There is no dative form of **was**, nor does **was** usually occur with a preposition. It is replaced by **wo-** or **wor-** before a vowel. In colloquial German **was** is sometimes used with a preposition irrespective of the case, e.g. Mit **was** schreibst du?

Examples

- referring to people:
  Wessen Buch ist das?   *Whose book is that?*
  Wer wohnt in diesem Haus?   *Who lives in this house?*
  Wen sah er gestern abend?   *Whom did he see yesterday evening?*
  Wem gab er das Buch?   *To whom did he give the book?*

  Also in indirect questions:
  Ich fragte ihn, **wen** er gestern gesehen habe   *I asked him whom he saw yesterday*
  (For the use of the subjunctive in reported speech, see pp118–123.)

- referring to things:
  Was liegt auf dem Tisch?   *What is on the table?*
  Was kann er sehen?   *What can he see?*
  Womit schreibst du?   *What are you writing with?*
  Worauf liegt das Buch?   *What is the book on?*

- **Welcher** *which* and **was für** *what sort of.* Both can be used as interrogative pronouns or adjectives. **Welcher** declines like **dieser**. Look at these examples:

Welches Bier willst du trinken?   *Which beer do you want to drink? (adjective)*

Hier sind zwei Bücher. **Welches**   *Here are two books. Which would you*
möchtest du zuerst lesen?   *like to read first? (pronoun)*

Was für   When this phrase is used with **ein**, the **ein** must be used in the appropriate case and must agree with the noun it qualifies. The **für** in this phrase is not followed automatically by the accusative case.

Was für ein Hund ist das?   *What sort of dog is that? (nom. sing.)*

Was für Blumen sind das?   *What kind of flowers are those? (nom. plur.)*

Mit **was für** einem Kugelschreiber   *What sort of ballpoint pen are you*
schreibst du?   *writing with? (dat. sing.)*

Please note both of these can be used in exclamations:

Welche Überraschung! **Was für** eine Überraschung!   *What a surprise!*

DEMONSTRATIVE PRONOUNS

dieser *this one,* **jener** *that one,* **solcher** *such a,* **derjenige** *that,* **derselbe** *the same.*
dieser, **jener** and **solcher** all decline like **dieser**.
Both parts of the other two decline according to gender and case.

Look at these examples:

Frau Kittel kauft zwei Kleider,   *Mrs. Kittel buys two dresses,*
    dieses kostet DM 200, **jenes** kostet   *the latter costs 200 marks, the former*
    nur DM 100.   *costs only 100 marks*
     (i.e. 'this one' and 'that one').

Der Fall als **solcher** interessiert mich.   *The case as such interests me.*

Ich habe mit **demjenigen** gesprochen,   *I spoke with the one who showed me*
    der mir das Auto gezeigt hat.   *the car.*

Dieses Buch ist **dasselbe**, das ich   *This book is the same one that I bought*
    gestern kaufte.   *yesterday.*

POSSESSIVE PRONOUNS

All the possessive adjectives listed with the mixed declension of adjective endings above on p80 can be used as pronouns. As pronouns they have the endings of **dieser**.

meiner	*mine*	uns(e)rer	*ours*		
deiner	*yours* (familiar)	eu(e)rer	*yours* (familiar)	Ihrer	*yours* (formal)
seiner	*his, its*	ihrer	*hers*	ihrer	*theirs*

Examples:

Unser Garten ist größer als **Ihrer**.   *Our garden is bigger than yours.*

Ich habe meinen Bleistift vergessen,   *I have forgotten my pencil, he has forgotten*
    er hat **seinen** auch vergessen.   *his too.*

Remember the possessive pronoun agrees in number and gender with the noun it is replacing, the case depends on the function it performs in the sentence.
Please note the following idioms:

Das gehört mir.   *That is mine (belongs to me).*

ein Freund von mir   *a friend of mine*

einer meiner Freunde   *a friend of mine*

Freunde von mir   *friends of mine*

INDEFINITES

These fall into two groups, those used only as pronouns and those used as pronouns and adjectives:

pronouns only		*pronouns and adjectives*			
jedermann	*everyone*	all	*all*	jeder	*each*
jemand	*someone*	ander	*other*	manch	*many a*

niemand	*no-one, nobody*	beide	*both*	mehrere	*several*
keiner	*none, nobody*	dergleichen	*suchlike*	viel, viele	*much, many*
man	*one*	ein bißchen	*a little*	wenig, wenige	*little, few*
meinesgleichen	*people like me*	einige	*some*	etwas	*some*
nichts	*nothing*	ein paar	*a few*		

Pronouns only

- **Jedermann** sah das, was geschehen war.   *Everybody saw what had happened.*
- Wenn einem nicht wohl ist, bleibt **man**   *If one is not well, it is better to stay at home.*
  besser zu Hause.

  Note that **man** can only be used in the nominative. It corresponds to the French 'on'. The other cases are **einen, eines** and **einem**, see above. The possessive adjective 'one's is **sein**:

  Man muß arbeiten, um **sein** Geld zu verdienen.   *One must work to earn one's money.*

- Aus **nichts** wird **nichts** (Proverb)   *Nothing comes of nothing.*

  Please note **nichts** + an adjective – the adjective has a capital letter and the case ending is the strong declension:

  Ich habe **nichts Neues** gesehen.   *I have seen nothing new.*

Pronouns and adjectives

- **all, alles, alle:**

all diese Leute	*all these people*
Ist **alles** da?	*Is everything there?*
Sie sind **alle** angekommen.	*They have all arrived.*
Alle zwei Wochen	*every other week, every second week*

- **ander** is mostly used as an adjective:

der **and(e)re** Tisch	*the other table*
mein **anderes** Kleid	*my other dress*
alle **anderen**	*all the others*

- **beide** usually has the endings of **dieser** but can be declined like an adjective with the usual case endings:

Beide sind schon weg.	*Both have already gone.*
Meine **beiden** Schwestern haben die Grippe.	*Both my sisters have the 'flu.*

- **ein bißchen, ein wenig, ein paar, einige, etwas:**

ein bißchen Glück	*a bit of luck*
Er hatte noch **ein wenig** Geld.	*He still had a little money.*
Er kaufte **ein paar** Blumen.	*He bought a few flowers.*
Er wollte **einige** Freunde besuchen.	*He wanted to visit some friends.*
Ich will dir **etwas** sagen.	*I want to say something to you.*

- **jeder** declines like **dieser** and is only used in the singular:

Sie gab **jedem** Jungen einen Bleistift.	*She gave each boy a pencil.*
In diesem kleinen Dorf kennt **jeder jeden**.	*In this little village everyone knows everyone else.*

- **mancher** is declined like **dieser**:

Ich habe **manche** schönen Tage am Rhein verbracht.	*I have spent many a lovely day on the banks of the Rhine.*

- **mehrere** also has the same endings as **dieser** and is used only in the plural:

  Mehrere warteten auf den nächsten Zug.   *Several were waiting for the next train.*

- **viel** and **wenig** are usually uninflected in the singular but have the endings of **dieser** in the plural:

Er trinkt **viel** Wein.	*He drinks a lot of wine.*
Viele sind gekommen.	*Many came.*
Sie hat **wenig** Geduld.	*She has little patience.*
Er hat **wenige** Freunde.	*He has few friends.*

2.7 NUMERALS AND EXPRESSIONS OF TIME

CARDINAL NUMBERS

These are as follows:

0 null	11 elf	22 zweiundzwanzig
1 eins	12 zwölf	30 dreißig*
2 zwei	13 dreizehn	40 vierzig
3 drei	14 vierzehn	50 fünfzig
4 vier	15 fünfzehn	60 sechzig*
5 fünf	16 sechzehn*	70 siebzig*
6 sechs	17 siebzehn*	80 achtzig
7 sieben	18 achtzehn	90 neunzig
8 acht	19 neunzehn	100 hundert
9 neun	20 zwanzig	
10 zehn	21 einundzwanzig	

Those marked with an * need care with the spelling.

101 hunderteins	999 neunhundertneunundneunzig
102 hundertzwei	1000 tausend
141 hunderteinundvierzig	1003 tausenddrei
200 zweihundert	1099 tausendneunundneunzig

454 123 vierhundertvierundfünfzigtausendeinhundertdreiundzwanzig

1 000 000 eine Million

3 000 000 drei Millionen

4 234 500 vier Millionen zweihundertvierunddreißigtausendfünfhundert

1 000 000 000 eine Milliarde

3 000 000 000 drei Milliarden

Notes

- In long numbers in figures there are spaces but no commas after three digits in German.

- After **Millionen** you need to start a new word.

- **Million** and **eine Milliarde** are used as separate nouns with the plural ending where appropriate.

- It is much more common in German to write complex numbers in figures rather than write them out in full.

- **Zwo** replaces **zwei** where confusion might occur, particularly in public announcements or on the telephone.

- Long numbers such as telephone numbers are often spoken in pairs. This is not done for the dialling code but the rest of the number is spoken as in this example:
  Number 0049/25 13 45 27 is pronounced as: Null Null vier neun, fünfundzwanzig dreizehn fünfundvierzig siebenundzwanzig

- Years are usually stated in hundreds:
  In 1996... : Im Jahre neunzehnhundertsechsundneunzig...

- Cardinal numbers can be used as nouns in certain circumstances. When they refer to the numeral as such they are feminine and have a plural in **-en**.
  In Deutsch hat er nie **eine Sechs** gehabt. *He has never had a 6 in German.*
  Beim Abitur hat er vier **Zweien** und *In his Abitur (A level equivalent) he got*
  eine Eins gekriegt. *4 twos and a 1.*

- The form **eins** is used only in isolation as a numeral. When used attributively with a noun it must be inflected like the indefinite article.
  Sie saßen alle auf **einem** Tisch. *They were all sitting on **one** table.*

- The suffix **-mal** is added to the cardinal number to translate once, twice, three times etc. **einmal, zweimal, dreimal** u.s.w.

ORDINAL NUMBERS

These are almost all formed by adding **-te** to the cardinal numbers up to 19 and **-ste** from 20 upwards; above 100 the number could end with part of a compound from a number less than 20. In this instance the **-te** ending will be used.

Examples:
2nd **der zweite,**   4th **der vierte,**   20th **der zwanzigste,**
119th **der hundertneunzehnte**

Exceptions to the above are:
1st **der erste**   3rd **der dritte**   7th **der siebte**

Notes

- Ordinal numbers are usually used as adjectives and take the normal endings.
- They are frequently written as a figure with a full stop as in the date at the beginning of a letter, e.g. den **8.** Januar *the 8th of January.*
- They can be combined with a superlative in phrases like
  die **viert**größte Stadt in Frankreich...   *the fourth largest town in France...*
- The suffix **-ens** can be added to the stem to translate **firstly, secondly,** etc.
  erstens, zweitens, drittens, and so on. More formally you could use **zum ersten, zum zweiten, zum dritten** as an alternative here.
- **mal** can be combined with the ordinal numbers meaning 'time':
  das erste**mal** *the first time,* zum ersten**mal** *for the first time,* zum dritten**mal** *for the third time,* zum letzten**mal** *for the last time.*

FRACTIONS

Almost all fractions in German – except 'half' – are formed by adding **-el** to the ordinal number:
das Drittel (-), das Viertel (-), das Zwanzigstel (-) *third, quarter, twentieth*

Notes

- Used as nouns they are neuter and have no ending in the plural:
  Zwei Drittel der Klasse waren abwesend. *Two thirds of the class were absent.*
- When followed by a noun they are used adjectivally but do not have any endings, they are also written with a small letter:
  Er ist mit einem viertel Liter Milch   *He arrived with a quarter of a litre of milk.*
    angekommen.
  They can be combined into one word with certain kinds of obvious measurements of quantity as in 'mit einem **Viertelliter**' in the above example.
  Dreiviertel *threequarters* is usually treated as one word and is often combined with Stunde to translate *three-quarters of an hour:*
  In einer **Dreiviertelstunde** wird er   *He will be home in three-quarters of an hour.*
    zu Hause sein.

HALF

Care is needed when translating 'half' into German. It can either be done through the noun **die Hälfte** or the adjective **halb**.

Look at these examples:

- using the noun die **Hälfte:**
  Er hat nur **die Hälfte** des Romans gelesen.   *He has read only half the novel.*
  Die Hälfte der Klasse ist nach Deutschland   *Half the class has gone to Germany.*
    gefahren.

- using the adjective **halb**:
  Er saß eine **halbe** Stunde im Warterzimmer. *He sat half an hour in the waiting room.*
  ein **halbes** Dutzend Eier   *half a dozen eggs*
- *one and a half*, $2\frac{1}{2}$, $3\frac{1}{2}$ etc. are **anderthalb, zweieinhalb, dreieinhalb** u.s.w.
  respectively. They are not declined:
  Er wohnte seit **achteinhalb** Monaten hier. *He had lived here for eight and a half months.*

DECIMALS

The decimal point in German is a comma:
5,9 = *5.9* spoken as **fünfkommaneun** *five point nine*

OTHER USEFUL NUMERICAL ITEMS

-fach used with a cardinal number is '-fold':
eine **einfache** Karte   *a single ticket*, i.e. 'one way' not a return ticket.
ein **dreifacher** Salto   *a triple (threefold) somersault*

-erlei used with a cardinal number is *kinds of*:
zweierlei, dreierlei, and by analogy **allerlei** mean *two, three and all kinds of*

EXPRESSIONS OF TIME

Time by the clock

	The 12-hour clock	The 24-hour clock
1.00am	Es ist ein Uhr	Es ist ein Uhr
3.00pm	Es ist drei Uhr	Es ist fünfzehn Uhr
4.05pm	Es ist fünf nach vier	Es ist sechzehn Uhr fünf
5.15pm	Es ist Viertel nach fünf	Es ist siebzehn Uhr fünfzehn
	Es ist Viertel sechs	
2.30pm	Es ist halb drei	Es ist vierzehn Uhr dreißig
6.45pm	Es ist Viertel vor sieben	Es ist achtzehn Uhr fünfundvierzig
	Es ist dreiviertel sieben	
7.55am	Es ist fünf vor acht	Es ist sieben Uhr fünfundfünfzig
12.00 noon	Es ist Mittag	Es ist zwölf Uhr
12.00 midnight	Es ist Mitternacht	Es ist vierundzwanzig Uhr

Days of the week

All of these are masculine.

Sonntag	*Sunday*	Montag	*Monday*	Dienstag	*Tuesday*
Mittwoch	*Wednesday*	Donnerstag	*Thursday*	Freitag	*Friday*
Sonnabend,	*Saturday*				
Samstag					

Months of the year

All of these are masculine.

Januar	*January*	Mai	*May*	September	*September*
Februar	*February*	Juni	*June*	Oktober	*October*
März	*March*	Juli	*July*	November	*November*
April	*April*	August	*August*	Dezember	*December*

Public Holidays

Neujahr	*New Year's Day*	Christi Himmelfahrt	*Ascension Day*
Rosenmontag	*Carnival Monday*	Mariä Himmelfahrt	*Assumption Day*
Aschermittwoch	*Ash Wednesday*	Allerheiligen	*All Saints' Day*

Karfreitag	*Good Friday*	der 1. Advent	*1st Advent Sunday*
Ostern	*Easter*	Buß- und Bettag	*Day of Penitence and*
Ostersonntag	*Easter Sunday*		*Prayer*
Ostermontag	*Easter Monday*	der Heilige Abend	*Christmas Eve*
Fronleichnam	*Corpus Christi*	der erste Weihnachtstag	*Christmas Day*
der erste Mai	*May Day*	der zweite Weihnachtstag	*Boxing Day*
Pfingsten	*Whitsun*	Silvester	*New Year's Eve*

der Tag der deutschen Einheit   *German Unification Day* (3.10)

Dates

Der wievielte ist heute?   *What's the date today?*
Heute ist der 3.(dritte) Januar.   *Today is the third of January.*
Sein Sohn wird am Sonntag, dem 7. (siebten) Januar um 16.35 Uhr in London ankommen.
His son will arrive in London on Sunday the 7th of January at 4.35 pm.

On a letter heading the date is usually written in the accusative as shown here:
den 3. Januar. Note the full stop after the 3.

Other expressions of time

Wieviel Uhr ist es?   *What time is it?*
Wie spät ist es?   *What time is it?*
Um wieviel Uhr beginnt der Film?   *At what time does the film begin?*
Ich komme gegen acht Uhr an.   *I shall arrive about eight o'clock.*
Er wurde im Jahre 1936 geboren.   *He was born in 1936.*

Definite time is conveyed by the accusative case in German.

- To show duration or length of time:
  Den ganzen Tag blieb er im Bett.   *He stayed in bed all day* (literally *the whole day*).

- To indicate a specific period of time:
  Nächstes Jahr werde ich auf die Universität gehen. *Next year I shall go to university.*

- **Anfang, Mitte, Ende** are used in the accusative without a preposition in German in phrases such as:
  Wir werden Anfang August unsre   *We shall begin our holidays in Switzerland*
    Ferien in der Schweiz beginnen.   *at the beginning of August.*

- guten Morgen *good morning*, guten Tag *good day*, guten Abend *good evening*
  and gute Nacht *good night* are all time phrases in the accusative.

Indefinite time is conveyed by the genitive case in German.

eines Tages *one day*, eines Nachts *one night* (even though 'Nacht' is feminine)
eines Freitags *one Friday*
Some of these genitive forms have become adverbs such as:

morgens, vormittags	*in the mornings*	nachmittags	*in the afternoons*
abends	*in the evenings*	nachts	*at night*
wochentags	*on weekdays*	werktags	*on working days*

heute, gestern, morgen are adverbs meaning *today, yesterday* and *tomorrow*. They can be combined together and with other expressions to give us a range of time phrases:

heute morgen	*this morning*	heute nachmittag	*this afternoon*
heute abend	*this evening*	heute nacht	*tonight*
gestern morgen	*yesterday morning*	gestern abend	*yesterday evening*
morgen früh	*tomorrow morning*	übermorgen	*the day after tomorrow*
vorgestern	*the day before yesterday*	heute vor acht Tagen	*a week ago today*
heute in acht Tagen	*today week*		

For more examples of time phrases with prepositions see 2.14 on pp129–139.

2.8 VERBS

Verbs are the most important words in any sentence. Without a finite verb, i.e. one which has a subject, there can be no sentence. The finite verb in a sentence or clause shows the action or state of being in that sentence, telling us what is being done, who or what is doing it and the time sequence in which the action is set, in the past, the present or the future. The verb will also tell us the 'mood', the person(s) involved and whether it is 'active' or 'passive'. Let us look at each of these in a little more detail.

THE PERSONS

The subject of a verb indicates the person(s) involved. There are three 'persons' and they can be either singular or plural. The verb must agree with its subject in 'person' and 'number'.

- The **first person** indicates that the speaker is performing the action of the verb. In English we use *I* (sing.) and *we* (plur.), in German **ich** and **wir**.
- The **second person** is *you* in English and one of **du, Sie** or **ihr** in German. This is the person who is being spoken to who is performing the action.
- The **third person** indicates that someone else is performing the action not the speaker, nor the person being spoken to. In English these are *he, she, it, one* (sing.) or *they* (plur.) remembering that these are pronouns and the nouns which they are replacing can also be the subject of a verb in the **third person**. In German they are **er, sie, es, man** and **sie** (they) or any noun they are replacing.

THE TENSES

Tenses indicate the time of the action of the verb. The tenses and their uses which you will need to know for A/AS-level are explained in detail later in this section.

THE MOODS

There are three 'moods' in which verbs are conjugated. They are:

- the indicative mood which states a fact and is the most common form of the verb in all tenses: e.g. Ich habe geschlafen. *I have slept.*
- the subjunctive mood which indicates a possibility or a report. This too has a full range of tenses, is rare in English but has some specific uses in German which you need to be familiar with and know how to use.(See 2.11 on pp118–123):
  Er sagte, er **wäre** krank.   *He said he was ill.*
- the imperative mood which expresses a command:
  Gib mir das Buch!   *Give me that book!*

ACTIVE AND PASSIVE

Most verb constructions are in the 'active voice' where the subject is performing the action. In the 'passive voice' we can talk about an action without revealing who is doing it.

Active: Der Gemüsehändler verkaufte Kartoffeln auf dem Marktplatz.
               The greengrocer was selling potatoes in the market square.

Passive: Kartoffeln wurden auf dem Marktplatz verkauft.
               Potatoes were being sold in the market square.

If we want to indicate the 'agent' by whom the action is performed, we insert the words **vom Gemüsehändler** into the passive version of the sentence.

               Kartoffeln wurden vom Gemüsehändler auf dem Marktplatz verkauft.
               Potatoes were being sold in the market square by the greengrocer.

For a full explanation of the passive voice refer to 2.10 on pp116–118.

WEAK, STRONG AND MIXED VERBS

When we look up verbs in a German dictionary we find them listed in their infinitive form. This does not tell us what sort of verbs they are. We need to know which category they belong to, in order to be able to conjugate them. The only way of doing this is to learn which verbs are **strong** or **mixed** and assume that all the others will be **weak**. Fortunately the **weak** verbs are by far the largest group overall. Let us now look at the formation of the tenses of these three types of verb in some detail.

Weak verbs

Basically all weak verbs are regular and follow the same pattern of endings in each tense. Tenses are either **simple** – the present and the past imperfect – or **compound**, where an auxiliary verb is required to form the tense. The compound tenses are the future, the conditional and the perfect tenses which include the pluperfect, future perfect and conditional perfect. Here is an example of a **weak verb** in all its indicative forms.

spielen *to play*

spielen is the infinitive which is made up of the stem **spiel-** and the ending **-en**. the other non-finite parts of this verb are the two **participles**. The **present participle** always ends in **-d** which is added to the infinitive to form **spielend** *playing*. This is used largely as an adjective in German and does not form part of any tense as it does in English. The **past participle** of a weak verb like 'spielen' is formed by **ge-** stem **-t**, making **gespielt** *played*. The past participle is used in the compound perfect tenses.

Present tense

	Singular		*Plural*	
1st person	ich spiel**e**	(I play)	wir spiel**en**	(we play)
2nd person	du spiel**st**	(you play)	ihr spiel**t**	(you play)
3rd person	er/sie/es spiel**t**	(he/she/it plays)	sie spiel**en**	(they play)

   2nd person   Sie spiel**en** (you play)
(singular or plural)

All weak verbs have these endings in the Present tense as highlighted above.

The present tense endings are: -e, -st, -t, -en, -t, -en

Imperfect tense or **simple past tense**

Meaning: I played (etc.)

Singular	*Plural*
ich spiel**te**	wir spiel**ten**
du spiel**test**	ihr spiel**tet**
er/sie/es spiel**te**	sie spiel**ten**

                    Sie spiel**ten**

The imperfect tense endings of all weak verbs are:
                 -te, -test, -te,   -ten, -tet, -ten

Perfect tense
This tense is mostly formed with the present tense of **haben** plus the past participle.

Meaning: I have played (etc.)

Singular		*Plural*	
ich habe	⎫	wir haben	⎫
du hast	⎬ **gespielt**	ihr habt	⎬ **gespielt**
er/sie/es hat	⎭	sie haben	⎭

              Sie haben **gespielt**

Pluperfect tense
This tense is mostly formed with the imperfect tense of **haben** plus the past participle.

Meaning: I had played (etc.)

Singular		*Plural*	
ich hatte	⎫	wir hatten	⎫
du hattest	⎬ **gespielt**	ihr hattet	⎬ **gespielt**
er/sie/es hatte	⎭	sie hatten	⎭

                 Sie hatten **gespielt**

Future tense

This is formed with the present tense of **werden** plus the infinitive.

Meaning: I shall play, you will play (etc.)

Singular			*Plural*		
ich werde	⎫		wir werden	⎫	
du wirst	⎬ spielen		ihr werdet	⎬ spielen	
er/sie/es wird	⎭		sie werden	⎭	

Sie werden spielen

Future perfect tense

This is mostly formed with the future tense of **haben** plus the past participle.

Meaning: I shall have played (etc.)

Singular			*Plural*		
ich werde	⎫		wir werden	⎫	
du wirst	⎬ gespielt haben		ihr werdet	⎬ gespielt haben	
er/sie/es wird	⎭		sie werden	⎭	

Sie werden gespielt haben

Conditional tense

This is formed with the imperfect subjunctive of **werden** plus the infinitive (for the subjunctive mood refer to pp118–123).

Meaning: I should play, you would play (etc.)

Singular			*Plural*		
ich würde	⎫		wir würden	⎫	
du würdest	⎬ spielen		ihr würdet	⎬ spielen	
er/sie/es würde	⎭		sie würden	⎭	

Sie würden spielen

Conditional perfect tense

This is formed with the conditional tense of **haben** plus the past participle.

Meaning: I should have played, you would have played (etc.)

Singular			*Plural*		
ich würde	⎫		wir würden	⎫	
du würdest	⎬ gespielt haben		ihr würdet	⎬ gespielt haben	
er/sie/es würde	⎭		sie würden	⎭	

Sie würden gespielt haben

Imperative or command forms

Spiele!	*play!*	This is the familiar form singular
Spielt!	*play!*	This is the familiar form plural
Spielen Sie!	*play!*	This is the polite form singular or plural
Spielen wir!	*let us play!*	This is the 1st person plural form

Haben, sein and werden

It is clear from the above that auxiliary verbs are used in German to form the compound tenses. There are three important auxiliary verbs **haben**, **sein** and **werden**.

Tenses of **haben** or **sein** are used to form the perfect and pluperfect tenses; tenses of **werden** are used to form the future and conditional tenses and these are combined with either **haben** or **sein** to form the future perfect and the conditional perfect tenses.

Because of their importance they are given in full below. They also happen to be slightly irregular. Learn them carefully!

Infinitive	**haben** (basically weak)	**sein** (irregular strong)	**werden** (irregular strong)
	to have	*to be*	*to become*
Present participle	habend	seiend	werdend
	having	*being*	*becoming*
Past participle	gehabt	gewesen	geworden
	had	*been*	*become*

Present tense

	haben	**sein**	**werden**
ich	habe *I have* etc	bin *I am* etc	werde *I become* etc
du	hast	bist	wirst
er	hat	ist	wird
wir	haben	sind	werden
ihr	habt	seid	werdet
Sie	haben	sind	werden
sie	haben	sind	werden

Imperative

	habe! habt! haben Sie!	sei! seid! seien Sie!	werde! werdet! werden Sie!

Imperfect tense

ich	hatte *I had* etc	war *I was* etc	wurde *I became* etc
du	hattest	warst	wurdest
er	hatte	war	wurde
wir	hatten	waren	wurden
ihr	hattet	wart	wurdet
Sie	hatten	waren	wurden
sie	hatten	waren	wurden

Perfect tense

ich	habe gehabt usw.	bin gewesen usw.	bin geworden usw.
I	*have had etc.*	*have been etc.*	*have become etc.*

Pluperfect tense

ich	hatte gehabt usw.	war gewesen usw.	war geworden usw.
I	*had had etc.*	*had been etc.*	*had become etc.*

Future tense

ich	werde haben usw.	werde sein usw.	werde werden usw.
I	*shall have etc.*	*shall be etc.*	*shall become etc.*

Future perfect tense

ich	werde gehabt haben usw.	werde gewesen sein usw.	werde geworden sein usw.
I	*shall have had etc.*	*shall have been etc.*	*shall have become etc.*

Conditional tense

ich	würde haben usw.	würde sein usw.	würde werden usw.
I	*should have etc.*	*should be etc.*	*should become etc.*

Conditional perfect tense

ich	würde gehabt haben usw.	würde gewesen sein usw.	würde geworden sein usw.
I	*should have had etc.*	*should have been etc.*	*should have become etc.*

Strong verbs

Strong verbs in German are characterised by a change of stem vowel in the formation of the simple tenses. Not all strong verbs have a vowel change in the **present tense**, but they all do in the **imperfect tense**. This is very like some English verbs which have similar changes: *I drink, drank, have drunk.* In German: ich trinke, trank, habe getrunken. Let us use **trinken** as our example to explain how a **strong** verb works.

Present tense		**Imperfect tense**		**Imperative – command**	
ich	trinke	ich	trank	*singular* (fam.)	trinke!
du	trinkst	du	trankst	*plural* (fam.)	trinkt!
er/sie/es	trinkt	er/sie/es	trank	*polite* (sing./pl.)	trinken Sie!
wir	trinken	wir	tranken	*Let us drink!*	trinken wir!
ihr	trinkt	ihr	trankt		
sie	trinken	sie	tranken		

If we compare these tenses with the weak verb **spielen** earlier in this section, we can see the following similarities and differences:

- In the **present tense** the endings are the same for both **weak** and **strong verbs**:
  -e, -st, -t,   -en, -t, -en
  These are added to the **stem** of the verb.

- The endings of the **imperative** are the same:
  -e familiar form singular, **-t** familiar form plural, **-en Sie!** polite form sing./plur.
  trinke! trinkt! trinken Sie!

- The endings in the **imperfect tense** are different and there is a change of **stem** vowel from **-i** to **-a** in this example. Please note the endings of **all strong verbs** in the **imperfect** are: **-, -st, -,   -en, -t, -en**

- The other tenses of **strong verbs** are formed in the same way as the **weak verbs** except that the **past participle** of a **strong verb** ends in **-en**. The past participle of **trinken** is therefore **getrunken**. Please note that the stem vowel has changed to **-u-**.

This change of stem vowels is characteristic of all strong verbs and occurs in some present tense forms as well as the imperfect and some past participles. Let us now look at the other tenses of **trinken**:

Future tense
ich werde trinken usw.   *I shall drink etc.*

Future perfect tense
ich werde getrunken haben usw.   *I shall have drunk etc.*

Perfect tense
ich habe getrunken usw.   *I have drunk etc.*

Pluperfect tense
ich hatte getrunken usw.   *I had drunk etc.*

Conditional tense
ich würde trinken usw.   *I should drink etc.*

Conditional perfect
ich würde getrunken haben usw.   *I should have drunk etc.*

- When you learn **strong** verbs you need to know therefore the **principal parts**. There is a complete list of these on pp113–116. They are:

infinitive	3rd pers. sing. present tense	3rd pers. sing. imperfect tense	past. part. *with sein	meaning
trinken	trinkt	trank	getrunken	*to drink*
fahren	fährt	fuhr	*gefahren	*to go*

Changes in the present tense and imperative of strong verbs

- Stem vowel **-e-** changes to **-i-** or **-ie-** in the **2nd** and **3rd person singular** of the **present tense** and in the **familiar form singular** of the **imperative** and the **-e** ending is dropped. Look at these examples:

Stem vowel **-e-** (short) changes to **-i-**, e.g. sprechen *to speak* and essen *to eat*:

Present	ich	spreche	esse
	du	sprichst	ißt
	er/sie/es	spricht	ißt
Imperative		sprich!	iß!

Stem vowel **-e-** (long) changes to **-ie-**, e.g. sehen *to see* and lesen *to read*:

Present	ich	sehe	lese
	du	siehst	liest
	er/sie/es	sieht	liest
Imperative		sieh!	lies!

There are a few exceptions to these rules which should be carefully noted as follows:

- These **strong** verbs with stem vowel **-e-** do **not** change the vowel:

bewegen	*to induce*	gehen	*to go*	genesen	*to recover*	heben	*to lift*
melken	*to milk*	scheren	*to shear*	stehen	*to stand*	weben	*to weave*

- Three **strong** verbs with stem vowel **-e-** (long) change to **-i-** as in:

  geben   *to give*   du gibst, er gibt, gib!
  nehmen *to take*   du nimmst, er nimmt, nimm!
  treten   *to step*   du trittst, er tritt, tritt!

- Most **strong** verbs with stem vowels **-a-** and **-au-** add an **Umlaut** in the **2nd** and **3rd person singular** of the **present tense**:

  backen *to bake*   du bäckst, er bäckt,   fallen *to fall*   du fällst, er fällt
  schlafen *to sleep*   du schläfst, er schläft   tragen *to carry*   du trägst, er trägt

  There is one strong verb in this group which does **not** add the Umlaut:
  schaffen *to create*   du schaffst, er schafft

Mixed conjugation verbs

These nine verbs are conjugated with the **weak** verb endings but change the stem vowel in the imperfect and the past participle like a **strong** verb, hence the name **mixed conjugation**.

Infinitive	Meaning	Present	Imperfect	Perfect
brennen	*to burn*	brennt	brannte	hat gebrannt
bringen	*to bring*	bringt	brachte	hat gebracht
denken	*to think*	denkt	dachte	hat gedacht
kennen	*to know*	kennt	kannte	hat gekannt
nennen	*to name*	nennt	nannte	hat genannt
rennen	*to run*	rennt	rannte	ist gerannt
senden	*to send*	sendet	sandte	hat gesandt
wenden	*to turn*	wendet	wandte	hat gewandt
wissen	*to know*	weiß	wußte	hat gewußt

Variations in the conjugation patterns of strong and weak verbs

- Addition of 'e':
  This is done in both strong and weak verbs when the stem ends in **-d** or **-t**, or **-m** or **-n** preceded by a consonant other than **l** or **r**. The extra 'e' is used before the endings **-t**, **-st** and with a weak verb throughout the past tense and in the past participle.

  Here are some examples: **arbeiten** *to work* (weak verb)

  Present   du arbeitest, er arbeitet, ihr arbeitet
  Imperative   arbeitet! (familiar plural)
  Past   ich arbeitete, du arbeitetest, er arbeitete, wir arbeiteten, usw.
  Past participle   gearbeitet

  finden *to find* (strong verb)
  Present   du findest, er findet, ihr findet
  Imperative   findet! (familiar plural)
  Please note when a vowel change occurs in a strong verb the the additional 'e' is **not** used, e.g. **halten** *to hold*: **du hältst, er hält**, no extra 'e', but **ihr haltet** no vowel change, so the extra 'e' is inserted.

  atmen *to breathe* (weak verb) du atmest, er atmet, ihr atmet, ich atmete, geatmet usw.

- Verbs with the stem ending in **-s**, **-ß**, **-x**, or **-z**, will drop the 's' of the **-st** ending after **du**:
  rasen *to race* du rast, grüßen *to greet* du grüßt

- No **ge-** in the **past participle**:
  The prefix **ge-** is omitted in verbs where the first syllable of the stem is unstressed. In most instances these verbs either begin with an inseparable prefix or are verbs ending in **-ieren** which are generally of foreign origin. In all other respects these verbs conjugate according to the rules governing weak or strong verbs.
  e.g. (weak – inseparable) bedeuten *to mean*, ich habe bedeutet;
        (strong – inseparable) gelingen *to succeed*, es ist ihm gelungen;
        (ending in **-ieren**) studieren *to study*, ich habe studiert
  For more information about separable and inseparable verbs see pp105–108.

THE FORMATION AND USE OF TENSES

From the conjugation patterns above we can now summarise how tenses are formed in German and compare their uses with English usage.

The present tense

This is formed by adding the following endings to the stem of either a strong or weak verb:
-e, -st, -t,   -en, -t, -en
There is only **one** form of the present tense in German unlike English where we have three versions of each tense. Look at these examples:

German: Er spielt Fußball, nicht Tennis.
In English this can mean: (a) *He plays football, not tennis.*
                                 (b) *He is playing football, not tennis.*
                                 (c) *He does play football, not tennis.*

The exact meaning of the English depends on the context and could be summarised as an action which is happening now (b), the continuous present, an habitual action (a), or the emphatic statement (c) also known as the 'do' form.

If you want to ask a question in English or make a negative statement, you have to use either the 'do' form or the 'continuous' form and they will mean slightly different things:

Does he play football? Is he playing football? (a question)   Spielt er Fußball?
He does not play football. He is not playing football. (negative)   Er spielt nicht Fußball.

The present can also refer to the immediate future:

He plays football this evening.   Heute abend spielt er Fußball.

The imperfect tense

This is also known as the simple past tense. The weak verb endings are:
-te, -test, -te,   -ten, -tet, ten
For strong verbs you need to learn the stem vowel change and add the endings:
-, -st, -,   -en, -t, -en
This tense is easily the most widely used past tense in formal writing and has real importance for your written work. It can be used in a variety of ways to translate the English forms of the past tense. **Er spielte Fußball** can mean, *he was playing football, he used to play football, he played football, he did play football.*

The perfect tense

This tense is formed with the present tense of **haben** or **sein** plus the past participle.
The past participle of a weak verb is formed **ge-** stem **-t**.
The past participle of a strong verb is formed **ge-** stem **-en**.

e.g. Er hat Fußball gespielt. (weak verb with **haben**)
    Er ist nach Österreich gereist. (weak verb with **sein**)
    Wir haben seinen Onkel gesehen. (strong verb with **haben**)
    Wir sind nach Hause gegangen. (strong verb with **sein**)

This tense is mostly used in spoken language and informal writing such as letters to refer to actions in the past, that are over or completed. The four examples could be translated in a number of different ways:
He has been playing football. He travelled to Austria. We have seen his uncle. We did go home.

The pluperfect tense

This tense is formed with the imperfect of **haben** or **sein** plus the past participle:
Er hatte Fußball gespielt.   *He had been playing football.*
Er war in die Schweiz gefahren.   *He had gone to Switzerland.*

It is usually used as in English in combination with the imperfect or the perfect to describe actions which happened before other actions in the past:

Bevor er nach Hause kam, hatte er drei Wochen in Frankreich verbracht.	*Before he came home he had spent three weeks in France.*

The future

This tense is formed with the present tense of **werden** plus the infinitive:
Er wird Fußball spielen. Er wird nach Frankreich fahren.

As its name implies this tense refers to an event or an intention in the future some time away from the present. So 'next week' *he will play football* or 'next year' *he will be going to France.*

The future perfect

This tense is formed with the future tense of **haben** or **sein** plus the past participle:

Er wird Fußball gespielt haben.	*He will have been playing football.*
Er wird nach Frankreich gefahren sein.	*He will have travelled to France.*

This is not a common tense in English or in German but it refers to something that will have happened in the future:

Nächste Woche wird er 20 Seiten gelesen haben.	*Next week he will have read 20 pages.*

The conditional tense

This tense is formed with the imperfect subjunctive of **werden** plus the infinitive:
Er würde Fußball spielen, wenn er nicht krank wäre. Er würde nach Frankreich fahren, wenn er genug Geld hätte.

The use of this tense is dealt with in more detail in the section on the subjunctive, but as these examples show the conditional denotes what *would happen*, if a condition is involved as in: *He would play football if he weren't ill. He would be going to France if he had enough money.*

The conditional perfect

This tense is formed with the imperfect subjunctive of **haben** or **sein** plus the infinitive:
Er würde Fußball gespielt haben, wenn er nicht krank gewesen wäre.
Er würde nach Frankreich gefahren sein, wenn er genug Geld gehabt hätte.

In practice this form of the conditional perfect is rarely used and is replaced by the pluperfect subjunctive, the examples would then read:
Er hätte Fußball gespielt, wenn er nicht krank gewesen wäre.
Er wäre nach Frankreich gefahren, wenn er genug Geld gehabt hätte.

The use of this tense is explained in more detail later on p122. As with the conditional tense it denotes what *would have* happened if a condition had been met as in: *He would have played football if he had not been ill. He would have been going to France if he had had enough money.*

The imperative

This is used to give commands. In German there are three forms of telling people to do things: the familiar form singular ('du' form), the familiar form plural ('ihr' form) and the polite form singular or plural ('Sie' form).

- The 'du' form is used to tell someone you know well to do something. In German writing it ends in **-e** for both weak and strong verbs, e.g. spiel**e**! and trink**e**!
  Strong verbs which have a stem vowel in **-e-** which changes do not have this **-e** ending in the 'du' form of the imperative, e.g. **Gib** mir das Buch! **Lies** das Buch!
  It is also usual to drop this **-e** ending in spoken German, e.g. **Komm** schnell! **Schlaf** gut! etc.

- The 'ihr' form is used for telling more than one person you know well to do something. It is simply the 'ihr' form of the present tense without the **ihr**, it therefore ends in **-t**. e.g. Gebt mir eure Bücher! *Give me your books!*

- The 'Sie' form is the polite or formal way of telling people to do something. It is simply the 'Sie' form of the present tense inverted and followed by an exclamation mark, e.g Meine Damen und Herren, **folgen Sie** mir bitte! *Ladies and gentlemen, follow me please!*

- Finally there is the 1st person plural form of the imperative meaning *'Let us do something...* There are two ways of expressing this:

  the present subjunctive in the 1st person plural inverted and followed by an exclamation mark.

  e.g. Seien wir glücklich! *Let us be happy!* Gehen wir ins Kino! *Let us go to the cinema!* In most instances the present subjunctive is the same as the present indicative.

  The command forms of *lassen* can be used especially in spoken German, e.g. Laß uns Fußball spielen! Laßt uns Fußball spielen! or Lassen Sie uns Fußball spielen! They all mean *Let us play football!* The difference depends on who is being spoken to.

'haben' or 'sein' in the perfect tenses?

Most verbs form their perfect tense with **haben**. There are four groups of verbs where you must use **sein** instead. They are all **intransitive verbs** which means they do not have an object in the accusative case.

- intransitive verbs of **motion**:
  Ich **bin** die Treppe hinuntergegangen.   *I went downstairs.*
  Er **ist** nach Frankreich gefahren.   *He went to France.*

- intransitive verbs expressing **a change of state**:
  Sie **ist** gestern abend gestorben.   *She died yesterday evening.*
  Die Blumen **sind** verwelkt.   *The flowers have faded.*

- most verbs meaning 'to happen', 'succeed' or 'fail':
  Wir **sind** uns gestern in der Stadt   *We met each other in the town yesterday*
    begegnet.   (i.e. by chance).
  Es **war** ihm gelungen.   *He had succeeded.*
  Wann **ist** das passiert?   *When did that happen?*
  Der Versuch **ist** mir mißlungen.   *My attempt has failed.*

- the verbs **bleiben, sein** and **werden**
  Ich **bin** in Münster geblieben.   *I stayed in Münster.*
  Sein Sohn **war** krank gewesen.   *His son had been ill.*
  Er **ist** Pfarrer geworden.   *He has become a vicar.*

Please be careful to ensure that the verb is intransitive when forming the perfect tenses with **sein**. There are a few verbs which can be used either transitively or intransitively. When these are used transitively in the perfect tenses then **haben** must be used. Look at these examples:

Er **ist** nach Frankreich gefahren   *He went to France.*
  (intransitive).
Er **hat** seinen neuen Volkswagen nach   *He drove his new Volkswagen to France.*
  Frankreich gefahren (transitive).

SEPARABLE AND INSEPARABLE VERBS

These two categories of verb are conjugated in a similar way to other weak and strong verbs. They all have a prefix which is either separable or inseparable.

Prefixes which are always **inseparable** are:
be-, emp-, ent-, er-, ge-, ver-, zer-

The only difference between these and any other kind of verb is that they do not have a **ge-** in the past participle and the prefix is **unstressed** when spoken:
Er hat begonnen.   *He has begun.*
Die Bombe hatte das Gebäude zerstört.   *The bomb had destroyed the building.*

Separable prefixes

Separable prefixes are more of a problem. Most separable prefixes are words in their own right such as prepositions, adverbs, nouns or adjectives.

Rules regarding separable prefixes are as follows:

- In pronunciation they are always stressed, e.g. **teil**nehmen *to take part.*

- In a main clause (including statements, questions and commands) the prefix must be placed at the end of the clause:
  Wir kommen um halb acht **an.**   *We are arriving at half past seven.*

- In a subordinate clause the separable prefix is joined to the finite verb at the end of the clause:
  Bis jetzt habe ich meinen Freund nicht gesehen, der letzte Woche zu Hause **an**kam.
  Up to now I have not seen my friend who arrived home a week ago.

- The separable prefix is joined to the infinitive form with or without **zu** and precedes the **ge-** of the past participle. Both are written as one word:
  Leider kann er nicht **aus**gehen.   *Unfortunately he cannot go out.* (infinitive no **zu**)
  Er mußte früh aufstehen, um pünktlich in der Schule **anzu**kommen.
  He had to get up early to arrive at school on time. (infinitive with **zu**)

- The commonest prefixes which are always **separable** in German are given in the list below with an example of a separable verb:

prefix	infinitive	meaning
ab-	abfahren	*to depart/leave/drive off*
an-	ankommen	*to arrive*
auf-	aufhören	*to stop/cease*
aus-	ausgehen	*to go out*
bei-	beitragen	*to contribute*
dar-	darstellen	*to represent*
davon-	davonlaufen	*to run away*
ein-	einsteigen	*to get into*
entgegen-	entgegenkommen	*to approach*
fern-	fernsehen	*to watch television*
fest-	festhalten	*to hold on to*
fort-	fortsetzen	*to continue*
heim-	heimgehen	*to go home*
her-	herstellen	*to produce/manufacture*
hin-	hingeben	*to give up*
los-	losgehen	*to set out*
mit-	mitteilen	*to inform*
nach-	nachdenken	*to consider*
nieder-	niedersinken	*to sink down*
statt-	stattfinden	*to take place*
teil-	teilnehmen	*to take part*
vor-	vorhaben	*to have in mind*
weg-	weglaufen	*to run away*
weiter-	weiterkommen	*to progress*
zu-	zugeben	*to admit*
zurück-	zurückgehen	*to go back*
zusammen-	zusammenstoßen	*to collide*

Please note that **her-, hin-** and **vor-** can be combined with other prepositions to form a number of other separable prefixes:
hinausgehen *to go out,* **vorbei**fahren *to go past*

The above list is not intended to be exhaustive but it does give you a good idea of how separable verbs are formed.

Separable or inseparable prefixes

There is a third group of prefixes which can be either separable or inseparable.
When the prefix is stressed in pronunciation it will be separable. The prefixes which fall into this category are:
durch-, über-, um-, unter-, voll-, wider-, wieder-
Let us look at each of them in turn, the stressed syllable has a • under it:

durch- generally has the idea of *through.*
It is mostly a separable prefix, e.g. 'durchblicken *to look through,*
'durchfallen *to fall through,* 'durchführen *to carry out,* 'durchrosten *to rust through.*

As a separable prefix it conveys the idea of getting through to the other side of something.

When it is used as an inseparable prefix it has the meaning of getting through something but not necessarily all the way through:
durchlöchern *to make holes in,* durchkreuzen *to cross out,* durchleben *to experience.*

The same general distinction applies to verbs which have two meanings one as a separable, the other as an inseparable verb:
durchsetzen (sep.) *to carry through,* durchsetzen (insep.) *to intersperse/infiltrate:*
Die Regierung setzte umstrittene Maßnahmen **durch.**
The Government put through controversial measures. (separable)
Die Verwaltung war von subversiven Elementen **durch**setzt.
The administration was infiltrated by subversive elements. (inseparable)

über- is mostly **inseparable.**
It has a number of meanings as an inseparable prefix:

- repetition | überarbeiten | *to rework* | überdrucken | *to overprint*
- more than enough | übersättigen | *to satiate* | übertreiben | *to exaggerate*
- failing to notice | übersehen | *to overlook* | überhören | *not to hear*
- 'over' | überreichen | *to hand over* | überdenken | *to think over*

As a **separable** prefix it usually means 'over' in a literal sense:
überquellen *to overflow,* überkippen *to topple/keel over*

The verbs in this group with two meanings are separable with the literal meaning of 'over' and inseparable with a more figurative meaning, here are some examples:

	separable	inseparable
überfahren	*to cross over*	*to knock down*
überfluten	*to overflow*	*to flood/inundate*
überlegen	*to lay over*	*to consider*
übersetzen	*to ferry across*	*to translate*

um-
This prefix is fairly evenly divided between verbs forming **separable** and **inseparable** compounds. Those which are solely **separable** denote the idea of 'turning' or 'changing state':
umadressieren *to readdress,* umändern *to alter/modify,* umblicken *to look around,*
umbringen *to kill,* umdrehen *to turn round,* umsteigen *to change* (trains etc.)

Those which are solely **inseparable** express the idea of encircling or surrounding:
umarmen *to embrace,* umdrängen *to crowd around,* umgeben *to surround*

Those verbs with two different meanings are **separable** or **inseparable** in expressing the same ideas as above.

	separable	inseparable
umbauen	*to rebuild*	*to enclose*
umfahren	*to run over/knock down*	*to travel round*
umkleiden	*to change one's clothes*	*to cover*
umlaufen	*to knock over/circulate*	*to orbit*

unter-

Those verbs which are only **separable** have the literal meaning of under:

unterbringen *to accommodate,* untergehen *to sink/ decline/ set* (of the sun)

The larger group is **inseparable** and has a range of meanings:

unterbrechen *to interrupt,* unterdrücken *to suppress,* unterrichten *to teach* etc.

A large number can be either **separable** or **inseparable**. The meaning is more literal if they are **separable** and more figurative if they are **inseparable**.

	separable	inseparable
unterhalten	*to hold underneath*	*to entertain*
unterbinden	*to tie underneath*	*to stop/ prevent*
unterlegen	*to put underneath*	*to underlay*
unterschieben	*to push underneath*	*to attribute to*

voll- is mostly **separable**.

volladen *to load up,* vollstopfen *to cram full,* volltanken *to fill up* (car)

A small number are only **inseparable** meaning *complete, finish, accomplish:*

vollbringen *to achieve/ accomplish,* vollenden *to complete,* vollziehen *to carry out.*

wider- forms mostly **inseparable** verbs.

Only two verbs are **separable**, widerhallen *to echo,* widerspiegeln *to reflect*

wieder- is a **separable** prefix.

Only one verb wiederholen *to repeat* is **inseparable**.

IMPERSONAL VERBS

All these verbs are used only in the third person singular mostly with the subject **es**. They include the following:

- those describing the weather:
  Es blitzt. Es donnert. Es friert. Es regnet. *There is lightning. It is thundering. It is freezing. It is raining.*

- those describing other natural phenomena:
  Es zieht. *there's a draught.* Es brennt. *Something is burning.*
  Es riecht nach Blut. *It smells of blood.*

- those describing noises:
  Es klingelt. *The bell is ringing.* Es klopfte an der Tür. *There was a knock at the door.*

- with **sein** or **werden** followed by a noun or adjective, corresponding to the English use of *it*:
  Es ist früh. *It is early.* Es ist seine Frau. *It's his wife.*

es ist/sind, es gibt

These mean *there is* or *there are.* They have precise uses in German which are not interchangeable.

- **es gibt** makes a general statement without reference to a particular place:
  Es gibt Tage, wo alles gut geht. *There are days when everything goes well.*

- **es gibt** also refers to the permanent existence of something in a large area:
  Es gibt zwei Kathedralen in Westminster. *There are two cathedrals in Westminster.*

- **es gibt** is used to record the likely outcome or consequence of an event:
  Heute gab es drei Tote bei einem Unfall *Today there were three killed in an*
      auf der Autobahn.   *accident on the motorway.*

- **es ist** or **es sind** are more specific and refer to the presence of something at a particular time and place. If they are not used to start a clause, then the **es** can be omitted. Look at these examples:
  Es war eine Katze in der Küche.
  Eine Katze war in der Küche.
  There was a cat in the kitchen.

es ist/es sind are used as follows.

- to refer to a temporary presence in a large space:
  Es waren Boote auf dem See.   *There were boats on the lake.*

- to refer to a permanent or temporary presence in a restricted place:
  Es ist jemand an der Tür.   *There is someone at the door.*
  Es sind viele Bücher in der Bibliothek. *There are lots of books in the library.*

N.B. **es gibt** means *there is/there are*; **es ist** means *there is;* **es sind** means *there are*. All three can be used in the various tenses according to the context.

Useful idioms using impersonal verbs

es fehlte uns an Liebe	*we lacked love*
es gefällt ihm in Wien	*he likes it in Vienna*
es geht mir sehr gut, danke	*I am very well, thank you*
wie geht es Ihnen?	*how are you?*
es geht um Leben und Tod	*it's a matter of life and death*
es handelt sich um Vorurteil	*it's a matter of prejudice*
es kommt darauf an	*it depends*
es lohnt sich	*it is worthwhile*
es macht nichts	*it doesn't matter*
es wurde darüber gesprochen	*it was talked about*
es ist ihr gelungen	*she has succeeded*
es tut mir leid	*I am sorry*
es tut ihr weh	*it hurts her*
es tut mir wohl	*it does me good*
es fällt mir ein	*it occurs to me*
das reicht ihnen	*that's enough for them*
es schmeckte wunderbar	*it tasted wonderful*

REFLEXIVE VERBS

There are three types of construction in German where reflexive verbs are used:

- where the action of the verb reflects back to the subject:
  sich waschen *to wash oneself* (see p88 under reflexive pronouns in the accusative)

- verbs where the reflexive pronoun is in the dative alongside an accusative object:
  Ich habe mir die Hände gewaschen. *I have washed my hands.*
  (see p88 under reflexive pronouns in the dative)

- verbs which have an accusative reflexive pronoun and cannot be used without it:

sich bedanken	*to say 'thank you'*	sich beeilen	*to hurry*
sich befinden	*to be situated*	sich benehmen	*to behave*
sich eignen	*to be suited*	sich erkälten	*to catch a cold*
sich verabschieden	*to say goodbye*		

USES OF THE INFINITIVE

The simple infinitive is the form of the verb which is listed in a dictionary. For most verbs it ends in **-en**, though **sein, tun** and those verbs whose stem ends in **-el** or **-er** have an infinitive ending in **-n**.

The infinitive with 'zu'

Generally the infinitive in German is preceded by the particle **zu**. Look at these examples carefully to familiarise yourself with the position of the infinitive in a clause and where the **zu** goes with different sorts of construction.

- Ich habe nichts **zu tun**. *I have nothing to do.* (main statement, infinitive at the end)

- Er hatte keine Lust, ins Kino **zu gehen**. *He did not want to go to the cinema.*
  N.B. In this example the infinitive is placed at the end of an infinitive clause which must be separated from the rest of the sentence by a comma.

- Obgleich das nicht leicht **zu verstehen** war, ging er sehr früh nach Hause.
  Although that was not easy to understand he went home very early.
  In this example the infinitive is in a subordinate clause – note its position before the finite verb, and also that it is an inseparable verb.

- Sie hatte vor, ihn morgen **anzurufen.** *She intended to ring him up tomorrow.*
  In this example the infinitive of a separable verb is written as one word with the **zu** placed after the prefix. The infinitive is placed at the end of the infinitive clause.

- An infinitive clause with **zu** can be the subject of a verb; when it comes first in the sentence, no comma is required:
  So etwas **zu tun** ist unverzeihlich.   *To do such a thing is unforgivable.*

  This construction can also be used to express an English clause with the *ing*-form as the subject of the verb:
  Ihm den Weg nach Hause **zu zeigen**   *Showing him the way home will be difficult.*
  wird schwierig sein.

- A similar infinitive clause is also used with verbs which have a prepositional object,
  Ich erinnere mich daran, sie vor zwei   *I remember having visited her in Berlin*
  Jahren in Berlin besucht **zu haben.**   *two years ago.*
  N.B. This is a compound perfect infinitive 'to have done something'.

- **um ... zu** basically means *in order to* and must be separated from the rest of the sentence by a comma:
  Er setzte sich hin, **um** die Zeitung **zu lesen.** *He sat down (in order) to read the paper.*

- **ohne ... zu** means *without*:
  Er ging, **ohne** ein Wort **zu sagen.**   *He went without saying a word.*

- **(an)statt ... zu** means *instead of*:
  Er blieb zu Hause, **(an)statt** in die   *He stayed at home instead of going to school.*
  Schule **zu gehen.**

The infinitive without zu

Like all infinitives these are placed at the end of the clause in which they occur. When used in a subordinate clause or compound tense, they are placed before the finite verb. For full details about the rules of word order in German see pp139–144. The infinitive without **zu** is used in the following constructions.

- With the modal auxiliaries see 2.12 pp123–125 for details:
  Wir werden nicht **kommen können.** *We shall not be able to come.*

- After **lassen.**
  – meaning *let* or *allow*:
  Meine Mutter ließ mich zu Hause **bleiben.** *My mother let me stay at home.*
  – meaning *cause, make, have something done*:
  Sie ließ sich die Haare **waschen.** *She had her hair washed.*

- In commands to replace an imperative:
  Nicht **rauchen!**   Bitte **anschnallen!**   Nicht **hinauslehnen!**   Bitte **einsteigen** und die Türen **schließen!** *No smoking. Fasten seat-belts! Do not lean out of the window! Please get in and close the doors!*

The infinitive as a noun

- The infinitive used as a noun is neuter, it frequently corresponds to the English *ing*-form used as a noun:
  das **Singen** des Männerchors war ausgezeichnet.
  The singing of the male voice choir was outstanding.

- It can also be combined with a preposition to translate the English *ing*-form or replace certain types of clause.
  – with **bei:**
  Beim Verlassen des Hauses bemerkte er das Auto auf der anderen Seite der Straße.
  On leaving/As he left the house he noticed the car on the other side of the street.

– with **zu** expressing purpose:
Ich gebrauche das Messer **zum Kartoffelschälen**.
I use the knife for peeling potatoes.

THE PRESENT AND PAST PARTICIPLES

These two participles can be used in German as adjectives, adjectival nouns and in clauses. There is also the problem that the present participle in English is used much more widely than in German and it is therefore important to know how to translate it into German.

Participles as adjectives

- Almost all present and past participles can be used as adjectives and they will have the usual endings when used attributively:
ein **lachendes** Kind *a laughing child*, der **aufgeregte** Junge *the excited boy*
N.B. *das Kind ist lachend* is **not possible** in German. 'The child is laughing' is the progressive form of the present tense in English and must be rendered in German by **das Kind lacht**.

- A number of both kinds of participle have become adjectives in their own right often with a meaning which is distinct from the original verb. They then become independent adjectives with a comparative and superlative and can be used with the verb **sein**. Examples of these are given in the following lists:

abwesend	*absent*	bedeutend	*significant*	rührend	*touching*
ansteckend	*infectious*	beruhigend	*reassuring*	spannend	*exciting*
anstrengend	*strenuous*	dringend	*urgent*	überraschend	*surprising*
anwesend	*present*	drückend	*oppressive*	überzeugend	*convincing*
auffallend	*conspicuous*	entscheidend	*decisive*	umfassend	*extensive*
aufregend	*exciting*	reizend	*charming*	verlockend	*tempting*

These are no longer true present participles and must not be confused with the real thing. It is correct to say:
Der Film war spannend. *The film was exciting.*

angebracht	*appropriate*	ausgezeichnet	*excellent*	gelehrt	*scholarly*
angesehen	*respected*	bekannt	*famous*	geschickt	*clever*
aufgebracht	*outraged*	belegt	*occupied*	verliebt	*in love*
aufgeregt	*excited*	erfahren	*experienced*	verrückt	*insane*

These are no longer true past participles but adjectives:
Er hatte einen ausgezeichneten Aufsatz geschrieben. *He had written an excellent essay.*

- A participle can be used to form an extended adjectival phrase before a noun in German which replaces a phrase or a subordinate clause in English:
ein **über dem Sofa hängendes Bild**   *a picture hanging over the sofa*
Ich habe diesen **von meinem Onkel**   *I enjoyed seeing this film which was*
empfohlenen Film mit Genuß gesehen.   *recommended by my uncle.*

German versions of the English 'ing- form'

- For two simultaneous actions use two main clauses in German:
Er legte das Buch auf den Tisch   *Putting the book on the table he began*
und begann zu lächeln.   *to smile.*

- You can also use a subordinate clause beginning with **als, wenn, indem, nachdem** or **während** depending on the context:
Als er zum Bahnhof ging, sah er   *Going to the station, he saw his old*
seinen alten Freund, Otto.   *friend, Otto.*
Indem sie ihm die Hand reichte,   *Offering him her hand she asked him to take*
bat sie ihn, Platz zu nehmen.   *a seat.*
Wenn man oben auf dem Kirchturm   *Standing on the church tower, you can*
steht, sieht man das ganze Dorf.   *see the whole village.*
Nachdem sie sich gesetzt hatte,   *Having sat down, she began to cry.*
begann sie zu weinen.

Während er auf einer Parkbank saß, schlief er ein.	*While sitting on a park bench, he fell asleep.*

- You can use a subordinate clause with **da** where a reason or cause is involved:

Da wir wußten, daß es dunkel wurde, machten wir uns auf den Weg nach Hause.	*Knowing that it was getting dark, we set off for home.*

- You can use a relative clause:

Ein Mann, der eine Zeitung las, saß ihm gegenüber.	*A man reading a newspaper was sittng opposite him.*

- You can use a **daß** clause:

Ich erinnere mich daran, daß er mich sah. *I remember him seeing me.*
You must use **daß** in this example because the subject of the two verbs is different.
If the subjects are the same, then an infinitive can be used:
Ich erinnere mich daran, ihn gesehen zu haben *I remember having seen him.*

- You can use the past participle after **kommen** to show how the action takes place:
Sie kam ins Bettzimmer gelaufen.   *She came running into the bedroom.*

VERBS WHICH GOVERN THE DATIVE

Many of these verbs are quite common and it is important to learn them carefully. It is useful to know that in many instances the dative object is a person who is advantaged or disadvantaged through the action of the verb. The following are the most frequently used:

ähneln	*to resemble*	folgen	*to follow*	kündigen	*to give notice*
antworten	*to answer*	gehorchen	*to obey*	nutzen/nützen	*to be of use*
begegnen	*to meet*	gehören	*to belong to*	passen	*to suit*
danken	*to thank*	gelten	*to be (meant) for*	schaden	*to harm*
dienen	*to serve*	gleichen	*to be equal to*	schmeicheln	*to flatter*
drohen	*to threaten*	gratulieren	*to congratulate*	trauen	*to trust*
einfallen	*to occur*	helfen	*to help*	vertrauen	*to have trust in*
sich ergeben	*to surrender*	imponieren	*to impress*	wehtun	*to hurt*

Trinken schadet **der Gesundheit**.	*Drinking is harmful to your health.*
Er half **seiner Mutter** in der Küche.	*He helped his mother in the kitchen.*
Sie hat **ihm** nicht geantwortet.	*She did not answer him.*

VERBS WHICH GOVERN THE GENITIVE

There are very few of these and they are not in general use except in set phrases or formal written German:

bedürfen	*to need*	entbehren	*to lack*
gedenken	*to remember*	sich bemächtigen	*to seize*
sich annehmen	*to look after*	sich rühmen	*to boast about/of*
sich erwehren	*to refrain from*	sich vergewissern	*to make sure of*
sich schämen	*to be ashamed of*		

Set phrases worth knowing:

jemanden **der fahrlässigen** Tötung anklagen	*to accuse someone of manslaughter through culpable negligence*
jemanden **der Freiheit** berauben	*to rob someone of their freedom*
jemanden **des Landes** verweisen	*to expel someone from the country*

2.9 STRONG AND IRREGULAR VERBS

The following is a list of strong and irregular verbs, giving details of their principal parts. These are the verbs which you should know for your A/AS-level examinations. The list is alphabetical by infinitive and includes the meaning, the third person singular of the present, imperfect and perfect tenses in the indicative, as well as the past subjunctive of Konjunktiv II. Only the basic verb is listed in full, as compounds usually have the same vowel changes and pattern of endings. Where this is not the case there is a note about it. In the perfect tense *hat* or *ist* is included before the past participle to indicate the auxiliary verb used to form the perfect tenses, where both are listed *haben* will be used if the verb is **transitive**, i.e. has a direct object, *sein* will be used if the verb is **intransitive**.

infinitive	meaning	present	imperfect	konjuktiv II	perfect
anbieten	*to offer*	(separable, see *bieten* below)			
anerkennen	*to recognise*	erkennt an	erkannte an	erkennte an	hat anerkannt
anfangen	*to begin*	(separable, see *fangen* below)			
anhalten	*to stop*	(separable, see *halten* below)			
annehmen	*to accept*	(separable, see *nehmen* below)			
anrufen	*to call/ring*	(separable, see *rufen* below)			
aufstehen	*to get up*	(separable, see *stehen* below)			ist aufgestanden
aussehen	*to look*	(separable, see *sehen* below)			
backen	*to bake*	bäckt	backte (buk)	büke	hat gebacken
befehlen	*to command*	befiehlt	befahl	beföhle	hat befohlen
(N.B. fehlen *to lack* is a weak verb: fehlte, hat gefehlt)				(befähle)	
begehen	*to commit*	(inseparable, see *gehen* below)			hat begangen
beginnen	*to begin*	beginnt	begann	begänne	hat begonnen
				(begönne)	
beißen	*to bite*	beißt	biß	bisse	hat gebissen
bekommen	*to get*	(inseparable, see *kommen* below)			hat bekommen
sich benehmen	*to behave oneself*	(inseparable, see *nehmen* below)			
bergen	*to rescue/hide*	birgt	barg	bärge	hat geborgen
bersten	*to burst*	birst(berstet)	barst	bärste	hat geborsten
besitzen	*to own/possess*	(inseparable, see *sitzen* below)			
bewegen	*to induce*	bewegt	bewog	bewöge	hat bewogen
(N.B. bewegen *to move* is a weak verb: bewegte, hat bewegt)					
biegen	*to bend/turn*	biegt	bog	böge	hat/ist gebogen
bieten	*to offer*	bietet	bot	böte	hat geboten
binden	*to bind/tie*	bindet	band	bände	hat gebunden
bitten	*to ask/request*	bittet	bat	bäte	hat gebeten
blasen	*to blow*	bläst	blies	bliese	hat geblasen
bleiben	*to stay/remain*	bleibt	blieb	bliebe	ist geblieben
braten	*to roast*	brät	briet	briete	hat gebraten
brechen	*to break*	bricht	brach	bräche	hat gebrochen
brennen	*to burn*	brennt	brannte	brennte	hat gebrannt
bringen	*to bring*	bringt	brachte	brächte	hat gebracht
denken	*to think*	denkt	dachte	dächte	hat gedacht
dreschen	*to thresh*	drischt	drosch	drösche	hat gedroschen
dringen	*to penetrate*	dringt	drang	dränge	hat/ist gedrungen
einfallen	*to occur to*	(separable, see *fallen* below)			ist eingefallen
einladen	*to invite*	(separable, see *laden* below)			
einschlafen	*to fall asleep*	(separable, see *schlafen* below)			ist eingeschlafen
einsehen	*to see/recognise*	(separable, see *sehen* below)			
einsteigen	*to get in*	(separable, see *steigen* below)			ist eingestiegen
eintreten	*to go in/occur*	(separable, see *treten* below)			ist eingetreten
empfangen	*to receive*	(inseparable, see *fangen* below)			
empfehlen	*to recommend*	(inseparable, see *befehlen* above)			
entkommen	*to escape*	(inseparable, see *kommen* below)			
entscheiden	*to decide*	(inseparable, see *scheiden* below)			

entschließen	*to decide*	(inseparable, see *schließen* below)			
sich entschließen	*to decide/determine/resolve to*		(inseparable, see *schließen* below)		
entstehen	*to originate/arise*	(inseparable, see *stehen* below)			ist entstanden
erfahren	*to learn/find out*	(inseparable, see *fahren* below)			hat erfahren
erhalten	*to receive/maintain*		(inseparable, see *halten* below)		
erkennen	*to recognise*	(inseparable, see *kennen* below)			
erklingen	*to ring out/resound*		(inseparable, see *klingen* below)		
erlöschen	*to go/die out*	erlischt	erlosch	erlösche	ist erloschen
erscheinen	*to appear*	(inseparable, see *scheinen* below)			ist erschienen
erschrecken	*to be startled*	erschrickt	erschrak	erschräke	ist erschrocken
(N.B. erschrecken *to frighten* is a weak transitive verb: erschrickte, hat erschreckt)					
essen	*to eat*	ißt	aß	äße	hat gegessen
fahren	*to go/drive*	fährt	fuhr	führe	ist gefahren
fallen	*to fall*	fällt	fiel	fiele	ist gefallen
fangen	*to catch*	fängt	fing	finge	hat gefangen
fechten	*to fight/fence*	ficht	focht	föchte	hat gefochten
fernsehen	*to watch television*		(separable, see *sehen* below)		
fertigbringen	*to manage/get done*		(separable, see *bringen* above)		
finden	*to find*	findet	fand	fände	hat gefunden
fliegen	*to fly*	fliegt	flog	flöge	ist/hat geflogen
fliehen	*to flee*	flieht	floh	flöhe	ist geflohen
fließen	*to flow*	fließt	floß	flösse	ist geflossen
freibekommen	*to get released*	bekommt frei	bekam frei	bekäme frei	hat freibekommen
fressen	*to eat*	frißt	fraß	fräße	hat gefressen
	(of animals)				
frieren	*to freeze*	friert	fror	fröre	hat/ist gefroren
gebären	*to give birth*	gebärt(gebiert)	gebar	gebäre	hat geboren
geben	*to give*	gibt	gab	gäbe	hat gegeben
gedeihen	*to thrive*	gedeiht	gedieh	gediehe	ist gediehen
gefallen	*to please*	(impersonal, see *fallen* above)			hat gefallen
gehen	*to go*	geht	ging	ginge	ist gegangen
gelingen (impers)	*to succeed*	gelingt	gelang	gelänge	ist gelungen
gelten	*to be valid*	gilt	galt	gälte(gölte)	hat gegolten
genießen	*to enjoy*	genießt	genoß	genösse	hat genossen
geschehen	*to happen*	geschieht	geschah	geschähe	ist geschehen
gewinnen	*to win*	gewinnt	gewann	gewänne	hat gewonnen
				(gewönne)	
gießen	*to pour*	gießt	goß	gösse	hat gegossen
gleichen	*to resemble*	gleicht	glich	gliche	hat geglichen
gleiten	*to glide/slide*	gleitet	glitt	glitte	ist geglitten
(N.B. begleiten *to accompany* is weak: begleitete, begleitet)					
graben	*to dig*	gräbt	grub	grübe	hat gegraben
greifen	*to seize/grab*	greift	griff	griffe	hat gegriffen
halten	*to hold/stop*	hält	hielt	hielte	hat gehalten
hängen (intrans)	*to hang*	hängt	hing	hinge	hat gehangen
(N.B. hängen *to hang* is a weak transitive verb: hängte, hat gehängt)					
heben	*to lift*	hebt	hob	höbe	hat gehoben
heißen	*to be called*	heißt	hieß	hieße	hat geheißen
helfen	*to help*	hilft	half	hülfe (hälfe)	hat geholfen
kennen	*to know*	kennt	kannte	kennte	hat gekannt
klingen	*to sound*	klingt	klang	klänge	hat geklungen
kneifen	*to pinch*	kneift	kniff	kniffe	hat gekniffen
kommen	*to come*	kommt	kam	käme	ist gekommen
kriechen	*to creep/crawl*	kriecht	kroch	kröche	ist gekrochen
laden	*to load*	lädt	lud	lüde	hat geladen
lassen	*to leave/let*	läßt	ließ	ließe	hat gelassen
(N.B. veranlassen *to cause* is an inseparable weak verb: veranlaßte, veranlaßt)					
laufen	*to run*	läuft	lief	liefe	ist/hat gelaufen
leiden	*to suffer*	leidet	litt	litte	hat gelitten
leihen	*to lend/loan*	leiht	lieh	liehe	hat geliehen
lesen	*to read*	liest	las	läse	hat gelesen
liegen	*to lie*	liegt	lag	läge	hat gelegen
liegenlassen	*to leave behind*	(separable, see *lassen* above)			hat liegengelassen

losfahren	*to set off*	(separable, see *fahren* above)		
loswerden	*to get rid of*	(separable, see *werden* below)		
lügen	*to tell lies*	lügt	log	löge	hat gelogen
meiden	*to avoid*	meidet	mied	miede	hat gemieden
messen	*to measure*	mißt	maß	mäße	hat gemessen
nehmen	*to take*	nimmt	nahm	nähme	hat genommen
nennen	*to name/call*	nennt	nannte	nennte	hat genannt
pfeifen	*to whistle*	pfeift	pfiff	pfiffe	hat gepfiffen
preisen	*to praise*	preist	pries	priese	hat gepriesen
quellen	*to well up*	quillt	quoll	quölle	ist gequollen
raten	*to advise*	rät	riet	riete	hat geraten
reiben	*to rub*	reibt	rieb	riebe	hat gerieben
reißen	*to tear*	reißt	riß	risse	hat/ist gerissen
reiten	*to ride*	reitet	ritt	ritte	hat/ist geritten
rennen	*to run*	rennt	rannte	rennte	hat/ist gerannt
riechen	*to smell*	riecht	roch	röche	hat gerochen
ringen	*to wrestle*	ringt	rang	ränge	hat gerungen
rinnen	*to flow/trickle*	rinnt	rann	ränne(rönne)	ist geronnen
rufen	*to call*	ruft	rief	riefe	hat gerufen
schaffen	*to create*	schafft	schuf	schüfe	hat geschaffen

(N.B. schaffen *to manage/work* is a weak verb: schaffte, geschafft)

scheiden	*to separate*	scheidet	schied	schiede	hat/ist geschieden
scheinen	*to shine/seem*	scheint	schien	schiene	hat geschienen
schelten	*to scold*	schilt	schalt	schölte	hat gescholten
scheren	*to shear/clip*	schert	schor	schöre	hat geschoren

(N.B. sich scheren *to care/bother about* is weak: scherte sich, hat sich geschert)

schiefgehen	*to go wrong*	(separable, see *gehen* above)			ist schiefgegangen
schieben	*to shove/push*	schiebt	schob	schöbe	hat geschoben
schießen	*to shoot*	schießt	schoß	schösse	hat/ist geschossen
schlafen	*to sleep*	schläft	schlief	schliefe	hat geschlafen
schlagen	*to hit/beat*	schlägt	schlug	schlüge	hat geschlagen
schleichen	*to creep*	schleicht	schlich	schliche	ist geschlichen
schleifen	*to grind/sharpen*	schleift	schliff	schliffe	hat gaschliffen

(N.B. schleifen *to drag* is a weak verb: schleifte, geschleift)

schließen	*to shut*	schließt	schloß	schlösse	hat geschlossen
schlingen	*to wind/wrap*	schlingt	schlang	schlänge	hat geschlungen
schmelzen	*to melt*	schmilzt	schmolz	schmölze	hat/ist geschmolzen
schneiden	*to cut*	schneidet	schnitt	schnitte	hat geschnitten
schreiben	*to write*	schreibt	schrieb	schriebe	hat geschrieben
schreien	*to shout/scream*	schreit	schrie	schriee	hat geschrie(e)n
schreiten	*to stride*	schreitet	schritt	schritte	ist geschritten
schweigen	*to be silent*	schweigt	schwieg	schwiege	hat geschwiegen
schwellen	*to swell*	schwillt	schwoll	schwölle	ist geschwollen
schwimmen	*to swim*	schwimmt	schwamm	schwömme (schwämme)	ist/hat geschwommen
schwinden	*to dwindle/fade*	schwindet	schwand	schwände	ist geschwunden
schwingen	*to swing*	schwingt	schwang	schwänge	hat geschwungen
schwören	*to swear*	schwört	schwor	schwüre (schwöre)	hat geschworen
sehen	*to see*	sieht	sah	sähe	hat gesehen
senden	*to send*	sendet	sandte	sendete	hat gesandt

(N.B. regular forms 'sendete, gesendet' are used in a technical sense i.e. *broadcast*)

singen	*to sing*	singt	sang	sänge	hat gesungen
sinken	*to sink*	sinkt	sank	sänke	ist gesunken
sitzen	*to sit*	sitzt	saß	säße	hat gesessen
spazierengehen	*to go for a walk*	(separable, see *gehen* above)			ist spazierengegangen
spinnen	*to spin*	spinnt	spann	spönne(spänne)	hat gesponnen
sprechen	*to speak*	spricht	sprach	spräche	hat gesprochen
springen	*to jump/spring*	springt	sprang	spränge	ist gesprungen
stattfinden	*to take place*	(separable, see *finden* above)			hat stattgefunden
stechen	*to sting/prick*	sticht	stach	stäche	hat gestochen
stehen	*to stand*	steht	stand	stünde(stände)	hat gestanden

stehlen	*to steal*	stiehlt	stahl	stähle(stöhle)	hat gestohlen
steigen	*to climb/rise*	steigt	stieg	stiege	ist gestiegen
sterben	*to die*	stirbt	starb	stürbe	ist gestorben
stinken	*to stink*	stinkt	stank	stänke	hat gestunken
stoßen	*to push/bump*	stößt	stieß	stieße	ist/hat gestoßen
streichen	*to stroke*	streicht	strich	striche	ist/hat gestrichen
streiten	*to argue*	streitet	stritt	stritte	hat gestritten

teilnehmen	*to take part*	(separable, see *nehmen* above)			
tragen	*to carry/wear*	trägt	trug	trüge	hat getragen

  (N.B. beantragen *to apply for* and beauftragen *to commission* are inseparable and weak)

treffen	*to meet/hit*	trifft	traf	träfe	hat getroffen
treiben	*to drive/drift*	treibt	trieb	triebe	hat/ist getrieben
treten	*to step/kick*	tritt	trat	träte	ist/hat getreten
tun	*to do*	tut	tat	täte	hat getan

übernehmen	*to take on/accept*	(inseparable, see *nehmen* above)	
umsteigen	*to change (trains)*	(separable, see *steigen* above)	
unterbringen	*to accommodate*	(inseparable, see *bringen* above)	
unterhalten	*to support/entertain*	(inseparable, see *halten* above)	
sich unterscheiden	*to differ from*	(inseparable, see *scheiden* above)	

verbieten	*to forbid*	(inseparable, see *bieten* above)			
verbringen	*to spend (time)*	(inseparable, see *bringen* abova)			
verderben	*to spoil*	verdirbt	verdarb	verdürbe	hat/ist verdorben
vergessen	*to forget*	vergißt	vergaß	vergäße	hat vergessen
vergleichen	*to compare*	(inseparable, see *gleichen* above)			
verlassen	*to leave*	(inseparable, see *lassen* above)			
verlieren	*to lose*	verliert	verlor	verlöre	hat verloren
verschwinden	*to disappear*	(inseparable, see *schwinden* above)			ist verschwunden
versprechen	*to promise*	(inseparable, see *sprechen* above)			
verstehen	*to understand*	(inseparable, see *stehen* above)			
verzeihen	*to forgive*	verzeiht	verzieh	verziehe	hat verziehen
vorbeifahren	*to drive past*	(inseparable, see *fahren* above)			
vorkommen	*to happen*	(separable, see *kommen* above)			ist vorgekommen
vorlesen	*to read out*	(separable, see *lesen* above)			
vorschlagen	*to suggest*	(separable, see *schlagen* above)			

wachsen	*to grow*	wächst	wuchs	wüchse	ist gewachsen
waschen	*to wash*	wäscht	wusch	wüsche	hat gewaschen
weisen	*to point*	weist	wies	wiese	hat gewiesen
wenden	*to turn*	wendet	wandte	wendete	hat gewandt

  (N.B. 1 the regular forms *wendete, gewendet* are more common meaning *turn over/round*)
  (N.B. 2 the regular forms are used with entwenden *to steal/purloin* and verwenden *to use/employ*)

werben	*to recruit*	wirbt	warb	würbe	hat geworben
werden	*to become*	wird	wurde	würde	ist geworden
werfen	*to throw*	wirft	warf	würfe	hat geworfen
wiegen	*to weigh*	wiegt	wog	wöge	hat gewogen

  (N.B. wiegen *to rock* is a weak verb: wiegte, gewiegt)

wissen	*to know*	weiß	wußte	wüßte	hat gewußt

ziehen	*to pull*	zieht	zog	zöge	hat/ist gezogen
zwingen	*to force*	zwingt	zwang	zwänge	hat gezwungen

2.10 THE PASSIVE

In the normal course of things we use the active voice to describe what is going on. However, the passive voice allows us to describe an activity without necessarily saying who is doing it (i.e. the agent). There are two passives in both English and German but in English we only use the verb *to be* to form the passives, whereas in German **werden** is used to form the 'actional' passive which describes an event and **sein** to form the 'statal' passive which describes a state; both are followed by the past participle of the verb concerned.

THE PASSIVE WITH WERDEN

The tenses of the passive are mainly the same as the active and they are used in the same way.

Fußball wird gespielt.	*Football is (being) played.* (Present)
Fußball wurde gespielt.	*Football was (being) played.* (Imperfect)
Fußball wird gespielt werden.	*Football will be played.* (Future)
Fußball würde gespielt werden.	*Football would be played.* (Conditiomal)
Fußball ist gespielt **worden.**	*Football has been played.* (Perfect)
Fußball war gespielt **worden.**	*Football had been played.* (Pluperfect)
Fußball wird gespielt **worden** sein.	*Football will have been played.* (Future Perfect)
Fußball würde gespielt **worden** sein.	*Football would have been played.* (Conditional Perfect)

In practice the future, future perfect and conditional perfect are rarely used. Please note that in all the perfect tenses of the passive the **ge-** of **geworden** is omitted as highlighted above.

Most transitive verbs can be used in the passive, the direct object in the accusative becomes the subject of the passive construction, the subject in the active becomes the agent or the means by which the action is done in the passive. Look at these examples:

Active: Der Mann sah einen Hund im Garten.
The man saw a dog in the garden.

Passive: Ein Hund wurde vom Mann im Garten gesehen.
A dog was seen by the man in the garden.

Active: Die Bomben zerstörten die Stadt.
The bombs destroyed the town.

Passive: Die Stadt wurde durch Bomben zerstört.
The town was destroyed by bombs.

Please note that **von** plus the dative translates as 'by' with an agent (person) and **durch** plus the accusative translates as 'by' with things or the 'means'.

N.B. Verbs which take a dative object cannot be used in the passive in German in the same way. The passive is conveyed through an impersonal construction in the 3rd person singular:

'Man kann Ihnen helfen' in the active becomes 'Es kann Ihnen geholfen werden' in the passive meaning *You can be helped.*

Similarly when a verb which takes a direct (acc.) and an indirect (dat.) object is used in a passive construction, only the accusative object can become the subject of a passive verb in German. In English either object can be used as the subject in the passive. Look at these examples:

Er gab meinem kleinen Bruder (dat.) ein neues Spielzeug. (acc.)
He gave my little brother a new toy. (active)

Meinem kleinen Bruder (dat.) wurde ein neues Spielzeug gegeben.
My little brother was given a new toy. (passive)

THE PASSIVE WITH SEIN

This is used to show a state of being when no action is usually involved,
so 'Die Tür **ist** geschlossen' indicates that the door is closed not open and no action was carried out. However, 'die Tür **wird** von mir **geschlossen**' indicates the closing of the door by me; the door is actually 'being closed' hence the need to use the passive with **werden** to show the action.

The tenses of *sein* plus the past participle of the verb concerned are used to form the 'statal' passive.

AVOIDING THE PASSIVE

There are basically three ways of avoiding the passive in German.

- use 'man':
  Bei uns wurde eingebrochen. *We were broken into/burgled.*
  or, to avoid the passive – Man brach bei uns ein.

- use a reflexive verb:
  Wie erklärt sich das?   *How is that explained?*

- an infinitive with **zu** after **sein** can have a passive meaning in certain contexts with the sense of 'is to be' in English:
  Dieses Buch ist bis morgen zu lesen.   *This book is to be read by tomorrow.*

2.11 THE SUBJUNCTIVE

THE FORMATION OF THE SUBJUNCTIVE

The formation of the subjunctive in German is very straightforward. There are two forms known in German as Konjunktiv I and II

❶ Konjunktiv I comprises the present, perfect and future tenses of the subjunctive.
The endings of Konjunktiv I are:
-e, -est, -e,   -en, -et, -en
All verbs have these endings with the exception of **sein** which is irregular. There are no vowel changes for strong verbs in the subjunctive.
- **Present subjunctive**: ich spiel**e**, du spiel**est**, er spiel**e**, wir spiel**en**, ihr spiel**et**, sie spiel**en** (weak verb)
  ich trink**e**, du trink**est**, er trink**e**, wir trink**en**, ihr trink**et**, sie trink**en** (strong verb)
  ich **sei**, du **seiest**, er **sei**, wir **seien**, ihr **seiet**, sie **seien** (**sein** irregular)
- **Perfect subjunctive**: er **habe** gespielt (weak verb) er **sei** gegangen (strong verb)
  i.e. the present subjunctive of **haben** or **sein** plus the past participle of the verb concerned.
- **Future subjunctive**: er **werde** spielen (weak verb) er **werde** trinken (strong verb)
  i.e. the present subjunctive of **werden** plus the infinitive of the verb concerned.

❷ Konjunktiv II comprises the past (imperfect), pluperfect and conditional tenses
The endings of Konjunktiv II are the same as for Konjunktiv I:
-e, -est, -e,   -en, -et, -en
- **Imperfect subjunctive**: ich spiel**te**, du spiel**test**, er spiel**te**, wir spiel**ten**, ihr spiel**tet**, sie spiel**ten** (weak verb)
  N.B. The imperfect indicative and the imperfect subjunctive of a weak verb are identical. The imperfect subjunctive of strong verbs is formed by taking the stem of the imperfect indicative and adding the subjunctive endings with an Umlaut on the stem vowel where this is possible.
  Examples:

verb		**trinken**	**biegen**	**bleiben**	**gehen**
Past indicative		trank	bog	blieb	ging
Konjunktiv II	ich	**tränke**	**böge**	**bliebe**	**ginge**
	du	**tränkest**	**bögest**	**bliebest**	**gingest**
	er	**tränke**	**böge**	**bliebe**	**ginge**
	wir	**tränken**	**bögen**	**blieben**	**gingen**
	ihr	**tränket**	**böget**	**bliebet**	**ginget**
	sie	**tränken**	**bögen**	**blieben**	**gingen**
	(Sie	**tränken**	**bögen**	**blieben**	**gingen**)

There are a number of other common verbs which have the Umlaut in the imperfect subjunctive. They are:
- the three auxiliary verbs: sein – er wäre, haben – er hätte, werden – er würde,
- the following modal verbs which have an Umlaut in the infinitive:
  dürfen – er dürfte, müssen – er müßte, können – er könnte, mögen – er möchte,
- and a small number of others mostly strong verbs:
  bringen – er brächte, denken – er dächte, helfen – er hülfe, stehen – er stünde,
  sterben – er stürbe,   wissen – er wüßte

- **The pluperfect subjunctive:** er **hätte** gespielt (weak verb) er **wäre** gegangen (strong verb)
  i.e. the imperfect subjunctive of **haben** or **sein** with the past participle of the verb concerned.
- The compound form, known as the conditional tense: er **würde** spielen (weak verb) er **würde** trinken (strong verb)
  i.e. the past subjunctive of **werden** plus the infinitive of the verb concerned.

Note:

- Konjunktiv I uses the present subjunctive formation for each of the three tenses it comprises.
- Konjunktiv II uses the past (imperfect) subjunctive formation for the three tenses it comprises.

THE USES OF THE SUBJUNCTIVE

English students are always puzzled by the subjunctive because they do not know what it is in English, it rarely changes the meaning and they have to learn therefore the specific types of construction where it is used in German. It does exist in English in the song title 'If I **were** a rich man' for example, but its uses are obscure.

Uses in German are in particular constructions and although in general the indicative is the 'normal' mood in speaking and writing German A-level and AS-level students will be expected to know and be able to use the subjunctive in its prescribed forms.

The subjunctive in German is used as follows:
(i) in reported speech or questions (ii) to express conditions (iii) after **als ob** *as if* (iv) to moderate the tone of a statement or request (v) to express a wish or give instructions or commands.

Let us look at each of these in turn.

Reported speech

Reported or indirect speech occurs when we report what someone said by putting it into a sentence of our own rather than quoting what was actually said. Direct speech appears in quotation marks in our writing but indirect speech does not. Compare these two examples:

Direct speech: He said, "I have finished my homework".
Indirect speech: He said (that) he had finished his homework.

We recognise the indirect speech in English because it is introduced by a verb of saying. In German we use the forms of the subjunctive to express the indirect speech.

Look at these examples:

Direct speech: Er sagte: „Ich habe meine Hausaufgaben fertig gemacht".
Indirect speech: Er sagte, daß er seine Hausaufgaben fertig gemacht **habe**.
       or: Er sagte, er **habe** seine Hausaufgaben fertig gemacht.

The second sentence here omits the *daß* which changes the word order. In the direct speech the verb is in the perfect indicative. The perfect subjunctive is used in both indirect (or reported) speech examples.

One of the problems of reported speech in German is that there are two separate sorts of usage, one in formal written language and one colloquial. Inspite of the fact that not all native speakers of German understand the rules of both sorts you will have to know both sets.

Reported speech in formal written language

Konjunktiv I in one of its three forms should be used to render reported speech wherever possible, which means **wherever the form of the subjunctive is different from the indicative**. The tense of the subjunctive chosen should reflect what the original speaker

actually said. What you need to do is to try and establish what was originally said and apply the following pattern. On the left are examples of what was said in direct speech, on the right the corresponding tense converted into the subjunctive in reported speech.

What was originally said (Direct speech)	**Formal written reported speech** (Konjunktiv I)
present indicative: Ich lese ein Buch *I am reading a book*	**present subjunctive:** Er sagte, er **lese** ein Buch *He said he was reading a book*
future indicative: Ich werde ein Buch lesen *I shall read a book*	**future subjunctive:** Er sagte, er **werde** ein Buch **lesen** *He said he would read a book*
past imperfect indicative: Ich las ein Buch *I was reading a book*	**perfect subjunctive:** Er sagte, er **habe** ein Buch **gelesen** *He said he had read a book*
perfect indicative: Ich habe ein Buch gelesen *I have read a book*	**perfect subjunctive:** Er sagte, er **habe** ein Buch **gelesen** *He said he had read a book*
pluperfect indicative: Ich hatte ein Buch gelesen *I had read a book*	**perfect subjunctive:** Er sagte, er **habe** ein Buch **gelesen** *He said he had read a book*

Points to note at this stage are:

- The example above is with a strong verb, any weak verb would follow the same pattern.
- The reported speech version of the imperfect, perfect and pluperfect indicative tenses is the same, i.e. the perfect subjunctive from Konjunktiv I is used.
- All these examples so far have been in the third person in reported speech where the form of Konjunktiv I is **distinctive**.

We must now look at what happens if the form of Konjunktiv I is **not** distinctive from the indicative. The rule is: **If the form of Konjunktiv I is the same as the indicative then you must use the corresponding form of Konjunktiv II.** Here is the pattern again in a different person, first with a weak verb **spielen** then with a strong verb **trinken**.

What was originally said (Direct speech)	**Formal written reported speech** (Konjunktiv II)
present indicative: Wir spielen Tennis *We are playing tennis* Wir trinken Wein *We are drinking wine*	**past/imperfect subjunctive:** Sie sagten, sie **spielten** Tennis *They said they were playing tennis* Sie sagten, sie **tränken** Wein *They said they were drinking wine*
future indicative: Wir werden Tennis spielen *We shall play tennis* Wie werden Wein trinken *We shall drink wine*	**conditional:** Sie sagten, sie **würden** Tennis **spielen** *They said they would play tennis* Sie sagten, sie **würden** Wein **trinken** *They said they would drink wine*
past/imperfect indicative: Wir spielten Tennis *We played tennis* Wir tranken Wein *We drank wine*	**pluperfect subjunctive:** Sie sagten, sie **hätten** Tennis **gespielt** *They said they had played tennis* Sie sagten, sie **hätten** Wein **getrunken** *They said they had drunk wine*
perfect indicative: Wir haben Tennis gespielt *We have played tennis* Wir haben Wein getrunken *We have drunk wine*	**pluperfect subjunctive:** Sie sagten, sie **hätten** Tennis **gespielt** *They said they had played tennis* Sie sagten, sie **hätten** Wein **getrunken** *They said they had drunk wine*

pluperfect indicative:	pluperfect subjunctive:
Wir hatten Tennis gespielt	Sie sagten, sie **hätten** Tennis **gespielt**
We had played tennis	*They said they had played tennis*
Wir hatten Wein getrunken	Sie sagten, sie **hätten** Wein **getrunken**
We had drunk wine	*They said they had drunk wine*

Points to note are:

● The Konjunktiv I forms of the present, future and perfect subjunctive tenses are the same in the third person plural as the tenses in the indicative:
present **sie spielen/trinken**, future **sie werden … spielen/trinken**, and perfect **sie haben … gespielt/getrunken**. We therefore have to use the Konjunktiv II forms of the tenses in the subjunctive in reported speech in formal writing.

● The subjunctive forms of both Konjunktiv I and II are in themselves enough to indicate that a statement is being 'reported' which immediately casts doubt on what was actually said. This is why the use of the subjunctive forms is so prevalent in the press. By using them they imply 'reported speech' which does not have to be strictly 'true':

● The word *daß* has been deliberately omitted in the above examples; if it is used after *sagen* then the finite verb must be placed at the end of the *'daß clause'*:
Er sagte, **daß** er ein Buch gelesen **habe**. *He said, that he had read a book.*

● Take special care not to be misled by the tense in English, learn the pattern as laid out above and write down what you think the original speaker said. This will then give you the corresponding tense in the subjunctive.

Reported speech in colloquial language

In everyday spoken German either the **indicative** or **Konjunktiv II** is used in reported speech. The forms of Konjunktiv I are not used, the indicative is preferred and the tense of the original direct speech is usually retained. When Konjunktiv II is used in past contexts it is often in the 'conditional' form with *würde*. Look at the pattern again:

What was originally said (Direct speech/Indicative)	Colloquial reported speech
present:	**present indicative or conditional:**
Ich spiele Tennis	Sie hat gesagt, sie **spielt** Tennis
	Sie hat gesagt, sie **würde** Tennis **spielen**
I am playing tennis	*She said she was playing tennis*
future:	**future indicative or conditional:**
Ich werde Tennis spielen	Sie hat gesagt, sie **wird** Tennis **spielen**
	Sie hat gesagt, sie **würde** Tennis **spielen**
I shall play tennis	*She said she would play tennis*
perfect:	**perfect indicative or pluperfect subjunctive:**
Ich habe Tennis gespielt	Sie hat gesagt, sie **hat** Tennis **gespielt**
	Sie hat gesagt, sie **hätte** Tennis **gespielt**
I have played tennis	*She said she had played tennis*
pluperfect:	**pluperfect indicative or subjunctive:**
Ich hatte Tennis gespielt	Sie hat gesagt, sie **hatte** Tennis **gespielt**
	Sie hat gesagt, sie **hätte** Tennis **gespielt**
I had played tennis	*She said she had played tennis*

Please note that the tenses in colloquial reported speech are very like those used in English. The examples above are with a weak verb, any other verb could be substituted in a different context.

Indirect questions

The use of the forms of the subjunctive in indirect questions follows the same pattern as reported speech or indirect statements as above:

Er fragte ihn, wie alt sein Bruder sei.	*He asked him how old his brother was.*
Der Mann fragte sie, ob sie Angst habe.	*The man asked her if she was afraid.*
Sie fragte ihn, ob seine Eltern zu Hause wären.	*She asked him if his parents were at home.*

Expressing conditions

There are three kinds of conditional clause in German. Each of them is introduced by **wenn** meaning *if*. Look at these examples:

- **Open conditions** are conditions which are likely to be met and therefore are not expressed in German in the conditional or the subjunctive.
  English: *If she is ill, she will not go to school tomorrow.*
  German: Wenn sie krank ist, (so) wird sie nicht morgen in die Schule gehen.
  The tenses used here are the present and future indicative in both languages.

- Expressing **possibilities**
  The condition in this kind of clause is 'unreal' expressing what might, or might not, happen, i.e. a possibility. Here the forms of Konjunktiv II are used in German.
  English: *If he had the time, he could work in the garden.*
  German: Wenn er Zeit **hätte**, (so) **könnte** er im Garten arbeiten.
  The tenses used here are the imperfect subjunctive and the conditional.

- Expressing **regrets**
  The conditional clause expresses regret for what might have happened but didn't.
  The pluperfect form of Konjunktiv II is used in both conditional and main clauses.
  English: *If he had come home, she would have seen him.*
  German: Wenn er nach Hause **gekommen wäre**, (so) **hätte** sie ihn **gesehen**.

A streamlined version of these conditional clauses is possible by omitting *wenn*. When you do this the word order is changed and the word **so** or **dann** is introduced at the beginning of the main clause. The '*wenn* clause' begins with the finite verb. Here are the conditional sentences above without *wenn*:

Ist sie krank, **so** wird sie nicht morgen in die Schule gehen.
Hätte er Zeit, **so** könnte er im Garten arbeiten.
Wäre er nach Hause gekommen, **so** hätte sie ihn gesehen.

dann can replace **so** in these examples without any other change:
Ist sie krank, **dann** wird sie nicht morgen in die Schule gehen. (usw.)

Both the **so** and the **dann** are optional but quite common.

After als ob meaning *as if, as though*

In German the conjunction **als ob** introduces a subordinate clause where the verb is in a form of Konjunktiv II. Look at these examples:

- If the action after **als ob** takes place at the same time as the action in the main clause, the imperfect subjunctive is used:
  Er tat, als ob er krank **wäre**.   *He acted as if he was ill.*

- If the action in the '**als ob** clause' took place before the action in the main clause, the pluperfect subjunctive is used:
  Er tat, als ob er krank **gewesen wäre**.   *He acted as if he had been ill.*

- If the action in the '**als ob** clause' will take place after the action in the main clause, the conditional is used:
  Er tat, **als ob** er krank **sein würde**.   *He acted as if he would be ill.*
  Es sieht aus, als ob es schneien würde.   *It looks as if it will snow.*

Streamlining these clauses is also possible by omitting **ob**, but please note the change to the word order – the finite verb in the '**als ob** clause' is placed next to **als**:

Er sprach, **als wäre er** krank.
Er sprach, **als wäre er** krank **gewesen**.

Softening the tone of a statement, a request or a question

You can use the forms of Konjunktiv II to make these less blunt:

Das **wär's** für heute.	*That's enough for today, maybe.*
Eine Frage **hätte** ich doch noch.	*I'd like to ask another question.*
Könnten Sie mir bitte sagen, wo das Freibad liegt?	*Could you please tell me where the open air swimming pool is?*

The subjunctive in expressing wishes or commands

- Konjunktiv I is used to express a wish mostly in the third person:

Gott **sei** dank!	*Thank God!*
Es lebe die Königin!	*Long live the queen!*

- A conditional clause with **wenn** is frequently used with Konjunktiv II to express a wish, one or more of **bloß, nur** or **doch** is usually inserted giving it the meaning of *if only*:

Wenn er doch nur schwimmen **könnte.**	*If only he could swim.*
Wenn er bloß sein Abitur **bestanden hätte.**	*If only he had passed his A-levels.*

  Please note that as in other 'wenn clauses' wenn can be omitted and the word order changes in the same way:

  Hätte er bloß sein Abitur **bestanden.**

- Konjunktiv I is used in commands in the first person plural:

Spielen wir Fußball!	*Let us play football!*
Seien wir dankbar, daß nichts Schreckliches passiert ist!	*Let's be thankful that nothing awful happened!*

2.12 MODAL AUXILIARIES

There are six modal verbs which, like *haben, sein* and *werden*, are auxiliary verbs.

They are:

dürfen	*to be allowed to*	**müssen**	*to have to*
können	*to be able to*	**sollen**	*to be supposed to*
mögen	*to like to*	**wollen**	*to wish/want to*

The present indicative of each verb is slightly irregular, as follows:

ich	darf	kann	mag	muß	soll	will
du	darfst	kannst	magst	mußt	sollst	willst
er/sie/es	darf	kann	mag	muß	soll	will
wir	dürfen	können	mögen	müssen	sollen	wollen
ihr	dürft	könnt	mögt	müßt	sollt	wollt
sie	dürfen	können	mögen	müssen	sollen	wollen

They have a full range of tenses and moods. The imperfect indicative is formed with the weak verb endings and no Umlaut on the stem:

ich durfte, konnte, mochte, mußte, sollte, wollte etc.

The perfect indicative is formed with *haben* in each case, but the past participle is hardly ever used. This is because these verbs are usually accompanied by a **dependent infinitive**. When this happens the past participle is replaced by the infinitive in the perfect tenses:

Er hat nicht gehen **können.**	*He has not been able to go.*

THE USES OF MODAL VERBS

The main use of all modal verbs is with a dependent infinitive. Remember there is no **zu** before the infinitive after a modal verb and the plain infinitive must stand at the end of the clause in which it is used:

Er darf nicht ausgehen.	*He is not allowed to go out.*
Wir können noch nicht nach Hause gehen.	*We cannot go home yet.*

123

In the perfect tenses the infinitive of the modal verb is used instead of the past participle. Like the past participle it will stand at the end of the clause after the dependent infinitive:

Er hat es tun **müssen**.	*He has had to do it.*
Wir hatten es tun **wollen**.	*We had wanted to do it.*

You will notice from these last two examples that there are two infinitives at the end of the clause, this pattern is retained in a subordinate clause when a compound tense is used. The finite verb precedes the two infinitives at the end of the clause. With a modal verb this can happen in the perfect tenses, the future and the conditional tenses when they are used in a subordinate clause:

Ich weiß nicht, ob ich den Brief **werde schreiben müssen**.
I do not know whether I shall have to write the letter.

Obgleich er gestern **hätte kommen sollen**, ist er noch nicht angekommen.
Although he ought to have come yesterday, he has not yet arrived.

Let us now look at each modal verb in turn and explore their uses.

Dürfen

Denotes permission to do something – in the negative it is a prohibition meaning 'must not':

Darf ich heute abend ins Kino gehen?	*May I go to the cinema this evening?*
Er durfte im Garten Fußball spielen	*He was allowed to play football in the garde*n
Wir dürfen nicht hier Fußball spielen	*We must not play football here*
Ich hätte es tun dürfen	*I should have been allowed to do it*

Können

Denotes ability, knowledge and possibility:

Er kann sehr schnell laufen	*He can run very fast*
Sie kann Deutsch	*She can speak German*
Sie könnte jetzt in Bonn sein	*She could/might be in Bonn now*

The last example is in the imperfect subjunctive (Konjunktiv II) and expresses a remote possibility.

With a compound infinitive, the perfect for example, *können* expresses possibility:

Er kann seine Freunde gesehen haben   *He may have seen his friends*

Look at these uses of *können* in the subjunctive and the notes which explain what each of them means:

Er könnte es getan haben	*He could have done it*	(It was possible that he did it)
Er hätte es tun können	*He could have done it*	(He would have been able to do it)

Mögen

Denotes liking, possibility or probability. The most frequent use of *mögen* to express liking is the imperfect subjunctive usually with *gern(e)*:

Ich möchte gerne in die Schweiz fahren   *I should like to go to Switzerland*

Other tenses are possible:

Sie mag ihn	*She likes him*
Er mochte dieses Gebäude nicht	*He didn't like that building*
Ich hätte es tun mögen	*I should have liked to do it*
Das mag (wohl) sein	*That may well be*

Müssen

Denotes necessity or compulsion, being obliged to do something:

Das muß schwer sein	*That must be difficult*
Er muß in die Schule gehen	*He has to go to school*
Wir mußten lachen	*We couldn't help laughing (We had to laugh)*
Ich hätte es tun müssen	*I should have had to do it*
Er muß nicht in die Schule gehen	*He doesn't have to go to school (doesn't need to...)*

N.B. the difference between:

Er muß ein Wörterbuch kaufen	*He has to buy a dictionary (needs to…)*
Er hat ein Haus zu verkaufen	*He has a house to sell*

Remember: 'must not' usually means 'is not allowed to' and is therefore **dürfen nicht** in German.

Sollen

Denotes an obligation or intention and means *to be to, to be supposed to, shall,* and in the subjunctive *should, ought*:

Er soll nach Italien fahren	*He is to go to Italy*
Der Prinz soll reich sein	*The prince is supposed to be rich*
Er sollte später eine Reise machen	*He was to go on a journey later*
Um wieviel Uhr soll ich kommen?	*What time shall I come? (am I to…)*
Er sollte das nicht tun, weil es gefährlich ist	*He should not do that because it is dangerous*
Er sollte es gestern getan haben	*He should/ought to have done it yesterday* (we would expect him to have done it)
Er hätte es gestern tun sollen	*He should/ought to have done it yesterday* (he ought to have done it, but he didn't)

Wollen

Denotes wish, willingness, intention:

Wollen Sie mitkommen?	*Will you come with me?*
Er will alles sehen	*He wants to see everything*
Wir wollen eben ausgehen	*We are on the point of going out (about to…)*
Ich hätte es tun wollen	*I should have wanted to do it*

If the subject is not a person then *wollen* will frequently be rendered by 'need'

Tomaten wollen viel Sonne	*Tomatoes need a lot of sun*

Other words which have a modal force

These are words which help to express the speaker's attitude to what is being said.

- **also** *so, thus, then* (it does not mean *also*):

Also blieb ich in der Schule	*So I stayed at school*
Also, gut!	*Well all right then!*

- **auch** as an adverb means *too, also, as well*:

Er mußte auch nach Hause gehen	*He had to go home too*

  Examples of other uses:

Hörst du auch zu?	*You are listening, aren't you?* (asks for confirmation)
Ich habe es auch nicht getan	*But I didn't do it, you know* (emphasises something)
Er kann nicht schwimmen – Ich auch nicht	*He can't swim – neither can I* (meaning *neither* or *nor*)

- **denn** *then, well then, so* – frequently used in questions toning them down and referring back to what has just been said:

Wie geht es dir denn?	*Well, how are you then?*
Was ist denn los?	*So what's the matter then?*

- **doch** usually expresses a contradiction or disagreement of some kind, but can be used for emphasis:

Er ist doch nicht gekommen	*He has not come after all*
Er kann doch singen	*He can sing* (emphasising what he can do)
Aber er hat es doch selber gesagt	*But he said so himself, you know*
Öffne doch das Paket!	*Do open the parcel!* (adding urgency to the command)
Und doch habe ich nichts gemacht	*And yet I did nothing*

doch is also used like 'si' in French to contradict a negative question:

Hast du ihn nicht gesehen?	*Haven't you seen him?*
Doch, ich habe ihn gestern gesehen	*Yes, I saw him yesterday*

- **eben** *just, exactly*:

Das ist es eben, was er sagte	*That is just/exactly, what he said*

- **eigentlich** *actually, in actual fact*:

Wie alt ist sie eigentlich?	*How old is she in actual fact?*
Wohnt Karl eigentlich schon lange in Berlin?	*Has Karl actually been living a long time in Berlin?*

- **erst** *only, not before, not until*:

Sie werden erst morgen ankommen	*They will not arrive till tomorrow*
Er hat erst zehn Seiten gelesen	*He has read only ten pages*

- **gar** is used to intensify a negative:

Ich habe gar nichts gegessen	*I have eaten nothing at all*

- **mal** moderates the tone of a sentence:

Sag mir mal, was geschah!	*Just tell me what happened!*

- **noch** corresponds to *still* or *yet*:

Er schläft noch	*He is still asleep*
Sonst noch etwas?	*Anything else?*
Noch ein Glas Milch, bitte	*Another glass of milk please*

- **schon** can mean *already* but has a wider range of use showing that something has happened or is happening rather sooner than expected:

Es hatte schon geregnet	*It had already been raining*
Bist du schon einmal in Bonn gewesen?	*Have you been to Bonn before?*

- **überhaupt** usually means *at all, any how, really*:

Wenn er etwas überhaupt trinkt, wird es nur Limonade sein	*If he drinks anything at all it will only be lemonade*
Das war überhaupt ein häßlicher Vorfall	*That was really an ugly incident*
Er hätte es überhaupt nicht tun sollen	*He ought not to have done it at all*

- **übrigens** usually means *by the way, incidentally*:

It is used to introduce a casual note into the conversation

Er hat mir übrigens erzählt, daß er dieses Jahr nicht komme	*By the way, he told me he wasn't coming this year*

- **vielleicht** *perhaps*:

Sie haben vielleicht recht	*You may be right/You are perhaps right*
Könnten Sie mir vielleicht erklären, wie lange die Aufführung dauert?	*Could you perhaps explain to me how long the performance lasts?*

- **wohl** is to do with probability and means usually *I suppose, probably, possibly*:

Sie wissen wohl, was geschah	*I suppose you know what happened*
Wer hat diesen Brief wohl gesandt?	*Who can possibly have sent this letter?*

As an adverb it usually implies *well, fully* or strengthens an affirmative:

Schlaf wohl!	*Sleep well?*
Hast du gut geschlafen? – Jawohl!	*Did you sleep well? – Yes indeed!*
Das habe ich mir wohl überlegt	*I have considered that fully*

- **zwar** used with *aber* has the idea of *although, though, it is true*:

Sie ist zwar sehr schön, aber sie kann nicht spielen	*Though she is very beautiful, she can't act*

Used with **und** before it, it means *namely, in fact, actually*:

Er kommt heute abend, und zwar um halb neun	*He is coming this evening, actually at half past eight*

2.13 CONJUNCTIONS

A conjunction is usually a small word used to join clauses together to make longer, often more complex sentences. There are basically two types in German: co-ordinating conjunctions and subordinating conjunctions.

CO-ORDINATING CONJUNCTIONS

Co-ordinating conjunctions link main clauses and are followed by main clause word order. (see 2.15 for the full details about word order). Most of them can also link single words or phrases. A few of them can only be used in this way and cannot link clauses. Here is a list of the ones you need to know for A/AS-level:

aber	*but*	nämlich	*as*
allein	*but*	oder	*or*
bald … bald	*now … now*	sondern	*but*
beziehungsweise	*or*	sowie	*as well as*
denn	*as, for*	sowohl als/wie	*as well as*
doch	*but*	teils … teils	*partly … partly*
entweder … oder	*either … or*	und	*and*
jedoch	*but*	weder … noch	*neither … nor*

Examples:

- **aber, allein, doch, jedoch** all usually mean *but, however*:

  Ich habe davon gehört, aber ich glaube es nicht — *I have heard about it but I do not believe it*

  Meine Mutter war schlank, meine Schwester aber war dick — *My mother was slim, but my sister was fat*

  Dieses Buch ist gut, aber teuer — *This book is good but dear*

  Er verlor jedoch die Nerven — *He lost his nerve however*

  N.B. *allein*, *doch* and *jedoch* are found mostly in literature as an alternative to *aber*.

- **bald … bald** *now … now*:

  Es ist ihm bald kalt, bald warm — *Now he is cold, now hot*

- **denn, nämlich** *as, because, for*:

  Er kann heute nicht kommen, denn er ist viel zu krank — *He cannot come today, as/because/for he is much too ill*

  N.B. A '*denn* clause' cannot begin a sentence; it is a main clause and it can be replaced by a clause with *nämlich*:

  Er kann heute nicht kommen, er ist nämlich zu krank — *He cannot come today, as he is much too ill/he is namely too ill*

- **oder, beziehungsweise, entweder … oder** *either … or*:

  Wir können heute abend ins Kino gehen, oder wir können zu Hause bleiben — *We can go to the cinema this evening or we can stay at home*

  - **beziehungsweise** is used to indicate mutually exclusive alternatives:

    Es kostet 200 DM bzw.175 DM mit Rabatt — *It costs 200 marks or 175 with discount*
    The abbreviation *bzw.* is common in written German.

  - **entweder … oder** *either … or* offers alternatives which are mutually exclusive:

    Nächstes Jahr reist er entweder nach Frankreich oder nach Spanien — *He is either travelling to France or Spain next year*

- **sondern** means *but* and is used after a negative to contradict:

  Sie ist nicht schön, sondern häßlich — *She is not beautiful, but ugly*

  N.B. the similar phrase **nicht nur … sondern auch** *not only … but also*:

  Sie ist nicht nur reich, sondern auch gierig — *She is not only rich but greedy too*

- **teils … teils** *partly … partly*:

  Das Wetter wird heute teils sonnig, teils wolkig — *The weather today will be partly sunny, partly cloudy*

- **und, sowie, sowohl … als/wie (auch)** *as well as* – **und** is the usual word for *and*, the others are really only used in written German to emphasise the connection between two elements in a stronger way than *und*:

  Mein Onkel und mein Bruder werden   *My uncle and my brother will*
   nächste Woche ankommen   *be arriving next week*
  Goethe hat sowohl Dramen wie/als   *Goethe has written plays as*
   Gedichte geschrieben   *well as poetry*
  N.B. *auch* frequently follows *sowie, sowohl … als/wie…*

- **weder … noch** *neither … nor*
  Er ißt weder Fisch noch Fleisch   *He eats neither fish nor meat*

SUBORDINATING CONJUNCTIONS

Subordinating conjunctions introduce subordinate clauses in which the finite verb is placed at the end of the clause. The difference between a main clause and a subordinate clause is that a **main clause** can stand on its own. It is independent of any other part of the sentence. Frequently it is a sentence itself.

'Paul helps his father in the garden' is a main clause, statement or sentence. But 'If he finishes his work…' is a **subordinate clause** which demands a follow-on statement to complete the sense. The most important of the subordinating conjunctions are listed below:

als	*when, as*	seit(dem)	*since*
als ob	*as if*	sobald	*as soon as*
als wenn	*as if*	sowie	*as soon as*
auch wenn	*even if*	solange	*as long as*
bevor	*before*	so daß	*so that, with the result that*
ehe	*before*	sooft	*as often as*
bis	*until, till*	während	*while*
da	*as, since*	wenn	*when, if*
daß	*that*	wenn auch	
damit	*in order that, so that*	selbst wenn	} *even if*
falls	*in case that, if*	wann	*when* (indirect question)
indem	*while*	weil	*because*
nachdem	*after*	wie	*as*
ob	*whether, if*	wie wenn	*as if, though*
obgleich			
obschon	} *although*		
obwohl			

These can be grouped according to their uses as follows:

Conjunctions of time

als, bevor, ehe, bis, indem, nachdem, seit(dem), sobald, sowie, solange, sooft, während, wenn, wie, wann

Examples:

- **als** can mean *when* or *as* and always refers to a single occurrence in the past:
  Als er in Münster ankam, holten wir ihn am Bahnhof ab
  When he arrived in Münster we met him at the station

- **wenn** can mean *when (ever)* or *if* (especially in conditional clauses). It is used for *when* in clauses referring to present or future time, or repeated occasions in the past, where it has the alternative meaning *whenever*:
  Wenn er krank ist, muß er zu Hause bleiben
  When he is ill, he has to stay at home
  Wenn er zum Bahnhof ging, pflegte er immer eine Zeitung zu kaufen
  When(ever) he went to the station, he used always to buy a newspaper

- **wann** *when* introducing an indirect question:
  Er fragte mich, wann der Zug abfahre   *He asked me when the train departed*

- **bevor** before:
  Bevor er zu Bett ging, trank er ein Glas Milch
  Before he went to bed, he drank a glass of milk

- **ehe** is simply a literary alternative to *bevor*

- **indem** is now used only to link two simultaneous actions and to express '*by ...ing something*':
  Er wurde naß, indem er ins Wasser fiel   *He got wet by falling into the water*

Conjunctions which indicate a cause or reason

- **da, weil** – the difference between these two is the same in German as is conveyed by the English meaning *as* or *since*, and *because*:
  Da er in Bonn übernachtet, kann er meinen Brieffreund dort besuchen
  As/Since he is staying overnight in Bonn, he can visit my penfriend there
  Er konnte nicht ausgehen, weil er so krank war
  He could not go out, because he was so ill

Conjunctions introducing clauses of purpose and result

- **damit** *so that, in order that* introduces a clause expressing purpose:
  Ich gab ihr Unterricht in Französisch, damit sie sich mit den Franzosen verstehen konnte
  I taught her French in order that she could get on with the French people

- **so daß** *so that, such that* introduces a clause of result:
  Er war sehr krank, so daß er nicht kommen konnte
  He was very ill, so that (with the result that) he could not come

Conjunctions introducing conditional clauses

falls, wenn, wenn ... auch, auch wenn, selbst wenn

- **falls** can replace **wenn** meaning *if* in situations where there could be some ambiguity in the meaning of *wenn:*
  Falls er mich anruft, (so) sage ich dir Bescheid   *If he rings me, I shall let you know*

- **Wenn ... auch, auch wenn, selbst wenn** all mean *even if:*
  Wenn ich ihn auch morgen sähe, würde er mit mir nicht sprechen wollen
  Even if I saw him tomorrow, he would not want to speak to me

Conjunctions of manner or concession

- **als ob** *as if* is dealt with in the section on the subjunctive.

- **obgleich, obwohl, obschon** all mean *although*. **Obwohl** is the one in current use in modern German, though you will find the others in formal written registers:
  Obwohl es noch dunkel war, bin ich sofort aufgestanden
  Although it was still dark, I got up immediately

2.14 PREPOSITIONS

Prepositions are usually small words which govern nouns or pronouns. They normally precede them and express a relationship between them and other nouns and pronouns indicating *where, how* or *when* something is happening. In both English and German prepositions are used in a variety of ways and the rules governing their use are very diverse. There is no short cut to mastering the use of prepositions in either language other than to learn which case they 'take' in German and the main ways in which they are used.

What you must do is learn by heart which prepositions belong to each group. In this section they have been grouped according to the case which they govern. The literal and figurative senses of each preposition have been kept together as have the uses with verbs. It is important not to be overwhelmed by the uses of prepositions. Be systematic in your learning and try to use them in all aspects of your work.

PREPOSITIONS TAKING THE ACCUSATIVE ONLY

Common		Less common	
bis	*as far as, till*	per	*by*
durch	*through, by*	pro	*per*
entlang*	*along*	wider	*against*
für	*for*		
gegen	*against, towards*		
ohne	*without*		
um	*round, about, at*		

*entlang is sometimes used, though rarely, followed by a dative.

Examples:

- **bis**

Er bleibt bis Montag	*He is staying till next Monday*
Bis morgen!	*See you tomorrow!*

  N.B. When *bis* is followed by a noun with an article or other determining word, it is linked with another preposition which determines the case:

Sie ging bis an die Tür	*She went right up to the door*
Wir gingen bis zum Ufer des Rheins	*We walked as far as the bank of the Rhine*

- **durch**

Wir gingen durch den Wald	*We walked through the wood*
Er wurde durch eine Erkältung gewarnt	*He was warned by a cold*

  (For details about the use of **durch** in the passive see pp116–118)

- **entlang**

Er fuhr die Straße entlang	*He drove along the street*

  When used before a noun **entlang** can be followed by the dative, but only when it is indicating position alongside an extended object like a frontier.

Wir stationieren Truppen entlang der Grenze	*We are stationing troops along the border*

- **für**

Er arbeitet für sie	*He works for her*
Tag für Tag	*day by day*
sich für etwas begeistern	*to be enthusiastic about something*
jemandem für etwas danken	*to thank someone for something*
sich für etwas entscheiden	*to decide on something*
halten für	*to consider (that)*
sich für etwas interessieren	*to be interested in something*
für jemanden/etwas sorgen	*to look after someone/something*

- **gegen**

Wir laufen gegen den Wind	*We are running against the wind*
Sie gewannen gegen alle Erwartungen	*They won against all expectations*
Er fährt gegen Osten	*He is driving towards the east (eastwards)*
Gegen acht Uhr muß ich abfahren	*I must leave about eight o'clock*

- **ohne**

Er kam ohne mich	*He came without me*

- **um**

Sie saßen um den Tisch	*They were sitting round the table*
Er kommt um acht Uhr an	*He is arriving at eight o'clock*
Er kommt um Weihnachten	*He is coming around Christmas*

  N.B. *um* means 'at' with actual clock times, but 'around' or 'about' with other time phrases.

sich um jemanden ängstigen	*to be worried about someone*
sich um etwas bemühen	*to take trouble over something*
sich um etwas handeln (impersonal)	*to be a question of*
jemanden um etwas bitten	*to ask someone for something*
um etwas kämpfen	*to fight for something*
um etwas konkurrieren	*to compete for something*
ums Leben kommen	*to die*
sich um jemanden/etwas kümmern	*to take care of someone/something*
sich um jemanden/etwas sorgen	*to be worried about someone/something*
um Geld spielen	*to play for money*
um etwas streiken	*to strike over something*

- **per**

Mainly used in commercial terms:

per Adresse, per Einschreiben	*by recorded delivery*
per Anhalter fahren	*to hitchhike*

- **pro**

Sie kosten 50 Pfennig pro Stück	*They cost 50 pfennig each*
20 Mark pro Person	*20 marks per person*
Die Reisekosten sind 30DM pro Tag	*Travelling expenses are 30 marks per day*

- **wider**

Nowadays only found in set phrases:

wider meinen Willen	*against my will*
wider alles Erwarten	*against all expectations*
wider mein besseres Wissen	*against my better judgement*

PREPOSITIONS GOVERNING THE DATIVE ONLY

Common

aus	*out of, made of*	nach	*to, after, according to*
außer	*except for, out of*	seit	*since, for*
bei	*by, at, at the house of*	von	*from, of, by*
gegenüber**	*opposite, towards*	zu	*to, at, for, towards*
mit	*with, by*		

Less common

ab	*from*	zufolge	*according to*
binnen	*within*	mitsamt	*together with*
dank	*thanks to*	nahe	*near to*
entgegen**	*contrary to*	nebst	*in addition to*
entsprechend	*according to*	zuliebe*	*for the sake of*
laut	*according to*	zuwider*	*contrary to*

[handwritten: to do with (not in der Nähe)]

** may precede or follow the noun
* follows the noun

- **aus**

Er lief aus dem Haus	*He ran out of the house*
Er kommt aus Bonn	*He comes from Bonn*
Die Handtasche ist aus Leder	*The handbag is made of leather*
aus diesem Grunde	*for this reason*
aus etwas bestehen	*to consist of something*
aus etwas entnehmen	*to infer from something*
sich aus etwas ergeben	*to result from something*
aus etwas folgern	*to conclude from something*
aus etwas schließen	*to conclude from something*

- **außer**

Keiner außer ihm	*nobody except him*
Ich war außer mir	*I was beside myself*
Die Maschine ist außer Betrieb	*The machine is out of service*
außer Atem, Gefahr, Sicht, Übung	*out of breath, danger, sight, practice*

- **bei**

Potsdam liegt bei Berlin	*Potsdam is near/by Berlin*
Er stand bei dem Fenster	*He was standing by the window*
Er wohnt bei uns	*He is living at our house/with us*
Ich habe kein Geld bei mir	*I have no money on me*
beim Frühstück/Mittagessen	*at breakfast/lunch*
bei schlechtem Wetter	*in bad weather*

- **gegenüber**

Er wohnt gegenüber dem Rathaus	*He lives opposite the town hall*
Sie saß ihm gegenüber	*She sat opposite him*

gegenüber can come before or after the noun; it tends to follow words denoting people, in other instances it precedes the word it governs:

Ihm gegenüber bist du ganz groß	*Compared to him you are quite tall*
Er ist dem Polizisten gegenüber sehr höflich	*He is very polite towards the policeman*

- **mit**

Er kam mit mir	*He came with me*
Er schrieb mit einem Bleistift	*He wrote with a pencil*
Sie sprach mit lauter Stimme	*She spoke in a loud voice*

Meaning *by* in phrases of transport:

mit der Bahn/dem Zug	*by rail/train*
mit dem Auto/Bus	*by car/bus*
mit dem Flugzeug	*by plane*
mit der Post	*by post*
mit der Luftpost	*by airmail*

Other phrases:

mit dreißig Jahren	*at the age of thirty*
mit der Zeit	*in (the course of) time*
etwas mit Absicht tun	*to do something on purpose*
mit etwas anfangen	*to make a start on something*
mit etwas aufhören	*to stop doing something*
sich mit jemandem/etwas abfinden	*to come to terms with someone/something*
sich mit etwas befassen	*to deal with something*
sich mit etwas beschäftigen	*to occupy oneself with something*
jemandem mit etwas drohen	*to threaten someone with something*
mit jemandem/etwas rechnen	*to reckon on/with someone/something*
mit jemandem telefonieren	*to speak on the phone with someone*
mit jemandem übereinstimmen	*to agree with someone*
sich mit jemandem unterhalten	*to talk to someone*
etwas mit etwas vergleichen	*to compare something with something*
sich mit jemandem verheiraten	*to get married to someone*
sich mit jemandem verloben	*to get engaged to someone*
jemanden mit etwas versehen	*to provide someone with something*
mit jemandem zusammenstoßen	*to collide with someone*

- **nach**

Meaning *to* a place with neuter names of countries and towns with no article:

Er fuhr nach Berlin, nach Italien	*He went to Berlin, to Italy*
Er ging nach Hause	*He went home*

Other phrases with the meaning *towards, in the direction of*:

Er fuhr nach Norden/Süden nach Osten/Westen	*He travelled northwards/southwards eastwards/westwards*
Er ging nach oben, nach unten	*He went upstairs, downstairs*
Er ging nach rechts, nach links	*He went to the right, to the left*

Meaning *after*:

Nach einer Weile schlief sie ein	*After a while she fell asleep*
Er kam nach mir an	*He arrived after me*

Meaning *according to*:

Nach seinem Brief ist er krank	*According to his letter he is ill*

In this sense it often follows the noun it governs:

Meiner Meinung nach	*in my opinion*
dem Gesetz nach	*according to the law*

Other phrases:

sich nach etwas erkundigen	*to ask about something*
sich nach jemandem erkundigen	*to enquire after someone*
nach jemandem fragen	*to ask after someone*
nach etwas greifen	*to make a grab for*
nach den Sternen greifen	*to reach for the stars*
nach etwas hungern	*to hunger for something*
nach etwas riechen	*to smell of something*
nach etwas/jemandem rufen	*to call for something/someone*
nach etwas schmecken	*to taste of something*
nach jemandem schreien	*to shout for someone*
nach etwas schreien	*to cry out for something*
sich nach etwas/jemandem sehnen	*to long/pine for something/someone*
nach etwas streben	*to strive for something*
nach etwas suchen	*to search for something*
nach dem Arzt telefonieren	*to phone for the doctor*
nach etwas verlangen	*to ask/long/crave for something*

● **seit**

Seit dem Krieg wohnt er in Bonn	*Since the war he has been living in Bonn*

N.B. Beware the tense in these phrases:

Er wohnt seit vier Jahren in Köln	***He has been living** in Cologne for four years*
Seit einem Jahr **wohnte er** bei uns	***He had been living** with us for one year*

● **von**

Wir fuhren von Paris nach Berlin	*We travelled from Paris to Berlin*
Er war ein Mann von zwanzig Jahren	*He was a man of twenty years of age*
Sie war eine Frau von kleiner Gestalt	*She was a woman of small stature*
von Zeit zu Zeit	*from time to time*
von Anfang bis Ende	*from beginning to end*
von Anfang an	*right from the start*
von heute auf morgen	*from one day to the next, overnight*
Sie tat es von selbst	*She did it of her own accord*
Der Brief wurde von ihm geschrieben	*The letter was written by him*

(See pp116–118 for use of *von* in the passive.)

jemanden von etwas abhalten	*to keep someone from something*
von etwas abhängen	*to be dependent on something*
von etwas befreien	*to free from something*
sich von jemandem/etwas distanzieren	*to dissociate oneself from someone/something*
sich von etwas erholen	*to recover from something*
von etwas erzählen	*to tell of/about something*
von etwas hören	*to hear of/about something*
von etwas lesen	*to read about something*
von jemandem/etwas träumen	*to dream about/of someone/something*

● **zu**

Direction towards meaning *to*:

Er ging zum Bahnhof	*He went to the station*
Er ging zum Arzt	*He went to the doctor's*

Meaning *at* in some expressions of time, place and price/measure:

zu Ostern, zu Weihnachten	*at Easter, at Christmas*
zu dieser Zeit	*at this time*
zu Hause	*at home*

zu beiden Seiten	*on either side*
Briefmarken zu 60 Pfennig	*stamps at 60 pfennigs each*
zum halben Preis	*at half price*
ein Päckchen Mehl zu 500 Gramm	*a 500 gram bag of flour*

Meaning *for* denoting a purpose:

Stoff zu einem neuen Kleid	*material for a new dress*
Was gibt es heute zum Frühstück?	*What's for breakfast today?*
Ich gebrauche dieses Messer zum Brotschneiden	*I use this knife for slicing bread*
zum Beispiel, zum Spaß	*for example, for/as a joke*

Other phrases:

Er sah zum Fenster hinaus	*he looked out of the window*
zu Fuß, zu Pferd	*on foot, on horseback*
zu meinem Erstaunen	*to my surprise*
zu seiner großen Freude	*to his great pleasure*
jemandem zur Seite stehen	*to give someone one's support*
jemanden zu etwas berechtigen	*to entitle someone to something*
jemanden zu etwas einladen	*to invite someone to something*
zu etwas führen	*to lead to something*
jemanden zu etwas herausfordern	*to challenge someone to something*
zu etwas neigen	*to have a tendency to something*
jemanden zu etwas veranlassen	*to lead someone to something, to cause someone to do something*
jemanden zu etwas verführen	*to seduce/tempt someone to something*

PREPOSITIONS GOVERNING THE ACCUSATIVE OR THE DATIVE

an	*at, by, on, to*	in	*in, into*	unter	*under, below, among*
auf	*on, at, in*	neben	*near, beside*	vor	*in front of, before*
hinter	*behind*	über	*over, about*	zwischen	*between*

These prepositions in their literal meanings refer mainly to places. The general rule as to which case should be used after them is straightforward. If the prepositional phrase explains **where** something is happening, then the **dative** must be used. If it indicates place **where to**, **motion towards**, then the **accusative** must be used. Look at these examples:

Er ging an **die** See (accusative)	*He went to the seaside*
Er wohnt an **der** See (dative)	*He lives by the sea/at the seaside*
Er legt das Buch auf **den** Tisch (accusative)	*He puts the book on (to) the table*
Das Buch liegt auf **dem** Tisch (dative)	*The book is on the table*

Sie setzt sich auf **eine** Bank (accusative) **im** Schatten (dative) einer Eiche
She sits down on a bench in the shade of an oak tree
In this example *sitting down on(to)* is 'motion towards' the bench while *in the shade* is 'place where'.
Be careful with verbs of motion because there are instances when there is no **motion towards**:

Er ging neben **seinem Bruder** die Straße entlang	*He was walking beside his brother along the street*

This is **dative** because he is not walking towards his brother but alongside him.
Similarly: Der Vogel kreiste über **dem Baum**   *The bird circled over the tree*
The circling is static above the tree, so therefore the **dative** must be used in German.

Let us now have a more detailed look at each of these prepositions and their uses with each case separately.

- **an** (plus dative)
  The main meaning of **an** is *on* in the sense of against a vertical surface, as opposed to *on top of* which is **auf** in German. In this way **an** can also mean *at*:
  Das Bild hängt an der Wand   *The picture is hanging on the wall*

Er steht an der Tür	*He is standing at the door*
Er wartet an der Bushaltestelle	*He is waiting at the bus-stop*
Er wohnt an der Mosel	*He lives by/on the Mosel*

On the underside of is also **an:**

Die Lampe hängt an der Decke	*The lamp is hanging from the ceiling*
Die Sterne funkeln am Himmel	*The stars are twinkling in the sky*

To be employed *at* an institution is **an:**

Er ist Lehrer am Gymnasium	*He is a teacher at the grammar school*

In expressions of time **an** is used with days and parts of the day:

am nächsten Morgen, am Wochenende *the next morning, at the weekend*

Other useful phrases:

Er ging an dem Rathaus vorbei	*He walked past the town hall*
an Bord	*on board*
an seiner Stelle	*in his place*
an etwas arbeiten	*to work on something*
jemanden an etwas erkennen	*to recognise someone by something*
an etwas erkranken	*to fall ill with something*
sich an etwas freuen	*to get pleasure from something*
an etwas gewinnen	*to gain in something*
an jemandem/etwas hängen	*to be very attached to someone/something*
Er hängt am Leben	*He clings to life*
an etwas leiden	*to suffer from something*
an etwas mitwirken	*to play a part in something*
an jemandem/etwas riechen	*to sniff (at) someone/something*
an etwas sterben	*to die of/from something*
an etwas teilnehmen	*to take part in something*
an Charme verlieren	*to lose some charm*
Es fehlt mir an Mut	*I am lacking in courage*

- **an** (plus accusative)

Er ging ans Fenster	*He went to the window*
Wir fuhren an die Küste	*We drove to the coast*
Er schrieb einen Brief an mich	*He wrote a letter to me*
Er verdient an die 6000DM im Monat	*He earns about 6000 marks a month*
an etwas/jemanden denken	*to think of something/someone*
Sie erinnert mich an meine Schwester	*She reminds me of my sister*
Ich erinnere mich an meine Schwester	*I remember my sister*
sich an etwas/jemanden gewöhnen	*to get used to something/someone*
an jemanden/etwas glauben	*to believe in someone/something*

- **auf** (plus dative)

auf means literally *on top of* which in German is used in a number of phrases where in English we use *in* or *at*:

Er war auf dem Lande	*He was in the country*
Der Junge spielte auf der Straße	*The boy was playing in the street*
Die Kühe waren auf der Wiese	*The cows were in the meadow*
Er stand auf dem Platz	*He was standing in the square*
Wir sind auf der Post/auf der Bank	*We are at the post office/bank*
Er studiert auf der Universität	*He is studying at the university*
Er ist auf dem Rückweg nach Bonn	*He is on the way back to Bonn*
Er wurde auf frischer Tat ertappt	*He was caught in the act*
auf der anderen Seite	*on the other hand*
auf etwas beruhen	*to be based on something*
auf etwas bestehen	*to insist on something*

- **auf** (plus accusative)

Means literally *on to* and expresses **motion towards:**

Er ging auf die Post/die Bank	*He was walking to the post office/bank*
Er lief auf die Straße	*He ran into the street*

Er stellte die Flasche auf den Tisch	*He put the bottle on(to) the table*
Er fährt auf eine Woche an die See	*He is going to the seaside for a week*
Sie kam auf mich zu	*She came up to me*
Er hat auf deutsch gesprochen	*He spoke in German*
auf jeden Fall	*in any case*
auf diese Weise	*in this way*
auf eigene Gefahr	*at one's own risk*
auf eigene Kosten	*at one's own expense*
auf den ersten Blick	*at first sight*
auf etwas achten	*to pay attention to something*
auf jemanden achten	*to keep an eye on someone*
auf etwas/jemanden aufpassen	*to look after someone/something*
sich auf etwas/jemanden beziehen	*to refer to something/someone*
auf etwas drängen	*to press for something*
sich auf etwas/jemanden erstrecken	*to apply to something/someone*
auf etwas folgen	*to come after something*
sich auf etwas freuen	*to look forward to something*
sich auf etwas gründen	*to be based on something*
jemanden auf etwas hinweisen	*to point out something to somebody*
auf etwas hoffen	*to hope for something*
sich auf etwas konzentrieren	*to concentrate on something*
auf etwas reagieren	*to react to something*
auf jemanden/etwas schimpfen	*to curse about someone/something*
sich auf etwas spezialisieren	*to specialise in something*
sich auf etwas/jemanden verlassen	*to rely on something/someone*
auf etwas/jemanden verzichten	*to do without something/someone*
auf etwas/jemanden warten	*to wait for something/someone*
auf etwas/jemanden zählen	*to count on something/someone*
auf etwas zurückkommen	*to come back/refer to something*

- **hinter** (plus dative)

Er stand hinter seiner Frau	*He stood behind his wife*
Ich ging hinter meinen Brüdern her	*I was walking behind my brothers*
	(place where, therefore dative)

- **hinter** (plus accusative)

Er fuhr den Wagen hinter das Haus	*He drove the car behind the house*
	(place where to, therefore accusative)

- **in** (plus dative)

Means basically *inside*, within something:

Er ist in der Stadt, im Kino, in der Kirche	*He is in town, in the cinema, in the church*
Er ist in der Nähe	*He is in the neighbourhood, nearby*
Er arbeitet im Freien	*He works in the open air/out of doors*
Er lebt im Ausland	*He lives abroad*
im Fernsehen, im Radio	*on television, on radio*
in der Schule, im Konzert, in der Kirche	*at school, at the concert, at church*
im ersten Stock	*on the first floor*
in diesem Augenblick	*at this moment*
heute in acht Tagen	*a week today*
im allgemeinen	*in general*
im Durchschnitt	*on average*
nicht im geringsten	*not in the slightest*
in gewissem Maße	*to a certain extent*
in diesem Zusammenhang	*in this context*
sich in etwas täuschen	*to be mistaken about something*

- **in** (plus accusative)

Conveys the idea of *into* something:

Er fuhr in die Schweiz	*He went to Switzerland*
Er reiste ins Ausland	*He travelled abroad*

Er ging ins Theater, ins Büro	*He went to the theatre, to the office*
Ich schnitt mich in den Finger	*I cut my finger*
in die Schule/die Kirche/die Stadt gehen	*to go to school/church/town*
ins Reine schreiben	*to make a fair copy*
ins Deutsche übersetzen	*to translate into German*
etwas in Gebrauch nehmen	*to put something into use*
sich in Bewegung setzen	*to begin to move*
sich in etwas mischen	*to meddle in something*
sich in jemanden verlieben	*to fall in love with someone*
sich in etwas vertiefen	*to become engrossed/absorbed in something*

- **neben**

Means *next to* or *beside* followed by the **dative** and it indicates 'place where':

Er saß neben mir	*He was sitting next to me/beside me*
Ich ging neben meinem Onkel her	*I was walking beside my uncle* (place where)

It can also mean *apart from/besides*:

Neben meiner kleinen Schwester waren alle Anwesenden Erwachsene	*Apart from my little sister all those present were adults*

- **über** (plus dative)

Means *over, above* or *across* and refers to position only when followed by the **dative**:

Das Bild hängt über dem Sofa	*The picture is hanging over the sofa*
Er wohnt über der Grenze	*He lives across the border*
über dem Meeresspiegel	*above sea level*

- **über** (plus accusative)

Implying movement it means *above, over, across* or *beyond*:

Er hängte das Bild über den Tisch	*He hung the picture over the table*
Sie liefen über die Straße	*They ran across the street*
Er ist über Franfurt geflogen	*He flew via Franfurt*
Er blieb über Nacht	*He stayed overnight*
Kinder über acht Jahre	*children over eight*

It can also mean *about/concerning*:

Er hatte eine Ansicht über Straßenunfälle	*He had a view about road accidents*
sich über etwas/jemanden ärgern	*to be annoyed about something/someone*
sich bei jemandem über etwas beklagen	*to complain about something to someone*
über etwas denken	*to think about something*
sich über etwas/jemanden freuen	*to be pleased about something/someone*
jemanden über etwas informieren	*to inform someone about something*
über etwas nachdenken	*to think over something*
über etwas schreiben	*to write about something*
über etwas sprechen	*to discuss something*
sich über etwas streiten	*to argue over something*
über etwas urteilen	*to judge something*
über etwas verfügen	*to have something at one's disposal*
über etwas wissen	*to know about something*
sich über etwas wundern	*to be surprised at something*

- **unter** (plus dative)

Conveys the idea of *underneath, below* or *beneath*:

Der Hund lag unter dem Tisch	*The dog lay under the table*
200 Meter unter dem Gipfel	*200 metres below the summit*
Das Paket wiegt unter einem Kilo	*The parcel weighs less than a kilo*

It can have two other meanings – *among* and to indicate circumstances:

Unter Freunden geschieht das nicht	*That does not happen among friends*
unter diesen Umständen	*in these circumstances*
unter allen Umständen	*in any case*
unter dieser Bedingung	*on this condition*
unter vier Augen	*in private*
unter anderem	*amongst other things*

- **unter** (plus accusative)
  Means *under* indicating 'place where to':
  Er schob den Stuhl unter den Tisch   *He pushed the chair under the table*

- **vor** (plus dative)
  Referring to place it means *in front of*:
  Er stand vor der Tür   *He stood in front of the door*

  Referring to time it means *before, ago*:
  vor vielen Jahren   *many years ago*
  vor kurzem   *a short time ago*
  vor dem Krieg   *before the war*

  It can indicate a cause or reason usually meaning *for* or *with*:
  Sie tanzte vor Freude   *She danced for joy*

  Other phrases:
  jemanden vor etwas bewahren   *to protect someone from something*
  sich vor etwas ekeln   *to be digusted by something*
  vor jemandem fliehen   *to flee from someone*
  sich vor jemandem/etwas fürchten   *to be afraid of someone/something*
  Angst vor jemandem/etwas haben   *to be afraid of someone/something*
  sich vor jemandem/etwas hüten   *to beware of someone/something*
  jemanden vor jemandem/etwas retten   *to save somebody from someone/something*
  sich vor jemandem schämen   *to be ashamed in front of someone*
  sich vor jemandem/etwas verbergen   *to hide oneself from someone/something*
  vor etwas warnen   *to warn of something*

- **zwischen**
  Means basically *between* and refers to 'place where' when followed by the **dative**:
  Er saß zwischen meiner Mutter und mir   *He sat between my mother and me*
  Er ging zwischen seinen Eltern her   *He was walking between his parents*
  Die Blumen wuchsen zwischen   *The flowers were growing amongst*
    den Bäumen   *the trees*

  When followed by the **accusative** it indicates direction:
  Ich setzte mich zwischen meinen   *I sat down between my uncle and my aunt*
    Onkel und meine Tante

PREPOSITIONS GOVERNING THE GENITIVE ONLY

Most common

(an)statt	*instead of*	trotz	*in spite of*
während	*during*	wegen	*on account of, because of*

These are normally followed by the genitive, but are found with the dative in colloquial speech.

Less common, referring to place

außerhalb	*outside*	innerhalb	*inside*
oberhalb	*above*	unterhalb	*below*
beiderseits	*on both sides of*	diesseits	*on this side of*
jenseits	*on the other side of, beyond*	unweit	*not far from*

This group can often be followed by *von* plus the dative rather than the genitive.

- **(an)statt**
  Statt is more common than **anstatt**, both mean exactly the same – *instead of*:
  Statt eines Mantels trug er nur   *Instead of an overcoat he wore only*
    eine Jacke   *a jacket*

- **trotz**
  trotz des schlechten Wetters   *inspite of the bad weather*

- **während**
  während der Sommerferien   *during the summer holidays*
  N.B. *während* cannot be used to denote a period of time as in *during the day*; this must be rendered in German by 'am Tag'; similarly *during the evening* will be 'am Abend' etc.

- **wegen**
  Wegen seines Vaters habe ich nichts gesagt *Because of his father I said nothing*
  Note: **meinetwegen** *on my account*, **deinetwegen** *on your account*, **seinetwegen** *on his account*, **unsertwegen** *on our behalf*, and so on.

- **außerhalb** and **innerhalb**
  Both of these can refer to place or time:

  Er wohnt außerhalb der Stadt *He lives outside the town*
  Außerhalb der Sprechstunden ist der *Outside the consultation time the doctor is*
  Arzt frei *free/available*
  Innerhalb dieses Hauses wohnen drei *Three families live inside this house*
  Familien
  Innerhalb eines Monats muß das Haus *The house must be built inside a month*
  gebaut werden

- **oberhalb** and **unterhalb**
  Both of these mean more specifically *above* and *below, underneath* than *über* and *unter* referring to position:

  Die Burg liegt oberhalb des Dorfes *The castle is situated above the village*
  Unterhalb der Baumgrenze wachsen *All kinds of flowers grow below the*
  allerlei Blumen *tree line*

- **beiderseits, diesseits** and **jenseits**
  These three refer specifically to place:

  Beiderseits der Straße sind große *There are large houses on both sides of*
  Häuser *the street*
  Diesseits und jenseits der spanischen *On this side and the other side of*
  Grenze liegen die Pyrenäen *the Spanish border lie the Pyrenees*

- **unweit**
  Unweit des Bahnhofs ereignete sich *Not far from the railway station a road*
  ein Verkehrsunfall *accident occurred*

Least common

There are some forty other prepositions which take the genitive. They are mostly used in formal registers in written German and in official or commercial contexts. A selection of them with their main meaning is listed here:

angesichts	*in view of*	anläßlich	*on the occasion of*
ausschließlich	*exclusive of*	einschließlich	*including*
gelegentlich	*on the occasion of*	halber*	*for the sake of*
hinsichtlich	*with regard to*	links	*on/to the left of*
namens	*in the name of*	rechts	*on/to the right of*
seitens	*on the part of*	seitlich	*to/at the side of*
um...willen*	*for the sake of*	vorbehaltlich	*subject to*
zugunsten	*for the benefit of*		

* **halber** follows the noun:
Er ist Geschäfte halber verreist *He is away on account of his business*
*um meines Bruders willen *for my brother's sake*

Please note both *halber* and *um ... willen* can be used with the personal pronouns to form words like 'um meinetwillen' *for my sake* etc. and 'meinethalben' *for my sake* etc. This is the same construction as 'meinetwegen' above. Note *halber* becomes *halben* in this instance.

2.15 WORD ORDER

The rules concerning word order in German are very important. They are formal and rarely alter. Unlike English, German does not depend on the order of the words to convey the sense. Reverse the positions of the subject and the direct object of a verb in English and you change the meaning completely. Look at these simple examples:

- The girl saw the man in town
- The man saw the girl in town

Now look at these two German sentences:

- Das Mädchen sah den Mann in der Stadt
- Den Mann sah das Mädchen in der Stadt

In German both sentences mean exactly the same and both are correct German, even though the word order has changed. The reason for this is that the case endings in German tell us what the subject and the direct object of the verb are. **den Mann** in both German sentences is in the accusative case and is therefore the direct object not the subject of the verb, **das Mädchen** is the subject of the verb in each sentence because it is in the nominative case. From this very simple example we can see that the sense is not dependent on the word order in German as it is in English.

RULES GOVERNING WORD ORDER

The rules of word order in German are bound up with the structure of each clause and the position of the finite verb and any other part of the verb, e.g. infinitives, past participles or separable prefixes which the clause may contain. The framework of the clause is determined by the fixed position of these various elements of the verb within it.

There are basically three types of clause structure where the position of the verb and its parts are fixed:

Main clause statements

In a main clause statement the finite verb must be the second idea. Frequently the subject will be the first idea:

Der junge Mann **stand** vor dem Rathaus. *The young man was standing in front of the town hall.*

If the subject is not the first idea in a main clause statement, then the subject must follow the finite verb in what is known as inverted word order, or **inversion**. The finite verb remains the second idea.

Gestern **stand** der junge Mann vor dem Rathaus. *Yesterday the young man was standing in front of the town hall.*

Questions and commands

In both questions and commands the finite verb is the first idea. In a question **inversion** occurs because the subject follows the finite verb; it is also possible for an interrogative word or phrase to come before the finite verb. Look at these examples:

Geht sie bald nach Hause? *Is she going home soon?*

Was **sieht er** unter dem Tisch? *What does he see under the table?*

In a command the verb is the first idea or element in the clause:

Gib mir das Buch! *Give me the book!*

Öffnen Sie doch das Paket! *Do open the parcel!*

Subordinate clauses

In a subordinate clause the finite verb is placed at the end. This is known as **transposed word order**:

Der Junge war nicht in der Schule, weil er krank **war**. *The boy was not in school, because he was ill.*

All of these examples are uncomplicated and only use simple tenses. What happens when we use complex sentences and compound tenses?

The tenses of a verb, as we have seen, can be formed with auxiliary verbs and the infinitive or the past participle of the verb concerned. Some verbs also have a separable prefix and we therefore need to know the rules about the position of these parts of the verb in any clause framework.

The rule is:

**Infinitives, past participles and separable prefixes
go to the end of the clause in which they occur.**

Here are some examples.

- Main clause statements:

  Nächste Woche werde ich in Bonn **sein** (future tense – infinitive)
  Gestern mußte er früh **aufstehen** (separable verb infinitive with a modal verb)
  Heute bin ich früh **aufgestanden** (past participle – separable verb)
  Um neun Uhr kommt er **an** (separable prefix)

- Questions and commands:

  Warum konnte er nicht **kommen?** (infinitive with a modal verb)
  Was hast du in der Zeitung **gelesen?** (past participle)
  Warum bist du so spät **angekommen?** (past participle – separable verb)
  Um wieviel Uhr stehst du **auf?** (separable prefix)
  Laß uns Tennis **spielen!** (infinitive – command)
  Steh **auf!** (separable prefix – command)

- Subordinate clauses:

  In a subordinate clause it is very possible that there will be more than one part of the verb being used, especially in compound tenses. When this happens there is a fixed order. In general the finite verb will come last and the non-finite parts will precede it. BUT if there are two infinitives at the end of a clause, then the finite verb will precede them. Look at these examples to see how it works:

  (a) Er kam früh in der Schule an, weil der Wecker ihn um 6 Uhr **aufgeweckt hatte.**
  He arrived at school early, because the alarm clock had woken him up at 6.

  (b) Er konnte seine Frau nicht sehen, weil sie **ausgehen mußte.**
  He couldn't see his wife, because she had to go out.

  (c) Heute abend kann er nicht ausgehen, weil sein Aufsatz **geschrieben werden muß.**
  He cannot go out this evening, because his essay has to be written.

  (d) Er hatte sich langweilt, weil kein Tennis **gespielt worden war.**
  He had become bored, because no tennis had been played.

  BUT

  (e) Er mußte das Haus verlassen, das er **hätte verkaufen sollen.**
  He had to leave the house that he ought to have sold.

Looking at each example in turn we see in (a) a pluperfect tense used with the finite verb **hatte** at the end after the past participle of a separable verb. This pattern would be repeated for any verb (except a modal verb) in any of the perfect tenses.

In (b) we see that the finite verb is the modal auxiliary **mußte** which follows the dependent infinitive **ausgehen** (also a separable verb).

In (c) we have a passive infinitive **geschrieben werden** (*to be written*) followed by **muß** (the modal auxiliary) which is the finite verb.

In (d) we have a pluperfect passive construction with the two past participles **gespielt worden** followed by the finite verb, the auxiliary **war.**

Finally in (e) we have the pluperfect subjunctive of **sollen** which creates the situation where there are **two infinitives** at the end of the clause. In this instance and only when this happens do you place the finite verb **before** the two infinitives as **hätte** is in this example.

Remember compound tenses occur when you have to use an auxiliary verb; see the relevant sections earlier in the book about the formation of tenses.

Before going on to look at word order within a clause we need to emphasise the concept of **inversion** which is the fundamental difference between English and German. English students find this more difficult to grasp than anything else about word order in German, the fact that the finite verb is the **second idea** in a main statement. The first idea in a clause can be any number of different elements, but the main finite verb must come next. Look at these examples which illustrate the point:

(a) Als der Mann durch den Park ging, **sah** er seinen Freund.
When the man walked through the park he saw his friend.

(b) Obwohl er sehr müde war, **wollte** er nicht zu Bett gehen.
Although he was very tired he did not want to go to bed.

These two examples are complex sentences which contain a main clause and a subordinate clause. When this kind of sentence begins with the subordinate clause ending in a verb, the verb of the main clause will be the next word, i.e. the **second idea**. This creates a pattern of '**verb, verb**' which is very common in German. In most instances these two verbs will be finite.

(a) Am Wochenende **soll** ich nach Münster fahren, um meine Tante zu besuchen.
I am supposed to be going to Münster to visit my aunt at the weekend.

(b) Etwas ärgerlich **holte** er uns mit dem Auto von der Telefonzelle ab.
Somewhat annoyed he picked us up from the telephone kiosk by car.

(c) Mehr als 500 Spiele **hat** er in weniger als 18 Monaten gesammelt.
He has collected more than 500 games in less than 18 months.

These examples are simple sentences where the finite verb is the **second idea** and the subject therefore follows the verb. In (a) and (b) the first element in each sentence is an adverbial phrase of time and manner respectively, in (c) it is the direct object of the verb *sammeln*, because the reporter in the newspaper article wanted to emphasise the large number of games which had been collected in the 18 months, so he put them at the start of the sentence.

It is important for you to recognise and understand these word order patterns in German, as it will help your own writing and speaking as well as enabling you to understand more easily what you hear and read.

WORD ORDER WITHIN THE CLAUSE

● In main clauses which begin with a co-ordinating conjunction the rules for main statements apply; the conjunction has no effect on the word order:
Er kann nicht heute kommen, **denn er ist** viel zu krank.
He cannot come today, for he is much too ill.

● In subordinate clauses linked by a co-ordinating conjunction the final position of the verb will apply in each clause:
Ich weiß, daß er nicht kommen **kann** und daß du darüber sehr enttäuscht sein **wirst**.
I know that he cannot come and that you will be very disappointed about it.

● In direct speech the main statement word order applies:
Er sagte: „Gestern **ging** ich in die Stadt, um Einkäufe zu machen".
He said: "I went to town yesterday to do some shopping".

● In indirect speech without **daß** the verb is second in the subordinate clause:
Er sagte, er **sei** krank. *He said he was ill.*

● In conditional clauses when **wenn** is omitted the finite verb comes first:
Wäre er gestern gekommen, so hätten wir ihn gesehen.
If he had come yesterday we would have seen him.

● Similarly when **ob** is omitted in a clause introduced by **als ob**, the finite verb follows **als**:
Er sah aus, als **hätte** er nichts gegessen. *He looked as if he had eaten nothing.*

The order of direct and indirect objects in the accusative and dative

Basically there are three patterns to remember:

❶ If both objects are nouns, then the **dative** precedes the **accusative**
(Nouns – Dative Accusative NDA).
Als er **dem Jungen das Buch** gab, sagte er... *When he gave the boy the book he said...*

❷ If both objects are pronouns, the cases are reversed, the **accusative** precedes the **dative** (Pronouns – **A**ccusative **D**ative PAD).

Als er **es ihm** gab, sagte er...   *When he gave it to him, he said...*

❸ If one object is a pronoun and the other a noun, the pronoun will always come first and the case will be irrelevant.

Als er **es** dem Jungen gab, sagte er...
When he gave it to the boy , he said...
Als er **ihm** das Buch gab, sagte er... } Pronoun first
When he gave him the book, he said...

Pronouns within a clause

Personal and reflexive pronouns will usually precede other kinds of pronoun and nouns within a clause.

● In a main clause the reflexive or personal pronoun object immediately follows the finite verb in normal word order, i.e. subject, verb, object:
Er hat **sich** gewaschen.
Ich habe **sie** gesehen.

● When there is inverted word order, then the reflexive pronoun or personal pronoun object will follow the subject if it is another pronoun, or precede the subject if it is a noun:

Dann setzte er **sich**.   *Then he sat down.*
but: Dann setzte **sich** mein Vater.   *Then my father sat down.*
or Dann setzte **sich** dieser.   *Then the latter sat down.*
                                (demonstrative pronoun – *dieser*)
Dann gab er **ihm** ein Buch. **but**: Dann gab ihm mein Vater ein Buch.

● In subordinate clauses it is usual in good style in German to place the reflexive pronoun or the personal pronoun object before a noun subject:
Da **sich** meine Schwester erkältet hat, ...   *As my sister has caught a cold...*

● In subordinate clauses if the subject is a personal pronoun, then the reflexive pronoun or personal pronoun object will immediately follow it:
Weil er **mir** das Buch gegeben hat, ...   *Because he has given me the book...*

● If both objects are pronouns (reflexive or personal), then PAD applies:
Sobald er **sich** (acc.) **mir** (dat.)   *As soon as he had introduced himself*
   vorgestellt hatte, ...   *to me...*

Adverbial phrases

The order of adverbial phrases or individual adverbs does not follow any strictly hard and fast rule. The order often has more to do with emphasis than any grammatical requirement. However, as a general statement which will apply in most instances adverbials of time, manner and place will be placed in that order in a German clause which is the opposite of the order in English. Look at these examples:

Mein Onkel kam um neun Uhr mit dem Zug in Berlin an.
               (1)   (2)   (3)

Very frequently the time phrase is placed at the beginning of the clause, followed by inverted word order. This tends to give the sentence more balance:
Um neun Uhr kam mein Onkel mit dem Zug in Berlin an.
My uncle arrived in Berlin by train at nine o'clock.

It is also possible that an adverb of manner will follow an adverb of place, especially when the adverb is closely linked with the meaning of the word it qualifies:
Gestern abend hat meine Schwester in ihrem neuen Bett **gut** geschlafen.
My sister slept well in her new bed last night.

The position of 'nicht'

In essence *nicht* and the other negatives are adverbs of manner. Here are some straightforward examples which illustrate the general principles of placing *nicht* in a clause.

In main clauses:

Wir haben ihn lange **nicht** gesehen.	*We have not seen him for a long time.*
Heute abend kannst du **nicht** hinausgehen.	*You cannot go out this evening.*
Stehen Sie bitte **nicht** auf!	*Please don't get up!*
Gestern war es **nicht** kalt.	*It wasn't cold yesterday.*
Sie ist **nicht** meine Frau.	*She is not my wife.*
Gestern ist sie **nicht** in die Schule gegangen.	*She didn't go to school yesterday.*
Er mag mich **nicht** sehr.	*He doesn't like me very much.*

In these examples *nicht* is placed immediately before a past participle, an infinitive, a separable prefix, an adjective used predicatively, a noun, a complement to a verb and an adverb. If none of these occurs in a main clause, then *nicht* is placed last.

Wir sehen ihn **nicht**.	*We do not see him.*
Vergiß mich **nicht**!	*Don't forget me!*

In subordinate clauses the position of *nicht* is very comparable, but the rules about the position of the finite verb and its parts will mean that the negative cannot go right to the end. Look at these examples:

Wenn er es **nicht** sieht, ...	*If he does not see it...*
Wenn er es **nicht** gesehen hätte, ...	*If he had not seen it...*
Wenn er **nicht** hätte kommen können, ...	*If he had not been able to come...*
Da es **nicht** so kalt ist, ...	*As it is not so cold...*
Weil sie **nicht** meine Tochter ist, ...	*Because she is not my daughter...*
Obwohl er **nicht** schnell läuft, ...	*Although he does not run quickly...*
Obwohl er **nicht** in die Schule geht, ...	*Although he is not going to school...*
Obwohl er **nicht** in die Schule gegangen ist, ...	*Although he has not gone to school...*

To a large extent placing a negative within a clause is common sense, as long as you remember the other rules of word order which override everything else.

2.16 PUNCTUATION

THE RULES

The rules about punctuation in German are very uncomplicated.

- Capital letters and fullstops are used at the beginning and end of a sentence as in English.
- All nouns and proper nouns in German are written with capital letters.
- The semi-colon is rarely used in German.
- The colon, not a comma, is used to introduce direct speech after a verb of saying or asking:
  Er sagte: „Ich verstehe das nicht, könnten Sie es wiederholen, bitte?"
- The first set of speech marks, inverted commas, is placed on the line not, above it as in English. This applies in German to both single and double inverted commas:
  Er fragte: „Warum bist du so traurig?"
  Er fragte: „Kennen Sie Bachs ‚Messe b-Moll'?"
- The exclamation mark is used much the same way as in English, i.e. after exclamations and commands.
  Ach!   Donnerwetter!   Verflucht! Schlaf gut!
- The question mark is used as in English. (see above)

Use of the comma

Only the use of the comma is specific to German in certain respects listed below:

- Each clause within a sentence should begin and end with a comma. In German this indicates the grammatical units of the sentence:
  Der Mann, der in der Goethestraße wohnt, heißt Klaus.

- Clauses linked by **und** and **oder** do not have a comma if the subject of the second main clause is understood or if the subordinate clauses are in parallel:
  Er stand auf und ging ins Badezimmer.
  Er wird nicht nach Berlin fahren, weil er keine Fahrkarte hat oder weil er zu krank ist.

- Infinitive constructions with **um ... zu** and others similar are counted as non-finite clauses and are separated from the rest of the sentence by a comma:
  Er warf den Ball über die Hecke, ohne darüber nachzudenken.

  Other infinitive constructions need care:
  - a plain infinitive with **zu** or dependent on an auxiliary verb does not have a comma:
    Er begann zu lachen.
    Er konnte nicht nach Hause gehen.
    BUT if there are other parts to the plain infinitive construction with **zu**, then a comma is required:
    Er begann, seine Kleider in seinen Koffer einzupacken.
  - when an infinitive clause forms the subject of the finite verb, no comma is required:
    Ihm ein Geschenk zu geben war dumm.

- As in English interjections, exclamations, explanatory phrases, phrases in apposition and words or phrases in parentheses are usually separated from the rest of the sentence or clause by commas, if they are obviously recognised as a separate entity from them:
  Hallo, wo sind wir denn jetzt?
  Gestern sahen wir Diana, die Prinzessin von Wales, in London.

- Two or more adjectives used attributively before a noun are separated by a comma, if they are of equal importance:
  Wir können gute, billige Kleider auf dem Marktplatz kaufen.
  BUT if the second adjective is linked to the noun to form a single idea then no comma is required:
  Wir können auch gute niederländische Käsesorten auf dem Marktplatz kaufen.

CHAPTER 3

LISTENING

Units in this chapter

3.1 INTRODUCTION

As has been stated earlier in this book, listening is a skill that requires lots of practice. It also requires a wide vocabulary. In our own language we do not listen carefully to everything that we hear. Much of what people say is redundant. We all use phrases and expressions that give us time to think of the next thing we are going to say. Very often when listening to a person we are able to complete his/her sentence before he/she does, because we can work out what is coming. We are able to follow what we hear with only one ear and pick out the bits that are important for us.

THE DIFFERENCE BETWEEN LISTENING TO A TAPE AND LISTENING TO A PERSON

In a foreign language we do not have the same ability and we need, therefore, to concentrate extremely hard all the time on what is being said. That is why it can be so exhausting staying in a foreign country with native speakers! Listening also requires using our short-term memories. Even in our own language it is surprisingly difficult to remember everything that has been said to us without making notes. We can usually follow the gist without any problem but the details often get forgotten or changed. You only have to think of the game 'Chinese whispers' to realise how a message can get changed when being transmitted by speech from one person to another.

Listening to a tape is always going to be more difficult than listening to somebody speaking to you face to face because you will not be able to get from their expressions and gestures all the non-verbal communication that often we are not aware of, but which helps to convey more than mere words can say.

3.2 THE LISTENING EXAMINATION

Most Examining Boards use 'authentic' passages for their examinations. They were originally intended for native German speakers and will have been taken from German radio or some other German speaking source. Some Boards re-record passages in a studio to improve the technical quality. In the process the speed of delivery may well have been slowed down, which is to your advantage. The most common complaint from candidates is that foreigners speak too quickly!

The passages are usually either shorter passages such as advertisements, traffic reports, news items, announcements and weather forecasts, or longer passages such as reports or interviews.

WHAT YOU WILL BE REQUIRED TO DO

The questions that are set will require different skills from you. You will be asked to:

- pick out details from a passage;
- render the gist of a passage or summarise its main points;
- draw inferences from what you have heard (that is to be able to make statements about things that are not explicitly stated in the text) and understand the relationship between the various parts of the passage.

Some Boards expect you to answer in English, other Boards may require German. Some will allow you to have your own tape which you can stop and start as you need to. Others have the tape played two or three times to a group of candidates and use pauses for you to write your answers. Find out how the listening examination is organised by your Board and practise. Any 'mock' examinations that you can take before the real thing will give you a good idea of how to organise your time and what problem areas you need to give more attention to.

MAKING NOTES WHILE LISTENING

You will inevitably need to take notes to help your memory, particularly where you do not have control of your own tape. Most Examining Boards allow you to make notes while the tape is being played to you. Listening in German and making notes in English is very difficult. While you are trying to think of the English for some of what you are listening to, you miss what follows. It is a good idea to make your notes in German and then translate them into English after the final re-play. This also gives you the chance to look up any unknown words if you are allowed a dictionary in the examination as is now often the case. Make sure that you cross out notes that are not meant to be marked.

THE IMPORTANCE OF CHECKING WHAT YOU HAVE WRITTEN

When you are nervous and under pressure in an examination it is very easy to write answers that do not make sense. You certainly do not have to write complete sentences all the time. Using the words of the question in your answer is definitely to be avoided as a great waste of time. Some time spent at the end of the examination reading through what you have written could be time well spent. When you are asked to write your answers in German it is often the case that grammatical accuracy is ignored provided that what you have written would make sense to a native German speaker. It will normally be marked only for comprehension. Nevertheless it is a good principle to try always to write correct German. Accuracy is something that cannot be switched on and off at will; it has to be practised. In some of the new syllabuses all written German carries some marks for accuracy.

USING ALL THE INFORMATION THAT YOU ARE GIVEN

When you are in the examination use all the information given to you on the question paper to prepare for what you are about to listen to. Usually you will be told what each extract is about. It may have a title. Ask yourself what the title indicates about the passage you are going to hear. Look carefully at the questions you are being asked. They will tell you something about the listening text. Pay careful attention to the number of marks being given for each answer. If there are four marks it is unlikely that one piece of information will be enough to get maximum marks. It is probable that four items of information are being asked for. Note the questions that ask for a number or a time and pay careful attention. Numbers and times can be difficult in German.

THE TYPES OF EXERCISES USED IN THE LISTENING EXAMINATION

The types of exercises that occur in listening examinations are:

- questions in English/answers in English;
- questions in German/answers in German;
- deciding whether a statement is true or false;
- filling in gaps in a parallel text or filling in gaps in the original text;
- completing sentences with the appropriate information;
- filling in grids with information from the text;
- writing a summary of the text in English/German;
- explaining or defining phrases or sentences from the original text;
- finding the equivalents in the original for English or German phrases;
- multiple choice questions, i.e. choosing the correct answer from a number of possibilities;
- broken sentences – matching up the beginnings and endings of sentences;
- ticking items in a list or a grid;
- inserting figures/graphics etc. on maps.

With the kind of objective answers being asked for in the listening paper it is more easily possible to score high marks than say in an examination paper that requires you to write essays. It is worthwhile, therefore, to give this part of the examination particular attention.

3.3 WORKED EXAMPLES

Included with this book is a CD containing examples of the kind of passages set in listening examinations. To save space these are recorded without the gaps that some Boards put into their longer passages. Each passage is recorded also only once.

The worked examples are at the beginning of the CD. Read the questions through before listening to each extract twice. Allow about a minute between playings. Try to answer the questions before looking at the candidate's answers and examiner's comments. You can check your own answers against the transcripts provided and compare them with those of the examiner.

The answers and mark schemes are not necessarily the official ones. The Examining Boards are unable to respond to any queries about them.

EXAMPLE 1

A short news broadcast with four items; questions in English to be answered in English.

You will hear four news items from the radio. Play all four extracts through once, go back to the beginning and listen to the first extract again. At the end of the first extract stop the recording and try to answer question 1. Follow a similar procedure for each extract. This test is from a Board that does not allow you to control your own tape in the examination.

Rubric: Answer the following questions in English. Your answers should give all **relevant** information but need not be in the form of complete sentences. You may make notes at any time during this paper.

News item 1: Question 1. Describe how the accident near Osnabrück occurred. (2)

News item 2: Question 2. What happened to the soldier as he was walking back to his barracks in the Heimfelderstraße? (2)

Question 3. What happened subsequently to the soldier? (2)

News item 3: Question 4. Why are the UN troops from Pakistan being sent to Somalia? (2)

Question 5. What are 4.5 million people in Somalia threatened with and why? (2)

News item 4: Question 6. What caused the severe weather conditions? (1)

Question 7. What was the result of the heavy rain in Blankenese? (2)

Question 8. Why was the fire brigade called out? (2)

ULEAC

Candidate's answers

1 Describe how the accident near Osnabrück occurred.

Candidate: A car driven by a 24 year old collided with another car containing a family.

Mark scheme: A car went on to the wrong side of the road/and there was a collision with another car. (1+1)

Examiner: Only one of the two marks available can be given for this answer. The candidate failed to indicate **how** the accident occurred.

2 What happened to the soldier as he was walking back to his barracks in the Heimfelderstraße?

Candidate: He was attacked and robbed.

Mark scheme: He was attacked by five men/and robbed of 390 marks. (1+1)

Examiner: This answer fails to give enough detail. The number of men who attacked and the amount of money stolen are important details. Only half marks for this answer.

3 What happened subsequently to the soldier?

Candidate: He had to go to hospital.

Mark scheme: He had to go to hospital/but was discharged the same day. (1+1)

Examiner: There is only enough information here for one mark.

4 Why are the UN troops from Pakistan being sent to Somalia?

Candidate: To stop shipments of aid from being attacked by armed bands.

Mark scheme: To prevent aid transports/from being attacked by armed gangs. (1+1)

Examiner: This is a good answer and gets full marks.

5 What are 4.5 million people in Somalia threatened with and why?

Candidate: With famine, because of the civil war in Somalia.

Mark scheme: Starvation/because of the drought. (1+1)

Examiner: The candidate got part of the information and would receive one mark. The word *Dürre* in the passage obviously proved too difficult. It looks as if the candidate guessed at the reason for the famine. Intelligent guessing is sometimes essential rather than failing to make an attempt at the answer. The candidate made an intelligent guess. Unfortunately it was wrong. This answer underlines the importance of having a good vocabulary so that a word like *Dürre* would be known. Some of the Boards now allow candidates to use dictionaries in the examination, so that this word could have been looked up. Nevertheless, using a dictionary is time-consuming so it is wise to know as many words as possible, rather than having constantly to consult a dictionary and risk not completing the examination paper.

6 What caused the severe weather conditions?

Candidate: An increase in temperature.

Mark scheme: The drop in temperature. (1)

Examiner: No mark for this answer. The candidate seems to have understood only the first part of *Temperatursturz.*

7 What was the result of the heavy rain in Blankenese?

Candidate: More streets were flooded.

Mark scheme: Several streets/were flooded. (1+1)

Examiner: Only one mark for this answer for failing to understand that *mehrere Straßen* means *several streets* and not *more streets.*

8 Why was the fire brigade called out?

Candidate: To pump away the masses of water.

Mark scheme: To pump out the water/from the cellars. (1+1)

Examiner: Only half the information is given in this answer, so the candidate will receive only one mark of the available two.

Total: 8 marks out of 15

EXAMPLE 2

A discussion with German students about environmental problems; questions in German to be answered in German.

This is an authentic text set by a Board that issues a cassette to each candidate and allows them to listen to the cassette as often as required. You will probably need to listen to the text once. Then play the extract again and stop the CD when you hear the information for the first question. Adopt a similar procedure for the other questions. Pay attention to the accuracy of what you write. Although the majority of the marks is given for the correct information some marks are also awarded for correct German.

Rubric: Hören Sie dieser Diskussion mit deutschen Studenten über Umweltprobleme gut zu, dann beantworten Sie folgende Fragen:

(a) Welche zwei Umweltprobleme werden von der Frau in der Diskussion erwähnt? (2)

(b) Wer hat diese Probleme verursacht, ihrer Meinung nach? (2)

(c) Welche zwei Möglichkeiten gibt es, die zum besseren Umweltschutz führen können? (2)

(d) Welche Frage erhebt sich in bezug auf die erstgenannte Möglichkeit? (1)

(e) Wie kann man die Industrie dazu zwingen, umweltfreundlichere Produkte herzustellen? (2)

(f) Nennen Sie die Initiative, die zum Kauf umweltfreundlicher Produkte anreizen soll.(1)

Oxford

Candidate's answers

(a) Welche zwei Umweltprobleme werden von der Frau in der Diskussion erwähnt?

Candidate: Qualität der Luft und des Wassers und Waldsterben.

Mark scheme: Die Qualität der Luft und des Wassers/das Problem des Waldsterbens. (1+1)

Examiner: The information given is correct and the quality of the German is fine. Full marks.

(b) Wer hat diese Probleme verursacht, ihrer Meinung nach?

Candidate: Industrie – auch der Individuum.

Mark scheme: Die Industrie/der Normalverbraucher/der Individualverbraucher. (1+1)

Examiner: The first part of what the candidate has written answers the question, but the second part is not strictly correct. Only one mark out of two would be awarded. The German is also faulty. It should be *die Industrie*. The gender of *Individuum* is *das*. 1 mark.

(c) Welche zwei Möglichkeiten gibt es, die zum besseren Umweltschutz führen können?

Candidate: 1 Durch bessere, strengeren Gesetze.
　　　　　　　2 Werbung, um die Verbraucher aufzuklären.

Mark scheme: Man könnte Gesetze einführen/
　　　　　　　　und das Verhalten der Verbraucher durch Werbung ändern. (1+1)

Examiner: The candidate has obviously understood the text and has given a reasonable, but not perfect answer. The first part gives the required information, but the adjectival ending on *strengeren* is wrong. It should be *strengere*. The second part of the answer is not as explicit as it could be. What the candidate has written implies that if consumers are given the information about products through advertising, then their behaviour will change, but it has been left to the examiner to infer that. This candidate would probably be given the benefit of any doubt. It is always wise to make your answers clear. Full marks, but the answer could be improved.

(d) Welche Frage erhebt sich in bezug auf die erstgenannte Möglichkeit?

Candidate: Wie effektiv sie sind, und wie weit sie kontrolliert werden können.

Mark scheme: Wie weit könnten die Gesetze kontrolliert werden? (1)

Examiner: The information is correct and the German is good. Full marks.

(e) Wie kann man die Industrie dazu zwingen, umweltfreundlichere Produkte herzustellen?

Candidate: Man könnte versuchen, die Leute aufzuklären, daß es andere Produkte gibt, die die Umwelt weniger schädigen. Deshalb werden die Leute andere Produkte kaufen und hoffentlich wird die Industrie freiwillig wählen, umweltfreundlichere Produkte zu kaufen.

Mark scheme: Wenn die Leute es wissen, können sie andere Produkte kaufen,/
　　　　　　　　die weniger schädlich sind. (1+1)

Examiner: An excellent answer, more detailed than the mark scheme and showing a good understanding of the text, with good German. Full marks.

(f) Nennen Sie die Initiative, die zum Kauf umweltfreundlicher Produkte anreizen soll.

Candidate: Die blauen Umwelt Engel.

Mark scheme: der blaue Umweltengel. (1)

Examiner: The candidate has given the required information, although with three grammatical errors: the wrong gender (*die* instead of *der*), the incorrect adjectival ending (*blauen* instead of *blaue*) and the splitting of the compound noun (*Umweltengel*). Full marks for comprehension, but some marks would be lost for accuracy of written German.

Total: 9 marks out of 10.

EXAMPLE 3

From a radio phone-in programme. A gap filling exercise.

Another authentic text. Here the candidates have not only to understand the listening text, but also a written text and establish what the missing word is.

A preliminary examination of the written text will help you to work out the kind of word you are looking for, whether it is a verb, noun, adjective or adverb and so on. The context will give you useful information about the facts being sought. All of the words that you need to find and the information are in the recorded text. When you have studied the gapped text listen to the extract twice. Try to fill in the gaps during the second hearing. Stop the CD as you need to.

Rubric: Hören Sie sich dieses Telefongespräch über einen Schüleraustausch mit Frankreich an, dann ergänzen Sie die Lücken in der folgenden Zusammenfassung des Ausschnittes mit Wörtern oder Ausdrücken, die zeigen, daß Sie den Ausschnitt verstanden haben. Sie dürfen ein Wort aus dem Text benutzen, wenn das am besten paßt.

Susanne Pötz ist –1– Jahre alt. Sie ist –2– , weil sie jetzt wieder in –3– ist, nachdem sie an einem –4– in Frankreich teilgenommen hat. Die deutschen Schüler sind an einem –5– in Frankreich angekommen und haben das Wochenende –6– in einer –7– verbracht. In der folgenden Woche gab es viel Arbeit in der –8– , aber man hat auch –9– gemacht und viel –10– gehabt. Die französischen Partner werden am 8. –11– nach Koblenz kommen. Susanne hofft, daß der Kontakt –12– wird. Die deutschen Schüler haben –13– , Frankreich irgendwann wieder zu besuchen. Susanne ist keineswegs –14– , daß die deutschen Lehrer während der Abwesenheit der Austauschgruppe einfach –15– haben und daß sie jetzt die verlorene Schularbeit –16– muß. Es gefällt ihr aber, daß sie im Radio ihre –17– hören wird.

Oxford

Examiner's tips

1: because of *Jahre alt*, it looks as if a number is missing here.

2: because of *Sie ist*, probably an adjective is required.

3: because of the preposition *in*, possibly a place.

4: because of the indefinite article *einem*, probably a masculine or neuter noun in the dative case.

5: because of the indefinite article *einem*, probably a masculine or neuter noun in the dative case, possibly the name of a day.

6: not a noun, not a verb, not an adjective, possibly an adverb, saying how the weekend was spent.

7: because of the *einer*, a feminine noun in the dative case.

8: because of the definite article *der*, a feminine noun in the dative case.

9: because of the verb used (*machen*), it is likely to be a noun.

10: because of the verb used (*haben*), it is likely to be a noun.

11: because of *am 8.*, almost certainly a date, the name of a month.

12: because of the auxiliary verb used (*wird*), either an infinitive, to produce a future tense or a past participle to produce a passive form.

13: because of the auxiliary verb used (*haben*), it is likely to be a past participle, although it could be a prefix.

14: because of *sie ist*, it is likely to be an adjective.

15: because of the auxiliary verb used (*haben*), it is likely to be a past participle to make up a perfect tense.

16: because of the modal verb *muß*, it is likely to be an infinitive.

17: because of the possessive adjective *ihre*, it is almost certainly a feminine or plural noun, in the accusative case.

You can see from carrying out the above exercise first of all, how much you can predict what kind of information is being asked for from you and secondly whether you are looking for a number, a date, a place name, an infinitive or a noun. So it is worth spending a bit of time reading through the gapped text before listening to the recorded text. Below you can see what the correct answers are and what an actual candidate wrote. It is worth mentioning that for some gaps several alternatives are possible, and provided that they fit in with the meaning of the recorded text and make sense in the passage they will be allowed.

Candidate's answers

Candidate:	Mark scheme:
1: 16	1: 16
2: traurig	2: traurig
3: Deutschland	3: Deutschland
4: Austausch	4: Austausch
5: Samstag	5: Samstag
6: allein	6: einzeln
7: Familie	7: Familie
8: Schule	8: Schule
9: Ausflüge	9: Ausflüge
10: Spaß	10: Spaß
11: Juni	11: Juni
12: dauern	12: halten
13: entschieden	13: beschlossen/vor
14: glücklich	14: froh
15: gearbeitet	15: weitergemacht
16: machen	16: nachholen
17: Lied	17: Lieblingsplatte

Examiner: This candidate scored very well. Some answers were different from the mark scheme, but acceptable both from the point of view of comprehension of the recorded text and fitting grammatically into the gapped text.

6: *allein*, rather than *einzeln*.

12: *dauern*, rather than *halten*.

14: *glücklich*, rather than *froh*.

Some answers would gain comprehension marks because they made sense, but would be penalised for being grammatically incorrect:

13: *entschieden* is a past participle and fits in with the meaning of the text, but it should here have the reflexive pronoun *sich* with it.

17: *Lied* gives the correct meaning, but its gender is *das* whereas the word being sought is feminine *die*.

Only two answers were disallowed:

15: *gearbeitet* although it is grammatically correct does not convey the sense of *weitergemacht* and would not be allowed.

16: *machen* is grammatically correct, but it does not convey the same sense as *nachholen* (to catch up with, make up).

Total: 15 marks out of 17 for comprehension.

EXAMPLE 4

A report on the position of women in the former East German communist state, the German Democratic Republic.

This is another authentic text. The exercise requires you to complete sentences with the appropriate information. Most of the marks will be given for giving the correct answer in German that can be understood by a sympathetic native German speaker. But whenever you write German containing errors some marks will be lost for those mistakes.

Normally the sentences to be completed will be in the same order as the information occurs in the text. You should be able to answer in sequence as you listen to the CD. With this type of exercise, as with the last one, you need to be able to understand the printed German on the page in front of you as well as what you are listening to on the CD. It is, therefore, worth spending a few moments reading the German and sorting out what it means before listening to the recording. It is not always clear from the printed German what information is being asked for.

Listen to the CD twice and try to write your answers as you listen the second time. Stop the CD whenever you need to.

Rubric: Hören Sie sich diese Sendung über Frauen in der ehemaligen DDR (Deutsche Demokratische Republik) an, dann ergänzen Sie die folgenden Sätze mit Informationen aus dem Text.

(a) Der Report erschien .... (2)

(b) Im Report geht es um .... (1)

(c) Daß Gleichstellungsbeauftragte installiert wurden, könnte man .... (2)

(d) Die Frauendiskriminierung .... aber in Wirklichkeit
     hatten die Ostfrauen .... (2)

(e) Die Bildungsunterschiede zwischen Mädchen und Jungen .... (1)

(f) Das Qualifikationsniveau der Frau .... (2)

(g) Im Vergleich zu den Westfrauen .... (2)

(h) Früher war der Lebensweg der Ostfrauen sicher: sie .... (3)

(i) Nun fürchten sie sich, weil .... (2)

An examination of the sentences that you have to complete will reveal a few difficulties:

In (a) you will need to know that *erschien* is the imperfect tense of the verb *erscheinen* and means to appear; so you need to listen out for a date or a year. You will not be able to answer (b) unless you know the expression *es geht um etwas*, which means *it is a question of something*. The word order of (c) is unusual in that it begins with a subordinate clause introduced by *daß*, which may make the sentence more difficult to understand and complete. The other sentences are more straightforward although they contain some long words that will hopefully be mentioned in the text! For example: *Bildungsunterschiede, das Qualifikationsniveau*.

Oxford

Candidate's answers

(a) Der Report erschien...

Candidate: am 1. April letztes Jahr.

Mark scheme: im letzten Jahr/im 41. Jahr (1)
                 der DDR. (1)

Examiner: This answer would gain no marks. The candidate failed to grasp that it was in the last year that the DDR existed.

(b) Im Report geht es um...

Candidate: die soziale Situation der Frau.

Mark scheme: die soziale Situation der Frau. (1)

Examiner: Full marks for this answer.

(c) Daß Gleichstellungsbeauftragte installiert wurden, könnte man...

Candidate: über Probleme der Gleichberechtigung sprechen.

Mark scheme: als/für eine große Leistung (1)
betrachten/halten. (1)

Examiner: No marks for this answer. What the candidate has written does not make any sense, either as a sentence or as an answer.

(d) Die Frauendiskriminierung...
aber in der Wirklichkeit hatten die Ostfrauen...

Candidate: existiert offiziel nicht in der ehemaligen DDR ... Diskriminierung erfahren.

Mark scheme: existierte offiziell in der DDR nicht (1)
keine Gleichberechtigung. (1)

Examiner: Although there are some minor language mistakes this answer would receive full marks for comprehension. The verb *existiert* should be in the imperfect tense, and *offiziell* is spelt incorrectly in the candidate's answer.

(e) Die Bildungsunterschiede zwischen Mädchen und Jungen...

Candidate: war ziemlich groß.

Mark scheme: existieren nicht mehr. (1)

Examiner: No marks for this answer, which is the direct opposite of what is said in the text. The verb should also be *waren*.

(f) Das Qualifikationsniveau der Frau...

Candidate: war niedriger als das Qualifikationsniveau des Mannes.

Mark scheme: wurde oft ignoriert/war keine Garantie (1)
wenn sie sich um/für eine gutbezahlte Stelle bewarb. (1)

Examiner: No marks again for this answer. It shows a complete lack of understanding of this part of the text.

(g) Im Vergleich zu den Westfrauen...

Candidate: die Ostfrauen verdienten weniger, machten schlechter und schwerer Arbeit und arbeiteten nicht in Berufen, für die sie qualifiziert waren. Sie hatten das Recht für ein Arbeitsplatz und ihre eigene Geld zu verdienen.

Mark scheme: hatten die Ostfrauen das Recht auf einen Arbeitsplatz (1)
und auf eigenes Geld. (1)

Examiner: The candidate has written a lot and has given the information necessary for the two marks. From the answer it is clear that this part of the text has been fully understood. There are some grammatical mistakes:

verdienten die Ostfrauen	– the main verb should be the second idea in a sentence.
schlechter**e** und schwerer**e** Arbeit	– no adjectival ending on the two adjectives.
auf ein**en** Arbeitsplatz	– wrong preposition and wrong gender of *Arbeitsplatz*.
ih**r** eigene**s** Geld	– wrong gender of *Geld*.

(h) Früher war der Lebensweg der Ostfrauen sicher: sie...

Candidate: wurden Berufe haben, sie wurden verheiraten und Kinder haben.

Mark scheme: hatten einen Beruf, (1)
sie heirateten (1)
und sie hatten Kinder. (1)

Examiner: Although there are several mistakes in the German all the information is there and it can be understood. So full marks for comprehension, although overall some marks will be lost for the language errors.

hatten Berufe, heirateten und hatten Kinder – the candidate has tried to say in German: *they would have a career, marry and have children*. In German the imperfect tense is used to render that, not the verb *werden*.

(i) Nun fürchten sie sich, weil...

Candidate: alles nicht so sicher wie vorher ist; nicht nur das berufliche Leben, sondern auch die Familie ins Gesamt. Sie könnten arbeitslos werden und die Miete nicht mehr bezahlen können.

Mark scheme: der Beruf und die Familie in Gefahr sind (1)
sie arbeitslos werden könnten/
die Mieten steigen könnten. (1)

Examiner: This is quite a good answer and would get full marks for comprehension. The German too is quite good. The candidate has shown good control of the word order after *weil* and the answer makes good sense. The repetition of the verb *können* in the last sentence is clumsy and *insgesamt* has been spelt wrongly.

Total: 10 marks out of 17 for comprehension.

EXAMPLE 5

This is a new kind of listening exercise. You are asked to listen to the text and use the information contained in it to do a writing exercise of not more than 180 words. The text is an authentic one and is part of an interview in which the chairman of a commission inquiring into the AIDS problem talks about the commission's findings. The exercise consists of writing a letter to a newspaper offering an opinion about how informing young people about the AIDS problem leads to a change in their behaviour and saying what more could be done to reduce the danger of infection for young people.

Listen to the text once without making notes. Then listen to it a second time stopping the recording to make notes as necessary. Then do the exercise.

Rubric: Hören Sie zuerst dem folgenden Text über AIDS und die Arbeit der Enquete-Kommission zu. Inwieweit führt Aufklärung über AIDS zu einer Änderung im Verhalten der Jugendlichen Ihrer Meinung nach? Was könnte man sonst noch tun, um die AIDS-Gefahr für junge Leute zu reduzieren? Schreiben Sie einen Brief (von nicht mehr als 180 Wörtern) an eine Zeitung, in dem Sie Information aus dem Hörtext benutzen.

Oxford

Candidate's answer

Hamburg, den 18. Juni 1995

1   Sehr geehrte Damen und Herren,

Ich habe vor kurzer Zeit eine Sendung gehört, indem Dr Hans-Peter Vogt (CDU-Bundestagsabgeordnete aus Nordheim) uns über die Probleme von AIDS in Deutschland erklärt hat. Er hat gesagt, daß obwohl es mehr AIDS-Kranken als vorher
5   gibt, der Prozentsatz steigt nicht so schnell wie man vor einige Jahren erwartet hat. Meiner Meinung nach, der Hauptgrund für diesen kleinen Zuwachs ist der Tat, daß die Mehrheit (95%) der jungere Generation sehr viel über die Probleme von Aids wissen, und deshalb können sie sich vor dieser Krankheit schützen.

Aber wie wissen die jungere Generation mehr über die Problematik von AIDS? Die
10   Antwort ist leicht. Seit ungefähr 1980, als man mehr als vorher über AIDS gewußt hat, hat die Regierung sich entscheidet, Aufklärungskampagne zu fördern, die Leute über die Nachteile von dem Nehmen von Drogen und Geschlechtsverkehr ohne Verhütungsmittel zu erklären, und wie man AIDS bekommen kann.

Meiner Meinung nach sind Aufklärungskampagne und AIDS-Aktionswoche wie hier
15   in Hamburg die einzige Methoden, die jungere Generation über die Probleme von AIDS zu erklären. Ich schlage deshalb vor, daß sie regelmäßige Werbungen gegen ✓ AIDS in Ihrer Zeitung erscheinen.

Mit freundlichen Grüßen,

Examiner: Although there are numerous grammatical mistakes in what this candidate has written there is good communication. The letter writing conventions are good, although strictly speaking the correct ending for a letter with this beginning should be *Hochachtungsvoll*. Some of the vocabulary is also quite sophisticated and has not been lifted from the recording: *Aufklärungskampagne, fördern, Geschlechtsverkehr, Verhütungsmittel, deshalb*. Some good constructions have also been attempted, not always successfully: *Er hat gesagt, daß obwohl...* A German reading this would understand everthing that the candidate is trying to say. One gets the impression that the candidate has been concentrating on the content of the letter, what he/she wanted to say and has possibly not had enough time to think much about how best to phrase it and the mechanics of word order and endings.

This exercise is marked out of 20: 10 marks for language and 10 for content. It is clear that the candidate has understood a good deal of the recorded text, but perhaps not all of it. Some of the words and facts in the recording have been reproduced in the candidate's work:

Dr Hans-Peter Vogt, CDU-Bundestagsabgeordnete aus Nordheim; obwohl es mehr AIDS-Kranken als vorher gibt, der Prozentsatz steigt nicht so schnell wie man vor einige Jahren erwartet hat; die Mehrheit (95%) der jungere Generation sehr viel über die Probleme von AIDS wissen.

When the candidate goes on to say *und deshalb können sie sich vor dieser Krankheit schützen* it is clear that not everything on the recording has been fully understood, because the gist of what Dr Vogt is saying is that he is at this stage not sure if young people are altering their behaviour to protect themselves from AIDS.

For language this piece of work would receive 6 out of 10: Adequate. Some attempt to vary the language and produce more complex syntax, but inconsistent. Accuracy variable.

For Content: 6 out of 10: Adequate – somewhat lacking in imagination, but shows reasonable understanding of the content of the passage. The first part of the question *Inwieweit führt Aufklärung über AIDS zu einer Änderung im Verhalten der Jugendlichen Ihrer Meinung nach?* has not been properly addressed. Because the candidate has not completely understood the recorded text most of what he/she has written has concentrated on successfully changing behaviour by means of advertising campaigns.

Here is a corrected version of the candidate's work. There were approximately 24 mistakes. See if you can explain what each mistake is and why the original version was wrong:

1   Sehr geehrte Damen und Herren!

Ich habe vor kurzer Zeit eine Sendung gehört, in der Dr Hans Peter Vogt (CDU-Bundestagsabgeordneter aus Nordheim) uns über die Probleme von AIDS in Deutschland erzählt hat. Er hat gesagt, daß, obwohl es mehr AIDS-Kranke als vorher
5   gebe, der Prozentsatz nicht so schnell steige, wie man vor einigen Jahren erwartet habe. Meiner Meinung nach ist der Hauptgrund für diesen kleinen Zuwachs die Tatsache, daß die Mehrheit der jüngeren Generation (95%) sehr viel über die Probleme von AIDS weiß, und deshalb kann sie sich vor dieser Krankheit schützen.

Aber wie weiß die jüngere Generation mehr über die Problematik von AIDS? Die
10   Antwort ist leicht. Seit ungefähr 1980, als man mehr als vorher über AIDS gewußt hat, hat die Regierung sich entschieden, Aufklärungskampagnen zu organisieren, um die Leute über die Nachteile von dem Nehmen von Drogen und Geschlechtsverkehr ohne Verhütungsmittel aufzuklären, und darüber, wie man AIDS bekommen kann.

Meiner Meinung nach sind Aufklärungskampagnen und AIDS-Aktionswochen wie hier
15   in Hamburg die einzigen Methoden, die jüngere Generation über die Probleme von AIDS aufzuklären. Ich schlage deshalb vor, daß Ihre Zeitung regelmäßig Information gegen AIDS herausbringt.

              Hochachtungsvoll,

3.4   EXAMINATION PRACTICE

The following tests are for you to try as practice for the examination. Look carefully through the exercise before listening to the CD to understand exactly what you are supposed to do and to gain as much information about what you are going to hear as possible. Listen to the recorded extract once all the way through and try to understand as much as you can. Then listen a second time and stop the CD when necessary to make notes.

    When you have done a test you will find the mark scheme at the end of this chapter so that you can assess your own answers. There is also a transcript of the recorded text in Appendix 3 in case there were bits of the recording that you could not understand. The more practice you can get the better. If you did not fully understand the recording, listen to it again with the transcript in front of you.

TEST 1

Mittwochslotto (3 Punkte)

Ergänzen Sie die Kästchen mit einer Zahl.

| Ziehung A: | 8 | 12 | 17 | 20 | 25 | … |
| Zusatzzahl: | 23 | | | | | |

| Ziehung B: | 3 | 12 | 25 | … | 46 | 49 |
| Zusatzzahl: | … | | | | | |

Oxford

TEST 2

Das Wetter (4 Punkte)

Wo sind die folgenden Wetterverhältnisse zu finden? Ordnen Sie der richtigen Region die Buchstaben zu.

(a) bedeckt und regnerisch

(b) Wolken mit Regenschauern

(c) vereinzelt Regen

(d) Wolken

Region	Buchstabe
Nordwesten	…
Schleswig-Holstein	…
Westen	…
Alpen	…

Oxford

TEST 3

Falsch beschuldigt (16 Punkte)

Ergänzen Sie die Tabelle mit Informationen aus dem Text.

(a) Name der Radiosendung, in der zuerst über die Putzfrau berichtet wurde	(1)
(b) Arbeitsplatz und Arbeitsort der Putzfrau	(2)
(c) Alter der Putzfrau	(1)
(d) Was die Putzfrau gemacht haben soll	(2)
(e) Urteil des Staatsanwaltes	(1)
(f) Wie der Krankenhausleiter die Putzfrau bestrafte	(2)
(g) Warum der Krankenhausleiter das Urteil des Staatsanwaltes nicht akzeptieren wollte	(2)
(h) Definition von „Krankenhauskuratorium"	(1)
(i) Inhalt des Briefes, den die Putzfrau vom Krankenhaus erhielt	(2)
(j) Reaktion der Putzfrau, als sie den Brief erhielt	(2)

Oxford

TEST 4

Fußballfans in Bremen (5 Punkte)

Kreuzen Sie (X) die richtige Antwort an.

(a) Das Europa-Pokalspiel ist zwischen…

… Bremen und Stuttgart.
… Stuttgart und Zeebrugge.
… Bremen und Zeebrugge.

(b) Zur Zeit der Nachrichtensendung…

… fängt das Spiel eben an.
… ist das Spiel schon zu Ende.
… fängt die zweite Halbzeit an.

(c) Im Kaufhaus wurden gestohlen...
  ... Sportartikel.
  ... Mützen.
  ... Mützen und Schals.

(d) Das Spiel Stuttgart-Borussia Dortmund beginnt um...
  ... 19 Uhr 30.
  ... 19 Uhr.
  ... 9 Uhr.

(e) Um einen freien Stehplatz für das Spiel Stuttgart-Borussia Dortmund zu haben, braucht man...
  ... eine Stuttgarter Mütze.
  ... einen Stuttgarter Schal.
  ... einen Dortmunder Schal.

Oxford

TEST 5

Ozonschichtgefahr (5 Punkte)

Sind die folgenden Aussagen richtig (R) oder falsch (F)?   R/F

(a) Die niedersächsische Landesregierung fordert, daß bei Ozongefahr Kraftzeugfahrer langsamer fahren sollten.   ...

(b) Die Umweltministerin wird am Freitag einen Vorschlag über Fahrbeschränkungen machen.   ...

(c) Fahrbeschränkungen sollten für alle Bundesländer gleich sein.   ...

(d) Das sonnige Wetter am Wochenende in Niedersachsen hat das Problem besonders dringend gemacht.   ...

(e) Bei einem Ozonwert von 160 Mikrogramm pro Kubikmeter wird eine Ozonwarnung herausgegeben.   ...

Oxford

TEST 6

Kindheitserinnerungen (13 Punkte)

Fassen Sie den Text AUF ENGLISCH in nicht mehr als 90 Wörtern zusammen. Fangen Sie so an:

The man was born in Vienna in 1946 ...

Oxford

3.5 SUGGESTED ANSWERS

TEST 1

Mittwochslotto (3 marks)
38; 43; 18

TEST 2

Das Wetter (4 marks)
Nordwesten   – (d)
Schleswig-Holstein   – (c)

Westen   – (b)

Alpen   – (a)

TEST 3

Falsch beschuldigt (16 marks)

(a)	"Einspruch"	(1)
(b)	Krankenhaus/Dortmund	(1+1)
(c)	46	(1)
(d)	Geld/gestohlen	(1+1)
(e)	die Putzfrau war unschuldig	(1)
(f)	sie durfte/das Krankenhaus nicht mehr betreten	(1+1)
(g)	either: der Krankenhausleiter hat das Hausrecht	(2)
	or: der Verdacht/besteht noch	(1+1)
	or: das Hausrecht hängt nicht ab/von dem Urteil eines Staatsanwaltes	(1+1)
	or: any words that make clear that it's the head of the hospital who makes decisions of this kind; it has nothing to do with lawyers	
(h)	Aufsichtsrat (governing body)	(1)
(i)	sie durfte/das Krankenhaus wieder betreten	(1+1)
(j)	es hat sich gelohnt/gegen das Unrecht (den Krankenhausleiter) zu kämpfen	(1+1)

TEST 4

Fußballfans in Bremen (5 marks, 1 for each correct answer)

(a) Bremen und Zeebrugge

(b) fängt die zweite Halbzeit an

(c) Mützen und Schals

(d) 19 Uhr 30

(e) einen Stuttgarter Schal

TEST 5

Ozonschichtgefahr (5 marks, 1 for each correct answer)

(a) richtig

(b) falsch

(c) richtig

(d) richtig

(e) falsch

TEST 6

Kindheitserinnerungen (13 marks, 1 for each correct point up to a maximum of 13)

father a soldier/with occupying troops (forces)/mother Viennese/left Vienna aged 3/ came to England/grew up bilingual/not a (social) advantage to speak German/so soon after the war/he (and brother) refused to speak German/would have lost his German/ but for Viennese contacts (relations)/felt excluded/other children did not want to play with him/German now sought after/foreign languages now important/because of the Common Market

3.6 PRACTISING SOME BASIC SKILLS

Numbers, dates, the time and individual letters of the alphabet occur frequently in both listening and reading texts. Comprehension questions are often targeted at this sort of basic information, so it is worth spending some time on practising these four 'survival' skills.

Numbers: Listen to the CD and write down the numbers that you will hear. They get progressively more difficult. Try first of all without stopping the CD. If you miss one go back and listen to it again. You can listen to the CD several times over a period of time until you can get them all right straight off!

Telling the time: You will hear different clock times, expressed in different ways. Write them down as numerals (3.30 a.m.; 7.15 p.m.). Do not write them down in words.

Dates: You will hear different dates. Write them down as they are spoken.

The alphabet: You will hear the alphabet in full. Repeat the pronunciation for each letter. Then 12 individual letters are spoken. Write them down. Finally 15 names are spelt out. Write them down too.

You can find all the 'answers' in Appendix 3.

CHAPTER 4

READING

Units in this chapter

4.1 INTRODUCTION

Although reading is tested in a formal way in a reading paper it is also a skill that you will need in other parts of the examination. In the written and speaking parts, for example essay titles and stimulus material will probably be in German. If you cannot understand what you are being asked to do you could end up doing something which is completely off the subject, so reading is of crucial importance. As we have stated elsewhere this is a skill that needs lots of practice.

4.2 THE READING EXAMINATION

In the reading paper a candidate's reading skills are tested in a number of different ways. You will certainly need to understand what the text is all about (global comprehension). You may be asked for details from the text (detailed comprehension). You may be asked to make inferences about things which are not actually in the text, but which you can make assumptions about from your knowledge of the text. Some Examining Boards will ask you to translate parts of the text into English. As well as showing understanding of a text you may also be required to manipulate the language of the text to show how good your knowledge of grammar is. A further possibility is writing a letter or other piece of guided composition which is based on the information contained in the reading text. Make sure you know what you will be asked to do so that you can prepare properly.

THE TYPES OF EXERCISES USED

The types of questions that are being set in the new A-level syllabus examinations are different from those set in the past, such as questions in English to be answered in English, although some Boards still have that question type. The following question types are now likely to occur:

- true or false statements;
- texts with gaps (sometimes you will have a list of possible words from which to choose the correct ones);
- questions in German to be answered in German;
- sentences that you have to complete;
- boxes to be completed with information from the text;
- translating part of the text into English;
- finding words or phrases in the text that correspond to definitions in German or phrases in English;
- sentences that you have to rephrase, but retaining the original meaning;
- summaries.

A METHOD OF ACTIVE READING

Whatever questions are set on a text your first priority is to understand the content of the text. That may seem obvious, but it is surprising how often students only skim read, looking for answers to specific questions. Try to develop a method for tackling a reading text:

- read the instructions at the beginning of the paper carefully before you start so that you are quite sure about how much time you have and how many questions you are supposed to answer;
- read the title of each passage and the questions before you start; they will give you valuable clues about the contents of the passage;
- read the passage through at least twice; parts that you did not understand on the first reading will become clearer on subsequent readings;
- underline the parts of the passage that you are not sure about and go back and spend more time on those;
- keep an eye open for key words in each paragraph and underline them;
- try to follow the author's argument; remember most writers will introduce their topic in the first paragraph and there will be one main idea in each paragraph; the passage will probably end with a restatement of the main theme;
- watch out for examples that the author has used to illustrate his/her points;
- if there are words that you do not understand make an intelligent guess at them when you have understood as much as possible; do not make a guess until you have understood as much as you can (some Boards now permit German/English dictionaries in the examination. If your Board does, make sure that you are familiar with how it works. Be careful not to spend too much time looking up words so that you do not complete the paper);
- make reading an active process, underlining words and making notes beside the text as you work.

SOME EXAMINATION TECHNIQUES

1 Normally the questions set on a passage are in the same order as the information in the passage. You would not expect to find the information for question number 1 at the end of the passage. The passages and questions at the beginning of the paper are generally easier than those at the end. It is called an 'incline of difficulty' and is intended to ease you into the paper gently. So start at the beginning and work through the paper in a steady manner.

2 Be aware of how much time you have for each part of the paper and keep an eye on the clock. You can only get full marks if you complete the paper. Do not leave out questions. When in doubt, guess! You may be right. If you leave it out you will get no marks for it. If you guess you may gain some marks. Attempting old examination papers is good training in managing your time successfully in the examination.

3 The marks shown beside each question are a good indicator of the number of points required for a complete answer. If the question is in a part of the examination where the accuracy of the language is also given credit, it is likely that half the marks for the question will be given for language and the other half will be for producing the correct information. When the accuracy of the language is also being assessed take extra care in constructing your answers, paying attention to the rules of grammar.

4 Get into the habit of checking what you have written. When you write a letter in English it is surprising how often you will find a mistake if you read it through again before sealing it in the envelope. If it can happen in your own language think how much more likely it is to happen in a foreign language when you are under pressure in an examination. It is a habit that you need to practise. It is difficult to do it suddenly in an examination for the first time.

4.3 WORKED EXAMPLES

In this section you will find some typical examination texts with a candidate's answers and an examiner's comments. You could try to do each one yourself before you look at what the candidate wrote and what the examiner's comments were. Then compare what you wrote with the examples and work out what mark your work would have been awarded. In a later section of this chapter you will find some more tests without any answers or comments. These are intended for you to practise on. The answers and mark schemes can be found after the tests.

EXAMPLE 1

Geschichten von Menschen

This is an example of a reading text with questions in German to be answered in German.

Rubric: Lesen Sie den folgenden Text durch und beantworten Sie die Fragen dazu:

ZUFALL ODER PLANUNG?

Eutin am 22. Juni 1955: Der 24jährige Bankangestellte Helmut Schumacher aus Bremen übernachtet während einer Radtour in der Eutiner Jugendherberge. Da trifft eine Klasse dänischer Teenager ein, unter ihnen Ruth Christensen aus Kopenhagen. Zufall oder Planung? Beide sind zum Küchendienst eingeteilt und bei Helmut fängt es an zu knistern. Mächtig freut er sich, als Ruth nach getaner Arbeit mit ihm durch die Stadt bummelt. Adressen werden ausgetauscht, und nach einigen Wochen werden die Postsäcke zwischen Bremen und Kopenhagen schwerer. Ostern 1956 reist Helmut zu Familie Christensen und läßt sich begutachten. Er übernachtet im Hotel. >>Das wollte ihre Mutter so!<< Der jungen Beziehung tat das offenbar gar nicht gut, denn nun folgen drei Jahre Sendepause. Erst auf seinen eindringlichen, schriftlich geäußerten Wunsch >>and don't forget to come to Bremen!<< knattert sie im Juli 1959 mit ihrer Vespa in die Hansestadt. >>Da hat's so richtig gefunkt.<< Am 25. März 1960 wird geheiratet. Dreißig Jahre nach dem jugendherbergsgemäßen Erst-Flirt startet die ganze Familie zur Erinnerungstour nach Eutin. Das war im Juli 1985. Preisfrage: Wo wird 2000 das 40jährige Ehejubiläum gefeiert werden?

Beantworten Sie folgende Fragen. Sie dürfen Wörter oder Ausdrücke aus dem Text benutzen, aber das Abschreiben ganzer Sätze oder Abschnitte ist nicht erlaubt.

(a) Wie ist Helmut Schumacher 1955 nach Eutin gefahren? (1)

(b) Aus welchem Land kam Ruth Christensen? (1)

(c) Was haben Ruth und Helmut nach der Arbeit in der Küche gemacht? (2)

(d) Warum haben Ruth und Helmut sich drei Jahre lang nicht mehr geschrieben? (2)

(e) Warum ist Ruth 1959 nach Bremen gefahren? (2)

(f) Was ist am 25. März 1960 passiert? (2)

ULEAC

Candidate's answers

(a) Wie ist Helmut Schumacher 1955 nach Eutin gefahren?

Candidate: Er hat eine Radtour gemacht.

Mark scheme: Mit dem Fahrrad. (1)

Examiner: This answer is correct and would receive full marks, although it would have been better for the candidate not to use a phrase out of the text. 1 mark.

(b) Aus welchem Land kam Ruth Christensen?

Candidate: Denmark.

Mark scheme: aus Dänemark. (1)

Examiner: The candidate did not know the correct German spelling for Denmark. Nevertheless the information is correct. Since there are no penalties for language errors in this question the candidate will receive full marks. 1 mark.

(c) Was haben Ruth und Helmut nach der Arbeit in der Küche gemacht?

Candidate: Sie haben einen Spaziergang gemacht.

Mark scheme: Sie sind ... gebummelt/gegangen/spazierengegangen (1)
durch die Stadt. (1)

Examiner: Only one of the two pieces of information being asked for is contained in this answer, so only one mark out of two. 1 mark.

(d) Warum haben Ruth und Helmut sich drei Jahre lang nicht mehr geschrieben?

Candidate: Der jungen Beziehung tat das offenbar gar nicht gut.

Mark scheme: Unter der Aufsicht der Familie (1)
konnte ihre Beziehung nicht gedeihen. (1)

Examiner: The candidate's answer has been 'lifted' from the original and this is expressly forbidden in the rubric. When this happens candidates cannot usually be awarded more than half of the available marks if what they have written answers the question. The answer to this question is not stated explicitly in the text. We are told that Helmut went to visit Ruth and had to stay in a hotel because her mother wanted him to, presumably rather than staying in the family home. Candidates are here required to infer information from the text. It looks very much as if the young couple did not have enough time together on their own to develop the relationship. No marks.

(e) Warum ist Ruth nach Bremen gefahren?

Candidate: Um Helmut zu besuchen.

Mark scheme: Er hat sie in einem Brief (1)
eindringlich eingeladen. (1)

Examiner: What the candidate has written is correct, as far as it goes, but it does not give enough detail. The candidate has failed to appreciate that it was only after being urged in a letter to come that she actually made the journey. No marks.

(f) Was ist am 25. März passiert?

Candidate: Sie haben geheiratet.

Mark scheme: Sie haben geheiratet.

Examiner: The candidate has given a perfect response and receives 2 marks.

Total: 5 marks out of 10.

EXAMPLE 2

Leichte Beute für Süchtige (15 Punkte)

This is an authentic text, taken from a German newspaper, about the theft of bicycles in Hamburg. The exercise consists of putting the correct information into boxes. In order to complete this exercise successfully it is important that you understand the text and can pick out the details required. Read the text through twice before attempting the questions.

Immer mehr Fahrraddiebstähle

Leichte Beute für Süchtige

Die Polizei hat in der Nacht zum Dienstag zwei Fahrraddiebe auf frischer Tat ertappt. Sie hatten in Lokstedt zwei Räder gestohlen, die jeweils mehr als 1000 Mark kosten. Damit liegen die Diebe voll im Hamburger und Bundes-Trend: Teure Räder sind besonders „beliebt". Diebe haben 1991 in Hamburg knapp 18 000 Räder gestohlen, umgerechnet knapp drei Prozent mehr als 1990. Mit der Steigerungsrate liegt Hamburg unter dem Bundestrend.

„Wir haben zwei Tendenzen ausgemacht", sagt Polizeisprecher Peter König. Neben extrem teuren Rädern würden auch immer mehr Uralt-Drahtesel gestohlen. Während sich in erster Linie Drogensüchtige und Diebesbanden über Luxus-Räder hermachten, würden billige Exemplare vor allem von Betrunkenen und Geh-Faulen gestohlen: Zechern, die kein Geld mehr für die Heimfahrt haben, oder Leute, denen die U-Bahn vor der Nase weggefahren ist. Sie werfen das Rad, zu Hause angekommen, gleich wieder weg.

Viele Heroinsüchtige finanzieren ihre Sucht mit dem Verkauf gestohlener Räder. „Die werden in der Regel im Großraum verkauft", so König. Daneben gibt es Banden, die mit Kleinlastern unterwegs sind, um teure Räder „einzusammeln" und gen Osten zu transportieren. Zu dieser „Gruppe" scheinen die zwei Männer (38, 46) zu gehören, die Dienstag morgen von einer Streife in Lokstedt gefaßt wurden. In ihrem Laster lagen Bolzenschneider und teure Sporträder. Die Herkunft der Räder ist unklar.

„Das genau ist häufig unser Problem", sagt Polizeisprecher König: eine Vielzahl der Bestohlenen sei nicht in der Lage, ihre Räder vernünftig zu beschreiben. Und ohne Opfer kein Täter: Wenn die Polizei ein sicher-gestelltes Rad keiner Anzeige zuordnen kann und Zeugen fehlen, muß sie den Dieb laufen-lassen – und im schlimmsten Fall das Rad noch mitgeben.

Räder werden tagsüber in erster Linie dort gestohlen, wo viele beisammen stehen – bei Schwimmbädern, Bahnhöfen und Schulen. Dort falle es kaum auf, wenn manipuliert werde. 1991 gingen bei der Hamburger Polizei umgerechnet 50 Anzeigen pro Tag ein. An Spitzentagen im Sommer waren es mehr als 100. Für 1992 rechnet die Polizei mit einem leichten Anstieg.

Bundesweit hat 1991 der „Radklau" um mehr als fünf Prozent zugenommen – auf 436 200 gestohlene Räder, die aneinan-dergereiht eine Schlange von Hamburg bis München ergäben. Der Schaden liegt bei mehr als 200 Millionen Mark. In der Hitliste der „beliebtesten Städte" führt Münster vor Hamburg.

Rubric: Ergänzen Sie die Tabelle mit Informationen aus dem Text.

(a)	Wie sich die Anzahl der Fahrrad-diebstähle in Hamburg im Vergleich zu 1990 verändert hat.	
(b)	Grund, warum billige Fahrräder von Menschen ohne Geld gestohlen werden.	
(c)	Grund, warum billige Fahrräder von faulen Menschen gestohlen werden.	
(d)	Was mit solchen Rädern passiert, wenn sie nicht mehr gebraucht werden.	
(e)	Grund, warum Fahrräder von Süchtigen gestohlen werden.	
(f)	Wo diese teuren Räder hingebracht werden.	
(g)	Wie die Fahrräder transportiert werden.	
(h)	Gruppe, der die 2 Männer angehörten, die in der Nacht zum Dienstag verhaftet wurden.	
(i)	Ein großes Problem für die Polizei, wenn sie ein gestohlenes Rad wiederfindet.	
(j)	Wo Fahrräder hauptsächlich gestohlen werden.	
(k)	Jahreszeit, in der die meisten Fahrräder gestohlen werden.	
(l)	Trend der Fahrraddiebstähle für 1992 im Vergleich zu 1991.	
(m)	Höchste Anzahl der Fahrräder, die an einem Tag in Hamburg gestohlen werden.	
(n)	Wie sich die Anzahl der Fahrraddiebstähle 1991 im Vergleich zu 1990 in der BRD verändert hat.	
(o)	Eine Stadt, in der mehr Fahrräder als in Hamburg gestohlen werden.	

Oxford

Candidate's answers

(a) Wie sich die Anzahl der Fahrraddiebstähle in Hamburg im Vergleich zu 1990 verändert hat.

Candidate: 1991 gab es mehr.

Mark Scheme: 3% (half a mark); mehr (half a mark)

Examiner: The candidate would receive only half a mark for this answer, for not indicating by how much more bicycle thefts in Hamburg increased.

(b) Grund, warum billige Fahrräder von Menschen ohne Geld gestohlen werden.

Candidate: Weil sie die Heimfahrt nicht bezahlen können.

Mark scheme: Sie haben kein Geld für die Heimfahrt. (1)

Examiner: A good answer. 1 mark.

(c) Grund, warum billige Fahrräder von faulen Menschen gestohlen werden.

Candidate: Sie wollen nicht zu Fuß nach Hause gehen.

Mark scheme: Man hat die letzte U-bahn verpaßt. (1)

Examiner: This answer would receive no marks. The candidate has failed to understand the precise reason and has probably guessed on the basis of the word *faulen* in the question.

(d) Was mit solchen Rädern passiert, wenn sie nicht mehr gebraucht werden.

Candidate: Sie werfen das Rad, zu Hause angekommen gleich wieder weg.

Mark scheme: Man wirft das Rad weg. (1)

Examiner: This answer is correct, but it has been 'lifted' straight out of the text, which candidates are forbidden to do. The maximum mark here would be a half mark.

(e) Grund, warum Fahrräder von Süchtigen gestohlen werden.

Candidate: Um die Fahrräder zu verkaufen.

Mark scheme: Um ihre Sucht mit dem Verkauf der Räder zu finanzieren. (1)

Examiner: This answer is not precise enough and would receive no marks. Yes, the bicycles are sold, but the reason why is important.

(f) Wo diese teuren Räder hingebracht werden.

Candidate: Nach Ostdeutschland.

Mark scheme: Nach dem Osten. (1)

Examiner: The text states that the bicycles are taken *gen Osten*, which could be to East Germany, Poland or Russia. Nevertheless this answer deserves full marks. 1 mark.

(g) Wie die Fahrräder transportiert werden.

Candidate: Mit Kleinlastern.

Mark scheme: Mit Kleinlastern. (1)

Examiner: A good answer. 1 mark.

(h) Gruppe, der die 2 Männer angehörten, die in der Nacht zum Dienstag verhaftet wurden.

Candidate: Zu dieser Gruppe.

Mark scheme: Zu einer Diebesbande. (1)

Examiner: This answer is once again 'lifted' from the text and does not explain which group of bicycle thieves the two men belonged to. No marks.

(i) Ein großes Problem für die Polizei, wenn sie ein gestohlenes Rad wiederfindet.

Candidate: Sie weiß oft nicht, wer der Besitzer ist.

Mark scheme: Der Besitzer kann es nicht identifizieren. (1)

Examiner: Although this answer is phrased differently from the mark scheme, it does answer the question according to the text. So 1 mark.

(j) Wo Fahrräder hauptsächlich gestohlen werden.

Candidate: Bei Schwimmbädern, Bahnhöfen und Schulen.

Mark scheme: Bei Schwimmbädern, Bahnhöfen und Schulen (any 2 – half a mark each).
Examiner: A perfect answer. 1 mark.

(k) Jahreszeit, in der die meisten Fahrräder gestohlen werden.

Candidate: 1991.
Mark scheme: Im Sommer. (1)
Examiner: The candidate has not read the question properly. The information required is the season, not the year. No marks.

(l) Trend der Fahrraddiebstähle für 1992 im Vergleich zu 1991.

Candidate: Man rechnet mit einem leichten Anstieg.
Mark scheme: Es wird einen Anstieg geben. (1)
Examiner: Although this answer uses some of the language of the original text it has been manipulated by the candidate and has not been lifted word for word. It is a good answer and deserves full marks. 1 mark.

(m) Höchste Anzahl der Fahrräder, die an einem Tag in Hamburg gestohlen werden.

Candidate: 100.
Mark scheme: 100+. (1)
Examiner: This answer would only be given half a mark, because the text says that more than 100 bicycles are stolen on peak days. Half a mark.

(n) Wie sich die Anzahl der Fahrraddiebstähle 1991 im Vergleich zu 1990 in der BRD verändert hat.

Candidate: Es gibt 5% mehr.
Mark scheme: Es gibt mehr als 5% (half a mark) mehr (half a mark).
Examiner: Only half marks again for this answer, for not understanding that there were more than 5% more bicycles stolen in 1991 than in 1990. Half a mark.

(o) Eine Stadt, in der mehr Fahrräder als in Hamburg gestohlen werden.

Candidate: München.
Mark scheme: Münster (1)
Examiner: The candidate has obviously looked through the text for the name of a town in Germany and chose the most obvious one, a guess which was wrong. No marks.

Total: 8 marks out of a possible 15.

EXAMPLE 3

How much time is allocated!?
much much harder than
Ex. 2
AS of R2
A2 ?

Spieleparadies in der Stube (33 Punkte)

This text is about a young man who collects board games. There are two exercises: inserting words that are missing from the beginning of the text and completing sentences with the necessary information. Read the text carefully through at least twice and then attempt the two exercises.

Spieleparadies in der Stube

Thorsten Dreyer sammelt Gesellschaftsspiele wie andere Leute Bücher

① **Loxstedt. Wie ein Laden für Gesellschaftsspiele wirkt die Wohnung ¹ Thorsten Dreyer in Loxstedt. ² den Wänden stehen Regale voller Spiele aller Art, ³ dem Schreibtisch, dem Fußboden und selbst auf der Heizung stapeln sich die kleinen und großen Pappschachteln. Ein Paradies ⁴ jeden, der unterhaltsamen Zeitvertreib sucht.**

② Aber nicht von einem einzigen der Spiele würde sich der 29jährige Beamte vom Militärwetterdienst trennen. Er hat das Sammeln solcher Spiele nämlich ⁵ seinem Hobby erkoren.

③ Lachend empfängt der immer gutgelaunte Spielefan, der sich neben seiner Sammelleidenschaft noch der Jugendarbeit verschrieben hat, seine Besucher an der Wohnungstür. Eine Treppe höher kommen sie ⁶ dem Staunen dann gar nicht mehr heraus.

④ „Es war ⁷ einem Seminar, das ich ⁸ fast anderthalb Jahren für den Gemeindejugendring Loxstedt in Worpswede besucht habe. Dort wurde uns gezeigt, wie gut man Kinder und Jugendliche aller Altersgruppen ⁹ Spielen beschäftigen kann. Das hat mir so gut gefallen, daß ich begann, selbst Spiele zu sammeln", erinnert sich der Loxstedter. Von da an verschaffte er sich Spiele, wo er nur an sie herankommen konnte.

Auf Flohmärkten gestöbert

⑤ Viele fand er auf Flohmärkten, etliche bekam er von Bekannten, aber eine große Zahl kaufte er auch neu. „Das ist meist eine ziemlich teure Angelegenheit", meint er. In weniger als 18 Monaten kamen so mehr als 500 Spiele zusammen. Ihm selbst sind solche am liebsten, die kooperativ in Gruppen gespielt werden. „Man glaubt gar nicht, wie ein solches Spiel die Gemeinsamkeit fördert. Es gibt kaum etwas Schöneres, als gemeinsame Strategien zu entwickeln, um dem spielerischen Gegner ein Schnippchen zu schlagen."

⑥ Auch einige Raritäten gehören zu Thorsten Dreyers Sammlung, darunter ein Kartenspiel von 1963 und ein amerikanisches Wirtschaftsspiel von 1964. „Manchmal finde ich ein bereits viele Jahre altes Spiel, bei dem das Zubehör noch originalverpackt ist und das deshalb also noch nie gespielt worden sein kann", berichtet der Sammler.

Spielenachmittage

⑦ Wer nun denkt, daß all die schönen Spiele nur ungenutzt in Thorstens Wohnung stehen, täuscht sich. Seit kurzem bietet er in Zusammenarbeit mit der Jugendpflege der Gemeinde Loxstedt im Haus der Begegnung Spielenachmittage von 15 bis 18 Uhr an, für die Mitspieler kostenlos. Die nächsten Termine: 16. September, 14. Oktober, 11. November und 9. Dezember.

⑧ Ausweiten konnte der Spieler aus Leidenschaft sein Hobby, als es ihm gelang, freier Mitarbeiter eines großen Spieleverlages zu werden, in dessen Auftrag er nun neue Spiele testet. „Der Verlag schickt mir neue Spielentwürfe zu, die ich dann, je nach Zielgruppe, mit Freunden, Kindern oder auch ganzen Familien spiele und darüber ein Beobachtungsprotokoll ausfülle. Kommen darin Ungereimtheiten vor, kann es sein, daß der Autor des Spiels noch einmal neu nachdenken muß. Das macht natürlich unheimlich Spaß, weil man mit Spielen umgeht, die es eigentlich noch gar nicht gibt", erklärt Thorsten Dreyer. An Mitspieler mangelt es ihm nicht. „Jeder, der einmal ein neues Spiel mitgemacht hat, möchte das auch öfter. Ich habe deshalb eine große Auswahl", schmunzelt er.

⑨ Irgendwann, so hofft der Spielenarr außerdem, wird einmal sein ganz großer Wunsch in Erfüllung gehen. Er möchte mit einem Bus voller Spiele von Ort zu Ort fahren, um Spieltage oder -abende für alle Altersgruppen anzubieten. „Das wäre für mich das Höchste überhaupt", sagt er. Sein zweiter großer Wunsch ist, daß er auch Spiele für seine Sammlung angeboten bekommt, die aus der Zeit vor 1960 stammen.

⑩ Schon heute bietet er an, mit seinen Spielen zu Veranstaltungen, wie zum Beispiel Dorf- oder Vereinsfesten, zu kommen. „Wer so etwas möchte, kann mich gerne unter der Telefonnummer 0 47 44/35 36 anrufen. Das gilt natürlich auch für solche Leute, die mir weitere Spiele anbieten möchten."

(i) Ergänzen Sie die Lücken im Text mit einer Präposition aus dieser Liste. Benutzen Sie jede Präposition nur einmal. Vorsicht! Es gibt mehr Präpositionen als Lücken.

auf; an; aus; bei; durch; für; mit; seit; von; vor; zu.

(ii) Ergänzen Sie die folgenden Sätze mit den richtigen Informationen aus dem Text. Die Absätze, wo Sie die Informationen finden können, sind angegeben.

(a) [3. Absatz] Thorsten Dreyers Hobby ist nicht seine einzige Freizeitbeschäftigung, denn…

(b) [4. Absatz] Er begann sich für dieses Hobby zu interessieren, nachdem…

(c) [5. Absatz] Er findet es ein teures Hobby, weil…

(d) [7. Absatz] Die Spiele werden auch oft benutzt, weil…

(e) [8. Absatz] Jetzt bekommt er von einem Spieleverlag neue Spiele, die…

(f) [9. Absatz] Er möchte seine Sammlung noch ausweiten, indem…

Oxford

Candidate's answers

Candidate: 1) von; 2) auf; 3) an; 4) für; 5) vor; 6) aus; 7) bei; 8) seit; 9) durch.

Mark scheme: 1) von; 2) an; 3) auf; 4) für; 5) zu; 6) aus; 7) bei; 8) vor; 9) mit.

Examiner: The candidate has four answers correct out of a possible nine. The candidate still confuses the use of *auf* and *an* in gaps (2) and (3). *Auf* is used to mean on top of a horizontal surface whereas *an* is used to indicate on a vertical surface, such as a wall. It should have been: *an den Wänden* (on the walls) and *auf dem Schreibtisch* (on the desk). In gap number (5) there is confusion in the candidate's mind perhaps between *vor* and *für*, although it would have been impossible to use *für* in this gap because it takes the accusative case and the case of the word after the preposition is dative (*seinem Hobby*). In gap number (8) both *seit* and *vor* can be used with expressions of time, but they have very different meanings: *vor anderthalb Jahren* means *one and a half years ago*; *seit anderthalb Jahren* means *for the last year and a half*. In this text the former is the correct one. In gap (9) *durch* would have been possible if it had been *durch das Spielen*. The word after the gap is in the dative plural and requires a preposition that governs the dative case.

(a) Thorsten Dreyers Hobby ist nicht seine einzige Freizeitbeschäftigung, denn…

Candidate: er viel Jugendarbeit verschreibt.

Mark scheme: er arbeitet auch mit jungen Leuten. (2+2)

Examiner: In this exercise two of the marks are given for showing comprehension and two of the marks are awarded for the accuracy of the language. The German must be intelligible to a sympathetic native German speaker to gain any marks at all. What the candidate has written does not make any sense and would, therefore, get no marks. The text has used the expression *sich verschreiben* which means *to devote oneself to something*. In this case Thorsten has devoted himself to youth work. Without the reflexive pronoun *verschreiben* means *to prescribe*, which makes what the candidate has written nonsense. It is always a good idea to answer comprehension questions in your own words, rather than using the words of the text. There is also a bad grammatical error in the candidate's answer. The conjunction *denn* does not affect the position of the verb. The verb should come after *er*. No marks.

(b) Er begann sich für dieses Hobby zu interessieren, nachdem…

Candidate: er einem Seminar besucht hat.

Mark scheme: er ein Seminar besucht hat. (2+2)

Examiner: This answer gets full marks for comprehension (two for giving the correct information), but loses a mark for writing *einem Seminar* (the wrong case). 3 marks.

In some of the new syllabuses marks for this kind of grammatical mistake are not deducted question by question but for the paper as a whole. There might be a mark out of 10 for grammatical accuracy and that will be assessed globally for all the written German on the paper.

(c) Er findet es ein teures Hobby, weil...

Candidate: in weniger als 18 Monaten kamen so mehr als 500 Spiele zusammen.

Mark scheme: er viele Spiele neu kauft. (2+2)

Examiner: The candidate has copied this answer straight from the text, which is penalised (*Das Abschreiben ganzer Sätze oder Abschnitte ist nicht erlaubt.*) It also does not answer the question satisfactorily, because it does not state why it was an expensive hobby. No marks.

(d) Die Spiele werden auch oft benutzt, weil...

Candidate: er Spielenachmittage für junge Leute in seinem Haus organisiert.

Mark scheme: er Spielenachmittage für junge Leute organisiert. (2+2)

Examiner: This is a good answer which gives the correct information. Unfortunately it also gives some information which is wrong. The activity is not organised in his house, but *im Haus der Begegnung*. Instead of two marks for comprehension this candidate would receive only one. In this exercise a candidate cannot receive more marks for language than have been given for comprehension, so the total mark is 1 + 1.

(e) Jetzt bekommt er von einem Spieleverlag neue Spiele, die...

Candidate: er mit Freunden spielt und dann ein Beobachtungsprotokoll ausfülle.

Mark scheme: er mit Freunden, Kindern oder ganzen Familien spielt, um zu sehen, ob die Spiele gut sind. (2+2)

Examiner: The candidate's answer is good. It gets over the idea of playing the games and then writing a report about them, so it would get full marks for comprehension. Unfortunately there is a grammatical mistake in the last word. The candidate has copied the verb *ausfülle* from the text but has forgotten to change its ending from the *ich*-form to the *er*-form (*ausfüllt*). One mark will be deducted for grammatical inaccuracy. 3 marks.

(f) Er möchte seine Sammlung noch ausweiten, indem...

Candidate: er mit einem Bus voller Spiele von Ort zu Ort fährt.

Mark scheme: er Spiele aus der Zeit vor 1960 bekommt. (2+2)

Examiner: The candidate has been misled by the word *möchte* which occurs in both the text and the sentence to be completed. Unfortunately it is not the correct information. Thorsten would very much like to travel from place to place with a bus full of games, but that would not help him to widen his collection. No marks.

Total: 8 marks out of 24.

EXAMPLE 4

Der blonde Engel der deutschen Straßenkinder

This is a newspaper article about a German, Markus Seidel, who helps homeless children. The exercise consists of finding phrases in the text that correspond to the definitions given. Read the text through twice before attempting the exercise.

Rubric: Lesen Sie den Text durch und finden Sie im Text die Worte, die mit den folgenden Ausdrücken zusammenpassen.

Der blonde Engel der deutschen Straßenkinder

Markus Seidel ist Tag für Tag mit der Bahn und seinem Funktelefon in Deutschland unterwegs. In Donaueschingen zurück bleibt nur seine Stimme auf dem Anrufbeantworter: „Straßenkinder und alle, die nicht gern auf dieses Band sprechen, können mich unter folgender Nummer erreichen." Seidels Schützlinge sind Vergessene der Gesellschaft: Straßenkinder. Lange schien es sie nicht zu geben, die Zehn-bis Vierzehnjährigen, die oft unerträgliche familiäre Verhältnisse hinter sich gelassen haben und in Städten untergetaucht sind. Auf fast 2000 schätzt man ihre Zahl.

Straßenkinder in Deutschland. Eine 14jährige aus Berlin beichtet ihm, daß sie wegen der Kälte wieder „drückt". Monatelang war sie weg vom Heroin. Ein 12jähriger ist aus seiner Wohngruppe aus-gebüchst; von einem anderen hat Seidel nur ein Bild und weiß, daß er sich in Köln herumtreibt. Markus Seidel wird die drei Kinder aufsuchen. „Wir können nur in Einzelfällen helfen", bedauert er. „Unsere Arbeit hat ja eben erst begonnen; wir können nicht die Retter der Nation sein."

Straßenkinder in Deutschland – so heißt auch Markus Seidels Buch im Ullstein-Verlag. Als der 27jährige blonde Werbemann und Journalist das Thema recherchierte, kam er nicht wieder davon los. Seither tut er alles für diese Kinder, die nur zu gerne wieder ein Zuhause hätten; aufgegeben haben sich die wenigsten. Aber sie sind schwer zu finden, und ihr Vertrauen zu gewinnen ist ähnlich schwer. Sie meiden die Sozialbehörden, und „du erkennst sie nicht, wenn sie dir begegnen", sagt Seidel. „Meist sind es die weichen Charaktere, die auf der Straße landen; nicht die Hartgesottenen."

Seidel hat im Frühjahr in Donaueschingen den „Off-Road-Kids-Förderverein" gegründet. Erklärtes Ziel: „Konkrete Zukunftsperspektiven für Deutschlands Straßenkinder". Mit ein paar ehrenamtlichen Mitarbeitern betreibt er diesen „Notdienst". Ihm wird seinerseits geholfen von der Münchner Initiative „Children for a better world", entstanden im Januar 1994 auf Anregung des Verlegers Florian Langenscheidt. Die Deutsche Bahn spendierte den Helfern der Kinder sechs Jahresnetzkarten, Mannesmann Mobilfunk das Telefon. „Weihnachten ist bitter für die Kids,"weiß Seidel. Das Fest versuchen sie gemeinsam zu bestehen. Die Abstürze kommen dann danach.

(a) er fährt die ganze Zeit [1. Absatz] (1)

(b) Menschen, auf die man aufpaßt, damit ihnen nichts passiert [1. Absatz] (1)

(c) sie sind in großen Orten verschwunden [1. Absatz] (1)

(d) sie gesteht Markus etwas, was man nicht weiter erzählen darf [2. Absatz] (1)

(e) er hat die Menschen, mit denen er wohnt, verlassen [2. Absatz] (1)

(f) sie möchten noch einmal eine Wohnung haben [3. Absatz] (1)

(g) die staatlichen Institutionen, die dafür verantwortlich sind, Sozialbenachteiligten zu helfen [3. Absatz] (1)

(h) sein Zuhause verlieren [3. Absatz] (1)

(i) Menschen, die freiwillig arbeiten, ohne Gehalt oder Lohn für ihre Arbeit zu bekommen [4. Absatz] (1)

(j) er leitet diese Aktion, Menschen in Not zu helfen [4. Absatz] (1)

Candidate's answers

(a) Er fährt die ganze Zeit.

Candidate: Er ist unterwegs

Mark scheme: Er ist Tag für Tag unterwegs. (1)

Examiner: This response fails to give an equivalent for *die ganze Zeit* and receives therefore only half a mark.

(b) Menschen, auf die man aufpaßt.

Candidate: Vergessene der Gesellschaft.

Mark scheme: Schützlinge. (1)

Examiner: This answer is completely wrong. *Schützlinge* comes from the verb *schützen*, which means *to protect*. *Vergessene* comes from the verb *vergessen*, meaning *to forget*. No marks.

(c) Sie sind in großen Orten verschwunden:

Candidate: In Städten untergetaucht sind.

Mark scheme: In Städten untergetaucht sind. (1)

Examiner: A completely correct answer. 1 mark.

(d) Sie gesteht Markus etwas, was man nicht weiter erzählen darf.

Candidate: Sie beichtet.

Mark scheme: Sie beichtet ihm. (1)

Examiner: Although this answer contains the important verb *beichtet*, it leaves out *ihm* and so gets only half a mark again.

(e) Er hat die Menschen, mit denen er wohnt, verlassen.

Candidate: Er ist aus seiner Wohngruppe ausgebüchst.

Mark scheme: Er ist aus seiner Wohngruppe ausgebüchst. (1)

Examiner: Another good answer. Full marks.

(f) Sie möchten noch einmal eine Wohnung haben.

Candidate: Sie hätten gerne ein Zuhause

Mark scheme: Sie hätten gerne wieder ein Zuhause. (1)

Examiner: The candidate has once again left out an important element and therefore loses half a mark. The word *wieder* has been omitted.

(g) Die staatlichen Institutionen, die für die Sozialbenachteiligten verantwortlich sind.

Candidate: Die Sozialbehörden.

Mark scheme: Die Sozialbehörden. (1)

Examiner: Full marks.

(h) Sein Zuhause verlieren.

Candidate: Aufgegeben haben sich die wenigsten.

Mark scheme: Auf der Straße landen. (1)

Examiner: It looks as if the candidate has guessed, which is much better than leaving a blank. This answer comes in the text before the previous answer, which does not normally happen. The candidate should have chosen a phrase after *Sozialbehörden*. No marks.

(i) Menschen, die freiwillig arbeiten, ohne Gehalt oder Lohn.

Candidate: Mit ein paar ehrenamtlichen Mitarbeitern.

Mark scheme: Ehrenamtlichen Mitarbeitern. (1)

Examiner: In this answer the candidate has included too much material from the text and thus receives only half marks again.

(j) Er leitet diese Aktion, Menschen in Not zu helfen.

Candidate: Betreibt er diesen Notdienst.

Mark scheme: Er betreibt diesen Notdienst. (1)

Examiner: The candidate has copied the words as they were in the text and in this kind of exercise that is perfectly acceptable. Full marks.

Total: 6 marks out of 10.

4.4 EXAMINATION PRACTICE

TEST 1

Weight Watchers

This is an advertisement for a job with the organisation *Weight Watchers*. The exercise based on it consists of statements about the text which you have to assess as *falsch* or *richtig*. Read the text carefully and then attempt the exercise.

Werden Sie Partnerin von

WEIGHT WATCHERS

Sie können gemeinsam mit uns, einem führenden Beratungsunternehmen für Gewichtsreduktion und gesunde Ernährung, einen oder mehrere Beratungstreffpunkte übernehmen als

selbständige Beraterin

Wir stehen mit unserem Namen für ein ausgezeichnetes, in 30 Jahren bewährtes und wissenschaftlich anerkanntes Konzept zur langfristigen Gewichtskontrolle und gesunden Ernährung. Viele Krankenkassen erstatten einen Teil der Kursgebühren.

Ihre Tätigkeit, ob haupt- oder nebenberuflich, unterstützen wir u. a. durch Aus- und kontinuierliche Weiterbildung, Organisation, Werbung und Öffentlichkeitsarbeit.

Sie sind zwischen 25 und 40 Jahre jung und haben ihre berufliche Qualifikation als Ernährungsberaterin, Diätassistentin oder in verwandten Tätigkeiten erworben. Sie sind in der Lage, Selbsterfahrungsgruppen zu leiten. Sie zeichnen sich aus durch Eigeninitiative, Verantwortungsbewußtsein und Organisationstalent.

Wollen Sie mehr über diese Aufgabe und uns wissen?

Dann richten Sie bitte Ihre Kurzbewerbung an:
**WEIGHT WATCHERS (Deutschland) GmbH, Personalabtlg.,
Postfach 10 53 44, 40044 Düsseldorf.**

Weight Watchers

MEHR ALS NUR EINE DIÄT

Rubric: Sind die Aussagen zum Text falsch oder richtig? (10 Punkte)

(a) *Weight Watchers* ist ein neues Unternehmen auf diesem Gebiet.

(b) *Weight Watchers* sucht Frauen, die Angestellte des Unternehmens werden sollen.

(c) *Weight Watchers* interessiert sich nur für Gewichtsreduktion.

(d) Leute, die abnehemen wollen, bekommen oft finanzielle Unterstützung von ihrer Krankenkasse.

(e) Es spielt keine Rolle, wenn die Bewerberinnen eine andere Tätigkeit nebenbei ausüben wollen.

(f) *Weight Watchers* unterstützt erfolgreiche Bewerberinnen bei ihrer Arbeit durch Ausbildungsprogramme.

(g) Erfolgreiche Bewerberinnen müßten ihre eigene Werbung für das ganze Konzept von *Weight Watchers* organisieren.

(h) Die Arbeit besteht darin, einzelne Menschen zu beraten, die abnehmen wollen.

(i) Man muß selbständig arbeiten können, um diesen Posten zu bekommen.

(j) Die ganzen Organisationsarbeiten für die Beratungsgruppen werden von *Weight Watchers* unternommen.

TEST 2

Blindes Vertrauen (11 Punkte)

This is an authentic text about a blind woman, Marina Stawitzki, and her dog. The test consists of broken sentences, which you have to join up. Read the text carefully and then attempt the test.

Hamburger Abendblatt

Blindes Vertrauen

Wie Hunde sehbehinderte Menschen durch eine dunkle Welt führen

150 000 Deutsche leben in ewiger Finsternis. Keine Sonne, keine Gesichter – immer in Angst vor dem falschen Schritt. Aber blind sein heißt nicht hilflos sein. Wissenschaftliche

Studien beweisen: Führhunde können den Sehbehinderten ein fast „normales" Leben ermöglichen – wenn die Tiere richtig ausgebildet sind. Aber warum sieht man sie so selten?

Von RÜDIGER KAHL

HA **Essen** – Sie war gerade elf Jahre alt, als zum erstenmal die Bilder aus ihrem Schulbuch im Nebel versanken…

Als sie auch am hellichten Tage nicht mehr ohne Lampe lesen konnte, ging die Mutter mit ihr zum Arzt. Die Diagnose ein Schock: „Retinopathia pigmentosa" – kurz Röhren- oder Tunnelblick genannt. Eine Krankheit ohne Heilungschance.

Sie hat dennoch gekämpft, sich aufgelehnt und gewehrt. Vergebens…

Seit drei Jahren lebt Marina Stawitzki aus Essen in einer dunklen Welt. Ihr Lichtblick: Die 40jährige ist nicht allein. Ehemann Herbert (42) und Tochter Jana (6), beide können sehen, geben ihr Kraft und Lebensmut.

Und vor allem ist da ‚Amos', ein Golden Retriever mit eisernen Nerven. Der vier Jahre alte Blindenhund gibt ihr einen Teil der Freiheit zurück, die sie mit dem Augenlicht verloren hat. Sicher führt er sie über Fußwege und Straßen, lotst sie zielstrebig durch volle Kaufhäuser, sucht den freien Platz im Bus und weiß

genau, an welcher Haltestelle er aussteigen muß…

„Seit ich ‚Amos' an meiner Seite habe, bin ich selbständiger und selbstbewußter", sagt Marina Stawitzki. „Ich kann mit meiner Tochter heute 95 Prozent der Dinge tun, die auch eine sehende Mutter mit ihrem Kind machen kann. Ohne Hund war das unmöglich. Ich war immer von anderen Menschen abhängig."

Eine neue Studie der Universität Bonn bestätigt das. Professor Dr. Reinhold Bergler, Direktor des Psychologischen Instituts: „Der Hund ist für die Blinden ein Hilfsmittel mit Seele. Er führt viele aus ihrer Einsamkeit und Isolation heraus, denn über den Hund werden Kontakte zu Mitmenschen hergestellt, die sonst nie zustande kommen."

Dennoch tasten sich die meisten Sehbehinderten allein mit dem weißen Stock voran. Nur etwa 2200 Blinde (1,5 Prozent) lassen sich in Deutschland von einem Hund führen. Denn die hochqualifizierten Tiere sind teuer. Ausbildung und Nachbetreuung verschlingen bis zu 40 000 Mark. Auch wenn der Augenarzt einen Hund ausdrücklich verordnet,

bieten die Krankenkassen den Blinden oft erst einmal den Stock an. Einmalige Kosten: rund 1800 Mark.

Hinzu kommt, daß unseriöse Geschäftemacher den ernsthaften Ausbildern die Preise verderben. Auf dem ohnehin engen Markt werden kaum ausgebildete Tiere für 10 000 bis 15 000 Mark angeboten. Oft beherrschen sie nur ein oder zwei Kommandos. „So lange die Ausbildung nicht rechtlich geschützt wird, sind die seriösen Schulen in ihrer Existenz bedroht, die wilden Trainer machen das große Geschäft", sagt der weltweit renommierte Blindenführhundausbilder Walter H. Rupp aus Basel.

Um die schwarzen Schafe zu überführen, wurden von den Kassen inzwischen Qualitätskriterien erlassen und eine Abschlußprüfung für die Hunde eingeführt. Bisher ist daraus nicht mehr als eine Art freiwilliger Selbstkontrolle geworden, denn – so Rupp – „es fehlen unabhängige Experten, die die Prüfungen auch abnehmen können…"

Ein Dilemma, von dem Marina Stawitzki verschont blieb. „Amos" beherrscht seine Führungsauf-

gaben. Der Hund hat 26 000 Mark gekostet und sie brauchte keinen Pfennig dazu bezahlen. Für Futter und Arztkosten gibt es einen monatlichen Zuschuß von 250 Mark.

„Bei mir gab es glücklicherweise keine Probleme mit der Kasse. Aber ich weiß von Fällen, wo das anders gelaufen ist." Damit jeder Blinde den Hund bekommt, der ihm auch wirklich nützt, gründet Marina Stawitzki jetzt sogar einen eigenen Verein. „Ich möchte anderen blinden Menschen helfen, die sich im Alltag nicht so zurechtfinden wie ich." Vor allem will sie Verständnis schaffen. Daß es daran mangelt, bekommt sie täglich zu spüren.

So erteilte der Lebensmittelhändler, bei dem Marina Stawitzki jahrelang Stammkundin war, ihr plötzlich Hausverbot, als sie mit dem Hund in den Laden wollte.

Auch bei vielen Veranstaltungen, in Kinos, Theatern, Kirchen oder Gaststätten heißt es oft: Hunde müssen draußen bleiben.

Marina Stawitzki: „Selbst mein Augenarzt, der mir ‚Amos' ausdrücklich verordnet hat, sagte zu mir: ‚Mit dem Hund kommen Sie bei mir nicht in die Praxis…'"

Rubric: Welche Satzteile gehören zusammen? Vorsicht! Es gibt mehr Endungen als Anfänge. Tragen Sie den richtigen Buchstaben in die Kästchen ein!

1 Marina hat seit langem Sehschwierigkeiten, weil…

2 Marina kann Mut in ihrer schwierigen Situation zeigen, weil…

3 Sie kann sogar durch volle Kaufhäuser ohne Probleme kommen, weil…

4 Marina kann mit ihrem Hund mit dem Bus fahren, weil…

5 Marina kann wie eine normale Mutter fast alles tun, weil…

6 Blinde Menschen, die einen Blindenhund haben, sind auch nicht mehr so einsam, weil…

7 Nur wenige Blinde haben einen Hund, weil…

8 Einige Hunde sind nicht so gut wie andere, weil…

9 Neu ausgebildete Hunde müssen jetzt geprüft werden, weil…

10 Marina hat ihren Hund umsonst gekriegt, weil…

11 Marina hat einen Verein gegründet, weil…

(a) ein paar skrupellose Trainer sie nicht richtig ausgebildet haben.

(b) es einem Blinden erlaubt werden sollte, ein Geschäft mit seinem Hund zu betreten.

(c) sie anderen Blinden im Alltag helfen möchte.

(d) sie schon als Kind an Retinopathia pigmentosa erkrankte.

(e) Amos sie erfolgreich an ihr Ziel führt.

(f) sie einen Blindenhund hat.

(g) sie sehr teuer sind.

(h) die Krankenkasse alles bezahlt hat.

(i) er genau weiß, an welcher Stelle er aussteigen muß.

(j) ihr Mann und ihre Tochter sie unterstützen.

(k) die Krankenkassen sich vergewissern wollen, daß die Hunde eine volle Ausbildung gehabt haben.

(l) sie durch ihren Hund mit anderen leicht ins Gespräch kommen.

1	2	3	4	5	6	7	8	9	10	11

TEST 3

Für Norbert Stein wurde ein Alptraum Wirklichkeit (15 Punkte)

This is an article from a magazine about a father's narrow escape during an outing with his two young children. The test that follows is a cloze test (a text with gaps that you have to fill). Read the text carefully at least twice and then read the cloze test through carefully, trying to work out what sort of word is missing from each gap. Is a noun, a verb, an adjective or an adverb missing?

Für Norbert Stein wurde ein Alptraum Wirklichkeit

Während der Vater seinen kleinen Söhnen in die Straßenbahn half, fuhr der Waggon plötzlich ohne ihn ab

Sekundenlang war Norbert Stein zu keinem klaren Gedanken fähig. Entsetzt und starr vor Schreck blickte er der Straßenbahn nach, die schon einige Meter von ihm entfernt auf den Schienen weiterfuhr. „Ich war wie angewurzelt", erinnert sich Norbert Stein. „Da stand ich nun mitten auf der Straße, während meine beiden kleinen Kinder mutterseelenallein in einer Straßenbahn saßen."

Wenn sich der Bäckermeister an jenen Tag erinnert, taucht in seinen Augen noch einmal die Verzweiflung von damals auf: „Ich hatte an diesem Nachmittag frei und wollte mit meinen beiden Söhnen zu meiner Schwester in die Innenstadt fahren." Die Kinder waren guter Laune, Tim (2) konnte vor lauter Aufregung kaum still in sein-

er Karre sitzen und Florian (4) hüpfte vor Freude von einem Bein aufs andere. „Wir haben an der Straßenbahn-Haltestelle gewartet, bis die Bahn kam", erzählt Norbert Stein. „Ich hob erst den Kleinen, Tim, in die Bahn, dann half ich Florian beim Einsteigen…"

Was dann folgte, ist ein wahrgewordener Alptraum: „Ich drehte mich zur Seite, um Tims Buggy einzuladen. Doch plötzlich schloß sich die Tür, und ich konnte nur noch mit großer Mühe die Karre aus den bereits zusammengeklappten Trittstufen ziehen. Die Bahn fuhr sofort los, und ich sah nur noch den Haarschopf meines ältesten Sohnes verschwinden…"

Würden sich die beiden in den scharfen Kurven festhalten können? Würden sie

denken, ihr Vater hätte sie verlassen? Saßen in dem hinteren Abteil überhaupt Fahrgäste, die sich der beiden annehmen könnten? Und wenn ja: Würden seine Söhne nicht in die falschen Hände geraten? All diese Gedanken rasten durch Norbert Steins Kopf, während er voller Panik losrannte. Ganz in der Nähe der Haltestelle stand ein Bus. Verzweifelt trommelte der Vater gegen die Fahrertür. Doch zu seiner Empörung erklärte ihm der Fahrer: „Das geht mich nichts an!"

Wieder stand der hilflose Vater also vor verschlossenen Türen. Und immer wieder die Angst: Würden seine Kinder an der nächsten Haltestelle vielleicht aussteigen und in den Straßenverkehr geraten?

Norbert Stein wußte nicht mehr ein noch aus. Doch dann hatte er Glück im Unglück. Eine Golf-Fahrerin hatte den Vorfall beobachtet und hatte angehalten. Nachdem Norbert Stein eingestiegen war, fuhr sie mit Vollgas der Bahn hinterher.

„Wir sind vielleicht fünf Minuten gefahren, aber für mich war es eine Ewigkeit!" erzählt der 30jährige. Dann, an einer Haltestelle, die Erlösung: Ein älteres Ehepaar hatte sich der Kinder angenommen, wartete mit ihnen neben den Gleisen. Norbert Stein schloß seine Söhne glücklich in die Arme. Heute kann der Familienvater darüber schon fast wieder lachen: „Ab sofort steigen wir jedenfalls nur noch gleichzeitig in die Straßenbahn…"

Wolfgang Hartig

Rubric: Ergänzen Sie die Lücken…

Weil Norbert Stein einen –1– Nachmittag hatte, entschied er sich, seine –2– in der Innenstadt zu besuchen. Die Kinder, Tim (2) und Florian (4), –3– sich über den Besuch, als sie an der Straßenbahn-Haltestelle –4– haben. Als die Bahn kam, –5– Norbert den kleinen Tim aus seiner –6– und setzte ihn in die Bahn. Dem 4jährigen Florian half der Vater beim –7–.

Doch dann schlossen sich die Türen der Bahn, und sie –8– davon. Norbert war erstaunt und –9– . Er rannte zuerst zu einem Busfahrer, der sich weigerte, –10– zu helfen. Eine –11– , die den Vorfall gesehen hatte, hielt –12– und folgte mit Norbert der Straßenbahn. Nach fünf Minuten fanden sie an einer Haltestelle ein altes –13– , das sich um die Kinder –14– hatte . Norbert war so glücklich, daß seine schlimmsten –15– nicht in Erfüllung gegangen waren.

TEST 4

Immer noch Probleme für Karrierefrauen

This text is a newspaper article about women and their problems in combining a career with having a family. The exercise is in English and asks you to respond to questions about the text.

Rubric: Lesen Sie zuerst den untenstehenden Text.

IMMER NOCH PROBLEME FÜR KARRIEREFRAUEN

Obwohl der Anteil von Frauen in Führungspositionen in der deutschen Wirtschaft auf zwischenzeitlich vier Prozent gestiegen ist, sind die Arbeitsstrukturen noch immer weitgehend auf den Mann zugeschnitten. Stellenausschreibungen, die sich exklusiv an männliche Bewerber richten, sind nur die ersten Stolpersteine auf dem steinigen Weg karrierewilliger Frauen nach oben.

Weitere Nachteile erwachsen ihnen nicht selten aus dem überlieferten familiären Rollenbild, das sich hartnäckig behauptet und in der Praxis häufig so aussieht: Für jede anspruchsvolle Position, die der Arbeitgeber mit einem Mann besetzt, „kauft" er im Grunde eineinhalb Personen: den voll belastbaren, dynamischen Mann und die dazugehörige Ehefrau, die ihm den Alltagsärger vom Hals hält. Entscheidet sich der Personalchef hingegen für eine Frau, kauft er quasi nur eine „halbe Person", weil die Frau auch als Managerin ihre häuslichen Verpflichtungen kaum vernachlässigen kann. Und das schon gar nicht, wenn sie Kinder hat oder sich welche wünscht. Da nur sehr wenig Ehemänner zu einem Rollentausch bereit sind, sehen sich viele Frauen gezwungen, zwischen ehelicher Partnerschaft und beruflicher Laufbahn zu entscheiden, während Männer alles haben können!

Selbst wenn es einer Frau gelingt, Mann, Mutterschaft und Management unter einen Hut zu bringen, hat sie doch die größte berufliche Hürde noch vor sich: den Umgang mit der Macht. Selbst eine erfolgreiche Managerin gibt zu, daß sie als erste Frau in einer Männerdomäne Startschwierigkeiten hatte. Am Anfang war sie bei den Kongressen richtiggehend schüchtern und saß ohne Selbstbewußtsein zwischen den gutgekleideten älteren Herren. Die Reaktionen reichten von wohlwollender Duldung bis zu offener Ablehnung und augenzwinkernder Galanterie unter dem Motto: „Was haben wir denn da für ein hübsches Mäuschen am Tisch?"

Unter solchen Umständen wächst der Anreiz, eigenhändig neue Strategien zur Selstbehauptung zu entwickeln. Denn Unterstützung aus den Reihen derer, die die Managerin auf dem Weg nach oben hinter sich ließ, ist kaum zu erwarten.

Referring to the passage, but without translating, explain in English the following points:

(a) why an employer may prefer to employ a man rather than a woman in a high level post;   (4)

(b) why the writer claims that men can have everything;   (4)

(c) at what stage career women face the greatest hurdle, and what it is;   (4)

(d) how the successful manageress was treated at conferences;   (4)

(e) why such women have to take matters into their own hands.   (4)

UCLES

4.5 SUGGESTED ANSWERS

TEST 1

Weight Watchers (10 marks). 1 mark for each correct answer.

(a) falsch – it has been around for 30 years
(b) falsch – they want to employ independent advisers
(c) falsch – it is also interested in healthy eating
(d) richtig – (Viele Krankenkassen erstatten einen Teil der Kursgebühren)
(e) richtig – (Ihre Tätigkeit, ob haupt- oder nebenberuflich)
(f) richtig – (Ihre Arbeit unterstützen wir durch Aus- und kontinuierliche Weiterbildung)
(g) falsch – they say they will help with the advertising
(h) falsch – they will be working with groups
(i) richtig – (Sie zeichnen sich aus durch Eigeninitiative)
(j) richtig – (Ihre Tätigkeit unterstützen wir durch Organisation)

TEST 2

Blindes Vertrauen (11 marks). 1 mark for each correct letter.

1	2	3	4	5	6	7	8	9	10	11
d	j	e	i	f	l	g	a	k	h	c

TEST 3

Für Norbert Stein wurde ein Alptraum Wirklichkeit (15 marks). 1 mark for each correct word inserted. Accept any word that makes sense and agrees with the facts of the text. Ignore minor spelling mistakes.

1 freien
2 Schwester
3 freuten
4 gewartet/gestanden
5 hob
6 Karre
7 Einsteigen
8 fuhr
9 entsetzt
10 ihm
11 Golffahrerin
12 an
13 Ehepaar
14 gekümmert
15 Ängste/Träume

TEST 4

Immer noch Probleme für Karrierefrauen (20 marks). 1 mark for each of the following points made.

(a) The employer can make any demands on a man (1)
    His wife represents half a person extra because of her support at home (1)
    A woman can never neglect her household duties (1)
    Even worse for women when children arrive (1)

(b) Men can be single-minded in their attitude to the job (1)
    They do not have to make difficult decisions (1)

about home and work	(1)
They do not have to share any of the wife's home keeping role	(1)

(c) Even when she manages to combine home and work (1)
The woman has to face up to handling authority (1)
This is a problem for women in a man's world (1)
They may feel shy and lacking in self-confidence (1)

(d) She met a number of different reactions (1)
Sometimes good humoured tolerance (1)
Sometimes outright rejection (1)
Or an effort to be gallant (1)

(e) Because she cannot expect (1) support (1) (2)
From those left behind (1)
On her way to the top (1)

4.6 TRANSLATION

Some Boards include translation of a text or a section of a text as part of their reading paper, in addition to other comprehension questions. The advantage of translation as a testing method is that it shows how much of a text you really understand. To do it well everything has to be translated. It also reveals how well you can communicate the meaning of a foreign text in English, which is something that you might have to do in a job.

The two signs of a good translation are:

(a) Has everything been translated that needs to be?

(b) Does it read like a piece of original English? (It should not give the impression that it has been written by somebody who does not have English as his/her first language.)

Developing a method for translation comes with a bit of practice:

- Read the text through several times for complete understanding. Make notes as ideas occur to you and jot them down in the margin of the original. Underline difficult and key sections to remind you that they are important.

- In an examination write your translation on every other line so that you can make alterations easily without your work looking too untidy.

- Take care with tenses. Remember that German has no continuous forms (I am going, he was sitting, they have been running). In the English version they may be more appropriate than the simple form (I go, he sat, they have run).

- Be careful to translate everything that can be translated, particularly those short adverbs, such as *bloß, doch, ja*. At the end of each sentence that you translate check that your version contains a translation for each 'item' in the German.

- Idiomatic phrases can be a problem: *Lieber ein Spatz in der Hand als eine Taube auf dem Dach* would translate as: *better a sparrow in the hand than a pigeon on the roof*, which is not an English expression. The best equivalent would be: *better a bird in the hand than two in the bush*.

- Proper names can be difficult, particularly where there is an English equivalent, e.g. Charles for Karl. It is probably better to leave German names in their original form, but do translate titles, such as *Herr* (Mr) and *Frau* (Mrs).

- Names of people and places can be very confusing if you do not recognise them as such and you assume they are simply words that you do not know.

- Always work on the assumption that the passage you are translating makes sense; there is a tendency amongst students to assume that because it is a foreign text it will not necessarily make sense and to write down gibberish. If what you have written does not make sense it is wrong and you should change it so that it does make sense.

- If there are parts of the text that you really cannot understand do not leave gaps; understand as much as you possibly can and then make an intelligent guess about the rest. Beware of guessing early on and then making everything fit in with your guess. Now that most Boards allow bilingual dictionaries guessing should not be so necessary.

- Take care with words that look like an English word, but which have a completely different meaning in English; e.g. the German word *also* does not mean *also* in English; it means *therefore*.

- Your knowledge of German grammar will help you to sort out the relationship of words to each other in a sentence. The cases, for example, convey meaning: the dative indicates *to*, the genitive *of*. Knowing where to look in the sentence for the verb will help you to find the right one. Recognising conjunctions will help you to work your way through the structure of a complicated sentence.

- If you have time it is a good idea to re-read your version after completing it. If you can come back to it after concentrating on something else you will see it with a fresh eye and should spot errors more easily. Hopefully you might recognise where you have, perhaps, translated something directly and kept its German form, when it should be expressed differently in English.

EXAMPLE

The following example is an advertisement from a magazine. Read it through carefully twice and then translate it into English. When you have finished compare your translation with the two that follow. The first one is an example done by a student, using a dictionary, sticking closely to the original. Inevitably it is full of not very English expressions. Try to think of better ways of expressing the bits that have been underlined. Then compare your version with the final version.

KINDER STARK MACHEN

Der Griff zu Drogen hat viele Ursachen. Das Gefühl von Ohnmacht und Schwäche kann eine Ursache sein. Schlimm genug, daß es Drogen gibt, aber das allein macht nicht süchtig.

Kinder, die sich den Anforderungen des Lebens nicht gewachsen fühlen, suchen oftmals Zuflucht in Alkohol, Tabletten oder Drogen. Wer gelernt hat, Konflikte mit sich und anderen eigenverantwortlich zu lösen, braucht nicht Scheinlösungen in Suchtmitteln zu suchen.

Selbstvertrauen stärken, Konfliktfähigkeit fördern, die realistische Einschätzung der eigenen Stärken und Schwächen unterstützen heißt, Kindern die Chance geben, eine starke Persönlichkeit zu entwickeln. Es schützt sie mehr vor Drogen als alle Warnungen und Verbote. „Starke" Kinder können von sich aus „Nein" sagen.

Die Angst um ihr Wohl macht es schwer, sich auf die eigene Stärke von Kindern zu verlassen. Aufmerksamkeit und Verständnis für ihre Probleme, Schutz und Halt bei Eltern, Freunden, Erziehern sind Voraussetzungen dafür.

Miteinander reden kann Schwierigkeiten beseitigen, bevor Probleme daraus werden.

Wir können viel dagegen tun, daß Kinder süchtig werden. Kinder stark machen, zu stark für Drogen, ist ein Teil davon.

Kostenloses Informationsmaterial erhalten Sie bei der BZgA, 51101 Köln. ☎ **0221 892031**
Wenn Sie Fragen zur Suchtvorbeugung haben, wenden Sie sich an das Infotelefon der BZgA.
Eine Anzeige der Bundeszentrale für gesundheitliche Aufklärung im Auftrag des Bundesministeriums für Gesundheit.

Version 1

TO MAKE CHILDREN STRONG.

The reach for drugs has many causes. The feeling of powerlessness and weakness can be a cause. Bad enough that there are drugs, but that alone does not make addicted.

Children who do not feel themselves grown to the demands of life seek often refuge in alcohol, tablets or drugs. Who has learned to solve conflicts with himself and others on his own responsibility does not need to seek false solutions in addictive materials.

To strengthen self-confidence, to promote conflict capability, to support the realistic appreciation of own strengths and weaknesses is called to give children the chance to develop a strong personality. It protects them more from drugs than all warnings and prohibitions. Strong children can say no from themselves.

The fear around their welfare makes it hard to rely on the own strength of children. Attention and understanding for their problems, protection and security with parents, friends, educators are preconditions for it.

To speak with one another can remove difficulties before problems become out of them.

We can do much against it that children become addicted. To make children strong, too strong, for drugs is part of it.

Version 2

MAKING CHILDREN STRONG.

There are many reasons for taking drugs. A feeling of powerlessness and weakness can be one reason. It is bad enough that drugs exist, but that on its own does not force people into addiction.

Children who do not feel able to cope with the demands of life often seek refuge in alcohol, tablets or drugs. Whoever has learned to resolve conflicts with himself and others, on his own, does not need to look for false solutions in drugs.

Strengthening self-confidence, promoting the ability to resolve conflicts, encouraging the realistic appreciation of one's own strengths and weaknesses is the way to give children the chance of developing a strong personality. That will protect them from drugs more than any warnings and prohibitions. "Strong children" can say "No" without help from others.

It is difficult to rely on children's own strength when one is worried about their welfare. Paying attention to their problems and having understanding for them, finding protection and security with their parents, friends and teachers are the preconditions necessary for them to find this strength.

Speaking to each other can remove difficulties before they become problems.

We can do a lot to prevent children from becoming addicted. Making children strong, too strong for drugs, is a part of that.

4.7 TRANSLATION PRACTICE

Test translation 1

Translate the last two paragraphs of the reading text, EXAMPLE 3: *Spieleparadies in der Stube.*

Test translation 2

Translate the first paragraph of the reading text, EXAMPLE 4: *Der blonde Engel.*

Test translation 3

Translate the last three paragraphs of the reading text, TEST 2: *Blindes Vertrauen*.

MODEL TRANSLATIONS FOR THE TESTS

Translation 1

Spieleparadies in der Stube (last two paragraphs).
In addition the games fan hopes that at some time his great wish will be fulfilled. He would like to drive from place to place in a bus full of board games to offer activity days or evenings for all age groups. "That would be for me the tops" he says. His second great wish is also to acquire for his collection games from the period before 1960.

At the present time he is offering to come with his games to events such as village fêtes or club festivals. "Anybody who would like me to come can telephone me on 04744/3536. Anybody who would like to offer me more games can, of course, do the same."

Translation 2

Der blonde Engel (first paragraph).
Markus Seidel travels daily around Germany by train, carrying his mobile phone. The only thing he has left behind in Donaueschingen is his voice on the answering machine: "Homeless children and all those who don't like leaving a message on tape can reach me on the following number." Seidel's charges are the forgotten ones of society: homeless children. For a long time they seemed not to exist, the 10 to 14 year olds who have often run away from unbearable conditions in their families and who have gone underground in towns. Their number is estimated to be almost 2000.

Translation 3

Blindes Vertrauen (last three paragraphs)
Thus her grocer, to whom she has been going for years, suddenly refused her entry into his shop when she appeared with her dog.

Also at many events at cinemas, theatres, churches or pubs she is often told: Dogs must stay outside.

Marina Stawitzki: "Even my ophthalmologist who was the very one to prescribe Amos for me told me: 'You can't bring your dog into the practice.'"

4.8 SUMMARY PRACTICE

Another method used in reading examinations to test comprehension is to ask candidates to summarise the main points of a passage, either in German or English. This is a useful skill to have in everyday life.

You obviously do not need to understand every single word in this sort of exercise, in the way that is necessary for translation, but it is important that you read the text carefully to try to understand as much as possible before you start.

- Read the passage several times before starting.
- As you read underline the main point(s) in each paragraph.
- Jot down in note form the main point(s) paragraph by paragraph.
- Re-write your notes in your own words, as a continuous piece of writing.
- Write on every other line to make it easier to change what you have written.
- Try to follow the argument of the author and watch out for counter-arguments if there are any.

- In a summary illustrative examples are not necessary.

- Check the length and prune if necessary. Cutting out unnecessary adjectives and adverbs and using simple tense forms (*ging* instead of *ist gegangen*) will help.

- Most mark schemes will not expect you to make every point. You will probably have to make, say 20 out of 25 points.

MARK SCHEMES AND MODEL ANSWERS

Example 1

Read the following text carefully and then summarise it in not more than 140 words. After the text you will find the mark scheme and a possible model. Mark your summary and then compare it with the model.

Lesen Sie den folgenden Text, dann fassen Sie die Hauptpunkte in nicht mehr als 140 Wörtern zusammen. (15 Punkte)

Eine Ära der neuen Chancen und Pflichten

ap **Bonn** – In einem Appell an Regierung und Parteien hat die Bundesarbeitsgemeinschaft der Senioren-Organisationen (BAGSO) eine altenfreundlichere Politik für die mehr als 15 Millionen Deutsche im Alter von mehr als 60 Jahren gefordert. Jeder vierte Bürger werde zum Ende des Jahrhunderts dem Seniorenalter zuzuordnen sein und in 30 Jahren fast jeder dritte.

Gleichzeitig boten die Sprecher mehrerer Altenorganisationen die aktive Mitarbeit ihrer Mitglieder bei der Bewältigung von Zukunftsaufgaben an. Bundeskanzler Helmut Kohl und die zuständigen Ministerien sollten sich jedoch verstärkt der Probleme alter Menschen in der sich verändernden Gesellschaft annehmen.

Die Sprecher plädierten ferner für einen intensiveren Dialog mit Bundesfamilienministerin Hannelore Rönsch und die Beteiligung an altenpolitischen Vorhaben. Bundesfinanzminister Theo Waigel wurde aufgefordert, die Steuergesetze zugunsten alter Menschen zu überprüfen. Scharf kritisiert wurde, daß Ausgaben für ehrenamtliche Arbeit in der Altenbetreuung nicht steuermindernd geltend gemacht werden könnten.

Die Bundesrepublik entwickle sich zu einer „ergrauenden Gesellschaft", für die es historisch kein Beispiel gibt", mahnte Ingeburg Seldte von der Bundesseniorenvertretung. Diese Entwicklung setze einer herkömmlichen Betreuung und Altenhilfe Grenzen. „Es müssen neue Wege beschritten werden, wobei Staat, Wissenschaft und Interessengruppen über neue Rezepte nachdenken."

Als Schwerpunkte für die politische Arbeit nannte die Organisation die „überfällige Absicherung des Pflegerisikos", Verbesserung der Heimunterbringung und neue Wohnformen im Alter. Ferner müßten Prävention und Rehabilitationsmaßnahmen für ältere Bürger ausgebaut werden.

Mit Erreichen der beruflichen Altersgrenze seien sehr viele Menschen noch in der Lage und bereit, das sogenannte dritte Lebensalter sinnvoll zu gestalten. „Zu den neuen Chancen des Alters kommen auch Pflichten", betonte Frau Seldte. „Ein Generationenvertrag kann nicht nur die Jüngeren in die Pflicht nehmen." Die „jungen Alten" seien eine soziale Reserve, die bisher kaum genutzt worden sei. Aus dem Verständnis für die neue Situation in Deutschland seien Senioren bereit, freiwillig Aufgaben für die Gemeinschaft zu übernehmen.

Als Beispiel stellte Professor Peter Oltmanns die Aktion „Alt hilft Jung" vor, in der aus dem Beruf ausgeschiedene Führungskräfte der Wirtschaft ihr Wissen weitergeben.

Mark scheme: One mark for each of the following points, made in a form that could be understood by a sympathetic native German speaker. Any 15 points.

- BAGSO appealed to the government and political parties;
- for a more friendly policy towards old people;
- there are more than 15 million Germans over 60;
- every 4th German over 60 by end of century;
- and every 3rd German in next 30 years;
- BAGSO also offered its help in overcoming problems in the future;
- the government should accept the problems of the old;
- BAGSO want a dialogue with government ministers to shape policy;

- they want new financial policies to help old people;
- German society is getting older;
- there is no historic model to guide the government;
- a different approach is now needed;
- most important concerns of old people are;
- they need to be assured that they will be cared for;
- home care needs to be improved;
- new ways of accommodating old people need to be found;
- measures to prevent (their situation worsening) are needed;
- measures to rehabilitate them (after illness) are needed;
- after retirement they are ready to help society voluntarily;
- they have an obligation to society;
- former business people put their knowledge at disposal of the young in *Alt hilft Jung*.

Model answer

Die BAGSO (Bundesarbeitsgemeinschaft der Senioren Organisationen) forderte von der Regierung und den Parteien eine bessere Politik für die mehr als 15 Millionen Deutschen über 60. Bis zum Ende des Jahrhunderts sei jeder vierte Deutsche über 60, in 30 Jahren jeder dritte. Gleichzeitig bot die BAGSO die Hilfe der Senioren bei der Bewältigung der Zukunftsprobleme an. Sie wolle auch von der Regierung ein besseres Verständnis für die Probleme der Senioren. Diese wollen an der Gestaltung von Politik durch Diskussionen mit Ministern teilnehmen. So viele Alte gebe es noch nie. Die neue Situation brauche neue Denkarten. Für Senioren seien wichtig: Absicherung des Pflegerisikos, Verbesserung der Heimunterbringung und neue Wohnformen. Präventions- und Rehabilitationsmaßnahmen müßten verbessert werden. Viele Senioren wollen freiwillig Aufgaben für die Gemeinschaft übernehmen. Ein Beispiel dafür sei „Alt hilft Jung", eine Aktion, bei der ehemalige Geschäftsleute jüngeren mit ihrem Wissen helfen.

(140 Wörter)

Example 2

Fassen Sie die Hauptpunkte des folgenden Textes in nicht mehr als 110 Wörtern zusammen. (15 Punkte)

Standesbeamter heiratete die Braut, die er trauen sollte
Heinrich Gärtner (31) fand die hochschwangere Frau sofort sympathisch

Die Situation war äußerst unangenehm: Über 20 Hochzeitsgäste warteten in dem kleinen Raum im Standesamt. Der schwangeren Braut, Irene Sillkeit (alle Namen geändert), kullerten dicke Tränen über die Wangen. Verzweifelt suchte die 24jährige Trost an der Schulter ihres Vaters. Sie konnte noch gar nicht fassen, was passiert war: An diesem Tag sollte sie getraut werden – aber Peter Weigand, der Bräutigam, war einfach nicht erschienen. Seit mehr als einer Stunde wartete die Hochzeitsgesellschaft schon auf ihn.

Schließlich sagte der Standesbeamte Heinrich Gärtner (31) die Hochzeit mit Einverständnis der verzweifelten Braut ab. In seinem Büro bewirtete er sie und ihre Eltern mit Kaffee. Mit einfühlsamen Worten versuchte er, Irene Sillkeit zu trösten. Die hübsche Frau war ihm sofort sympathisch gewesen.

Die Verbindung von Irene Sillkeit und dem 27jährigen Peter Weigand hatte von Anfang an unter keinem glücklichen Stern gestanden. Das Paar lernte sich in einer Diskothek kennen, verliebte sich Hals über Kopf. Irene Sillkeit kümmerte es wenig, daß ihrem Freund schnell wechselnde Frauenbekanntschaften nachgesagt wurden. In ihrer Verliebtheit vertraute sie ihrem Gefährten bedingungslos.

Nach sechs Monaten wurde Irene Sillkeit schwanger. Nur zögernd willigte Peter Weigand in eine Hochzeit ein. Doch als es soweit war, brach er sein Versprechen – ohne ein Wort der Erklärung.

Irene Sillkeit fuhr an die Nordsee, um sich von der bitteren Enttäuschung zu erholen. Als sie ein Café betrat, traute sie ihren Augen nicht: Da saß Heinrich Gärtner, der Standesbeamte. Zufällig verbrachte er hier ein paar freie Tage. „Wir führten ein langes, intensives Gespräch und machten einen ausgiebigen Spaziergang am Strand", erinnert sich Irene Sillkeit. Heinrich Gärtner: „Schon bald war uns klar, daß wir zusammengehören."

Als die Wehen bei Irene Sillkeit einsetzten, brachte der Beamte seine Freundin in die Klinik. Sie bekam einen Sohn, Marco. Danach wollten die beiden ihr Glück besiegeln. Ein neuer Hochzeitstermin wurde anberaumt – und Heinrich Gärtner heiratete die Braut, die er ursprünglich trauen sollte. Irene Sillkeit ist heute wunschlos glücklich. Von Peter Weigand, dem Vater ihres kleinen Sohnes, hat sie nie wieder etwas gehört.

Conny Paul

Mark scheme: One mark for each of the following points, made in a form that could be understood by a sympathetic native German speaker. Any 15 points.

- 20 wedding guests waiting in registry office;
- (pregnant) bride weeping;
- bridegroom did not turn up;
- official cancelled wedding;
- bride, Irene Sillkeit, had got to know bridegroom, Peter Weigand;
- in a disco;
- she fell in love with him;
- did not listen to rumours of other women;
- trusted him;
- got pregnant after 6 months;
- he agreed to marry her;
- reluctantly;
- Irene went to Northsea coast;
- to recover from disappointment;
- met Heinrich Gärtner, registry office official, in a café;
- spending a few days there by chance;
- got into conversation with him;
- they fell in love;
- he took her to hospital for the birth of her son;
- they got married;
- both very happy;
- heard nothing of Peter Weigand.

Model answer

Zwanzig Hochzeitsgäste warteten am Standesamt auf den Bräutigam, Peter Weigand, der nicht kam. Die schwangere Braut, Irene Sillkeit, weinte. Der Standesbeamte, Heinrich Gärtner, sagte die Hochzeit ab. Irene hatte ihren Bräutigam in einer Diskothek kennengelernt. Sie war so verliebt, daß sie auf die Gerüchte nicht hörte, daß er anderen Frauen nachlaufe. Sechs Monate später wurde sie schwanger. Peter versprach widerwillig, sie zu heiraten, aber er kam nicht. Irene ging an die Nordsee, um ihre Enttäuschung zu vergessen. In einem Café begegnete sie dem Standesbeamten. Sie verliebten sich. Er brachte sie ins Krankenhaus für die Geburt ihres Sohnes. Später heirateten sie und waren glücklich. Sie denkt nicht mehr an Peter.

(109 Wörter)

Example 3

Fassen Sie die Hauptpunkte des Textes in nicht mehr als 80 Wörtern zusammen. (15 Punkte)

Das unglaubliche Glück
Witwe gewann mit letztem Geld 2,5 Millionen

Aus den Wolken muß es fallen, aus der Götter Schoß – das Glück.

Friedrich Schiller

rev. **Hannover** – Als es gestern vormittag an der Haustür klingelte, dachte sie: „Es ist soweit. Das muß der Gerichtsvollzieher sein!"

Irrtum. Es war Glücksbote Asmus Weber vom Niedersachsen-Lotto. Seine Nachricht für die 40jährige Sozialhilfeempfängerin, die ihre Miete nicht mehr bezahlen konnte: „Sie haben 2,5 Millionen Mark gewonnen!"

Weber: „Ich habe schon viel erlebt, aber solche Freude noch nie! Sie hat eine halbe Stunde nur geweint…"

Vor drei Jahren war die Frau aus einem Dorf bei Hannover Witwe geworden. Von einem Tag zum anderen stand sie mit den drei Töchtern (heute 13 bis17) alleine da. Im Sommer 1990 dann der zweite Schicksalsschlag: Beim Überqueren der Straße wurde sie von einem Auto angefahren und so schwer verletzt, daß sie noch heute nur mit Krücken laufen kann. Ihren Angestellten-Beruf mußte sie aufgeben. Endstation war das Sozialamt. Danach fehlten ihr sogar die 700 Mark Miete für die kleine Wohnung: „Mir blieb nur eins: aufhängen oder gewinnen."

Verzweifelt kaufte sie für 200 Mark Lose der Klassenlotterie, dazu ein Dauerlos der Glücksspirale für 89,50 Mark. „Es war fast mein ganzes Geld. Und dann habe ich gebetet…"

Den Volltreffer gab es jetzt von der Glücksspirale. Zuviel Risiko? Der französische Moralist Francois La Rochefoucault schrieb vor 325 Jahren: *„Mit dem Glück muß man es machen wie mit der Gesundheit: Es genießen, wenn es günstig ist, Geduld haben, wenn es ungünstig ist – und zu gewaltsamen Mitteln nur im Notfall greifen…"*

Mark scheme: One mark for each of the following points (any 15).

- there was a ring at the doorbell;
- she thought it must be the bailiff;
- it was the man from the lottery;
- she had won 2.5 million Marks;
- she cried for half an hour when she heard she had won;
- widowed three years before;
- had 3 daughters;
- in the summer 1991;
- run down by car;
- badly injured;
- can only walk with crutches;
- could no longer work;
- had to go to social security;
- had no money for the rent;
- used all her money for lottery tickets; then prayed;
- French moralist wrote 325 years ago;
- luck is like health;
- enjoy it when good;
- have patience when bad.

Model answer

Der Glücksbote vom Lotto klingelte. Die 40jährige Sozialhilfeempfängerin hatte 2,5 Millionen Mark gewonnen. Sie weinte. Vor 3 Jahren wurde sie mit 3 Töchtern Witwe. Im Sommer 1990 wurde sie angefahren und konnte nicht mehr ohne Krücken gehen und auch nicht arbeiten. Sie ging zum Sozialamt, weil sie die Miete nicht bezahlen konnte. Mit ihrem letzten Geld kaufte sie Lose für die Lotterie und betete. Man soll das Glück genießen, wenn es gut ist, und Geduld haben, wenn es schlecht ist.

(80 Wörter)

CHAPTER 5

SPEAKING

Units in this chapter

5.1 THE ORAL EXAMINATION

Your ability to speak German is tested in the oral examination, which with some Boards can carry as much as 35% of the total marks at A-level and up to 50% at AS-level, so it is a very important part of the examination.

Most oral examinations take between 15 and 25 minutes, which is not very long for so many marks and for someone to make a judgement on your ability after two or more years of study. Fortunately you will know well in advance when it is going to be held and can, therefore, prepare yourself for it.

The downside is that it is often conducted by a visiting examiner that you do not know; it is usually recorded on cassette and because so much is at stake it can be a stressful experience, particularly the time leading up to the examination itself.

However, the fact that the orals are recorded is in your favour. A percentage of the cassettes will be listened to by a moderator to make sure that the oral has been conducted as it should be and to make sure that the marks given are appropriate. It is a way for the Board to maintain a uniform standard across all its examiners. In addition when grades are being awarded all candidates who fall below a grade borderline will have all their work re-marked to make sure that there have been no mistakes. The cassette is then available so that the oral element can also be re-assessed.

ORAL EXAMINERS

Visiting examiners are usually practising or retired teachers who are anxious to see what you can do. They are not out to test what you do not know. They will want to put you at your ease so that you will perform well. If you have lots to say it will make their task much easier.

They are also not looking for native speaker competence, but rather the ability to communicate in German. Provided that you can express yourself it does not matter if your accent is not perfect and that you make mistakes. Communicating is the most important thing. You should obviously aim to make as few mistakes as possible and to sound as German as possible, but do not let the worry about making mistakes inhibit you so much that you are afraid to say anything.

THE STANDARD REQUIRED

If you listen to English people around you and in the media you will realise that even people who are very good speakers sometimes make mistakes. They will often not complete a sentence, will stop and go off at a tangent as something new occurs to them. They will sometimes trip up over the pronunciation of a word, will re-phrase things, say 'um' to give themselves time to think, will make grammatical mistakes and will misunderstand something and ask for it to be repeated. If that can happen to expert English speakers it is obviously more likely in a foreign language. We tolerate it in English provided that we are interested in and can follow what is being said. The same applies to an oral examination.

Also, some mistakes, such as with adjectival endings, are much less important in speech than in writing. If you can relax to some extent in the oral so much the better, although a certain amount of nerves will put an edge on your performance, for that is what it is – a performance.

PREPARING YOURSELF

As part of your preparation you need to find out:

- what your oral will consist of;
- how long it will last;
- how much preparation time you will have. Some Boards give you a few days to prepare a task. Others allow you only the time that the person ahead of you is being examined;
- whether you are allowed a dictionary during the preparation time;
- whether you will be allowed to take notes with you into the examination.

Part of your preparation should also entail getting hold of past papers to see what precise tasks have been set in the past. Going through them with a friend, a German national or the German assistant in your school or college will give you a good idea of what to expect and will help to boost your confidence.

Oral fluency cannot be acquired quickly just before the examination. Throughout your course you need to take a full part in oral lessons, build up a stock of expressions and phrases that will help you to express opinions, ask for information and explain things. A visit to a German-speaking country is an excellent way of improving your spoken German, particularly just before the examination. Record yourself on cassette and listen critically to improve your performance.

THE ASSESSMENT CRITERIA

Most oral examinations are marked under a number of different headings. Most Boards publish their mark schemes. It is worth getting hold of the mark scheme for your Board from your teacher or by writing to the Board itself. You will probably find they are divided up as follows:

Pronunciation and intonation: ranging from 'very good, only occasional errors' to 'barely comprehensible, extremely anglicised pronunciation and intonation'.

Accuracy: from 'highly accurate in more complex language with only a few minor errors' to 'very little evidence of grammatical awareness'.

Range of structures and vocabulary: from 'confident and appropriate use of a wide range of structures, idiom and vocabulary for purposes of discussion' to 'struggles to create sentences or use authentic words'.

Fluency/initiative: from 'spontaneous development of ideas and amplification of answers; sustains conversation; responds well to challenge; no hesitation or prompting'; to 'very little initiative; mainly short answers with no development in discussion; hesitant; frequent recourse to material consciously memorised and pre-rehearsed; difficulty in producing spontaneous language without prompting'.

Communication of content: from 'comprehensive; full discussion of ideas, including opinions, description, explanation and supporting reasons' to 'little information conveyed; virtually no ideas or opinions'.

SOME TIPS FOR THE ORAL

The best candidates will know their topic well, will have the facts at their finger tips and will be able to explain them. They will have opinions and will be able to defend them, answering questions fully and giving reasons for holding such opinions. They will listen carefully to what the examiner says and will try to elicit information and opinions from him or her. They will sound mainly German, make few or no pronunciation errors and will use idiomatic phrases and expressions. They will also use some more complicated structures where appropriate.

Many people get by in a foreign country using mainly signs and gestures and it is surprising how much you can achieve without a word of the language. That is not much use in an oral examination, but positive body language is important in making a good impression on the examiner. It is difficult for the examiner to be interested in what you are saying if you slouch in your chair, look bored and rarely smile. Maintain eye contact with the examiner. Do not keep your eyes fixed on a point just above his or her head. Smile, look interested in what you are saying and what the examiner says. Lean forward to show that you are interested.

Acting confident can boost your confidence. Dressing smartly will also make you feel more confident and will signal that you think it is an important occasion. Arrive in good time so that you do not get flustered before you start.

5.2 THE VARIOUS ORAL TASKS

The kinds of tasks that occur in oral examinations are as follows:
- role play with instructions in English;
- role play with instructions in German and some stimulus material in English;
- discussion based on a German text;
- reporting the content of an English text to a German who speaks no English;
- acting as interpreter between an English person and a German, neither of whom speaks the other's language;
- doing a presentation of a topic;
- discussion of a prepared topic;
- general conversation.

ROLE PLAY WITH INSTRUCTIONS IN ENGLISH

This kind of test will normally last between 5 and 10 minutes and you will have about 15–20 minutes in which to prepare it. You will be given a brief, which sets the scene and a task that you are to carry out. There will be a number of instructions with some indication of what the person that you are to speak to will require from you. The examiner will normally be playing this role and will supposedly speak no English. It is important, of course, to listen carefully to what is said to you in response to your questions or statements, so that you respond in the appropriate way.

The mark scheme for this sort of task will probably award half of the marks for successfully carrying out the instructions (completion of the task), so it is important that you prepare carefully and cover everything. The other half of the marks will be given for the quality of the language that you used (pronunciation, intonation, range of expressions, accuracy). Provided that you do all that is asked of you in clear, comprehensible German you will receive a good mark. When you are engaged in this kind of transactional language it is likely that you will need mainly simple everyday phrases. Do not be put off by words in English that you do not know the German for. You will probably be able to paraphrase them so that the person you are speaking to knows what you mean even if you have not known the correct word. If, for example, you needed to use the German for *woodpecker* and did not know the correct term, you would be readily understood if you said *ein Vogel, der Löcher in Bäume macht*.

The following example is typical of this kind of test. As you will see you are told the kind of thing that will be said to you, but you will need to listen carefully to what is said so that you respond in the best way possible. It is followed by a German dialogue which might have been used.

Rubric: Choose one of the role play situations described below. You may not take any notes into the examination room. The test will last approximately 5 minutes.

Brief: Your school organises a regular squash tour during the half-term week of the autumn term. Your teacher in charge has decided it would be a good idea to tour Germany this year. He/She has asked you to make some preliminary telephone enquiries.

Task: You must phone the *Deutscher Squash Rackets Verband* in Duisburg and ask to speak to the *Geschäftsführer*, Ulrich Stolte, to find out about the feasibility of organising such a tour. (NB: the examiner's role for this role play is recorded on the CD which accompanies this book.)

(a) **When you get the receptionist**, explain that you wish to speak to Herr Stolte personally. **When you are told he is not available**, ask if you can talk to someone about organising a tour to Germany. **When the receptionist says he/she can help you**, continue with your task. Introduce yourself, explain what your teacher has asked you to do. Give the exact dates you have in mind.

(b) **When you are asked about numbers**, say how many you plan to bring, explain that your squash team will consist of both girls and boys, aged between 15 and 18 and a half, and that you would like to play against players of a similar age, possibly in schools, and probably stay in Youth Hostels.

(c) **When the receptionist explains that squash is largely played through clubs and not schools**, say that you are happy with that. Say that you would like to play two fixtures a day in a maximum of three cities or towns, but preferably within a manageable range: you will be coming in a minibus and driving yourselves.

(d) **When the receptionist says he/she will put the addresses of six clubs in the Ruhr area in the post for you**, explain that you had a less industrialised area in mind; perhaps he/she might have suggestions for matches in Lower Saxony or even Schleswig-Holstein?

(e) **When he/she suggests you might like to consider playing against British Army clubs in Northern Germany**, say that you are anxious to play against German youngsters. Give him/her your name and your school address (be prepared to spell in German any word he/she does not understand) and thank the receptionist for his/her help.

O&C

The examiner will play an active part in the conversation, assuming the role of the receptionist.

Candidate: <u>Darf ich</u> Herrn Solte <u>sprechen</u>, bitte?

Examiner: Es tut mir leid. Herr Stolte ist im Moment nicht da.

Candidate: Ist noch jemand da, mit dem ich über die Möglichkeit sprechen könnte, eine Squashtournee in Deutschland zu organisieren.

Examiner: Kann ich Ihnen helfen?

Candidate: <u>Das ist nett von Ihnen</u>. Mein Name ist John Smith. Ich und andere Schüler von meiner Schule möchten Squash gegen deutsche Schüler spielen. Wir wollten <u>eigentlich</u> in den Herbstferien nach Deutschland kommen, <u>das heißt</u> in der letzten Woche im Oktober.

Examiner: Wieviele Schüler möchten daran teilnehmen, bitte?

Candidate: Etwa 12 insgesamt. Jungen und Mädchen zwischen 15 und 18 einhalb. <u>Wir würden gerne</u> gegen gleichaltrige deutsche Schüler <u>spielen</u>. <u>Wenn es möglich wäre</u>, <u>möchten wir</u> in deutschen Schulen <u>spielen</u>. <u>Wir hatten vor</u>, in Jugendherbergen zu übernachten.

Examiner: Tja, hier in Deutschland spielt man Squash hauptsächlich in Vereinen und nicht in Schulen.

Candidate: <u>Das ist uns egal</u>. Wenn möglich, möchten wir zweimal pro Tag in höchstens drei Orten spielen, die nicht zu weit voneinander liegen. Wir fahren <u>nämlich</u> mit dem Schulminibus nach Deutschland und möchten nicht zu lange unterwegs sein.

Examiner: Gut. Ich schicke Ihnen die Adressen von 6 Vereinen im Ruhrgebiet, die vielleicht Interesse daran hätten.

Candidate: Oh, <u>wir wollten eigentlich</u> nicht so gerne in einem Industriegebiet sein. <u>Hätten Sie</u> vielleicht andere Adressen in Niedersachsen oder Schleswig-Holstein?

Examiner: Sie könnten vielleicht gegen englische Soldaten in der britischen Armee in Deutschland spielen. Es gibt mehrere englische Kasernen in Niedersachsen.

Candidate: Das ist eine gute Idee, aber <u>wir interessieren uns dafür</u>, gegen deutsche Schüler <u>zu spielen</u>. Wir wollten Deutsche kennenlernen.

Examiner: Gut. Geben Sie mir Ihren Namen und die Adresse Ihrer Schule, und ich werde versuchen, Vereine in Niedersachsen für Sie zu finden.

Candidate: Das ist sehr nett. <u>Vielen Dank für Ihre Hilfe</u>. Ich heiße John Smith und die Adresse meiner Schule ist: Morden School, Long Way, London SW10 6DT, England. Noch einmal, danke schön für Ihre Hilfe und auf Wiederhören.

As you can see from the dialogue the language is fairly simple, with the minimum of idiomatic expressions. The bits underlined are the kind of phrases and constructions that are useful for this kind of exercise, no matter what the task consists of.

Here is another example of this sort of task.

Brief: You are on a visit to Germany in the Half Term of the Autumn Term. You see a poster for the Munich *Oktoberfest* sellotaped to a door inside a small railway station in southern Germany. The *Fest* is over, you would like the poster as a souvenir but do not feel you can simply take it.

Task: Persuade the ticket-seller to let you have it.

(a) Attract the ticket-seller's attention (**he/she is busy with some paperwork**) and explain what you have seen and what you would like. **He/She will be very reluctant**.

(b) Ask if you can talk to his/her boss, the station-master for instance, or someone in higher authority. **He/She will say there is no-one there**.

(c) Explain that the poster is out-of-date, surely, no-one else will want it, could he/she simply let you detach it. **He/She will be very unsure what to do**.

(d) Plead that you have been to the festival, it would be a wonderful souvenir, say how much you like Bavaria, etc. (i.e. appeal to his/her good nature).

(e) **If he/she is adamant that it is not possible**, ask if you can leave a note for the station-master explaining your request and saying that you will come back tomorrow.

(f) **If he/she seems to be weakening**, say that you cannot afford to offer him/her money for the poster but that, if he/she would like to, you could send him/her a poster from Britain in exchange to put up in the office or give to his/her children.

The examiner will play an active part in the conversation, assuming the role of the ticket-seller.

O&C

ROLE PLAY WITH INSTRUCTIONS IN GERMAN AND STIMULUS MATERIAL IN ENGLISH

This exercise is much more open-ended, so you will have longer to prepare, probably about 30 minutes. It is, obviously, important that you read the German instructions very carefully so that you understand precisely what you have to do. There are some things that you will have to find out from the examiner and some negotiation which could go in a variety of ways, depending on how the examiner reacts. Part of your preparation time should be spent in thinking about the ways in which he/she might react and having a strategy ready for dealing with whatever he/she says. You must familiarise yourself with the information in English that you will need to call on to help you to carry out the task.

The mark scheme allocates a good proportion of the total marks to task completion and the use of the stimulus material. The language marks are given for the range of structures, vocabulary, accuracy and fluency.

In the example below, which is supposed to take 10 minutes, you are meant to be an employee of a British airline at the Information desk at Heathrow. All flights have been cancelled because of fog. A German teacher with an exchange group of 13-year-old German pupils arrives at the airport expecting to catch the flight back to Düsseldorf. It is your task to give him the information necessary to make a decision about what to do.

ROLLENSPIEL – KANDIDATENBOGEN

Die Situation

Sie arbeiten für eine britische Fluggesellschaft am Informationsschalter des Flughafens Heathrow in London. Der/die Prüfer/in übernimmt die Rolle eines deutschen Lehrers/einer deutschen Lehrerin, der/die verantwortlich für eine Gruppe von dreizehnjährigen Schülern ist, die gerade ihren ersten Besuch nach Großbritannien gemacht haben. Die Schüler haben an einem Austausch teilgenommen und haben bei britischen Familien gewohnt.

Es ist sechs Uhr abends. Die Gruppe ist am Flughafen eingetroffen, um nach Hause zu fliegen und muß feststellen, daß der Flughafen aufgrund dichten Nebels geschlossen ist. Es besteht keine wirkliche Aussicht, daß vor dem nächsten Morgen irgendein Abflug zu einem Zielort erfolgen wird.

(NB: the examiner's role for this role play is recorded on the CD which accompanies this book.

Die Aufgabe

Der/die für die Gruppe verantwortliche Lehrer/Lehrerin erscheint am Informationsschalter und bittet Sie, ihm/ihr zu erklären, was passiert. Im Verlauf des Gespräches werden Sie folgendes von ihm/ihr herausfinden müssen:

- den Zielort der Gruppe;
- die Abflugszeit und die Flugnummer;
- die Größe der Gruppe.

Der Lehrer/die Lehrerin ist offensichtlich sehr besorgt über die Situation, und Sie werden mit ihm/ihr die verschiedenen Möglichkeiten diskutieren müssen, was die Gruppe machen könnte. Zum Beispiel:

- für diese Nacht zu ihren Gastfamilien zurückzukehren und am nächsten Morgen nach Hause zu fliegen;
- die Nacht im Aufenthaltsraum des Flughafens zu verbringen und den ersten Flug des nächsten Tages zu nehmen;
- sich in einem Flughafenhotel einzutragen;
- mit dem Zug und der Fähre zu reisen (und Versicherungsansprüche geltend zu machen).

Auf dem beigefügten Blatt finden Sie verschiedene Informationen, die Ihnen helfen können, mit den Problemen der Gruppe fertigzuwerden. Besprechen Sie die Situation mit dem Lehrer/der Lehrerin, und versuchen Sie, die unter den schwierigen Umständen bestmögliche Lösung zu finden.

Sie wollen selbstverständlich so hilfreich wie möglich mit Ihren Kunden umgehen. Ihre Gesellschaft wird Ihnen erlauben, in Ihrem Ermessen befindliche Zugeständnisse zu gewähren (zB kostenloses Essen, die Benutzung des Telefons) und die Vergütung der Flugscheine anzubieten, wenn diese nicht benutzt werden. Sie sind jedoch nicht befugt, kostenlose Übernachtungsmöglichkeiten zu bieten, da sich Hunderte von Passagieren in derselben Situation befinden.

Oxford

☞ Shopping at Heathrow

Heathrow Airport Limited offers passengers well known, branded shops, and high quality goods together with a well publicised guarantee of value.

By encouraging well-known high street shops like Austin Reed, Jaeger, Bally, Boots the Chemist and Olympus Sports to trade at the airport, Heathrow Airport Limited ensures that passengers are familiar with standards of quality and pricing.

☞ Eating at Heathrow

High Street names
In line with Heathrow's global policy to improve customer service, competing high street catering companies have been encouraged to run airport restaurants and bars. Heathrow Airport Limited believes this gives customers greater confidence in value for money and the quality of food and drink available. In 1991 famous name brands including Burger King, Upper Crust, Garfunkels, Harry Ramsdens, Tap and Spile and Haagen Dazs opened branches at Heathrow. In December 1992, McDonalds opened for business in Terminal 4.

☞ Hotel information and reservations

There are Hotel Reservations desks in the arrivals hall of each terminal. They can book a wide selection of hotels, from basic youth hostels to luxury hotels.

Airport Hotels

Prices are per person	Our Rating	Parking	Mon–Thurs Twin	Mon–Thurs Single	Fri-Sat Twin	Fri-Sat Single
Arlington	★★		24.75	48.00	19.75	39.50
		15 nights inc	30.00	56.00	29.00	54.00
Ibis	★★	£3.50 per day	25.25	49.50	20.75	41.00
Ambassador	★★★		25.50	51.00	20.50	41.00
		8 nights inc	30.00	60.00	25.00	50.00
Novotel Jul/Aug/Dec/Jan	★★★	8 nights free	34.75	67.00	28.00	49.00
			29.00	54.00	28.00	49.00
Master Robert	★★★		32.00	63.00	28.00	53.00
		15 nights inc	35.00	68.00	28.00	53.00
Excelsior Jul/Aug/Dec/Jan/Apr	★★★★		35.50	71.00	30.00	59.00
			34.00	68.00	28.00	58.00
		15 nights inc	42.00	84.00	36.50	73.00
Crown Club Supplement			12.50	25.00	7.50	15.00

☞ Public transport

Heathrow airport is very well served by public transport. The London Underground offers direct services into central London.

Examples of average journey times from Heathrow to:

▶ Piccadilly Circus   47 minutes
▶ King's Cross   55 minutes
▶ Liverpool Street   61 minutes

Trains run every 5 minutes at peak times and every 9 minutes at off peak times and at weekends.

☞ Entertaining Children at Heathrow

While there are presently no dedicated 'play areas' in the terminals at Heathrow, there are video game machines distributed around the terminals which are very popular with the younger visitors to the airport.

The spectators' viewing area, on the roof of Terminal 2, is also a good place to entertain children. They can enjoy an aerial view of airport activity and visit the area's cafeteria and shop. The viewing area can be reached by Clifton Road, next to Terminal 2. Admission is free.

☞ Flight times

Depart London	Arrive Düsseldorf
0630	0735
0725	0830
0845	1050
0915	1120

☞ Train departures

Via Dover–Ostend

Depart London Victoria Station	Arrive Düsseldorf
2205	1042

The examiner opens the conversation. The conversation might go something like this:

Examiner: Können Sie mir bitte sagen, was los ist? Sind alle Flüge gestrichen?

Candidate: Ja, wegen des Nebels. Die nächsten Flüge finden morgen statt, wenn das Wetter sich verbessert. Wohin wollten Sie fliegen?

E: Nach Düsseldorf.

C: Um wieviel Uhr ist Ihr Flug?

E: Um 19.15 Uhr.

C: Und was ist die Flugnummer?

E: Lufthansa 123.

C: Ja, dieser Flug ist gestrichen.

E: Mein Gott, das ist eine Katastrophe! Ich bin mit einer Austauschgruppe von 13jährigen Schülern unterwegs. Wir sind auf dem Weg nach Hause. Ich weiß nicht, was ich mit den Kindern machen soll.

C: Wieviele Schüler sind in der Gruppe?

E: 10.

C: Könnten die Kinder nicht zu ihren Gastfamilien zurückkehren und da übernachten? Sie könnten von hier aus telefonieren, und es ist sehr leicht nach London zu fahren. Sie könnten in 45 Minuten mit der U-bahn wieder in der Mitte von London sein.

E: Das wäre eigentlich sehr schwierig. Einige Kinder hatten Gastfamilien, die außerhalb von London wohnen. Es könnte schwierig sein, sie alle telefonisch zu erreichen, und es ist nicht sicher, daß sie ihren Gast wieder aufnehmen können. Und es wäre sehr umständlich, die Kinder wieder hinzubringen und morgen früh wieder zum Flughafen zu fahren.

C: Ja, das verstehe ich. Könnte ich dann vorschlagen, daß Sie die Nacht im Aufenthaltsraum des Flughafens verbringen. Es gibt viel für die Kinder hier zu tun, und sie könnten kostenlos in der Kantine zu Abend essen, und frühstücken könnten sie auch umsonst. Die Sessel im Aufenthaltsraum sind auch ganz bequem und in ihrem Alter schlafen Kinder fast überall gut. Es wäre für sie ein Abenteuer.

E: Das ist keine so gute Idee. Die Kinder haben heute eine lange Fahrt hinter sich und sind sehr müde und genervt. Es wäre schwierig, auf sie aufzupassen. Was könnten sie hier tun? Das sind letzten Endes 12 oder mehr Stunden. Wann ist der erste Flug morgen?

C: Um 6.30 Uhr. Ankunft in Düsseldorf 7.35 Uhr.

E: Und wir haben fast kein Geld mehr. Die Kinder haben jetzt bestimmt Hunger.

C: Eine andere Möglichkeit wäre im Hotel hier am Flughafen zu übernachten. Ich kann für Sie herausfinden, ob man Zimmer frei hat.

E: Die sind wohl alle sehr teuer.

C: Im Hotel Arlington kostet ein Einzelzimmer £19.75 und ein Doppelzimmer £39.50.

E: Tja, so viel Geld haben wir nicht. Würde die Fluggesellschaft die Übernachtungskosten zahlen, bitte? Wann sind die anderen Flüge morgen, bitte?

C: Es tut mir leid. Die Fluggesellschaft könnte das nicht bezahlen. Es gibt so viele Passagiere, die in der gleichen Lage sind. Morgen früh gibt es drei Flüge nach Düsseldorf, um 7.25, 8.45 und 9.15. Sie könnten auch mit dem Zug und der Fähre fahren. Vielleicht würde Ihre Versicherung diese Kosten bezahlen.

E: Was würde dann mit unseren Flugkarten passieren?

C: Ich kann Ihnen Ihr Geld dafür zurückgeben.

E: Danke. Wissen Sie, wann ein Zug nach Düsseldorf fährt?

C: Ja, um 22.05 fährt der nächste Zug von Victoria in London. Der sollte um 10.42 am nächsten Morgen in Düsseldorf ankommen. Das ist über Dover und Ostende. Mit der U-bahn können Sie Victoria erreichen.

E: Ja, aber das wäre sehr umständlich und anstrengend und wir kämen morgen früh genauso schnell mit dem Flugzeug dahin. Ich müßte eigentlich die Eltern der Kinder anrufen, damit sie Bescheid wissen, warum wir nicht heute wie geplant in Düsseldorf ankommen.

C: Sie dürfen gerne von hier aus telefonieren.

E: Danke, das ist sehr nett. Ich glaube, die Fluggesellschaft sollte auch die Übernachtung im Hotel bezahlen. Wir sind nicht Schuld daran, daß die Maschinen nicht fliegen können.

C: Ich verstehe Ihre Situation sehr gut, aber ich darf das nicht erlauben. Die Fluggesellschaft bezahlt gerne das Essen hier am Flughafen und wir werden es den Kindern im Aufenthaltsraum so bequem wie möglich machen, aber mehr darf ich nicht tun.

E: Na, gut. Dann bleiben wir hier am Flughafen und ich danke Ihnen für Ihre Hilfe.

Here is another example of this sort of task.

ROLLENSPIEL – KANDIDATENBOGEN

Hinweis an die Kandidaten

Die Aufgabe erfolgt vielleicht nicht in der unten angegebenen Reihenfolge. Jede beliebige Reihenfolge ist möglich, vorausgesetzt, daß Sie alle Einzelheiten der Aufgabe bearbeitet haben. Seien Sie flexibel und richten Sie sich nach dem Prüfer/der Prüferin.

Die Situation

Sie sind bei Ihrem/Ihrer Brieffreund/in in Deutschland. Der Vater der Familie raucht ziemlich viel. Sie kommen aus einer Nichtraucher-Familie.

Die Aufgabe

Eines Abends werden Sie gefragt, warum Sie Nichtraucher sind. Mit Hilfe von den Informationen in den Artikeln, die Sie gelesen haben, müssen Sie folgendes erklären:

- Kosten und Gefahren des Rauchens;
- Statistik von Ihrer Heimat (Bath in Wessex);
- Neue Gesetze in Frankreich vom 1. November.

Von dem Vater müssen Sie herausfinden:

- wann und warum er angefangen hat, zu rauchen;
- warum er immer noch raucht;
- ob er versucht hat, das Rauchen aufzugeben.

Sie machen sich Sorgen um die Auswirkungen des Rauchens sowohl auf ihn als auch auf die anderen Mitglieder der Familie. Der Vater raucht gern und will das Rauchen nicht aufgeben. Während des Gesprächs sollen Sie auch diskutieren:

- was man tun könnte, um Jugendlichen davon abzuraten;
- die Gefahren des passiven Rauchens;
- ob Raucher auch Rechte haben.

Der Vater gibt natürlich ungern sein Rauchen auf. Sie müssen ihn dazu überreden.

Oxford

Shocking new study into 'cost' of smoking

By Jayne Brierley

SMOKING is costing Bath District Health Authority £2.49m and 655 lives every year, according to figures released today.

One in seven deaths in Bath every year is related to smoking. In Wessex smoking directly kills 5,000 people every year.

According to the study, which is the first update on smoking statistics since 1985, someone dies from smoking every two hours. Lung cancer kills 1,500 Wessex people a year.

Nearly 400 beds in Wessex, enough to fill a district general hospital, are taken up every day by patients requiring treatment for smoking-related diseases. The £17 million cost of these beds does not take into account the costs of passive smoking and of lost work days due to ill health.

Dr Graham Winyard, director of public health at Wessex, said: "These statistics are appalling. Our tolerance of smoking, given its massive effect on health, is remarkable.

"Steps should be taken to increase the taxation on tobacco and ban the advertising and promotion of tobacco products.

"The direct ill-effects of smoking and other forms of tobacco on smokers are well known. The indirect harm that smokers do to those around them, including children, has been more recently demonstrated.

"Prevention is the only potentially effective route and should be possible as lung cancer is almost entirely a man-made disease, due largely to cigarette smoking."

Dog-End Days in France

Andrew Bell

French smokers are enjoying their last week of freedom before an anti-tobacco law restricting smoking in offices, cafés and other public places comes into effect.

It will have its most dramatic impact in offices and factories. There, smoking will no longer be permitted in areas where several people work together, and managements will be obliged to set aside sections to separate smokers from non-smokers. The habit will be completely banned in public areas at work such as reception rooms and canteens, but smoking will still be allowed in individual offices.

After November 1, French smokers may try and escape to a bar for a peaceful puff, but they will not necessarily be safe there either: proprietors are supposed to designate a smoking area with adequate ventilation. French smokers returning home will also find that they can no longer indulge their habit in the Paris Métro or in the suburban trains of the Ile de France region. Breaking the law in any of these places could entail a fine of more than £100.

The principal aim of the law is to protect France's non-smokers, many of whom are estimated to inhale a couple of Gauloises a day through passive smoking. The law also hopes to cut the number of French smokers and the cost of the habit in terms of lost working days and health expenditure. Government figures show that smoking causes 54,000 deaths a year in France. Forty per cent of the French smoke, and while that is not the highest figure in the EC, the government has been especially concerned by an estimate that two thirds of 18-year-olds take up the habit, a higher proportion than in any other European country.

Examiner's sheet

Situation

As on the Candidate's Sheet. You are the mother/father of the candidate's penfriend, and a heavy smoker. The candidate is currently staying with you and your family.

The task

You start by asking the candidate why s/he is so against smoking – after all, don't a lot of young people smoke? As the candidate explains, you comment and ask questions as follows:

- You know of course that smoking is supposed to be bad for you (but your father smoked 40 a day and lived to the age of 90!). **Does the candidate know any precise mortality figures?**
- You understand about the financial costs to the individual – cigarettes are getting very expensive – **but what other costs are there? What is this £17 million for?**
- You know **that an anti-smoking law came into effect in France last November, but what does it actually mean? Where exactly is smoking now forbidden?** Does it mean there is no smoking in offices at all?
- It all seems very hard – **why did they bring in such strict laws?**

The candidate will try to persuade you that your health is at risk and that you should give up smoking. In reply to the candidate's questions:

- **You started smoking when you were 15, because all your friends smoked;**
- **You continue to smoke because you enjoy it** – it's relaxing and you have a stressful job;
- **You have tried to give up from time to time, but it's very hard!** You end up eating too much instead and getting fat!

During the discussion you comment and ask questions as follows:

- Why should officials stop you doing something that gives you pleasure – it's an infringement of personal liberty;
- It's your life and you can do what you want with it;
- **You think the fuss about passive smoking is exaggerated**;
- And anyway your family has never objected!
- Where you come from smoking is part of the culture;
- **Smokers have rights as well as non-smokers** – it's not right that one group of people should be allowed to dictate other people's behaviour;
- Has anyone ever proved that smoking causes lung cancer? Some people die of lung cancer who never smoked;
- Smoking isn't as dangerous as taking drugs – lots of young people take drugs;
- Does your smoking in the house cause the candidate any problems? You could offer to open the windows!
- **You agree that young people should be discouraged from starting to smoke** (if only for financial reasons) – **does the candidate have any ideas of how this could be achieved?**

Eventually you admit that you haven't been feeling too well lately and agree that at least during the candidate's stay you will try to give up.

DISCUSSION BASED ON A GERMAN TEXT

The length of text that you will have to prepare varies from Board to Board. The discussion will last between seven and ten minutes. You will have time to read the material through and think about what line the discussion might take. With some Boards there will be some questions which are intended to guide you. In other examinations you have only the text. Certain Boards give you a choice of texts, say one from three, and several days of preparation time.

Your first priority is to read through the material carefully, understand as much as you possibly can and to think of what the issues are. Try, if you can, to adopt a particular attitude to the issue and think of arguments to defend your point of view. That way a discussion is more likely to be focused than if you have sympathy for all points of view. It is likely that you will, in any case, be asked what your attitude is and marks will be awarded for being able to defend a point of view.

Some mark schemes will have a statement similar to the following: **Aim:** To assess the variety and complexity of responses in which effective communication occurs: e.g. how far does the candidate go beyond narrative statements to express ideas and opinions, or to give explanations and descriptions? How far does the candidate enlarge appropriately on simple statements, or take the opportunity of entering into discussion? It is the responsibility of the examiner to ask questions which give the candidate opportunity to demonstrate his/her level of competence in the range of responses indicated above.

In the following example the issue being dealt with is the role of fathers. Three different fathers illustrate three different ways of being a father. The two questions that accompany the text help to set the scene.

Consider this material on the subject of the role of the father in today's family. Be prepared to discuss the material itself and issues relating to it.

DIE LÜGE VON DEN NEUEN VÄTERN

Liebe, wenn's die Zeit erlaubt

Sie sind bei der Geburt dabei, können wickeln und wurden als neue Väter-Generation gefeiert. Alles nur Fassade: Die meisten fliehen vor ihren Kindern – genauso wie ihre eigenen Väter

Papa auf Abruf
Andreas Stachowski hängt an seinen Töchtern Anja-Elsa und Lena Marie. Aber ganz für sie dasein möchte er nicht. Der Angestellte ist schnell genervt und flüchtet dann in seine Junggesellenbude

Erziehung ist Frauensache
Die wenigen Stunden, die Manfred Lampelmayer für seine Tochter Mariela Zeit hat, will er nicht auch noch mit Regeln und Prinzipien vollstopfen. Das ist die Angelegenheit seiner Frau Gabriela. Der Anwalt glaubt: Ein Kind ist besser dran, wenn es den Vater nicht ständig sieht

Immer für die Kids da
Ein Vater nach Maß: Edwin Beuter teilt sich mit Frau Annerose alle Elternpflichten. Seinen Lehrerjob gab er auf, um mehr Zeit für Daniel und Sarah zu haben

AEB

1   Welche Rolle sollte ein Vater spielen?

2   Was verstehen Sie unter „Liebe, wenn's die Zeit erlaubt"?

You need to think of the various 'angles' to the topic that you have been presented with and the kind of questions that might be put to you as part of a discussion. Having done that you need to decide on your attitude and opinion. What do you think? What answers would you give and how would you back up your answers? Think how you would answer the following questions. There would not be time for all of them. Make some notes then record your answers on cassette and listen to what you have said, noting how you could improve your answers. Do it again, making the improvements. (NB: the questions are recorded on the CD which accompanies this book.)

1   Was verstehen Sie unter „neuen Vätern"?

2   Was ist der Unterschied zwischen Andreas Stachowski und Edwin Beuter?

3   Wie unterscheiden sich Manfred Lampelmayer und Andreas Stachowski?

4   Wer ist der beste Vater, Ihrer Meinung nach? Und warum?

5   Was ist die Gefahr für Kinder, wenn sie den Vater nur selten sehen?

6   Sollte Erziehung der Kinder Frauensache sein?

7   Wie war Ihr Vater, als Sie jung waren?

8   Sollte eine Frau berufstätig sein?

9   Kann ein Mann die Rolle einer Mutter spielen?

10   Was halten Sie von einem Hausmann wie Edwin Beuter?

11   Was bedeutet „Papa auf Abruf"?

12   Was ist eine Junggesellenbude? Warum kann Andreas dahin flüchten?

13 Sollten eine Frau und ein Mann zusammenleben, bevor sie heiraten? Und warum?

14 Sollten sie heiraten, bevor sie Kinder haben? Und warum?

15 Wie wäre Ihre Haltung, wenn Sie mit Manfred Lampelmayer verheiratet wären?

16 Glauben Sie, daß ein Kind zwei Eltern braucht? Und warum?

Here is another example of this sort of task.

HAKAN IST EINER DER BESTEN IN DEUTSCH

Gemeinschaftshauptschule Wesseling bei Köln. Der jüngste Lehrer ist 39, die Klassen sind 28 bis 30 Schüler stark, der Ausländeranteil liegt in manchen bei über 50 Prozent. Aber was heißt hier Ausländer? Bei Claudia Rinn in der Klasse ist Hakan einer der Besten in Deutsch.

Frau Rinn spielt mit der 5b Buchstaben umstellen. Aus dem Wort „Ostern" sollen neue Begriffe gebildet werden. Die Klasse ist lebhaft, die Finger schnipsen, am Ende stehen über 20 Wörter an der Tafel. Die meisten stammen von Christian, Uwe und Hakan.

Elf Mädchen und 17 Jungen, 16 „Ausländer" und zwölf Deutsche. Die Mutter von Efthimios, den sie wegen seines schwer auszusprechenden griechischen Namens „Sammy" nennen, ist in Köln zur Schule gegangen. Nourdine, der Marrokaner, kam vor einem halben Jahr nach Deutschland, begleitet von seinem Großvater, und spricht kaum ein Wort Deutsch. Fehmi, der Albaner, ist 1992 mit seinen Eltern aus dem zerbrechenden Jugoslawien geflüchtet. Unter den drei polnischen Aussiedlerkindern sind zwei in Wesseling geboren, einer kam 1991 und lernt Deutsch im Förderkurs. Milena, Tochter eines brasilianischen Arztes, lebt seit 1990 in Deutschland. Die sieben Türken (sechs davon wurden in Deutschland geboren) sprechen gut Deutsch, es hapert allerdings mit dem Schreiben.

Kinder, die aus dem Ausland zu uns kommen, werden altersmäßig den Klassen zugeordnet, in die sie hineinpassen, ohne Rücksicht auf Sprach-oder Rechenkenntnisse. Sie bekommen zwar sechs Stunden Förderunterricht in Deutsch und Unterricht in ihrer Muttersprache. In Wesseling sind ein türkischer und ein griechischer Lehrer angestellt. Doch das reicht nicht aus, meint Frau Rinn, um ein Kind, das im Heimatland noch nicht einmal lesen und rechnen gelernt hat, in eine Klasse zu integrieren. „Wir brauchen eine Förderschule, die die Kinder auf den Unterricht an einer normalen Schule vorbereitet."Doch derzeit werden Förderkurse, die von den Gemeinden mitfinanziert wurden, aus Finanznot gestrichen.

Dazu kommen die kulturellen Unterschiede. Emel ist ihr vor zwei Wochen mitten im Unterricht umgekippt. Das zierliche Mädchen hatte auf Anweisung ihrer Eltern gehungert. Moslems essen und trinken im Fastenmonat Ramadan von Sonnenaufgang bis Sonnenuntergang nichts. In dieser Zeit fällt auch der Kochunterricht für sie an der Schule aus.

Nicht alle machen die strengen Sitten mit, einige Familien haben sich losgesagt. „Es gibt Väter, die ihren Töchtern alles verbieten – vom Schwimmunterricht bis zum Klassenausflug", sagt Frau Rinn, „und andere, da merken Sie gar nicht, daß das Mädchen aus einer türkischen Familie stammt."

Probleme mit Ausländerfeindlichkeit? – Das Wort möchte sie gar nicht hören, sagt Frau Rinn: „Die Kinder wachsen zusammen auf, leben zusammen, lernen miteinander, streiten sich und haben ihre Eigenheiten. Das ist völlig normal und hat nichts mit Ausländerfeindlichkeit zu tun."

ULEAC

REPORTING THE CONTENT OF AN ENGLISH TEXT

The scenario for this kind of exercise is that you have met a German who speaks no English. He/She has a newspaper article in English that he/she would like to have explained. You are requested to give the gist of the article in German.

Although you are not expected to translate the English text word for word into German you will gain marks for the details that you mention. If there are words that you do not know the German for you can either ignore them, if they are not too important, or you can paraphrase or describe them. The advantage of this kind of test is that you do not have to be able to give a word for word rendering.

Half the marks will probably be given for 'completion of the task', that is how much information you conveyed in comprehensible German. The other half will be given for the quality of the German that you used. If you are concentrating on conveying the information it is likely that you will use relatively straightforward German. If you can use the occasional subordinate clause and/or idiomatic expression, so much the better. Pronunciation and intonation will also be important.

In the following example the German has been kept as simple as possible. You are told not to translate, but you may make notes beside the text and refer to both the text and your notes when carrying out the task. Some of the language may at first sight seem difficult, such as: *surviving half a century on this planet, deserves recognition, marking the occasion, for the perils of life as an actor, pretending to be all ages from 40 to 70.* Look at the way they have been rendered into German. The sense of the English has been given rather than a word for word translation.

Rubric: Study the article below and then, in German, explain the main points to the examiner. You must not translate the article, but you may refer to it if you wish.

Dear Editor

Reaching the age of 50 is a significant event. Surviving half a century on this planet and 30 (or more) years working hard, raising a family, generally behaving in a sensible, conventional manner, deserves recognition.

A good way of marking the occasion, with an eye to a not-too-distant retirement, might be to invest in a savings scheme. Like many others I did just that – but I also did something else. I gave up my secure career as a school teacher for the perils of life as an actress.

That was last summer. Since then I have been on stage in classics and modern plays, as ladies and as whores, pretending to be all ages from 40 to 70. I have danced a manic twist and a stiff tango, been shot dead every night for a month, and have worn many different coloured wigs. I have also performed in numerous different locations. The search for acting work is permanent and in between I have done casual work in kitchens and canteens and signed on for the first time in my life. No matter how stressful this new life may seem, it is a tonic compared with the daily battle that teaching had become.

Fifty can be the first step on a downhill slide towards inactivity, but it does not have to be. For me, it has been the start of an uphill climb to never-ending creativity, the beginning of a whole new way of life.

NEAB

203

Example answer

In diesem Text handelt es sich um einen Brief an den Redakteur einer Zeitung. Die Verfasserin des Briefes meint, daß es ein wichtiges Ereignis ist, wenn man 50 wird. Man hat ein halbes Jahrhundert auf der Erde gelebt und hat 30 oder mehr Jahre dabei verbracht, fleißig zu arbeiten, um eine Familie aufzuziehen und zu ernähren. Man ist vernünftig und konventionell gewesen. Das sollte anerkannt werden.

Man könnte vielleicht diesen Geburtstag dadurch feiern, daß man Geld für die Rente investiert. Wie viele andere habe ich das auch gemacht. Ich habe auch etwas anderes gemacht – ich habe meinen sicheren Job als Lehrerin aufgegeben, um ein viel riskanteres Leben als Schauspielerin zu führen.

Das war im letzten Sommer. Seitdem habe ich in klassischen und modernen Theaterstücken gespielt – ich habe die Rollen von Heldinnen und Huren gespielt und mußte Personen zwischen 40 und 70 darstellen. Ich habe wie verrückt den Twist und steif den Tango getanzt. Man hat mich jeden Abend einen ganzen Monat lang erschossen. Ich habe viele verschieden farbige Perücken getragen. Ich habe überall gespielt.

Man muß als Schauspielerin ständig Arbeit suchen. Inzwischen habe ich in Küchen und Kantinen gearbeitet und mich zum ersten Mal als arbeitslos angemeldet. Dieses neue Leben kann anstrengend sein, aber im Vergleich zu dem täglichen Kampf als Lehrerin tut es mir gut.

Mit 50 kann man bergab gehen und nichts tun, aber es muß nicht sein. Für mich war es der Anfang einer neuen Lebensweise, ein Weg bergauf zu einer ständigen Kreativität. (NB: this report is recorded on the CD which accompanies this book. Please note that this recording contains more expression than you will be expected to show in the exam.)

ACTING AS AN INTERPRETER

In this real-life task you are given a little information about the people for whom you are to act as an interpreter. You may also be given some vocabulary items that you would not be expected to know.

The two people with whom you are working have a script which tells them exactly what to say and how much to say in one go. You will not be expected to remember too much before translating it. You may also ask for something to be repeated if you did not understand it or if you require clarification, but you must use the appropriate language to each person.

Much of what you have to translate into German will be of a basic nature such as giving personal details – name, address, profession etc. – and it is likely that the conversation will be of a fairly practical nature. It is the kind of task that is difficult to prepare for, except by doing some practice ones beforehand, but it does not involve you in learning material or facts. If you have good basic oral skills it should not be too difficult.

Inevitably there will be words or phrases that you will find difficult to translate, but you can always paraphrase or explain them. Provided that you convey the meaning and it is understood you have done your job.

Here is an example of one such task.

A Candidate's instructions

You are required to act as an interpreter from German into English and vice versa between a German teacher and an English teacher, neither of whom speaks each other's language. The roles of the teachers will be played by the two interlocutors.

During the course of the conversation you may ask each of the participants to repeat any of the statements they make or for any other clarification you require at any point but be sure to address each of them in the appropriate language.

Dictionaries **may not** be used.

Some of the vocabulary items you may need are listed below.

die Gesamtschule:	comprehensive school
dreigliedrig:	tripartite
der Druck:	pressure

Start by asking each participant his/her name and its exact spelling.

B Interlocutor's instructions

Interlocutors are required to read the following instructions:

A is the **German speaker** and **B** is the **English speaker**.

The candidate is required to translate from English into German and vice versa. Make sure you pause after each | to give the candidate sufficient time to render the statement in the appropriate language.

If the candidate requires clarification supply this in short, simple sentences.

(a) signifies that the examiner is to continue with this point **only if the previous statement has been understood and meaningfully conveyed**. This section usually refers back to a statement previously made which the candidate may/or may not have communicated successfully. If this has not been conveyed successfully then proceed to point (b) which represents the new point.

Transcript

A: Ich heiße Gerd/a Höhner

B: John/Julia Stevenson

A: Könnten Sie Frau/Herrn S fragen, wo er/sie wohnt und in was für einer Schule er/sie unterrichtet. |

B: I live in a town near Bristol | and I teach in a small comrehensive school in Bath | which is about 12 miles from my house. | I teach English. | Could you please ask Gerd/a where he/she lives and works. |

A: Ich wohne in Neumünster in Schleswig-Holstein | und ich bin an einer Grundschule in der Stadtmitte. | Ich gebe alle Fächer außer Musik. |

B: (a) How old are the children in your primary school? |
(b) Is it true that German teachers are better paid than their English colleagues? |

A: (a) Von 7 bis 10. |
(b) Da ich nicht weiß, wieviel ein englischer Lehrer monatlich verdient, | kann ich das schlecht beurteilen. | Ich verdiene zB DM 3000 netto pro Monat | – das entspricht ungefähr £1500 – | und ein Realschullehrer verdient so ungefähr DM 4000 monatlich | – also umgerechnet wäre das so ungefähr £2000. | Wieviel verdient ein junger Grundschullehrer bei Ihnen? |

B: (a) I'm not sure, | I think on average a beginner earns £10 000 per year. |
(b) What has Gerd/a done and seen so far during his/her visit?

A: Ich habe eigentlich sehr viel gemacht. | Bisher habe ich drei Grundschulen und eine Gesamtschule gesehen. |

B: (a) What opinion does he/she have of them? |
(b) What opinion does he/she have of the schools he/she has visited so far?

A: Die Gesamtschule war sehr interessant | und die Disziplin dort war wesentlich besser als bei uns. | Aber ganz ehrlich gesagt haben mir die Grundschulen mehr imponiert. | Die Klassen bei Ihnen sind aber viel größer als bei uns | – oft 35 Kinder in einer Klasse. | Mit so vielen könnte ich nicht fertig werden. |

B: (a) How many pupils does Gerd/a have in his/her class? |
(b) Do you have many comprehensive schools? |

A: (a) 22 |
(b) Nicht viele. | Wir haben ein dreigliedriges System. | Mit 10 Jahren verlassen die Schüler die Grundschule: | sie können auf einen von 3 Schultypen gehen – | das Gymnasium oder die Realschule oder die Hauptschule. |

B: (a) Could Gerd/a briefly explain the types of school. |
(b) Do you have any foreign children in your area? |

A: (a) Es ist eigentlich sehr kompliziert, | aber das Gymnasium | ist vorwiegend für akademisch begabte Kinder geeignet – wie Ihre 'Grammar schools' –; | die Realschule | für Schüler, die sich für technische und wirtschaftliche Fächer interessieren, | und die Hauptschule | vermittelt eine allgemeine Vorbereitung auf das Berufsleben. |
(b) In den Großstädten bestimmt | aber nicht so viele auf dem Lande. | In letzter Zeit besuchen immer mehr ausländische Kinder das Gymnasium. | Sind Sie der Meinung, daß das deutsche dreigliedrige System besser ist als das jetzige System in England? |

B: We have many types of schools in England. | I think that the comprehensive school | where I teach | is very good indeed. | There the pupils can develop without pressure. | They have a wide choice of subjects. | But we can talk about this later. | My wife/husband and I have invited some friends to dinner this evening. | Would you like to come? |

A: Ja, gerne. Das ist sehr liebenswürdig von Ihnen. | Wo wohnen Sie übrigens? |

B: I will pick you up. Is 7.30 OK? |

A: Prima. Ich freue mich sehr darauf, Ihre Frau/Ihren Mann und Ihre Freunde kennenzulernen. |

ULEAC

PRESENTING A TOPIC

For some Boards' orals you may have to give a presentation of about three minutes on your prepared topic. You will be expected to show evidence of the ability to present relevant facts, to express opinions and to offer points for discussion. This is a skill that will be useful to you later in life. It is worth preparing it well, because careful preparation will boost your confidence in what is a stressful situation.

It is not intended that you should recite a pre-learned passage, but you will probably need to write down beforehand what you intend to say to test it out for length if nothing else. If you learn it off by heart and recite it word for word it will be very obvious that it has been pre-learned. You need to know the material so well that you can talk about it and deliver it in as natural a way as possible. Noting down a few key words or short headings as prompts for use in the examination should give you the confidence not to need to pre-learn it, although undoubtedly you will be saying things that you have rehearsed beforehand.

When you write down what you are going to say, keep it simple, using the expressions, constructions and vocabulary that come naturally to you in speech. Have it checked for grammatical errors. Make sure that you do not overrun the allotted time. Do not use expressions that would be more appropriate to written German. If you do, your presentation will 'clash' sharply with what you go on to say when you discuss your topic.

What is being looked for is an interesting and lively presentation showing that you have prepared your topic thoroughly. You may bring in a limited quantity of illustrative material to help your presentation. This might include maps, diagrams, statistics, pictures or short articles. If you take in too much you may find it difficult to organise your material and you may spend more time searching for the appropriate item than actually speaking. Having some illustrative material is a good idea if there is suitable material available for your topic. It shows that you have done some preparation, gives you confidence, because it acts as a prompt for you, and it provides a bit of variety.

You may not take into the oral a prepared script, which you then read out. You are normally allowed a cue card in German with not more than five headings to remind you of the main points you wish to make. Remember the following:

- practise several times before you go in;
- time yourself;
- try not to be nervous;

- remember your audience;
- maintain eye contact;
- smile occasionally;
- look interested in what you are saying;
- three minutes will pass very quickly.

DISCUSSION OF A PREPARED TOPIC

Most Boards include a discussion of a prepared topic in the oral. It gives you the opportunity of doing research and finding out as much as possible about a subject that interests you. Knowing a subject well should make it easier for you to talk and have something interesting to say, which helps the examiner. In some syllabuses a good proportion of the marks will be given for what you know about the topic.

There are no examination questions as such, but there are ways to make sure that you are well prepared:

1. Have factual material to back up what you say (figures, percentages, facts).

2. Prepare some charts, pictures, photographs to take with you into the oral.

3. Choose a topic that you are interested in; you will speak with more enthusiasm.

4. Do not use the same topic for two languages; the risk is that you will mix up facts, figures even some of the language and you may give the impression of being stale!

5. Make a list of vocabulary, phrases and expressions that relate to your topic and learn them.

6. Think of the kind of questions that you might be asked and prepare your answers in advance.

7. Be prepared for some questions that will require you to offer and defend opinions, that will make you think on your feet. The examiner is required to give you the opportunity of gaining the higher marks for these skills.

8. Take a few notes into the examination with you to act as a prompt, if they are allowed. You will not be allowed to read out prepared statements.

9. Practise beforehand with a friend, the German assistant and/or your teacher so that you have had to formulate answers several times. The questions in the examination may not be the same, but the information for your answers will not change much.

The following are some typical topics with questions that should make you think:

Probleme der Jugendlichen

Arbeitslosigkeit:
Wie wirkt sich die Arbeitslosigkeit auf das Individuum aus?
Was ist das größte Problem für Arbeitslose? Und warum?
Was sollte die Regierung machen, um dieses Problem zu lösen?

Drogen:
Wie kann man Drogensüchtigen am besten helfen?
Sind Drogen das größte Problem für junge Leute? Warum/oder warem nicht?
Wie kann man das Problem von Drogen am besten bekämpfen?

Verhältnisse:
Warum gibt es so oft Konflikt zwischen den Generationen?
Was kann man tun, damit junge Leute sich in der Familie wohl fühlen?
Was ist das größte Problem für Jugendliche auf diesem Gebiet? Und warum?

Industrie und die Umwelt

Waldsterben:

Was muß getan werden, um die Wirkungen dieses Problems zu vermindern?

Wie zerstört die Industrie unsere Wälder?

Was ist wichtiger – die Industrie oder die Umwelt? Und warum?

Müll:

Was ist die beste Lösung für dieses Problem?

Warum halten Sie Müll für ein Problem?

Wer kann dieses Problem leichter lösen – die Industrie oder das Individuum?

Literatur

Warum haben Sie dieses Buch gewählt?

Könnte man einen guten Film daraus machen?

Wie hat das Buch Ihre Ideen verändert?

War die Hauptperson des Buches ein typischer Deutscher?

Was wollte der Verfasser dieses Buches mit seinem Buch aussagen?

GENERAL CONVERSATION

Many Boards have general conversation as an element of the oral. It can range over a vast number of topics, but the following are favourites with many examiners:

❶ Your school, the subjects you are doing, why you chose them.

❷ What your plans for the future are.

❸ Your hobbies.

❹ Any visits that you have made to Germany and your impressions of Germany and German life. A comparison between English and German life.

❺ Current affairs, items in the news, your opinion about them and how you think that they might be solved.

❶ **Your school:** Was für Fächer machen Sie in der Schule?

Warum haben Sie diese Fächer gewählt?

Welches ist Ihr Lieblingsfach? Und warum?

Was halten Sie von Ihrer Schule?

Wie würden Sie das englische Schulsystem verändern, wenn Sie Kultusminister wären?

Halten Sie das englische oder das deutsche Schulsystem für besser? Und warum?

❷ **Your plans for the future:** Was wollen Sie nächstes Jahr machen, nachdem Sie die Schule verlassen haben? Warum?

Welchen Beruf möchten Sie ergreifen? Und warum?

Wie wird Ihr Leben in 10 Jahren sein, wenn alles geht, wie Sie es sich vorstellen?

Glauben Sie, daß Jugendliche heutzutage mehr Chancen als ihre Eltern haben? Warum glauben Sie das?

❸ **Hobbies:** Was tun Sie in Ihrer Freizeit?

Warum gefällt Ihnen das? Wie sind Sie dazu gekommen?

Wie würden Sie versuchen, mich dazu zu überreden, das auch zu tun?

Sollte man Sport in seiner Freizeit treiben? Warum/oder warum nicht?

Sind Sie der Meinung, daß das Fernsehen ein gutes Hobby ist? Warum/oder warum nicht?

❹ **Visits to Germany:** Sind Sie je in Deutschland gewesen?

Wann? Wo? Für wie lange?

Was hat Sie am meisten beeindruckt? Und warum?

Was sind die größten Unterschiede zwischen Deutschland und England?

Wie ist das Familienleben anders als in England?

Möchten Sie gerne da wohnen? Warum/oder warum nicht?

Was halten Sie von der deutschen Wiedervereinigung?
Was sind die Unterschiede zwischen Ost- und Westdeutschland?

5 **Current affairs:** Was ist heute das größte Problem für Deutschland?
Was würden Sie tun, um dieses Problem zu beseitigen, wenn Sie Bundeskanzler wären?
Ist dieses Problem schlimmer in Deutschland als in England? Warum?

Was halten Sie von…? Was meinen Sie über…?

5.3 USEFUL EXPRESSIONS

General:

ich halte das für eine gute Idee	*I consider that a good idea*
es kommt auf das Wetter an	*it depends on the weather*
es kommt darauf an	*it all depends*
der Grund dafür ist, daß…	*the reason for that is…*

Introducing a text:

es handelt sich hier um die Rolle des Vaters	*it's a question here of the role of the father*
in diesem Text handelt es sich darum daß, der Vater nicht immer seine Rolle spielt	*in this text it's a question of the father not always playing his role*

Voicing an opinion:

ich bin der Meinung, daß…	*I am of the opinion that…*
meiner Meinung nach ist das eine gute Idee	*in my opinion that is a good idea*
ich glaube persönlich, daß…	*I personally think that…*
ich bin fest davon überzeugt, daß…	*I am firmly convinced that…*
ich würde sagen, daß…	*I would say that…*
ich finde es furchtbar, daß…	*I find it terrible that…*
ich halte es für besser, wenn man…	*I consider it better, if one…*
ich möchte lieber dies als das…	*I would prefer this to that…*

Showing agreement/disagreement:

das stimmt/nicht	*that is (not) correct*
ich stimme mit Ihnen (nicht) überein	*I (do not) agree with you*
ich bin damit (gar nicht) einverstanden	*I am (not at all) in agreement with that*
ich finde das gut/schlecht	*I find that good/bad*
es ist nicht zu leugnen, daß … aber…	*it cannot be denied that … but…*
ja, das finde ich auch…	*yes, I think so too*
ja, das kann man sagen	*yes that's true*
ich bin grundsätzlich dafür/dagegen	*I am basically in favour of it/against it*
ich bin grundsätzlich für diese Idee	*I am basically in favour of this idea*

Voicing concern:

es ist erschreckend, daß…	*it's shocking that*
es stört mich, daß…	*it disturbs me that*
ich mache mir Sorgen darüber, daß…	*I worry about the fact that…*

Talking about visual material:

dieses Bild/diese Statistik zeigt, daß…	*this picture/set of statistics shows…*
es scheint, daß dieser Prozentsatz steigt/sinkt	*it seems that this percentage is rising/falling*
für mich ist das wichtigste/interessanteste, daß…	*for me the most important/interesting thing is that…*
im Vergleich mit England	*in comparison with England*
verglichen mit England	*compared with England*

einerseits	*on the one hand*
andererseits	*on the other hand*
auf der anderen Seite	*on the other hand*
man darf aber nicht vergessen, daß...	*one must not forget, however, that...*
es ist wichtig zu verstehen, daß...	*it's important to understand that...*
Sie müssen verstehen, daß...	*you must understand that...*
es läßt sich nicht bestreiten, daß...	*you have to accept that...*

5.4 PRONUNCIATION, STRESS AND INTONATION

Success in your oral test will depend on your ability to speak German fluently. To help you do this, you need to be sure of the rules governing pronunciation, stress and intonation.

PRONUNCIATION – VOWEL SOUNDS

Most vowel sounds in German are pure, i.e. only one sound. There are only a few double sounding vowels, (see below). Most vowel sounds in German can be either long or short as in these examples:

a (long) as in *Rasen*, (short) as in *fast*;

e (long) as in *ebenso*, (short) as in *Ecke*,

e (unstressed) is always 'short' and is pronounced like the English *the* as in *Sessel*;

i (long) as in *ihr*, (short) as in *ich*;

o (long) as in *oben*, (short) as in *oft*;

u (long) as in *Uhr*, (short) as in *unter*.

In most examples the vowel sound is short when followed by two sounded consonants and long when followed by a silent *h* as in *Uhr* or a single sounded consonant as in *Samstag*.

Three vowels are written as double letters, and they are always long:

aa as in *Aal*, **ee** as in *Meer*, **oo** as in *Boot*.

The vowels **a**, **o**, and **u** can be modified by adding an Umlaut. The effect is to change the sound. All three can be short or long as in these examples:

ä (short) as in *Hände* pronounced like a short **e**, **ä** (long) as in *Fähre* pronounced like the English *air* or *heir*.

ö (short) as in *Hölle*, there is no equivalent sound in English, but if you know French then this sound is very like the *eu* in the word *adieu*. **ö** (long) as in *Höhle* is a longer version of the same sound.

ü (short) as in *Glück* is like the French *u* in *tu* or *vue*, lips pursed forward as for *oo* and then try to say *ee* without moving them. **ü** (long) as in *Glühbirne* is the same sound only longer.

y can be used as a vowel but usually only in words of foreign origin. It is pronounced as a long or short *ü* as in *Typ* (long) and *mystisch* (short).

ie is a common vowel sound pronounced like *ee* in English, it occurs in words like *Lied* or *diese*. This is always a long sound.

The diphthongs or double sounded vowels are really only three in number, although there is more than one way of spelling them. They are also all long sounds.

They are:

au, **ei**, and **eu** as in *Haus*, *Bein* and *treu*.

The nearest equivalent sounds in English are *house*, *nice* and *boy*.

The same sound as *ei* is spelt sometimes as *ai* in *Bai* or *Hai*, it can also be spelt **ay** or **ey** in proper names like *Bayern* or *Meyer*.

äu has the same sound as *eu* as in *Häuser*.

CONSONANTS

The single letter consonants and sounds as in English are **b, p, d, t, g, k**, but remember **b, d, g** are pronounced as **p, t, k** at the end of a word or syllable as in *Kalbfleisch*, *Band*, *klug*.

Remember also that **-ig** is pronounced as **-ich** as in *zwanzig*.

f is as in English.

h is silent at the end of a syllable and makes the preceding vowel long as in *sehen*, otherwise it is aspirated.

j is as the English *y* in *young* – *jung*.

l, m, n, are similar to English except that the German **l** is always the sound in English *bell* not *milk*.

The German **r** is usually an uvular **r** like the French **r** in *rue* as in *Rathaus* but in Austria, Switzerland and some parts of Southern Germany it can be trilled with the tip of the tongue as in Scotland. The English sound as in *rough* is unknown in German.

s is pronounced as *ss* in English at the end of a word or syllable as in *Gras* or as a soft **z** before a vowel as in *Gläser*.

v is unvoiced in German and is pronounced usually as **f** except in a few foreign words like *Vase*, *Violine*, *Alcoven* when it is as in English *vase*, *violin*, *alcove*.

w is the voiced consonant pronounced like the English **v**.

x is pronounced *ks* as in *Hexe*.

y is very rare as a consonant but is the same as in English.

z is pronounced as a *ts* as in *Zeit*.

Two or more consonants are as follows:

ch after **a, o,** or **u** is a guttural like the Scottish *loch*, after all other letters it is pronounced as the sound at the start of the word *huge* in English.

ch at the beginning of a word of foreign origin is pronounced as a *k* as in *Chor* or *Character*. In other examples particularly words of French origin it is pronounced as in *huge* above – *Chemie* and *Chirurg*, or as **sch** (see below) in *Chance* and *Chef*.

chs is pronounced as an *x* as in *sechs*

dt is pronounced as *t* as in *Stadt*.

qu is pronounced as English *kv* as in *Quatsch*.

sch is a heavy sounding English *sh* as in *Schule*.

sp and **st** at the beginning of a word or syllable are pronounced as the German *schp* and *scht* as in *sprechen* and *stehen*.

th is pronounced as *t* in foreign words like *Theater*.

Double consonants like **ll, pp, rr** etc. follow short vowel sounds as in *Welle*, *Mappe*, *schnurren*.

The choice between **ss** and **ß** needs care. The **ß** is used after a long vowel, before a third consonant or at the end of a word or a prefix as in *Füße, mußte, Haß, mißbrauchen*. **ss** is only used between two vowels when the first is short as in *wissen*.

On the CD which accompanies this book there is an exercise to practise the spelling of words with *ss* or *ß*.

In a dictionary long vowel sounds are usually indicated by underlining the vowel concerned as in *mehr* whereas a short vowel has a dot under it.

THE GLOTTAL STOP

The use of the glottal stop is important in German pronunciation. It prevents the slurring together of sounds as in English. For example *an apple* in English would be pronounced without a break between the two words, but in German *ein Apfel* would be pronounced as two distinct words with a glottal stop at the start of each of them. The glottal stop is a momentary closing of the glottis followed by a vigorous release of the next sound. It occurs before any word or part of a word beginning with a stressed vowel as in *'ein 'Apfel* or *ver'achten* or *Wild'ente*.

STRESS

There are generally two things to remember about where to put stress in pronouncing German.

1. In all simple and compound words and words adding prefixes or suffixes there is a strong stress on the first syllable as in *Kaufmann, unsere Mutter, ungeduldig, anfangen, regnerisch*.

2. But where a verb is formed with an inseparable prefix, the stress is placed on the first syllable of the simple verb as in *entscheiden*; other words formed from such verbs also have the stress on the second syllable as in *Entscheidung, Entscheidungsfrage, entscheidend*. (see Grammar Section for more examples of inseparable verbs).
   Exceptions to these rules are very few.

INTONATION

For English speakers intonation in German is quite difficult to get right. When you listen to German being spoken you can detect the rise and fall of the sound. You should notice that in general the sound rises at the end of the sense groups until you reach the end of the sentence when it falls. To represent the sound pattern as a series of lines, German would look something like this:

The sound pattern for English is very different, being much more singsong, rising and falling within the sense groups, like this:

You can check this for yourself by playing part of the listening CD in German and recording it onto a new tape. Using the transcript of the listening CD re-record the same passage of German yourself and compare the two with particular reference to the sound pattern or intonation. All English people have to concentrate very hard to get the sound pattern in German right.

CHAPTER 6

WRITING

Units in this chapter

6.1 INTRODUCTION

Writing accurately is the most difficult skill to acquire. In our own language it is the one that takes us years to perfect. Many adults have problems expressing themselves clearly on paper. How many times have you heard people bemoan their inability to spell correctly?

If it is a problem in our own language it is even more of a problem in German. We have to remember to apply all the rules of grammar, to spell correctly, to use the Umlaut properly, to punctuate our work and at the same time to convey our ideas clearly so that our reader can understand them easily.

In the new A-level syllabuses virtually all of the writing will be in German. You will not be required to write a great deal in English. It is important, therefore, not only to write accurately in the examinations that test writing but also in the other parts of the examination where listening and reading may be tested, for example, by answering questions in German. Grammatical and spelling mistakes will lose you marks in listening and reading papers, so it is worth trying to make everything you write as perfect as you can get it.

DIFFERENCE BETWEEN WRITING AND SPEAKING

The big advantage with writing is that you can keep going over it to find errors and thus polish it. When you are speaking it is difficult to get everything you say grammatically accurate and, provided that your mistakes do not prevent people from understanding you, that is acceptable. When writing you have more time to think about the grammatical rules than you do in a conversation.

6.2 THE WRITING EXAMINATION

Your written German may be tested in a number of ways. Most Boards allow you to write coursework, which gives you the advantage of being able to write without the pressure of the exam situation.(See the next section on **Coursework**). Other Boards set essay questions which you have to write within a certain time. An essay tests:

- how well you can write correct and idiomatic German in a formal register;
- how well you can use vocabulary and structures;
- how well you can construct a response to a task set, in a given time.

To do it well you need:

- to know the rules of grammar and how to apply them;
- to have a good vocabulary;
- to be able to use idiomatic expressions correctly;
- to express your ideas with the linguistic means at your disposal, which means using only the vocabulary and expressions you know to be correct;
- to plan your ideas;
- to progress from a draft to a finished product.

The kind of written tasks that you will be asked to do in an examination will be:

- responding to a stimulus, which will be either a reading or listening text;
- writing a traditional essay, which may be creative or discursive (presenting an argument);
- some kind of task-based assignment like producing a letter or fax;
- writing an essay on a topic that you have studied during your course.

CHECKING WHAT YOU HAVE WRITTEN

You should get into the habit of checking carefully what you have written to make sure that the following common errors have been avoided:

1 **Verbs:** Are they in the correct position? Do they have the appropriate ending to agree with their subject? Are they in the right tense?

2 **Prepositions:** Are they followed by the correct case? Accusative, Dative, Genitive?

3 **Nouns:** Do they all have capital letters? Are the genders, cases and plural forms correct?

4 **Umlauts:** Have they been used appropriately? They can change the meaning of a word: *mochte* (liked), *möchte* (would like); *wurde ... gesehen* (was seen – passive), *würde ... sehen* (would see – conditional); *Vater* (father), *Väter* (fathers).

5 **Punctuation:** Is there a comma between each clause? Commas are compulsory in German to separate clauses.

6 **Clauses:** Does the essay contain a reasonable number of subordinate clauses, with the verb at the end of the clause?

7 **Idiomatic expressions:** How many have been used?

Checking is a habit you need to acquire. If you practise it regularly whenever you write anything it should become automatic.

Analyse any written work you do during the course and learn from mistakes. Keep a notebook in which you write down your mistakes and how they can be avoided. Try not to make that same mistake a second time.

Record useful expressions and vocabulary in a notebook and learn them regularly. Make a conscious effort to include a certain number of expressions and structures in whatever written work you do: some subordinate clauses, a passive, a verb with the dative, a subjunctive, a *wenn*-clause.

THE MARK SCHEME

The mark scheme for most essays will be split into certain categories. The **content**, your ideas, what you say, will probably count for slightly under half of the total marks. The mark for content may itself be split into smaller sections, such as:

❶ **Relevance:** Does the essay stick to the point? Does it digress? Does it do what it was supposed to do to answer the question in the title?

❷ **Evidence/Illustration:** Does the essay contain evidence to support and illustrate the points being made or is it full of generalities?

❸ **Structure/Development of ideas:** Is the essay properly structured, with an introduction, a point per paragraph and a conclusion?

❹ **Knowledge of the subject:** Does the essay show that the writer knows what he/she is writing about? Is it full of padding?

❺ **Fulfils task:** (for assignments or non-discursive essays) Does it fulfil the task set?

Just over half of the marks will be given for the **language** of the essay and that mark may also be broken down into categories:

❶ **Vocabulary:** Is the vocabulary varied and interesting? Does it cover a good range? Is it appropriate to the subject? Are there any idiomatic expressions?

❷ **Range of expression/Syntax:** Is there a good variety of sentence pattern, tenses and verb forms? Are the sentences well linked? Does the essay read easily? Is there a confident use of more complex linguistic structures?

❸ **Grammatical accuracy:** Is there strong evidence of grammatical awareness? Are verb endings, cases, adjectival endings, word order correct? Are common genders correct?

6.3 PLANNING YOUR ESSAY

If you are going to produce a good piece of work, planning is essential. In an examination time is short and the temptation is to start writing immediately. But because most A-level language essays are limited to a fairly small number of words you will need to structure what you want to say if you are to present the arguments for and against effectively. A few minutes spent planning what you want to say and how you want to say it will enable you to produce a better finished product.

❶ Read carefully what you are being asked to do. It is surprising how many candidates do not take enough time to read the question properly and end up writing a completely irrelevant essay for which they will get few marks. If, for example, the essay title asks for the *Vor- und Nachteile* of a topic, you must make sure that you give both sides of the argument.

❷ Plan what you want to say. It does not have to be an elaborate plan. It may simply be a few jottings of ideas. Always write your ideas down in German. If you write them in English you will end up translating them, which is a difficult exercise and one likely to lead to mistakes. When you have jotted down your ideas try putting them into some kind of logical order. Remember some of the marks will be given for the structure of the essay.

❸ Think of how you might introduce them. It is important that the introduction prepares the reader for what is to follow, gives some idea of the attitude the writer is going to adopt and leads smoothly into the main part of the essay.

❹ In the main part of the essay will come the points you wish to make; usually one point per paragraph, supported by illustration, examples, facts or statistics. Again some marks will be given for the evidence you use to support your statements.

⑤ Think of how you can round the essay off. The points that you make towards the end of your essay are the ones that will have the strongest impact on your reader, so always keep your most telling ideas until near the end. If you are putting two sides of an argument always outline the side you are against at the beginning of the essay and save the side that you favour until the end. In your conclusion you can then draw together those arguments that prove your case. Even if you do not feel particularly strongly about either side of the argument it is always better to have an opinion, because that will make your essay more focused.

⑥ Write down some expressions and vocabulary that you might use and try to include them. Remember the language you use carries more marks than the ideas. Most writers have certain phrases, expressions and constructions that they are fond of. Good writers will have a wider range than other people. Some academics have done research into the frequency with which certain writers use certain types of language and there are computer programmes that can analyse a writer's work by establishing how often certain words are used. So do not be afraid to develop your own phrases. Normally clichés are frowned upon, but when you are learning a foreign language you need to learn the phrase that is used in certain situations. Build up your own store of such phrases.

⑦ Use a range of different structures, particularly subordinate clauses. A word of caution: always be aware of what you are trying to say. The best kind of language is that which expresses ideas clearly. There is a danger that you will be so concerned to use your constructions that you will 'drag them in' regardless of how well they fit in. Use a range of structures and expressions but take care that your ideas are easy to understand.

⑧ Give evidence to support what you are saying: examples, quotations, statistics.

⑨ Write on every other line so that you have the space to change things without making too much of a mess.

6.4 RESPONDING TO A STIMULUS

The kind of stimulus used for this sort of exercise varies. You may have to respond to a reading or listening text, or a collection of different materials (photographs, headlines, short texts) which highlight some aspects of the title that you are asked to write about.

Your first priority is to understand the stimulus used and to pick out the ideas and language contained in it. Use the material to your advantage, without copying too much word for word from the original. Some Boards will penalise more than five words 'lifted' together from the original. But some of the marks for 'content' will be given for what use you made of the ideas contained in the stimulus material.

You will often have a choice of stimulus. The rubric to the following example said, for example: *Wählen Sie entweder Aufgabe A oder B. Schreiben Sie auf deutsch einen Aufsatz von 240–260 Wörtern über das folgende Thema: Ist der Einfluß des Fernsehens tatsächlich so negativ wie behauptet wird?*

»Der Titel unserer nächsten Sendung lautet: Hat das Fernsehen die Lebensgewohnheiten in der Familie verändert?«

»Lauf schon, du fauler Sack...!«

3 Ein Jahr lang sollten 184 Männer und Frauen auf das Fernsehen verzichten. Doch statt erwarteter Familienidylle gab es Krach und neue Konflikte. Keiner hielt durch.

4

Das Lehrangebot der Fernuniversität ist durch den Einsatz technischer Medien orts- und zeitunabhängig.

»Du bist dir wohl klar darüber, meine Liebe, daß wir dann auch einen zweiten Fernsehapparat brauchen!«

(Source: Langenscheidt Illustrierte)

6 „Mit meinem Fernseher bekomme ich wenigstens etwas von der Welt zu sehen!"

(Source: Fernuniversität)

(Frau Ilse Rimprecht. 75 Jahre)

AEB

The number of words indicated for this essay task is quite limited. It is going to be difficult to cover the positive and negative side of the question in the space allowed. If you look now at the stimulus material you will see that it consists of three cartoons, one picture containing a short text and two other short texts.

❶ **First cartoon:** This cartoon, with the family watching television as they eat, makes the point that television dominates family life, often to the detriment of other activities. A negative effect of television.

❷ **Second cartoon:** The fat man in the armchair is a good example of somebody who takes very little exercise because of television. Another negative effect.

❸ **First short text:** This text illustrates the idea that families without a television set do not know how to occupy themselves. Another negative effect.

❹ **Picture:** Here we can see a positive effect of television: the ability to indulge in distance learning, because television enables students to watch and learn from talented teachers without leaving their homes.

❺ **Third cartoon:** The man is making it clear to his wife that they would have to buy another television set, if they bought the sofa. Everybody must have access to a television set. Another negative effect of television.

❻ **Last short text:** This quotation displays a positive effect of television in that it enables viewers, particularly lonely people, to see something of the outside world.

The stimulus material contains six points of view about television, four of which are negative and two of which are positive. If we were to note now some ideas to include in this essay, we might come up with the following:

Negative:

❶ Einfluß auf die Familie, man spricht nicht mehr miteinander.

❷ Passive Unterhaltung, man sitzt vor dem Fernseher, statt Sport zu treiben.

❸ Streit um das Programm.

❹ Schlechter Einfluß auf junge Menschen – Sex und Gewalttätigkeit.

Positive:

1 Guter Einfluß auf die Familie, man versammelt sich, um eine Sendung gemeinsam zu sehen; man spricht nachher über die Sendung.

2 Man bekommt etwas von der Welt zu sehen, neue Sportarten, die man vielleicht mal später selber macht.

3 Man erhält nützliche Informationen – Fernuniversität.

4 Mit zwei Fernsehgeräten oder einem Videorekorder kann man Streit um das Programm meiden.

5 Es ist noch nicht bewiesen worden, daß das Fernsehen einen schlechten Einfluß auf die Zuschauer ausübt. Man könnte das gleiche von Filmen und Büchern behaupten.

Having noted down these ideas you must now try to put them into some kind of structure. With nine ideas, plus an introduction and a conclusion it is going to be difficult to keep within the 240–260 words stipulated for this exercise. The following *Gliederung* or plan might now be produced:

Einleitung: Das Fernsehen ist sehr populär. Deswegen ist es auch ein umstrittenes Thema.

Negative Punkte:
- Schlechter Einfluß auf die Familie;
- Streit um das Programm;
- Passive Unterhaltung;
- Sex und Gewalttätigkeit.

Positive Punkte:
- Fernsehsendungen sind ein Gesprächsthema in der Familie;
- Man versammelt sich als Familie, um eine Sendung zu sehen;
- Ein Fenster auf die Welt;
- Sex und Gewalttätigkeit – noch nicht bewiesen.

Schluß: Meine Meinung: Es könnte einen schlechten Einfluß ausüben; man muß Sendungen auswählen. Alles mit Maßen. Es darf nicht unser Herr sein.

The following is one version of an essay on this topic:

> Es liegt auf der Hand, daß das Fernsehen sehr populär ist. Laut der Statistik haben 90% der Haushalte einen oder mehr Fernsehapparate, und der Durchschnittssbürger verbringt 15 bis 30 Stunden pro Woche vor dem Fernseher. Gerade deswegen, weil wir so viel Zeit beim Fernsehen verbringen, sollte man die Frage stellen: Ist dieser Einfluß positiv oder negativ?
>
> Gegner des Fernsehens argumentieren, daß die Lebensgewohnheiten der Familie durch das Fernsehen auf eine schlimme Weise verändert werden. Statt sich zu unterhalten, sehe man fern, sogar beim Essen. Man streite auch um die Programmwahl.
>
> Ihrer Meinung nach sollte man aktiv sein, statt sich passiv Sportsendungen anzushen. Es sei ungesund.
>
> Junge Kinder werden durch zu viel Sex und Gewalttätigkeit in einigen Sendungen schlecht beeinflußt. Aber das ist noch nicht bewiesen worden.
>
> Wie dem auch sei, vertreten die Befürworter eine ganz andere Meinung. In vielen Familien versammeln sich die Familienmitglieder gerade, um sich eine Sendung anzusehen. Nachher wird oft heftig über die Sendung diskutiert. Streite kommen nicht zustande, wenn man einen zweiten Fernseher oder einen Videorekorder hat.
>
> Reportagen, Dokumentarfilme und die Tagesschau sind sehr informativ. Dadurch bekommt man wichtige Informationen über die Welt. Man kann auch mit Hilfe von Fernsehsendungen sein Studium bei der Fernuniversität fortsetzen.

Meiner Meinung nach ist das Fersnsehen etwas Positives, aber Menschen, besonders Eltern, müssen auswählen, was gesehen wird. Wie bei Filmen und Büchern sollte der Staat Sendungen kontrollieren. Gewisse Sendungen dürfen nicht zu früh am Abend gebracht werden, bevor Jugendliche schon im Bett sind. Wie in allen Bereichen des Lebens sollte man alles mit Maßen tun.

253 words

The essay has some pertinent ideas and a clear structure. Some expressions have been used: *es liegt auf der Hand; laut der Statistik; gerade deswegen; beim Fernsehen; auf eine schlimme Weise; ihrer Meinung nach; wie dem auch sei; zustandekommen; etwas Positives; in allen Bereichen des Lebens; alles mit Maßen.*

Some good constructions have also been used: subordinating conjunctions: *daß, weil, bevor*; *um... zu...* + infinitive construction; *statt... zu...* + infinitive construction; four examples of a passive construction, including a perfect tense and the impersonal form; the passive in reported speech; some modal verbs. The essay should receive a good mark.

6.5 WRITING A TRADITIONAL ESSAY

Traditional essays are set by a number of Boards. If you have studied topics for the examination you will have to write essays on your topics, as well as on more general themes. A topic essay should be easier, because you should have lots of information and will know the specialised vocabulary of the theme you are writing about. In all other respects a topic essay will be tackled in exactly the same way as any other essay.

General essays will require you to produce some ideas about something you may not have thought about before. There will normally be a choice of titles. Select something that you have some ideas on and adopt an opinion about the theme. Your essay will be more focused than if you simply present both sides of the argument and leave the reader to make up his/her mind.

Example

Schreiben Sie auf deutsch einen Aufsatz von nicht mehr als 350 Wörtern zu einem der folgenden Themen:

ULEAC

❶ Pressefreiheit? Ja, aber in Grenzen. Was meinen Sie?

❷ Was sollte die Rolle der Polizei in der heutigen Gesellschaft sein?

❸ Schreiben Sie einen Zeitungsartikel über Ausländerfeindlichkeit in Deutschland.

❹ „Frauen haben es schwer in dieser Männerwelt". Nehmen Sie Stellung zu dieser Behauptung!

❺ Wird im Europa des zwanzigsten Jahrhunderts Deutsch die wichtigste Sprache sein? Geben Sie Gründe an!

❻ Schreiben Sie eine kurze Geschichte, die mit den folgenden Wörtern beginnt: „Ich saß jetzt zum allerersten Mal in einem deutschen Wagen auf einer deutschen Autobahn…

NEAB

If you were to take the first essay in the list and note down some pros and cons to consider in this essay you might end up with something like the following. Although the length this time is greater than in the previous example it is still not enough to go into great detail:

Vorteile:

❶ Meinungsfreiheit – ein Teil der Demokratie.

Nachteile:

❶ Konzentration der Presse beeinträchtigt Meinungsfreiheit.

2 Die Presse untersucht politische Skandale.

3 Presse gibt wichtige Informationen.

4 Kommentar über Politik usw.

5 Unterhaltung – Kreuzworträtsel, Kochrezepte usw.

2 Einzelne Menschen können sich gegen die Macht der Presse nicht verteidigen.

3 Die Presse möchte nur Zeitungen verkaufen, veröffentlicht Skandale.

4 Kann einen Gerichtsprozeß beeinflussen.

5 Hat oft eine voreingenommene politische Meinung.

A *Gliederung* for this essay title could now be produced:

Einleitung:
- Ein umstrittenes Thema;
- Konzentration der Presse.

Nachteile:
- Konzentration der Presse beeinträchtigt Meinungsfreiheit;
- Ohnmacht des einzelnen Menschen gegenüber der Presse;
- Sensationelle Berichte, oft über private Angelegenheiten;
- Einfluß auf einen Gerichtsprozeß;
- Vertritt oft eine politische Meinung/Partei.

Vorteile:
- Gibt wichtige Informationen und Unterhaltung;
- Teil einer Demokratie;
- Untersucht politische Skandale.

Schluß:
- Meine Meinung: Hat eine wichtige Rolle. Ist auch ein Geschäft. Muß Verantwortung haben. Nicht zu viele Zeitungen in wenigen Händen.

Die Presse ist seit langem ein umstrittenes Thema, weil man einsieht, daß eine Zeitung einen großen Einfluß auf die Meinungsbildung der Bevölkerung ausübt. Meinungsfreiheit ist ja ein Grundstein jeder Demokratie. Wenn ein Mensch oder ein Verlag mehrere Zeitungen besitzt, besteht die Gefahr, daß die neuesten Informationen nicht objecktiv veröffentlicht werden.

Eine deutsche nationale Zeitung wie die *Bild*-Zeitung wird täglich von drei oder vier Millionen Menschen gelesen. Dadurch kann man einen ungeheuren Einfluß auf die Haltung und Meinung der Leser ausüben.

Wenn eine Zeitung etwas Schlechtes aber auch Falsches über ein Individuum druckt, ist es sehr schwer, dieses zu berichtigen. Wenn man Glück hat, veröffentlicht die Zeitung eine Entschuldigung, aber sie ist normalerweise nicht auf der Titelseite und oft schwer zu finden.

Reporter versammeln sich oft in großen Mengen vor einem Haus, weil sie ein Interview oder ein Photo machen wollen. Oft wollen sie über private oder sogar intime Angelegenheiten einer Familie berichten.

Oft wird durch sensationelle Berichte ein Gerichtsprozeß so beeinflußt, daß die Geschworenen falsche Informationen von der Presse bekommen. Es ist schon mal vorgekommen, daß ein Angeklagter freigesprochen werden mußte, weil die Boulevardzeitungen, zu viele Informationen vor dem Prozeß veröffentlicht haben.

Auch vertreten die meisten Zeitungen eine bestimmte politische Meinung. Die Gefahr existiert, daß zu viele Zeitungen eine einzige Partei unterstützen.

Andererseits ist es aber nicht zu leugnen, daß wir wichtige Informationen und Kommentar von einer Zeitung erhalten. Eine bedeutende Aufgabe der Presse besteht darin, politische Skandale zu entdecken und die Wähler vor undemokratischen Aktionen einer Regierung zu warnen. Die Aktionen von Politikern müssen immer von der Presse untersucht werden. Wenn Politiker wissen, daß ihre Aktionen beobachtet werden, ist es für die Demokratie gut.

Meiner Meinung nach spielt die Presse eine Schlüsselrolle in unserer Demokratie und darf also ihre Freiheit nicht verlieren. Aber das Verkaufen von Zeitungen ist ein Geschäft, durch das sehr viel Geld verdient wird. Also müssen Zeitungen Verantwortung ausüben. Sie sollten es vermeiden, Berichte zu veröffentlichen, die falsch oder sensationell sind, nur des Geldes wegen. Und kein Mensch sollte zu viele Zeitungen besitzen, weil das ihm zu viel Einfluß gibt.

344 words

This essay contains approximately seven ideas about the press, it has a structure and the writer comes down firmly at the end on the side of preserving the freedom of the press. It contains some expressions: *seit langem; etwas Schlechtes; normalerweise; andererseits; es ist nicht zu leugnen; meiner Meinung nach; eine Rolle spielen; des Geldes wegen*. It also contains some good constructions: the subordinating conjunctions *wenn, daß* and *weil*; a number of relative clauses; several passive constructions; the modal verbs *müssen, wollen,* and *sollen*; an example of a verb with a preposition introducing an infinitive, *die Aufgabe besteht darin, etwas zu machen*; a verb with a preposition *warnen vor*; a noun formed from a verb *das Verkaufen von Zeitungen*. It should, therefore, get good marks for content and language.

6.6 TASK-BASED ASSIGNMENTS

This kind of activity tries to simulate real life and usually involves dealing with a letter or fax. You may have to summarise in English for your boss the contents of what has been received and then compose a reply in German. It is important that you understand the text of the material given and that you cover all the points in the letter that you are asked to write.

Example

You are the personal assistant to the Sales Manager at a ceramics factory and have just received the following letter.

Küsters GmbH
Friedensstraße 26
46673 Siegenfingen

DAK Ltd
F.A.O. Mr Harper
Bridge Rd
Guildford GU3 7HA

Siegenfingen, den 23.04.1994

Sehr geehrter Herr Harper,

Leider muß ich Ihnen mitteilen, daß Ihre Sendung in einem schrecklichen Zustand bei uns eingegangen ist. Nicht nur waren die Tassen und Teller mehrheitlich in den falschen Farben, sondern mindestens zehn Prozent war Ausschußware, die wir auf keinen Fall unseren Kunden anbieten können. Ob die Beschädigung während der Fahrt oder schon bei Ihnen aufgetreten ist, kann im Moment noch nicht geklärt werden. Wir werden der Sache noch im Detail nachgehen. Es kommt auch noch hinzu, daß die Kartons, in die die Ware gepackt war, ganz offensichtlich mehrere Stunden im Regen gestanden haben und die für den deutschsprachigen Raum besonders hergestellten Verkaufsverpackungen erheblich gelitten haben. Die Lieferfirma hat sich noch nicht dazu geäußert. Aus dem Fahrer des Transports konnten wir kein Wort herausbringen. Wir können diese Ware so nicht annehmen und erwarten sofortige Neulieferung innerhalb von sechs Tagen.

Mit freundlichen Grüßen

Siegmund Lorenz

Summarise the letter for your boss who does not understand German in not more than 55 words. Your boss then asks you to reply in **German** to the appropriate person using **all** and **only** the information contained in the following notes. Your letter should be roughly 110–130 words long, not counting the words in the address.

O&C

- apologise for the condition of the goods;
- explain that you have been in touch with the transport company and that they take part of the blame;
- the insurance will cover the rest of the damage;
- the new delivery will arrive in a few days time;
- the colours have been checked according to the order;
- you can assure that this will never happen again, especially as you have already taken on a different transport company for the future.

The summary might read as follows:

> Our delivery arrived in a terrible condition. Most cups and saucers were the wrong colour. 10% were rejects. Cannot yet say where the damage occurred. They will pursue it. The cartons had also been left standing out in the rain. They cannot accept the goods and expect a new delivery in six days.
>
> 53 words

The letter in reply would look something like the following:

DAK Ltd
Bridge Road
Guildford GU3 7HA

Herr Lorenz
Küsters GmbH
Friedensstraße 27
46673 Siegenfingen

Sehr geehrter Herr Lorenz,

Entschuldigen Sie vielmals, daß die Ware in einem schlechten Zustand war. Ich habe mich mit der Transportfirma in Verbindung gesetzt, und sie nimmt einen Teil der Schuld auf sich. Unsere Versicherung wird für den restlichen Schaden aufkommen.

Die neue Lieferung wird in ein paar Tagen ankommen. Die Farben sind der Bestellung entsprechend geprüft worden.

Ich kann Ihnen versichern, daß dies nicht wieder vorkommen wird, vor allem, da wir für die Zukunft schon eine andere Lieferfirma beauftragt haben.

Mit freundlichen Grüßen

John Harper

Provided that all the points are made in a form of German that could be understood and without too many mistakes the letter should get good marks. It is not necessary to use the kind of formal language that is usually found in business letters.

6.7 USEFUL EXPRESSIONS

For introductory paragraphs:

Ganz am Anfang möchte ich behaupten...	*Right from the start I should like to claim...*
Wenn man an dieses Problem denkt, darf man nicht vergessen, daß...	*When thinking about this problem one should not forget that...*
Diese Frage ist ein umstrittenes Thema	*This question is a controversial topic*
Diese Frage taucht regelmäßig in den Medien auf	*This question pops up regularly in the media*
Dieses Thema ist seit Generationen umstritten	*This topic has been controversial for generations*

In meinem Aufsatz möchte ich diese Frage unter die Lupe nehmen	*In my essay I should like to examine this question carefully*
Wenn man diese Frage betrachtet, ist es nicht zu leugnen, daß...	*When looking at this question it can not be denied that...*

For paragraph openings:

Untersuchen wir zuerst die positive/ negative Seite	*Let us first of all examine the positive/ negative side*
Man kann an mehrere Gründe denken, warum dieses Problem fortfährt	*One can think of several reasons why this problem continues*
Mehrere Gründe fallen mir ein, warum...	*Several reasons occur to me why...*
Dieses Problem bereitet mir großes Kopfzerbrechen	*This problem causes me a lot of worry*
Die Vor- und Nachteile müssen gegeneinander abgewogen werden	*The pros and cons must be considered*

For use within the essay:

erstens	*firstly*
zweitens	*secondly*
einerseits... andererseits...	*on the one hand... on the other hand...*
wie dem auch sein mag	*however that may be*
kurz	*in brief*
mit einem Wort	*in one word*
in bezug auf (+ accusative)	*with reference to*
bezüglich	*concerning, with reference to*
in dieser/mancher Hinsicht	*in this respect/in many respects*
vor allem	*above all*
zusätzlich	*in addition*
aus diesem Grund	*for this reason*
es liegt auf der Hand, daß	*it is obvious that*
bei dieser Gelegenheit	*at this opportunity*
das gilt auch für	*that also applies to*
ich bin davon überzeugt, daß	*I am convinced that*
infolge (+ genitive)	*as a result of*
dank (+ dative)	*thanks to*
als Folge der Klimaveränderung	*as a consequence of the change in climate*
auf diesem Gebiet	*in this area*
das liegt im Bereich des Möglichen	*that lies within the realm of the possible*

For indicating times and periods:

heutzutage	*nowadays*
früher	*formerly*
im 20. Jahrhundert	*in the 20th century*
in den 90er Jahren	*in the nineties*
vor hundert Jahren	*100 years ago*
in weniger als 100 Jahren	*in less than 100 years*
in der Gegenwart/Vergangenheit/Zukunft	*in the present/past/future*
unsere Vorfahren	*our ancestors*
die Generationen der Zukunft	*future generations*

For indicating numbers:

viele Menschen	*many people*
die meisten Leute	*most people*
die Mehrheit der Leute ist...	*the majority of people is...*
eine Minderheit	*a minority*
einige sagen... andere aber sind anderer Meinung	*some say... others however are of a different opinion*

For giving an opinion:

ich bin der Meinung, daß...	*I am of the opinion that...*
ich bin der Ansicht, daß...	*I am of the opinion that...*
meiner Meinung nach ist das falsch	*in my opinion that is wrong*
das entspricht nicht meiner Meinung	*that does not correspond with my opinion*
ich stimme mit diesen Leuten nicht überein	*I do not agree with these people*
sie sind sich darüber einig, daß mehr für den Umweltschutz getan werden muß	*they are agreed that more should be done for conservation*

For conclusions:

schließlich/endlich/zuletzt/zum Schluß	*finally*
zum Schluß kommen, daß...	*to come to the conclusion that...*
die Lösung ist klar/offensichtlich	*the solution is clear/obvious*
das letzte Wort ist noch nicht gesprochen	*the final decision has not yet been taken*
eine Entscheidung treffen	*to take a decision*
bevor es zu spät wird	*before it's too late*

CHAPTER 7

COURSEWORK

Units in this chapter

7.1   THE ADVANTAGES OF COURSEWORK

Some Examining Boards now offer candidates the possibility of doing the writing part of the examination in the form of coursework. This has several advantages:

- it means that you can complete an important part of the examination over an extended period of time;

- it therefore takes some of the pressure off you at the end of the course;

- you can consult dictionaries, reference books and notes while you are writing, which is a much more 'natural' way of writing than a traditional examination;

- you have much more opportunity to check and 'polish' what you have written, particularly if you are well organised and do not leave everything until the last minute.

Coursework is designed to give you the opportunity of researching a topic about Germany (or another German-speaking country) that interests you and of presenting facts, information and your opinions about one or more aspects of the topic. Normally you have more choice than would be the case in a traditional examination, particularly when it comes to the aspect that you wish to write about. You can, for example, choose the title of the essays that you write. The downside is that because you have access to reference books a higher standard of accuracy is expected than when writing under examination conditions, where you do not have so much time to consult dictionaries.

7.2 HOW TO APPROACH COURSEWORK

CHOOSING A TOPIC

Often the Examining Board will set out in its syllabus for each year a number of topics that candidates may choose from. They are expressed in very general terms such as *Die deutsche Industrie und die Umwelt*, *Das deutsche Schulsystem* or *Die Presse im deutschen Sprachraum*. When choosing which topic to do take into account not only what interests you but also how easy it will be to obtain authentic and up-to-date materials from which to inform yourself. Some of the marks given for coursework will go for what you know about the topic. Material is much easier to get hold of for some topics than others.

It is not advisable to get the majority of your information from English sources. If you do, you may end up knowing a lot about the topic but you will be lacking the vocabulary and expressions that are necessary to express your ideas and you will be tempted to translate your English ideas into German. This is not an easy task and one that is likely to lead to some very awkward and anglicised German. Reading about the topic in German is an essential part of coursework; it will help your reading skills and will give you the technical vocabulary and expressions you need to express your own ideas with confidence.

CHOOSING A TITLE

Another important aspect of writing a coursework essay is to choose the right kind of title. Some of the marks will be given for the powers of analysis that you show in your work. A title that invites you to describe something simply rather than analysing a problem will not allow you to gain the top marks for analysis. If you are writing an essay on, for example, *Umwelt* it would be far better to choose a title such as *Was für ein Problem ist Sauerregen für Deutschland?*, which is looking for analysis of the problem and some personal assessment on your part in order to answer the question posed in the title; rather than a title such as *Sauerregen in Deutschland* which might result in a simple description of the problem. Description on its own will rarely be sufficient at A-level for the top marks. A title in the form of a question is usually much better.

USING SOURCES AND QUOTATIONS

As you write your essay you will need to support your arguments with facts and quotations. If you use more than half a sentence from a source it is usually stipulated that you must indicate where it came from. If you bring in statistics or other factual information you will normally have to indicate where you found them.

At the end of your essay you should list the sources you used for your information in a bibliography. This must include, for books and periodicals, page number, publishers and dates, and, for newspaper articles, dates and sources. All quotations should be acknowledged by means of footnotes. Normally quotations should not be included as part of your word count.

LANGUAGE

At least half the marks, possibly more, will be awarded for the quality of the German that you use. Because it is coursework the Board can expect it to be more accurate and polished than the same piece of work written under examination conditions. As explained earlier it is a good idea to have a stock of idiomatic, all-purpose expressions and a number of constructions that will form a skeleton on which to hang your ideas.

Check everything that you are unsure of. If you are doubtful about the gender or plural of a word, look it up in a dictionary, and make a note of it for next time in your vocabulary notebook. Check all verbs, prepositions, adjectival endings as has already been stressed earlier. Getting things right at this stage is important. Once you have written them down it becomes more difficult to spot the errors.

WRITING THE ESSAY

Once you have a title and a plan you can start to write. You may want to show your plan to your teacher or discuss it with a friend to make sure that you are on the right lines. It is best to write a rough version first. If you are well organised and have planned your work well you should have enough time to leave your rough version untouched for two or three days. When you come back to it there will undoubtedly be things that you wish to change. You will probably find some mistakes that you overlooked the first time. A better word or expression may occur to you as you read it through again with a fresh mind and the critical eye of a new reader.

The Board's syllabus will give you information on how many words you have to write, whether you have to write on every other line and any other particular regulations governing the submission of coursework. Make sure you are familiar with them before handing your work in. When you have finished your final version, leave it for a day or so and read it through again to make sure you have not missed a word out here or there and have made no avoidable mistakes. When you have done all that, you can be reassured that you have done everything possible to produce a good piece of work.

7.3 AN EXAMPLE OF COURSEWORK

The following is an example of one student's coursework. As you will see from the detailed comments that follow, the piece is of a high standard and scored good marks. It illustrates very well the importance of a good plan, using facts to back up the points you make and choosing a title that poses a question. This candidate did not simply describe the problem but set out to analyse why it was a problem. A personal opinion was offered, the essay referred to Germany the whole time, and some of the ways in which the problem is being tackled in Germany were looked at.

Linguistically this candidate has a very good command of written German. There are very few grammatical errors: agreement of verbs with subjects, position of the verb, tenses, case mistakes or adjectival-ending mistakes. There is a good range of constructions: subordinating conjunctions, co-ordinating conjunctions, verbs with prepositions, passives, subjunctive, relative pronouns. Idioms are also used frequently.

The *Gliederung*, or plan, is quite detailed. Each point that is to be made is supported by a number of specific examples. The plan follows a traditional pattern of an introduction, four main points and a conclusion. This piece of coursework had to be between 500 and 700 words in length. This candidate kept just within the guidelines. With a difficult topic such as this one on *Arbeitslosigkeit in Deutschland*, which was written under the general heading of *Gesellschaftsprobleme* it is often difficult to keep what you want to say within the 700 words limit.

There are no quotations in the essay, but there is a detailed bibliography at the end showing an extensive selection of materials that were consulted.

Wie groß ist das Problem der Arbeitslosigkeit in Deutschland?

1 **Gliederung: Einleitung:**	Statistik über Arbeitslosigkeit in Deutschland (über 4 Millionen). – Welche Leute sind betroffen? – alle können betroffen werden; Frauen; Ausländer; Arbeitnehmer ohne ausreichende berufliche Qualifikation.

                                            – Die Wiedervereinigung – überholte
wettbewerbsunfähige staatliche
Unternehmen wurden geschlossen.
– Die Wirtschaftskrise der siebziger Jahre.

2 Warum ist es ein Problem?: Arbeitslose verlieren ihre Identität.
– keine Arbeit, keinen Wert.
– Menschen leiden, besonders Kinder und
  Frauen.
– Arbeitslosigkeit führt zu Depression.
– Depression führt zu Selbstmord und Drogen.
– Ehen gehen kaputt.
– Vergeudung von Talent – junge leute.

3 Probleme für den Staat: der Staat muß Arbeitslosengeld an 55.3% der
Arbeitslosen und 1793DM Arbeitshilfe an 22.2%
der Arbeitslosen bezahlen.
– der Staat erhält keine Steuereinnahmen von
  den Arbeitslosen.
– die Rechtsextremisten führen gewalttätige
  Ausschreitungen gegen die Ausländer aus.
– Immer mehr Arbeitslose können keine
  Unterkunft bezahlen – obdachlos.
– Arbeitslose könnten Verbrechen begehen, um
  Geld zu bekommen.
– Arbeitslose und ihre Familien werden krank
  und müssen gepflegt werden – Unsummen
  staatlicher Gelder werden für die Versorgung
  gebraucht.

**4 Was wird in Deutschland
gemacht?:** Verkürzung der Arbeitswoche, damit mehr
Arbeiter eingestellt werden können.
– 1994 verabschiedete der Bundestag ein
  Gesetz, um mehr Erwerbslose vermitteln zu
  können.
– praktische Hilfe bei der Suche nach einer
  Arbeit.
– Umschulungsprogramme sind eingeführt
  worden.
– mehr Kinderkrippen und Kindergärten sind
  einzurichten.
– das System der sozialen Sicherheit
  garantiert den von Arbeitslosigkeit
  Betroffenen eine ausreichende
  Existenzgrundlage.

5 Meine Meinung: – das Problem der Arbeitslosigkeit ist ziemlich
  groß in Westdeutschland aber bedeutend
  größer in Ostdeutschland.
– die Produktion stellt auf computergestützte
  Fertigung um.
– Wenn der Staat vor 4 Jahren keine
  überholten Unternehmen geschlossen hätte,
  wären heute 3,5 Millionen Ostdeutsche nicht
  arbeitslos gewesen.
– man muß lernen, seine Freizeit kreativ zu
  gestalten und immer wieder neue Berufe zu
  lernen.

- die Regierung muß dafür sorgen, daß jeder
die Möglichkeit zu arbeiten hat.

Wie groß ist das Problem der Arbeitslosigkeit in Deutschland?

Paragraph 1: <u>Während der 80er Jahre</u>[1], <u>als</u>[2] es keine Arbeitslosigkeit in dem sozialistischen Staat Ostdeutschland gab, wurde die Arbeitslosigkeit in Westdeutschland ein beachtlicher Grund zur Sorge, und die Zahl der Arbeitslosen stieg <u>intermittierend</u>[3] weiter: 1988 lag die Arbeitslosenquote <u>bei 8,7%</u>[4]. Seit der Wiedervereinigung erlebt Deutschland eine seiner größten Phasen der Arbeitslosigkeit, und nach <u>fachmännischen Schätzungen</u>[5] der HSBC Märkte lag die Arbeitslosenquote am Ende Februar 1995 bei 10% (mehr als 4 Millionen Leute). Regionale Unterschiede bestehen in der Arbeitslosenquote und <u>es ist nicht zu leugnen</u>[6], daß die Bundesländer mit überdurchschnittlicher Arbeitslosigleit Sachsen-Anhalt (21,7%) Sachsen (20,3%), Nordrhein-Westfalen (15,4%) und Bremen (14,3%) sind.

Paragraph 2: <u>Obwohl</u>[1] alle Leute leider von Arbeitslosigkeit <u>betroffen werden können</u>[2], <u>ob jung oder alt</u>[3] scheint es, <u>als ob</u>[4] unqualifizierte ältere deutsche Frauen besonders betroffen wären, denn 53,7% aller Arbeitslosen sind Frauen. Wegen der <u>zunehmenden</u>[5] Arbeitslosigkeit leiden Ausländer unter deutscher Feindseligkeit und Rassendiskriminierung, <u>wenn sie um Stellen konkurrieren</u>[6] und <u>das hat zur Folge daß</u>[7] 17,2% der Arbeitslosen Ausländer sind. Betroffen sind <u>vor allem</u>[8] die Arbeitnehmer ohne ausreichende berufliche Qualifikation, <u>die</u>[9] <u>48% der Arbeitslosen betragen.</u> Die Wirtschaftskrise der siebziger Jahre und die Ersetzung der menschlichen Arbeitskraft durch Technik haben <u>einen bedeutsamen Beitrag zur heutigen Massenarbeitslosigkeit geleistet</u>[10], außerdem führte die Wiedervereinigung zum Ergebnis, daß überholte wettbewerbsunfähige staatliche Unternehmen im Osten <u>geschlossen wurden</u>[11], und folglich gingen Arbeitsplätze verloren.

Paragraph 3: <u>Hier wäre zu bemerken</u>[1], daß Arbeitslosigkeit einen Identitätsverlust verursacht und, daß die Arbeitslosen das Gefühl haben, nicht gebraucht zu werden. Außerderm schlagen die Gefühle der 950 000 Dauerarbeitslosen leicht in Apathie um. Es wird zunehmend erkannt, daß die Deutschen, besonders <u>die auf das Gehalt ihrer Väter und Ehemänner angewiesenen Kinder und Hausfrauen</u>[2] leiden, wegen der Arbeitslosigkeit, und in den meisten Fällen <u>geraten</u>[3] Familien in finanzielle Schwerigkeiten, die zu Depression, <u>zum Scheitern</u>[4] der Ehe und schließlich zu Selbstmord führen können, aber was Sorgen bereiten sollte, ist, daß die jungen begabten Leute, <u>die</u>[5] <u>nie gearbeitet haben</u>, aus Verzweiflung <u>zu Drogen greifen</u>[6].

Paragraph 4: <u>Obwohl es ohne jeden Zweifel feststeht</u>[1], daß 1993 22,5% der Arbeitslosen keine Leistungen erhielten, mußte der deutsche Staat monatlich Arbeitslosengeld an <u>55,3%</u> der Arbeitslosen sowie 1793DM Arbeitslosenhilfe an <u>22,2%</u>[2] der Arbeitslosen bezahlen. Fachleute sagen, die Kosten der Arbeitsbeschaffungsmaßnahmen, Umschulung und Vorruhestandsgeld stiegen 1993 gegenüber dem Vorjahr um rund 35% auf 116 000 000 000 DM, weiter erhält der Staat keine Steuereinnahmen von den Arbeitslosen, und Wochenende für Wochenende protestieren die Rechtsextremisten gegen die Ausländer, <u>indem</u>[3] sie gewalttätige Ausschreitungen ausführen. <u>Wir können uns</u>

der Tatsache nicht verschließen[4], daß immer mehr der Arbeitslosen keine Unterkunft bezahlen können: folglich werden sie obdachlos, und es läßt sich kaum bestreiten[5], daß sie Verbrechen begehen könnten, um ihre finanzielle Situation zu verbessern, Die psychisch gestörten Arbeitslosen und ihre Familien, die einen Nervenzusammenbruch erleiden könnten, müssen gepflegt werden[6], dadurch werden Unsummen staatlicher Gelder für die kostspielige ärztliche Versorgung gebraucht.

Paragraph 5:   Da[1] das Problem der Arbeitslosigkeit beängstigende Ausmaße erreicht hat[2], ergreifen die Deutschen Maßnahmen[3] zum Abbau der Arbeitslosigkeit: Vom 1 April 1990 an gab es im öffentlichen Dienst eine Arbeitszeitverkürzung von 40 auf 39 Wochenstunden, und durch diese Arbeitszeitverkürzung wurden in Rheinland-Pfalz laut[4] Innenministerium, etwa 1000 Stellen im öffentlichen Dienst des Landes zusätzlich geschaffen, und im Juni 1994 verabschiedete der Bundestag mit den Stimmen der Regierung ein Gesetz, das die private Arbeitsvermittlung in Deutschland einführt, um mehr Erwerbslose vermitteln zu können. Die deutschen Berufsberater bieten praktische Hilfe bei der Suche nach einer Arbeit, dadurch können sie einem Jugendlichen ganz neue berufliche Möglichkeiten eröffnen, und man sollte auch nicht vergessen, daß Umschulungsprogramme vom deutschen Staat eingeführt worden sind[5], damit Arbeitslose mit dem technischen Wandel zurechtkommen können, und angesichts der Tatsache[6], daß viele Frauen mit Familien zurück in den Beruf wollen, sollen[7] mehr Kinderkrippen und Kindergärten eingerichtet werden und das deutsche System der sozialen Sicherheit garantiert den von Arbeitslosigkeit Betroffenen[8] eine ausreichende Existenzgrundlage.

Paragraph 6:   Meiner Meinung nach[1] ist das Problem der Arbeitslosigkeit ziemlich groß in Westdeutschland, aber das Problem ist bedeutend größer in Ostdeutschland, wo die Arbeitslosenquote bei 21,7% liegt und es[2] wächst ein Jahr ums andere[3], denn die Produktion stellt[4] auf computergestützte Fertigung um und, wenn[5] der Staat vor 4 Jahren keine überholten staatlichen Unternehmen geschlossen hätte[5], wären heute 3,5 Millionen Ostdeutsche nicht arbeitslos gewesen, aber man muß lernen, seine Freizeit kreativ zu gestalten und immer wieder neue Berufe zu lernen, vor allem[6] muß die Regierung dafür sorgen, daß[7] jeder die Möglichkeit zu arbeiten hat.

Deutsches Quellen Material

OXFORD BOARD INFORMATION PACKAGE

1   **Article:**   Arbeitslosigkeit sinkt nur langsam

2   **Article:**   Arbeitslos?
    Source: Junge Zeit, December 1986

3   **Article:**   Wann bekommt man Arbeitslosenhilfe?
    Source: Junge Zeit

4   **Article:**   Mehr als 660 000 Jugendliche suchen in diesem Jahr...

5   **Article:**   Mehr für Arbeitslose tun

6   **Article:**   Arbeitslosenrate bei Frauen steigt ständig.

7   **Article:**   Wer Computerfachmann werden will, wird als Friseur nicht zufrieden sein.

8 **Tabelle 150:** *Dauer der Arbeitslosigkeit 1985*
   Tabelle 151: *Langzeitarbeitslosigkeit (Sept 1987)*
   Tabelle 147: *Struktur der Arbeitslosigkeit*
   Article: *Arbeitsmarkt*
             Ostdeutscher Arbeitsmarkt 1991
             Arbeitslosenunterstützung
   Tabelle 151: *Arbeitslosengeld (1992)*
   Source: *Jahrbuch der Bundesrepublik Deutschland 1993/94*

9 **Deutschland-Atlas:** *Arbeitslosigkeit*   *Page 9*
   Article: *Arbeitsbeschaffungsmaßnahmen*   *Page 59*
   Article: *Arbeitslosenversicherung*   *Page 60*
   Article: *Arbeitsmarkt*   *Page 61*
   Article: *Arbeitszeit – Größere Flexibilität soll Stellen sichern und schaffen* *Page 66*
   Source: *Aktuell 95*

Some of the points worth commenting on are:

Paragraph 1: The paragraph sets the scene with some important statistics, making the points outlined in the first part of the plan that unemployment is a serious problem in Germany, particularly since re-unification and that the Eastern *Länder* are more seriously affected than in the West.

1 This is a good start: a preposition taking the genitive case and the idiomatic use of *80er*.

2 The first subordinating conjunction that sends the verb to the end of the clause. Confident use of the correct word order, with *gab* and *wurde* both in the correct position.

3 Not a good word to use here. It normally relates to machines and technology. Obviously found in a dictionary and not checked properly; *allmählich* would have been a more appropriate word.

4 A good use of the preposition *bei*.

5 An excellent idiomatic phrase.

6 A good construction, providing variety and giving the work a sound German quality.

Paragraph 2: This paragraph continues the introduction to the problem, looking at which people are particularly affected and why the re-unification brought unemployment in its wake.

1 A good start to the paragraph with this subordinating conjunction.

2 Very confident use of the modal verb *können* with a passive infinitive.

3 An effective idiomatic phrase.

4 This use of *als ob* with the subjunctive is a construction only really good candidates would attempt.

5 Good use of a present participle, with the correct adjectival ending.

6 Verbs with prepositions, used correctly, create a good impression and are typical of good German style.

7 Effective idiomatic phrase.

8 Effective idiomatic phrase.

9 Use of a relative clause, with the verb in the correct position.

10 A rather good and stylish construction.

11 Confident use of the passive.

Paragraph 3: This paragraph takes the reader into the main body of the essay and begins to analyse why unemployment is a problem in Germany.

1 Another good beginning to the paragraph with a subjunctive and the idiomatic use of the verb *sein* with *zu* + an infinitive, which has a passive meaning: *At this point it should be observed.*

2 A good use of an expanded adjectival construction. Only good candidates could use this construction successfully.

3 Another good verb with a preposition.

4 This use of a verbal noun is a sign of a strong candidate.

5 Another relative clause.

6 Another good verb with a preposition.

Paragraph 4: Here the reader is informed how unemployment is a drain on the government's resources with some detailed statistics to prove it.

1 A good beginning to the paragraph with this subordinating conjunction and an idiomatic phrase.

2 The statistics here are expressed correctly.

3 A good construction, which adds variety.

4 Another good, appropriate construction.

5 A common construction, but very suitable here.

6 Another modal verb, used with a passive infinitive.

Paragraph 5: The measures being taken by the German government provide the content of this paragraph, also supported by good examples.

1 Beginning a paragraph with a subordinating conjunction is obviously a favourite device of this candidate.

2 A very good idiomatic expression.

3 Another good idiomatic expression.

4 An unusual preposition, but very suitable here.

5 A good example of a perfect passive construction.

6 Another unusual preposition, used appropriately.

7 Good use of modal verbs.

8 A good example of an adjective used as a noun, with the correct adjectival ending.

Paragraph 6: This is the concluding paragraph, in which the candidate offers an opinion. It is the weakest part of the whole essay. It draws together the points made earlier, which is good, but the candidate's opinion is rather weakly tagged onto the end in the last three lines.

1 A good idiomatic phrase to introduce the candidate's opinions.

2 A rare grammatical error. This should be *sie* to refer back to *Arbeitslosenquote.*

3 Another pleasing idiomatic phrase, providing variety and an authentic German feel to the essay.

4 Another grammatical error. This verb has no object, so requires the reflexive pronoun *sich* to act as the object, which should be inserted here.

5 An excellent, advanced construction: a *wenn*-clause with the pluperfect subjunctive.

6 This is the second time this idiomatic phrase has been used, but it could hardly be said that it has been overused.

7 A very good example of a verb with a following preposition introducing a clause: *die Regierung sorgt dafür, daß...*

This essay was marked according to the following criteria of the Oxford Delegacy:

- **Vocabulary – maximum 10 marks:** This candidate was put into the 'very good' band (Good knowledge of idiom. Rich and sensitive use of language [adjectives, adverbs, verbs]. Displays ability to select unexpected words. Demonstrates thorough knowledge of topic-specific vocabulary.) The candidate was awarded 10 marks.

- **Range of expression – maximum 10 marks:** The candidate was again put into the 'very good' band. (Confident use of complex verb forms [e.g. passives, subjunctives]. Uses articulate language appropriate to conveying well developed and thoughtful ideas, without the style appearing too forced.) Full marks were given.

- **Accuracy – maximum 10 marks:** There were virtually no grammatical mistakes in this essay so the candidate was put into the 'very good' band and given full marks. (Can handle quite complex language with few errors.)

- **Structure of essay/paragraphing – maximum 5 marks:** This was a well constructed essay and was put into the 'very good' band. (Well-balanced and coherent piece, with a good sense of overall perspective. Ideas clearly linked throughout. All paragraphs well constructed. Essay has well developed introduction and conclusion.) The candidate received the top mark.

- **Relevance to question/title – maximum 5 marks:** This essay was entirely relevant and deserved full marks. (Clearly relevant throughout.)

- **Analysis and development of ideas – maximum 5 marks:** Here the essay was put into the 'good' category and was awarded 4 marks, because of the undeveloped personal opinion in the last paragraph. (Most ideas developed. Some attempt to examine implications/draw conclusions where appropriate. Can give opinions and develop them although not always with complete consistency.)

- **Factual content/illustration/detail – maximum 5 marks:** There was a lot of supporting factual detail which meant that the candidate again received full marks. (Very detailed, fully supported answer, demonstrating thorough knowledge of the subject. Occasionally uses unusual/less obvious illustrations.)

This was an excellent essay, which within the limit on the number of words allowed, covered the subject well. It was obviously well planned, expressed in varied, accurate, idiomatic German and deserved the very high mark it received.

7.4 INFORMATION SOURCES

A useful source of up-to-date facts and figures on all aspects of Germany, which is published each year is:

Harenberg Lexikon der Gegenwart
Aktuell '95
Fakten, Trends, Hintergründe
Harenberg Lexikon Verlag   ISBN 3-611-00336-0

It can be obtained from: **European Schoolbooks Ltd, The Runnings, Cheltenham, Gloucestershire GL51 9PQ.**

If you need information on a particular topic it is worthwhile contacting the **Goethe-Institut, 50 Princes Gate (Exhibition Road), London SW7 2PG**, which will probably be able to give you the name of an organisation to approach if it does not have the information itself.

The following institutions are useful sources of information on the environment:

- Greenpeace (Deutschland) e.V., Hohe Brücke 1, Haus der Seefahrt, 2000 Hamburg 11
- Bundesverband Bürgerinitiativen Umweltschutz e.V. (BBU), Friedrich-Ebert-Allee 120, 5300 Bonn 3
- Bund für Umwelt und Naturschutz Deutschland e.V. (BUND), Im Rheingarten 7, 5300 Bonn 3
- Umweltbundesamt, Bismarckplatz 1, 1000 Berlin 33

CHAPTER 8

LITERATURE

Units in this chapter

8.1 INTRODUCTION

Many Boards now give you the option of choosing topics for study during the course. Often one or more of the options is to study a work of literature. Many students avoid literature if they have the choice and go for an area of study that ties in with their other A-levels or interests.

If you enjoy reading there are some strong arguments for choosing the literature option for your area of study: literature gives an insight into the culture of a country; it is often very interesting, dealing with subjects of human interest seen from a German point of view; all the 'facts' that you will need for the examination or coursework are contained within the covers of one book, possibly two; writing an essay on a work of literature is no more difficult than writing on other, perhaps more technical topics; a work of literature can be quickly revised, re-read, before the examination.

CHOOSING A TEXT

It is very likely that your teacher will choose the book(s) to be studied. If you have the choice try to choose something that will be reasonably accessible in terms of the language and ideas, not too long and with a theme which gives you some scope for discussion. A modern play is often a good choice, because it can be read in two to three hours, which is the amount of time that it would take to perform it on stage. The works of Bertolt Brecht, Max Frisch and Friedrich Dürrenmatt all deal in reasonably easy language with social issues that can be discussed in an essay. The prose works of Heinrich Böll, Siegfried Lenz, Alfred Andersch, Friedrich Dürrenmatt or Ödön von Horvath also have good, strong social themes.

8.2 HOW TO STUDY A LITERARY TEXT

Having chosen your book the first thing is to become familiar with the text, which will mean reading it carefully. You might try reading it through fairly quickly the first time, not bothering to look up too many unknown words, concentrating on getting a broad idea of what it is all about. A second more detailed reading would then be necessary, looking up unknown words and trying to understand all the text. If there are sections that you find difficult to understand you could ask either your teacher or a German national to explain them to you.

Once you have read and understood the book you then have to think about the theme. What was the author trying to say? For what reason did the author write the book. It was not just to make money. He/She had some statement to make about society, relationships, the position of women, the importance of money. Each book will have a different main theme. Discussing the book with other people will help you to clarify your ideas and will give you the benefit of theirs, which may make you see what happens in the book in a different light. If you have read a book by any of the famous writers, some of whose names are listed above, there are commentaries on most of their works which examine all the various aspects of the texts. One series is called *Interpretationen*, published by the R. Oldenbourg Verlag München. Also most editions of their texts published for use by schools contain a useful introduction and notes on the text.

When you know what point the author is trying to make other things begin to fall into place. A work of fiction will contain **characters** and they are carrying the 'message' of the author. You need to understand the motivation of the various people in the book. Why do they do what they do? Their relationships to each other will also be important. Is there a main character? What role does he/she play in the book? How do they react with the minor characters? What is their role? Are the characters credible or do you get the impression that their only role is to portray an idea? Do the characters have any unusual features which make them unique or are they representative of a whole class or type of person? These are some of the questions that you need to think about to prepare yourself for the examination and writing an essay.

When you have considered the theme and characters you should look at the way in which the author chose to tell the story, the **technique**. Is the story told from the point of view of a narrator, who knows the whole story and can see into the minds of the characters, the omniscient narrator? Why? Has the author got the characters to narrate the story? Why? If it is a play has the author used some of the devices of epic theatre to narrate the story? What is the structure of the book? Are there flashbacks? Is there a story within a story? The technique will have been chosen because the author felt that it was the best way of communicating the theme of the book. Your job is to examine how the story has been told and explore how effective it is.

Finally you should look at what the book reveals about the country or the time in which it was set. Many books relate to a specific time or country. Alfred Andersch's book *Sansisbar, oder der letzte Grund*, for example, is set in Germany in 1937 and says a lot about what it was like to live in Germany at that time, with pictures of Hitler in public places, the Gestapo spying on the population and the persecution of the Jews and communists. Many of Heinrich Böll's short stories are set in postwar Germany and reveal very graphically what it was like to be living in Germany in that period. Ask yourself why the book you are studying is set in the location chosen by the author, what it reveals about the theme and the author's own country and what you learn about the place and the period in which it is set.

8.3 WRITING ABOUT LITERATURE

There is no mystique to literature and essays on literature. If you adopt a practical, down-to-earth approach and do not try to make everything you say profound or vague, it is no different from writing any other essay. A common problem with literary essays is that students spend far too much time re-telling the story. You can assume that your reader knows the story well, so it is not necessary to re-tell the whole story. You will need to use incidents or quotations from the book to back up what you are saying, but that is all.

Provided that you can back up what you say with evidence or quotations, what you say is as valid as anybody else's opinion. Often the book can be interpreted in several different ways. There is not always one correct answer to a question on a book. Studying a book under the four headings: **theme**, **characters**, **technique** and **background** should make it easy to get to grips with it. But before you can do that you must understand the German text and that means reading it carefully. When you come to write about the book you will want to give your opinion about it, whether you enjoyed it and why. It does not matter if you say you did not enjoy what may be an acknowledged masterpiece, provided that you can give reasons.

8.4 USEFUL VOCABULARY

One of the problems that students have when writing about a book is their lack of the necessary vocabulary for discussing the various aspects. Here are some of the more common words that you will need:

der Autor/Verfasser	*author*
die Handlung/Nebenhandlung	*plot/sub-plot*
es handelt sich in diesem Buch um	*in this book it is a question of*
bearbeiten/verarbeiten	*to deal with (a topic)*
es behandelt die Frage	*it deals with the question of*
es setzt sich kritisch mit (+ dative) auseinander	*it takes a critical look at*
es dreht sich um (+ accusative)	*it is about*
das zentrale Thema	*the central theme*
die Personen, Figuren, Gestalten	*characters*
der Charakter	*character (personality)*
die Charakterisierung	*characterisation*
die Hauptperson	*main character*
die Absicht des Autors	*the intention of the author*
eine Stimmung vermitteln	*to convey an atmosphere*
das Werk	*the work*
der Roman	*the novel*
das Theaterstück	*the play*
ein Stück aufführen	*to perform a play*
darstellen	*to portray, describe, represent*
schildern	*to describe, portray*
veröffentlichen	*to publish*
sein Verhältnis zu seiner Frau	*his relationship to his wife*
menschliche Beziehungen	*human relationships*
die Eigenschaft	*the characteristic*
sich entfalten	*to unfold*
entwickeln	*to develop*
etwas in Frage stellen	*to question something*
das Zitat	*quotation*

zitieren	*to quote*
analysieren	*to analyse*
eine Erzählung in der Ich-/Er-Form	*a narrative in the first/third person*
es spielt in (+ dative)	*it is set in*
der Schauplatz der Erzählung	*the scene of the narrative*
die Einfühlung in (+ accusative)	*empathy with*
es stellt hohe Ansprüche an den Leser	*it makes great demands on the reader*
anspruchsvoll	*demanding*
wir bekommen dadurch einen Einblick in (+ accusative)	*it gives us an insight into*
die Bühne	*stage*
konkrete Gegenstände als Symbole	*concrete objects as symbols of*
abstrakte Ideen	*abstract ideas*
betonen	*to emphasise*
verallgemeinern	*to generalise*
Gedanken anregen	*to inspire ideas*
herausfordernd	*challenging*
die Phantasie	*imagination*
erfunden	*imaginative, made up*
auf etwas (accusative) reagieren	*to react to something*
einfache/gehobene/komplizierte Sprache	*simple/elevated/complicated language*
ich finde es langweilig/interessant	*I find it boring/interesting*

8.5 EXAMPLE OF A LITERARY ESSAY

Here is an example of an essay on a literary topic. It is a coursework essay, which means that it is longer than an essay under examination conditions. It has been written on the play *Andorra* by the Swiss playwright Max Frisch. The title was chosen by the candidate, which is another advantage of doing coursework: **Andorra ist der Name für ein Modell. Was wollte Frisch mit dieser Anmerkung sagen?**

Gliederung:

Einleitung: Das Stück ist ein Beispiel von epischem Theater – der Autor wollte etwas über die Gesellschaft sagen.

1   Eine Gemeinde auf die Bühne bringen. Andorra stellt alle westlichen Staaten dar.
2   Die Personen haben keine Namen. Sie sind Typen.
3   Die Eigenschaften eines typischen Juden.
4   Wie Andri in Wirklichkeit war.
5   Die Vorurteile der Andorraner.
6   Antisemitismus. Die Haltung der Schweiz im 2. Weltkrieg.

Schluß: Die Vordergrundsszenen. Die Andorraner haben von der Geschichte nichts gelernt. Und die Zuschauer?

Max Frisch wurde von den Ideen von Bertolt Brecht, dem Gründer des epischen Theaters, stark beeinflußt. Brecht war der Ansicht, daß das Theater die Aufgabe haben sollte, die Zuschauer zu lehren. Er hielt es für falsch, daß man im Theater unterhalten werden sollte. Brecht wollte, daß der Zuschauer nie vergessen sollte, daß er sich in einem Theater befand, damit er über die Botschaft des Stückes nachdenken könnte. In seinen

Anmerkungen sagte Frisch: „Es braucht kein Anti-Illusionismus demonstriert zu werden, aber der Zuschauer soll daran erinnert bleiben, daß ein Modell gezeigt wird, wie auf dem Theater eigentlich immer."

Mit diesen Worten wollte Frisch sagen, daß wir in seinem Stück ein Modell der Gesellschaft sehen, eine Gemeinde, Andorra, das uns eine für alle anderen westlichen Länder typische Gesellschaft zeigt. Andorra ist ein wirkliches Land, das zwischen Frankreich und Spanien liegt, aber wie Frisch selber sagt, hat „das Andorra dieses Stücks nichts zu tun mit dem wirklichen Kleinstaat dieses Namens."

Weil Frisch eine typische Gemeinde auf die Bühne bringen wollte, haben die Personen in seinem Stück meistens keine Namen. Die meisten werden durch ihren Beruf gekennzeichnet, zum Beispiel, der Lehrer, der Pater, der Soldat. Sie sollen typische Menschen vertreten. Wenn sie Namen gehabt hätten, wenn sie Individuen gewesen wären, hätten wir vielleicht vergessen, daß sie die typischen Ansichten von Menschen in ihren Berufen vertreten sollten. In seinen Anmerkungen sagte Frisch: „Einige Rollen könnten zur Karikatur verführen. Das sollte unter allen Umständen vermieden werden. Es genügt, daß es Typen sind."

Andris Vater, weil er Angst vor seinen Mitbürgern hatte, hatte die Geschichte erzählt, daß Andri ein Judenkind sei, das der Vater vor den Schwarzen gerettet habe. Vom Anfang hatten die Andorraner ihn als Juden behandelt. Sie hatten eine vorgefaßte Meinung über Juden: sie hielten sie für feig, geil, geizig, ehrgeizig und ohne Gemüt. Sie erwarteten also diese Eigenschaften in Andri zu finden. Die Andorraner zeigen diese Eigenschaften selber.

In Wirklichkeit sehen wir, daß Andri nicht feig war: er kämpfte gegen den Soldaten und er hatte keine Angst vor dem Tod. Die Andorraner aber haben ihr Land gegen die Schwarzen nicht verteidigt, weil sie Angst hatten. Er war auch nicht geil: er versuchte nicht Barblin zu verführen. Der Soldat aber hat sie vergewaltigt. Andri war auch nicht geizig; er hat seine Trinkgelder in das Orchestrion geworfen. Der Wirt aber wollte das Land des Lehrers für nur 50 Pfund kaufen, weil er wußte, daß der Lehrer das Geld für Andris Lehre brauchte. Ehrgeizig war er auch nicht: er wollte nur Tischler werden, und in seinem ersten Monat lernte er, wie man einen guten Stuhl macht. Der Doktor aber hatte Professor werden wollen, aber ohne Erfolg.

Wir sehen in dem Stück wie die verschiedenen Personen Andri mit Vorurteilen betrachten, sogar der Pfarrer. In seinem ersten Gespräch mit Andri sagt er: „aber eine Unart, das muß ich leider schon sagen, habt ihr alle." Der Tischler wollte ihn nicht in seiner Werkstatt ausbilden; der Soldat verachtete ihn; der Wirt hat Lügen über ihn erzählt. Es ist kein Wunder, daß Andri sich endlich für einen Juden hielt. Nur Barblin, die ihn liebte, sah den wirklichen Menschen und nicht das vorgefaßte Bild.

Mit diesem Stück wollte Frisch zeigen, wie gefährlich es ist, wenn wir Vorurteile haben, denn dann sehen wir den wirklichen Menschen nicht. Wir sehen nur das, was wir sehen wollen. Vielleicht wollte er die Haltung der Schweizer im zweiten Weltkrieg kritisieren, die gar nichts gemacht haben, den verjagten Juden zu helfen. Vielleicht ist Andorra ein Modell für die Schweiz.

In seinen Stücken zeigt Brecht eine sozialistische Lösung für die Probleme, die er in seinen Stücken untersuchte. In *Andorra* aber scheint Frisch eine pessimistische Haltung zu haben. In den Vordergrundszenen, die eigentlich viel später als die Bilder stattfinden, sagen alle Andorraner außer dem Pater: „Ich bin nicht schuld." Sie haben von der ganzen Geschichte gar nichts gelernt. Vielleicht glaubte Frisch, daß wir, die Zuschauer, von seinem Stück auch nichts lernen werden.

653 words

This essay makes some very relevant points, which are backed up by quotations and references to the text. It is well structured. The German is accurate, with a range of constructions and expressions. It would get a good mark.

APPENDICES

APPENDIX 1

SUMMARY OF TOPICS BY BOARD

AEB

A Das Schulwesen in der BRD
B Das Jahr in einem deutschsprachigen Land
C Die Nazizeit in der Literatur
D Berlin 1945–1990: Geschichte einer Teilung
E Der deutsche Film
F Deutsche Dramatiker des 20. Jahrhunderts
G Eine Region im deutschen Sprachraum auf gesellschaftlicher
   und wirtschaftlicher Basis
H Ausländer in der BRD

Oral Topics

1 Conservation (of the built or natural environment)
2 The role of the media
3 Transport
4 The Third World
5 The changing role of women
6 Moderation and/or extremism in politics
7 The family unit
8 Education after 16
9 Minority groups and their problems
10 The role of leisure
11 The arts today
12 Health problems in today's society

Plus: Youth in Germany; the German cinema; German music; a novel, play or collection of short stories by a German-speaking writer; the contribution of a famous German-speaking person to his/her field.

UCLES

Core topics (A and AS)
A Human relationships
B Daily life
C Environment
D Work and leisure

Themes:
Die Frau in der Gesellschaft
Familienverhältnisse

Extension topics (A-level only)
E International affairs
F Scientific and technological innovations
G Aspects of Germany and the German-speaking world today

Themes:
Der Außenseiter
Gerechtigkeit und das Gesetz

ULEAC

AS and A

1 Family, home, old people, social problems, law and crime
2 Youth, education, health and welfare
3 The world of work
4 Transport and communications, basic geography

5 Current affairs, politics, the media
6 Everyday science and technology, including I.T.
7 The environment
8 Urban and rural life
9 Leisure and travel
10 National customs and traditions, religion, food and drink
11 The arts
12 European/international issues in the context of Germany

A Level only

1 Deutschland 1939–1953
2 Gastarbeiter, Aussiedler, Asylbewerber
3 Die Bundesrepublik seit der Wiedervereinigung
4 Thüringen und Sachsen: zwei der „neuen Bundesländer"
5 Der deutsche Film: ein von Edgar Reitz und ein von Wim Wenders
6 Brecht – Leben und Werk
7 Die Nazizeit in der Literatur
8 Der Kriminalroman in der deutschsprachigen Literatur

NEAB

Topics prescribed for 1997

1 Kindheit in Deutschland, 1939–50
2 Jugend, Gewalt und Ausländer seit 1980
3 Die Deutschen und die Umwelt

NICCEA

List A Writing topics

1 Television
2 War/disarmament
3 Pollution and conservation
4 City/country life
5 Role of women/family life
6 Holidays, leisure and sport
7 Third World
8 Crime, punishment and Human Rights
9 The world of work
10 Education

List B Literature and culture

1 Berlin – the whole city – 1945 to the present
2 Youth culture in Germany
3 Secondary education in Germany
4 Political developments in the two Germanies 1945–1961

OXFORD AND CAMBRIDGE

List A Topics

1 Die Familie und interpersonelle Beziehungen
2 Stadt- und Landleben
3 Umwelt und Umweltschutz
4 Ausbildung
5 Die Arbeitswelt
6 Gesellschaftliche Struktur
7 Medien und Freizeit
8 Transport und Reisen
9 Europa und internationale Beziehungen
10 Das politische Leben
11 Naturwissenschaft und Technologie
12 Geistige und kulturelle Traditionen

German for Professional Use: two additional topics – 13 Geographie 14 Geschichte

Themes

1 Adolescence   3 Conflict
2 Rural Life and Communities   4 Travel

OXFORD

Themes

The world of work; Transport and travel; Food and drink; Culture and the arts; Sport and pastimes; the Media; Social issues; Education and training; Environmental issues, Current affairs and Technology.

Topics: Literary (the examination will include one question focussing on each of the following aspects.)

1 Dramatic techniques
2 The portrayal of children/young people in literature
3 The portrayal of war and its effects
4 The portrayal of society in literature
5 Short stories
6 Characterisation and/or plot

Topics: Non-Literary

1 Deutschland seit 1945
2 Die Presse im deutschen Sprachraum
3 Probleme der Jugendlichen im deutschen Sprachraum
4 Das deutsche Schulsystem
5 Sport im deutschen Sprachraum
6 Die deutsche Industrie und die Umwelt
7 Eine Gegend oder eine Stadt im deutschen Sprachraum
8 Tourismus im deutschen Sprachraum

SEB

Oral topics

My future   Travel
Family   Home area

WJEC

1 Die Gesellschaft in der BRD   5 Bildung und Erziehung
2 Das politische Leben   6 Die Welt der Jugend
3 Das wirtschaftliche Leben   7 Freizeit und Urlaub
4 Die Umwelt   8 Die Medien

APPENDIX 2

The following is a list of all the literature texts currently in the Boards' syllabuses. The list is alphabetical by author's surname.

Andersch: *Sansibar oder der letzte Grund* (novel about Germany under Hitler)

Der Vater eines Mörders (a short story about how Hitler and Himmler were possible)

Andres: *Wir sind Utopia* (a novel about a former monk in the Spanish civil war)

Becker: *Bronsteins Kinder* (a novel about a young man whose father was killed for crimes committed during World War II)

Böll: *Das Brot der frühen Jahre* (short novel about the post war years in Germany)

Die verlorene Ehre der Katharina Blum (short novel about powerlessness of the individual against the press)

Der Zug war pünktlich (short stories about the effects of war on people)

Dr Murkes gesammeltes Schweigen (short stories criticising society)

Und sagte kein einziges Wort (short novel about the post war years in Germany)

Borchert: *Draußen vor der Tür* (play about post war Germany)

Selected short stories (short stories about the effects of war)

Braun: *Unvollendete Geschichte* (a short novel about growing up in the GDR)

Brecht: *Der kaukasische Kreidekreis* (a play about possessions belonging to those who can best use them)

Leben des Galilei (the responsibility of the scientist)

Mutter Courage (anti-war play)

Der gute Mensch von Sezuan (the difficulty of being good in a capitalistic world)

Der aufhaltsame Aufstieg des Arturo Ui (an anti-Nazi play)

Ausgewählte Gedichte (selected poems)

Büchner: *Woyzeck* (a play about the hero of the title, who is exploited, kills his unfaithful lover because of jealousy and dies)

Droste-Hülshoff: *Die Judenbuche* (a short novel about the life and death of Friedrich Mergel)

Dürrenmatt:	*Die Physiker* (a play about the responsibility of the scientist)
	Der Besuch der alten Dame (a play about the power of money and how it corrupts our ideals)
	Romulus der Große (a play about the problems of Western society)
	Der Verdacht (a short detective novel)
	Das Versprechen (a short detective novel)
	Der Richter und sein Henker (a short detective novel)
	Die Panne (short novel about justice)
Ende:	*Das Gauklermärchen* (a play about the apparent omnipotence of the chemical industry, a modern fairy tale)
Fallada:	*Kleiner Mann – was nun?* (novel about the difficult years after the first World War in Germany)
Frisch:	*Biedermann und die Brandstifter* (a play about political complacency and fear when faced with terrorism)
	Andorra (a play about antisemitism and prejudice in general)
	Homo Faber (a novel about an engineer who seduces his own daughter, without knowing who she is)
Goes:	*Unruhige Nacht* (anti-war novel, set in the Russian front of 1942)
	Das Brandopfer (a short novel about the experiences of war from a civilian point of view)
Goethe:	*Urfaust* (a play about a man who sells his soul to the devil)
Grass:	*Die Plebejer proben den Aufstand* (a play comparing the uprising of the plebeians against Coriolanus with the uprising in Berlin in 1953 against the Communist government)
	Katz und Maus (a short novel set in World War II)
Grün:	*Irrlicht und Feuer* (a novel about the hard and dangerous life of a Ruhr worker)
Hauptmann:	*Bahnwärter Thiel* (a short novel about a simple railway worker)
Heine:	*Buch der Lieder* (poems)
Hesse:	*Unterm Rad* (a novel about adolescence)
Hochwälder:	*Das heilige Experiment* (a play about the Jesuit settlements in Paraguay in the 18th century)
Hoffmann:	*Das Fräulein von Scuderi* (a story about a goldsmith who robs and murders to get his creations back)
Horvath:	*Jugend ohne Gott* (short novel about young people in Germany under Hitler)
	Der jüngste Tag (a play set in the 1930s about guilt and responsibility)
Kafka:	*Die Verwandlung* (a short novel about a man who wakes up to find he has become a beetle)
Kastner:	*Faber* (a novel about city life in Berlin in the 1930s)
Keller:	*Romeo und Julia auf dem Dorfe* (love story, set in Switzerland)
	Kleider machen Leute (a story about judging people by their outward appearance)

Klapproth: *Mit falschem Paß* (a story of a Kurdish refugee in Switzerland)

Kleist: *Das Erdbeben in Chili, Die Marquise von O* (two short novels or novellas, the first about two lovers in Chile, saved by an earthquake, then killed; the second about the effect of motherhood on the heroine of the title)

Prinz Friedrich von Homburg (a play about the relationship between the freedom of the individual and the laws of the state)

König: *Ich fühl mich so fifty-fifty* (a story about an East German girl anxious to flee to West Germany)

Lehnert: *Wie ein rostiger Nagel im Brett* (a short novel about a boy growing up during World War II on a farm)

Lenz: *Das Wrack* (a collection of short stories)

Der Mann im Strom (a novel about a diver getting too old for his work)

Zeit der Schuldlosen (a play about guilt and responsibility under a dictator)

Maltzan: *Schlage die Trommel und fürchte dich nicht* (an autobiography spanning the 1930s to the post war period)

Mann: *Tonio Kröger* (a short novel about the role of the artist in society)

Martin: *Blut ist dunkler als rote Tinte* (a short thriller)

Pausewang: *Die Wolke* (a short novel, set in the 1990s, after a nuclear accident in Germany)

Rosinkawiese (a short autobiographical novel about the author's upbringing in the Sudetenland)

Plenzdorf: *Die neuen Leiden des jungen W.* (a play about love and politics, the individual and society)

Remarque: *Im Westen nichts Neues* (novel set in the first world war)

Rinser: *Gefängnistagebuch* (an autobiographical account of her time in prison)

Salm: *Brandstiftung* (anti-racist novel about a young Turk in Germany)

Schiller: *Wilhelm Tell* (a play about the famous Swiss hero)

Schneider: *Vati* (story about the visit of Rolf Mengele to his father, Josef Mengele, the famous concentration camp doctor)

Sichrovsky: *Schuldig geboren* (non-fiction about children from Nazi families)

Storm: *Der Schimmelreiter* (short novel, set in Schleswig Holstein, about a ghostly figure)

Immensee (a short love story)

Wallraff: *Der Aufmacher* (a factual account, an exposure of Bild-Zeitung)

Zuckmayer: *Der Hauptmann von Köpenick* (a play about a tramp who impersonates a military captain, satire on society)

Zweig: *Angst* (a short story about the wife of a well-to-do solicitor, who is having an affair with a young pianist)

Brennendes Geheimnis (a short novel about young love)

Schachnovelle (a short novel set around a game of chess)

APPENDIX 3

LISTENING TRANSCRIPTS AND ANSWERS

Example 1

Nachrichten: Osnabrück – Vier Menschen sind bei einem Verkehrsunfall auf einer Landstraße nahe Osnabrück ums Leben gekommen. Ein 24jähriger war mit seinem Auto auf die Gegenfahrbahn geraten und frontal mit dem Wagen einer Familie zusammengestoßen. Die beiden Eltern, ihre siebenjährige Tochter und der Unglücksfahrer waren sofort tot.

Hamburg/Harburg – Fünf Männer haben einen 21jährigen Bundeswehrsoldaten überfallen und beraubt. Der junge Mann war am S-Bahnhof Heimfeld aus einem Bus ausgestiegen und wollte zu Fuß zur Kaserne an der Heimfelderstraße. Plötzlich tauchten die fünf Täter auf. Sie schlugen den Soldaten zusammen und raubten ihm 390 Mark aus der Geldbörse. Die Täter entkamen. Der 21jährige mußte ins Krankenhaus, wurde aber noch am selben Tag entlassen.

UNO-Soldaten nach Somalia – 500 pakistanische Blauhelme sollen in Somalia verhindern, daß Hilfstransporte von bewaffneten Banden überfallen werden. Durch die anhaltende Dürre in Somalia sind 4,5 Millionen Menschen vom Hungertod bedroht.

Hamburg – Der Temperatursturz brachte gestern nachmittag ein Unwetter. In dem Stadtviertel Blankenese überflutete der heftige Regen mehrere Straßen. Mehrere Keller liefen voll. Die Feuerwehr mußte zu rund 30 Sondereinsätzen ausrücken, um die Wassermassen abzupumpen.

Example 2

Umweltprobleme: Eine Diskussion mit deutschen Studenten

Ja, in der Bundesrepublik wird ja in letzter Zeit sehr viel über die Qualität der Luft, des Wassers und der Umwelt überhaupt gesprochen, z.B. haben wir das Problem des Waldsterbens und nicht zuletzt wird es ja also durch die Industrie aber auch durch den Individualverbraucher hervorgerufen – was denkt ihr darüber, wie die Regierung auf dieses Problem reagieren sollte?

– Hm, schwierig zu sagen. Es gibt auf der einen Seite Möglichkeiten halt, durch Gesetze restriktiv einzugreifen. Als die Frage, wie effektiv die sind, wie weit die kontrolliert werden könnten, z.B. was weiß ich, Abwässer im Rhein sind wahrscheinlich auch ohne staatliche Überprüfung möglich, selbst wenn es Gesetze gibt, die sie verbieten. Tja, andere Möglichkeiten...

– Ja, andere Möglichkeit wär' halt doch z.B. durch Werbung halt versuchen, die Verbraucher über Dinge aufzuklären und ihr Verhalten zu ändern.

– Ja, ich mein', was kann der Verbraucher machen, wenn die Industrie ihm diese Produkte verkauft, ich mein', der Verbraucher kann doch schlecht kontrollieren.

– Er kann wählen.

249

– Ja, man könnte beispielsweise versuchen, die Leute aufzuklären, daß es andere Produkte gibt, die die Umwelt weniger schädigen als diejenigen, die momentan verkauft werden und daß man da dann, falls die Industrie da nicht freiwillig reagiert, die Industrie dazu zwingt, andere Produkte herzustellen, wenn das möglich ist, die halt weniger schädlich sind.

– Diese Inititativen gibt es schon, es gibt ja diesen blauen Umweltengel auf Produkten und die dann also zum Kauf anreizen sollen.

Example 3

Schüleraustausch mit Frankreich: ein Telefongespräch

– Susanne Plötz, bei dir darf ich auch noch „du" sagen, ja?

– Ja, doch, ich denke.

– 15 Jahre, stimmt das? Hab' ich hier stehen.

– Nee, sechzehn.

– Geht aber trotzdem noch. Du warst gerade in Frankreich, hab' ich hier stehen.

– Ja.

– Du bist ziemlich traurig, daß du wieder hier in Deutschland bist?

– Ja, unter anderem, doch. Ja.

– Ja, warum?

– Das war 'ne ganz tolle Zeit. Wir waren zum Wochenaustausch da.

– Wo denn?

– In Macon. Das ist in Burgund. Wir haben uns super verstanden mit allen auch mit den Lehrern und so.

– Da ist ein Schüleraustausch, ja?

– Ja.

– Was macht man da? Lebt man da jetzt vordringlich bei einer französischen Familie oder muß man auch was arbeiten?

– Ja, also wir waren, wir sind samstags angekommen und hatten das Wochenende in den Familien, also wir waren jeder in einer Familie, nur einzeln, und in der Woche über hatten wir teilweise mit Schule, montags den ganzen Tag, also bis nachmittags ist das ja bei denen, und sonst hatten wir auch so Ausflüge so, jede Menge Kultur. Burgen besichtigen und Lamartine, Touren und so weiter, aber war es viel Kultur dabei, muß schon sagen, aber wir hatten noch trotzdem viel Spaß.

– Und habt sehr viele neue Freunde gewonnen, wahrscheinlich.

– Ja, jetzt ist es nur noch am Schreiben im Moment.

– Kommen die denn vielleicht auch mal 'rüber nach Deutschland?

– Ja. Das ist, vom Austausch her kommen sie am 8. Juni nach Koblenz, und wir wollen aber auch so weiter Kontakt halten. Also wir haben schon uns beschlossen, daß wir schon noch hinfahren in den Sommerferien oder irgendwann, wenn es klappt.

– Und heute ging's in der Schule da wieder richtig zur Sache?

– Ja, das fand ich etwas frustrierend, daß die Lehrer dann direkt weitergemacht haben und gemeint haben, es wär halt unser Pech, wenn wir was nachholen müssen.

– Ja, deswegen hast du auch beim Fruststopper angerufen und deswegen liegt jetzt auch ein schöner Titel für dich auf. Schau mir in die Augen, Kleines, und sag's mir ins Ohr. „As time goes by."

– „As time goes by".

– Mit Dooley Wilson aus „Casablanca".

– Danke.

Example 4

Frauen in der ehemaligen DDR

Im 41. und letzten Jahr der DDR wurde zum ersten Mal ein umfassender Bericht über die soziale Situation der Frauen veröffentlicht. Herausgegeben wurde dieser Frauenreport von der Gleichstellungsbeauftragten des Ministerrates. Die Installierung von Gleichstellungsbeauftragten beim Ministerrat und in den Städten ist eine Errungenschaft der Revolution. Denn im marxistischen Musterland DDR gab es offiziell keine Frauendiskriminierung. Tatsächlich aber waren die ostdeutschen Frauen von Gleichberechtigung noch weit entfernt. Ein Zitat aus dem Frauenreport.

„Trotz weitestgehender Aufhebung von Bildungsunterschieden zwischen Mädchen und Jungen blieben die geschlechtsspezifischen Differenzen in der beruflichen Qualifikationsstruktur nahezu erhalten. Das Berufswahlfeld für Mädchen konzentrierte sich nach wie vor auf die traditionellen und schlechter bezahlten Frauenberufe. Weitaus mehr Frauen als Männer arbeiteten in ihren Berufen unterhalb ihres Qualifikationsniveaus. In logischer Konsequenz lag auch das Einkommen deutlich niedriger."

Etwas hatten die ostdeutschen Frauen allerdings den Westfrauen voraus. Sie hatten das Recht auf einen Arbeitsplatz und damit das Recht auf eigenes Geld. Nun ist doch das gefährdet.

– Die Wende heißt für Frauen auch ja Unsicherheit und Unsicherheit ist völlig neu. Unsicherheit gab's noch nie. Bislang war der Lebensweg gesichert. Es war klar, daß man Beruf haben wird, daß das beruflich weitergeht, daß man heiraten wird, daß man Kinder haben wird, daß es mit den Kindern gehen wird und nu ist plötzlich alles unsicher und damit können Frauen nicht umgehen. Männer auch nicht. Aber für Frauen ist eben nicht nur der Beruf in Gefahr, sondern auch die Kinder stärker in Gefahr und die Familie insgesamt. Und die sagen uns zwar:„Ja, ich könnte arbeitslos werden" oder „Wie könnte denn das werden?" oder „Die Mieten werden steigen" aber was das in der Konsequenz heißt, darüber haben Frauen im Moment keine Vorstellungen und von daher auch keine Konzepte.

Berufstätigkeit war ein Teil der Identität von DDR-Frauen. Mit dem Übergang zur Marktwirtschaft tritt erstmals offene Arbeitslosigkeit auf. Der Arbeitsmarkt verändert sich radikal und zwar zu Ungunsten der Frauen, wie der offizielle Frauenreport feststellt.

Example 5

Der Bericht der AIDS Enquete-Kommission

Das letzte Thema in den heutigen Funkbildern betrifft die AIDS-Problematik. Nach etwa zweieinhalbjähriger Arbeit wird die AIDS Enquete-Kommission des deutschen Bundestages Ende Mai ihren Bericht der Bundestagspräsidentin vorlegen können. Maite Zeeg führte ein Gespräch mit dem Vorsitzenden dieser Enquete-Kommission, Dr Hans Peter Vogt, CDU Bundestagsabgeordneter aus Nordheim.

– Wie ist denn die Entwicklung bei AIDS? Gibt es mehr Krankheiten?

– Es gibt nach wie vor mehr Krankheiten, auch wenn die prozentualen Zuwächse glücklicherweise nicht so dramatisch sind, wie man das noch vor einigen Jahren erwartet hat, aber für uns ist ja auch nicht ausschlaggebend der Zuwachs der AIDS-Kranken, denn das sind ja die Kranken, die sich vor 5 bis 10 Jahren angesteckt haben, sondern für uns ist wichtig die Zuwachsrate der Infizierten. Hier gibt es Zuwächse, die im Bereich von 15 Monaten Verdoppelung liegen, also wie es nicht weniger als vor einigen Jahren befürchtet, aber es gibt überhaupt keinen Anlaß zur Entwarnung.

– Ja, und wie sieht es dort aus, beispielsweise bei den jungen Leuten? Sind denn diese bereit, sich nun vorzusehen? Gibt es genügend Schutzmaßnahmen?

– Ich glaube, daß die jüngere Generation die Problematik schon erfaßt hat. Wir können nicht messen, inwieweit die jüngere Generation – vor allem die Jugendlichen, auch die jetzt vor allem nachwachsenden Jugendlichen, die nicht in der ersten AIDS-Welle schon angesprochen worden sind – wie weit sie tatsächlich auch ihr Verhalten ändern. Daß sie die Problematik kennen, das kann man, glaub' ich, zu weit über 95% annehmen, aber ob sie auch tatsächlich ihr Verhalten dementsprechend einrichten, vermag man im

Augenblick nicht zu sagen. Ich habe die Hoffnung, es gibt einige Parameter, aus denen man schließen kann, daß die Jugendlichen schon die Problematik sehr ernst nehmen, aber die Evaluationen unserer Maßnahmen sind da noch nicht ausreichend.

Test 1

Mittwochslotto
Hier die Zahlen vom Mittwochslotto.

Ziehung A: 8 12 17 20 25 38. Zusatzzahl: 23
Ziehung B: 3 12 25 43 46 49. Zusatzzahl: 18

Test 2

Das Wetter
Heute nacht werden die Wolken, die im Nordwesten schon angekommen sind, allmählich den Himmel über Deutschland überziehen. Dabei wird es vereinzelt regnen und vor allem in Schleswig Holstein und im nördlichen Niedersachsen. Dabei wird der Wind im Norden allmählich stärker und dreht von Süd auf westliche Richtung. Und dieser böige Westwind treibt dann morgen Wolken mit einigen Regenschauern über den Norden und Westen Deutschlands. Vom Erzgebirge bis hinunter zum Bodensee bleibt es bedeckt und regnerisch und das vor allem in den Alpen.

Test 3

Falsch beschuldigt
„Das darf doch wohl nicht wahr sein." Das haben sich auch manche von Ihnen gedacht, sofern Sie vor einigen Wochen in unserer Reihe „Einspruch" hören konnten, was da einer Putzfrau in einem katholischen Krankenhaus passiert war. Es gibt Gründe, auf die Geschichte noch einmal zurückzukommen. Helmut Ulrich.

„Dazu bin ich wirklich sprachlos. Mit das hab' ich nie gerechnet." Emilie Krüger kann es kaum fassen, sie darf wieder das katholische Krankenhaus in Dortmund-Kirchlinde betreten. Vielleicht erinnern Sie sich noch. Vor fünf Wochen hatten wir in dieser Sendung über das traurige Schicksal der 46jährigen Putzfrau berichtet. Sie war beschuldigt worden, im Krankenhaus Dortmund-West Geld gestohlen zu haben. Doch der Vorwurf war falsch. Ein Staatsanwalt stellte ihre Unschuld fest. Der katholische Krankenhausleiter Werner Möllerfeld pfiff allerdings auf die Meinung des Staatsanwalts und weigerte sich beharrlich, sein zu Unrecht erteiltes Hausverbot wieder aufzuheben. „Für uns besteht dieser Verdacht weiterhin, auch wenn ein Freispruch erfolgt ist. Ich hab' das Hausrecht hier, und das Hausrecht ist ja unabhängig von einem Urteil eines Staatsanwaltes."

So der Krankenhausleiter in der Sendung vor fünf Wochen. Eine erwiesenermaßen Unschuldige öffentlich als Diebin zu verdächtigen, das ist nicht die feine katholische Art. Nach der Sendung tagte eilig das Krankenhauskuratorium, eine Art Aufsichtsrat, und kurz darauf konnte Emilie Krüger ein erfreuliches Schreiben entgegennehmen, unterzeichnet von Klinikchef Möllerfeld. Das gegen sie verhängte Hausverbot sei aufgehoben, heißt es darin in einer einzigen Zeile, ohne ein Wort der Entschuldigung. Aber immerhin, für die Putzfrau hat es sich gelohnt, gegen das Unrecht des Krankenhausleiters zu kämpfen.

„Ja, das hat si' gelohnt."

Test 4

Fußballfans in Bremen
Mehr als 30 belgische Fußballfans haben heute nachmittag vor dem Europa-Pokalspiel zwischen Werder Bremen und dem FC-Zeebrugge – die Spieler betreten übrigens just im Moment den Rasen zur zweiten Halbzeit – ein Kaufhaus in der Bremer Innenstadt gestürmt. Nach Angaben der Bremer Polizei waren die Fans in die Sportartikelabteilung gelaufen und hatten dort mehrere Schals und Mützen entwendet. Offenbar haben sie vielleicht eine Meldung der Stuttgarter Kickers falsch verstanden, in der sichern sie jedem Besucher, der im Besitz eines original Kickerschals ist, morgen für das wichtige Spiel um 19 Uhr 30 gegen Borussia Dortmund einen freien Stehplatz zu.

Test 5

Ozonschichtgefahr

Die niedersächsische Landesregierung fordert Fahrbeschränkungen bei Ozonwarnung. Umweltministerin Griefhahn kündigte an, daß sie auf der Umweltministerkonferenz des Bundes und der Länder am Donnerstag einen entsprechenden Vorschlag machen werde. Die Fahrbeschränkungen bei Ozonwetterlagen müssen bundeseinheitlich für alle Autos ohne geregelten Katalysator gelten. Durch das sonnige Wetter stiegen bereits am Wochenende in Niedersachsen die Ozonwerte auf bis zu 160 Mikrogramm pro Kubikmeter. Ab 180 Mikrogramm pro Kubikmeter werden an die Bevölkerung Ozonwarnungen herausgegeben.

Test 6

Kindheitserinnerungen

So, geboren bin ich 1946 in Wien, mein Vater war damals Soldat bei den britischen Besatzungstruppen und meine Mutter ist Wienerin. Also in meinem vierten Lebensjahr haben wir Wien verlassen und sind nach England gekommen, bin allerdings zweisprachig aufgewachsen. Aber das Interessante ist vielleicht, daß ich mich geweigert habe, als ich so ziemlich jung war, deutsch zu sprechen, weil so kurz nach Kriegsende war es nicht gerade ein sozialer Vorteil, deutsch zu sprechen. Mein Bruder und ich, wir haben uns geweigert, deutsch zu sprechen, und ich glaub', ich hätte mein Deutsch total verlernt, wenn wir den Kontakt zu unseren Verwandten in Wien nicht aufrecht erhalten hätten. Ja, ich hab' mich auch ziemlich ausgestoßen gefühlt damals. Die Kinder haben mit mir nicht spielen wollen. Aber jetzt sind meine deutschen Sprachkenntnisse gefragt, und zwar deswegen weil Fremdsprachen groß geschrieben sind wegen der EG, nicht?

Practising some basic skills

NUMBERS

3; 7; 11; 27; 32; 34; 43; 56; 65; 78; 87; 345; 952; 5 986; 12 011; 24 379; 125 621; 450 777; 689 112; 10 Millionen; 11,6 Millionen; 7,4 Millionen; 3,5 Millionen; 4,25 Millionen; 8,75 Millionen; ein Fünftel; drei Viertel; ein Zehntel; sieben Achtel

TIMES

halb drei (2.30); Viertel nach 5 (5.15); 25 Minuten vor 3 Uhr (2.35); 2 Minuten nach 6 (6.02); 23 Uhr 13 (11.13 p.m.); 17 Uhr 25 (5.25 p.m.); Viertel 6 (5.15); drei Viertel 7 (6.45); 1 Uhr 5 morgens (1.05 a.m.); 5 Uhr eins abends (5.01 p.m.); 5 Minuten vor Mitternacht (11.55 p.m.); zu Mittag (12 noon); 3 Uhr nachmittags (3.00 p.m.); 20 Uhr 19 (8.19 p.m.); 29 Minuten nach 7 (7.29); 5 Minuten vor halb 5 (4.25); Punkt 6 Uhr (6.00 exactly); gegen 5 Uhr (5.00 approx.); um etwa 2 Uhr morgens (at 2.00 a.m. approx.); 2 Minuten vor 11 (10.58)

DATES

 1 Montag, den 24. Juni, 1992
 2 Donnerstag, den 22. April, 1984
 3 Dienstag, den 31. März, 1979
 4 am Freitag, dem 17. Mai, 1936
 5 am Samstag, dem 28. Februar, 1965
 6 am Sonnabend, dem 1. Juli
 7 am Mittwoch, dem 11. Januar, 1961
 8 am 3.11.95
 9 den zwoten März, 1981
10 den 12.7.1946
11 im September
12 Ende Januar
13 den 10.2.39

14 am 26. August, 1941
15 nach dem 31. Oktober
16 vor dem 1. Dezember
17 zwischen dem 15. und 21. November
18 ab dem 1. April
19 in den 90er Jahren
20 im 20. Jahrhundert

THE ALPHABET:

A B C D E F G H I J K L M N O P Q R S T U V W X Y Z

1	I	7	W
2	E	8	J
3	U	9	Y
4	O	10	H
5	A	11	Q
6	V	12	Z

SOME NAMES:

1	Anna	9	Ellen
2	Maria	10	Dirk
3	Erika	11	Silke
4	Ulrika	12	Hermann
5	Ute	13	Inge
6	Uwe	14	Angelika
7	Henning	15	Ruth
8	Hannelore		

PRONUNCIATION PRACTICE:

1 The long **a**: Rasen, Abend, Tag
2 The short **a**: fast, man, das
3 The long **e**: ebenso, gehen,sehr
4 The short **e**: Ecke, fett, danke
5 The long **i**: ihr, dir, wir
6 the short **i**: ich, sich, Imitation
7 The long **o**: oben, ohne, oder
8 The short **o**: oft, doch, morgen
9 The long **u**: Uhr, Buch, suchen
10 The short **u**: unter, bunt, murren
11 A double **a**: Aal, Saal
12 A double **e**: Meer, Tee
13 A double **o**: Boot, Zoo
14 The short **ä**: Hände, Männer, Dächer
15 The long **ä**: Fähre, nächste, Dämon
16 The short **ö**: Hölle, zwölf, möchte
17 The long **ö**: Höhle, Röte, schön
18 The short **ü**: Glück, bücken, fünf
19 The long **ü**: Glühbirne, Grüße, Füße
20 The diphthong **ie**: Lied, diese, sie
21 The diphthong **au**: Haus, aus, brausen
22 The diphthong **ei**: Bein, dein, eine
23 The diphthong **eu**: treu, neun, heute
24 **b** at the end of a word: Kalb, Dieb, Grab
25 **d** at the end of a word: Band, und, rund
26 **g** at the end of a word: klug, Tag, mag
27 **-ig** at the end of a word: zwanzig, König, heilig
28 The consonant **j**: jung, Jahr, jagen

29 The consonant **l**: hell, Milch, lachen
30 The consonant **r**: Rathaus, rennen, reiten
31 **s** at the end of a word: Gras, Haus, bis
32 **s** at the beginning or in the middle of a word: Gläser, sie, rasen
33 The consonant **v**: Vater, vier, vernünftig
34 The consonant **w**: Wasser, wir, wenn
35 The consonant **x**: Hexe, boxen
36 The consonant **z**: zwei, zwölf, Zahn
37 **ch** after **a**, **o**, **u**, or **au**: acht, doch, Buch, Bauch
38 **ch** after all other letters: ich, dich, bricht
39 **ch** at the beginning of a word: Chor, Charakter, Chaos
40 The combination **chs**: sechs, Dachs, Luchs
41 The combination **qu**: Quatsch, quer, Qualm
42 The combination **sch**: Schule, schön, scheinen
43 **sp** at the beginning of a word: sprechen, spielen, spinnen
44 **st** at the beginning of a word: stehen, Stadt, stinken
45 The combination **th**: Theater, Thema, Theorie
46 The combination **ll**: Welle, hell, bellen
47 The combination **pp**: Mappe, Krippe, Grippe
48 The combination **rr**; schnurren, murren, Dürre

THE 'ß-SIGN'

1 müssen (between 2 vowels, first one short)
2 ich muß (at the end of a word)
3 ihr müßt (before a consonant)
4 der Fuß (at the end of a word)
5. die Füße (between 2 vowels, first one long)
6 der Fluß (at the end of a word)
7 fließen (between 2 vowels, first one long)
8 die Flüsse (between 2 vowels, first one short)
9 schließen (between 2 vowels, first one long)
10 er schließt (before a consonant)
11 geschlossen (between 2 vowels, first one short)
12 das Schloß (at the end of a word)
13 die Schlösser (between 2 vowels, first one short)
14 passieren (between 2 vowels, first one short)
15 passen (between 2 vowels, first one short)
16 das paßt mir nicht (before a consonant)
17 messen (between 2 vowels, first one short)
18 er mißt (before a consonant)
19 das Maß (at the end of a word)
20 lassen (between 2 vowels, first one short)

STRESS:

Kaufmann, unsere, ungeduldig, anfangen, regnerisch
entscheiden, die Entscheidung, Entscheidungsfrage, entscheidend,
beantworten, gestehen

INTONATION:

1 Obgleich wir während des Tages tüchtig gegessen hatten, waren wir immer noch bereit, am Abend mit unseren Freunden ins Restaurant zu gehen.

2 Der Mann, der hinter uns gefahren war, hatte die Seitenstraße nicht bemerkt und war daran vorbeigefahren.

3 Zu unserem Erstaunen hat der junge Arzt, der erst vor kurzem in die Praxis gekommen ist, keine Probleme dabei gehabt, eine richtige Diagnose bei einer selten vorkommenden Krankheit zu stellen.

INDEX

A Level German CD/Cassette

If you have purchased a copy of our Study Guide for A Level German and would like to buy the accompanying CD or cassette, or if you have bought the CD and would like to swap it for a cassette, please tick the relevant box below, complete the order form and return it to:

Letts Educational
Aldine House
Aldine Place
London W12 8AW
Telephone 0181 740 2266

Forenames (Mr/Ms) _____

Surname _____

Address _____

_____

_____ Postcode _____

Please swap the enclosed CD for a cassette: ☐

Please send me: Quantity   Price (incl VAT)   **Total**

A Level German CD ☐   _____   £4.00   _____

A Level German cassette ☐   _____   £4.00   _____

Add postage – UK and ROI   _____
75p for each CD/cassette

I enclose a cheque/postal order for £ _____
(made payable to Letts Educational)

Or charge to Access/Visa card No. ☐☐☐☐☐☐☐☐☐☐☐☐☐☐☐☐☐

Expiry date _____

Signature _____